an *agile* servant

COMMUNITY LEADERSHIP BY COMMUNITY FOUNDATIONS

edited by
RICHARD
MAGAT

Produced by
The National Agenda
for
Community Foundations'
Community Leadership Project
of the
Council on Foundations

The Foundation Center

Library of Congress Cataloging-in-Publication Data

An agile servant : community leadership by community foundations / edited
  by Richard Magat.
     p. cm.
  ISBN 0-87954-330-2 : $24.95. — ISBN 0-87954-332-9 (pbk.) : $15.95
    1. Community welfare councils—United States. 2. Endowments—United
States. 3. Community leadership—United States. 4. Community welfare
councils—United States—Case studies.
I. Magat, Richard.
HV97.A3A58 1989
361.8'0973—dc20   89-38377
                                             CIP

CONTENTS

Asset Growth

Assistance to Nonprofit Organizations

Catalyst on Critical Issues

Neighborhood Development

New Philanthropists

Preface

Although publication of this book coincides with the seventy-fifth anniversary of the community foundation field, it is also significant as a major product of the National Agenda for Community Foundations. The National Agenda itself is a rather extraordinary effort, not only in its dimensions—a $2.2 million enterprise over three years—but in its origins and governance. It is one of three special initiatives by the Council on Foundations; the other two, begun in 1987, concern giving by individuals and corporations. It is composed of five projects— On-Site Consulting, National Presence, Data Gathering, National Training, and Community Leadership.

As evident in its title, this book was commissioned under the Community Leadership subcommittee, whose goal is to stimulate discussion of the role of the community foundation in tomorrow's communities and to identify creative solutions to problems that confront foundations today. But the book also has ties to the other parts of the National Agenda. For the National Presence effort, which seeks to create a greater awareness of community foundations among donors and their advisors, we hope it will serve as a vehicle for greater visibility and understanding of community foundations. From the Data Gathering effort, which is charged with collecting, analyzing, and regularly publishing new information about community foundations, the book has drawn valuable material about the structure and operations of community foundations. In the process we have uncovered new areas where further research is needed. For the National Training and On-Site Consulting components, we hope that the book will serve as a conceptual tool for thoughtful management and decision-making; the former designs systematic learning opportunities for community foundation boards and staff to improve management, grantmaking, donor relations, and knowledge of the history and mission of philanthropy and the community foundation movement; the latter provides seasoned community foundation personnel on request to foundations seeking counsel on grantmaking, asset development, staffing, and management operations.

To serve this range of purposes, we were determined to assemble a work of informed, thoughtful, and candid analyses. Especially in Part I of this book, we intend not only to address current issues within the field but also to anticipate future challenges. In Part II, we seek to provide tangible cases of leadership by community foundations in various aspects of their work—grantmaking, convening, mediating, asset development, and nonmonetary assistance to nonprofit organizations. Contributors to both parts were urged to include difficulties and missteps as well as successes. As an additional means of ensuring against self-congratulation, we invited a critic of foundations, Robert Bothwell, to share his concerns about community foundations. We have also included a chapter of personal statements of donors—the men and women who are part of the constituency community foundations were established to serve in the first place, but who in turn serve their communities through community foundations.

Although this book is intended principally for present and future community foundation staff, board and distribution committee members, and donors, we believe it has an important secondary audience, consisting of public policymakers, colleges and universities in the growing movement to make organized philanthropy part of the academic research and training agenda, the professional and mass media, and such other funding agencies as private foundations and corporate contributions programs.

The philanthropic leaders who have contributed essays to this volume have earned our deep gratitude, but our debt extends also to innumerable others—the executive directors represented in the sixteen case studies, who opened their records to independent writers and who accepted candid and sometimes critical comments on their work, and to the men and women who helped shape the contents and commented on drafts.

It is fitting that I single out a special group of volunteers with respect to this book—my fellow Community Leadership subcommittee members: Frederick Adams of the Hartford Foundation for Public Giving; Dwight Allison, Boston Foundation and Palm Beach Community Foundation; Malvin E. Bank, Thompson, Hine & Flory; Marion G. Etzwiler, The Minneapolis Foundation; Virginia L. Hubbell, Sonoma County Foundation; Dorothy A. Johnson, Council of Michigan Foundations; Mariam C. Noland, Community Foundation for Southeastern Michigan; Dan Sweat, Central Atlanta Progress, Inc.; and Paul Ylvisaker, Harvard University.

To edit this volume, we were fortunate in enlisting Richard Magat, who has spent most of his professional life in and around organized philanthropy—as a staff member of the country's largest private foundation, as the president of one of the smallest, as a writer of books and articles about philanthropy, and book editor of *Foundation News* magazine.

Although the National Agenda has operated mainly though time-consuming volunteer efforts of dozens of community foundation leaders, the Council on Foundations has been an energetic partner, and the National Agenda has benefited from the active encouragement of James Joseph, president, and Alice Buhl, senior vice-president of Member Programs and Services, and the substantial contribution of their staff. In particular everyone is in debt to Joanne Scanlan for her day-to-day administration of this far-flung project. Her skill and patience in the face of a complex, often trying, enterprise have helped produce tangible results from an ambitious, even visionary, plan. She would also be the first to share this credit with her efficient, ready staff, Julie Wernick, Nancy Jakubowski, and Susanne Stelling.

And finally, of course, this all could not have happened without the generous funding contributed by 125 community foundations, six large private foundations, and the Council on Foundations itself.

We hope that this book will itself prove to be "an agile servant" to the improvement and future development of community foundations. We intend it not as a blueprint or a fixed body of doctrine, but as a provocative starting point for the discussion and introspection vital to a field that has evolved dramatically through several phases in its first 75 years and may be expected to undergo at least equally important changes in the decades to come.

Steven A. Minter, Chair
National Agenda

Acknowledgments

Despite the vicissitudes of dealing with 24 contributors and a clutch of community foundation heads whose work was being analyzed, the editing of this book has been a labor of interest and discovery. My odyssey took me through a part of organized philanthropy of which I had been only moderately familiar even in 30 years' work in foundations. For allowing me the privilege of making this journey and for their counsel and support, I am grateful to the Community Leadership subcommittee of the National Agenda for Community Foundations, whose names are given in the Preface. Especially I wish to thank its chair, Steven A. Minter, whose calm judgment in the face of a daunting array of responsibilities, including the contribution of an essay to this book, was a comfort all along the way and an example I wish I was able to follow. Another substantial debt is owed, of course, to the other contributors to the volume, not only for their talents but for their patience in a flurry of drafts and deadlines. For unflagging support and guidance, a special bow in the direction of Joanne Scanlan, who never ran out of reserves of energy and almost serene competence in the face of multitudinous details on the five-headed National Agenda, and others on her staff, and to the Council on Foundations officers named in the preface.

I cite also the CEOs of the 16 community foundations covered in the case studies (Chapters 11–26) for their generous cooperation, even in the few cases where differences arose, and of the 13 foundations represented by donors' statements (Chapter 6), and those mentioned in the Introduction. For information, advice, or leads I am pleased to add appreciation to Thomas Beech, Prudence Brown, Helmer Ekstrom, Suzanne Feurt, Judith Healey, Cynthia Mayeda, Carol Farquhar, Brian O'Connell, Barry Pribyl, Lois Roisman, James Shannon, Mal Salter, Lorie Slutsky, Eugene Struckhoff, and Paul Verret.

This work began a few months after I became a Visiting Fellow at the Foundation Center, to which I am indebted generally for a hospitable environment. Particular thanks go to Rick Schoff for the skilled hand with which he guided this book into production, and to Liz Thackston and Caryn Golden for valuable secretarial assistance.

As always, my wife, Gloria, was remarkably understanding and supportive in the face of a schedule that cut deeply into my family responsibilities.

R.M.
New York, April 1989

Contributors

MARK BERNSTEIN, a free-lance writer in Yellow Springs, Ohio, is a contributor to *Smithsonian Magazine* and a contributing editor of *Ohio Magazine.*

PATRICIA BILL is director of communications at the Minnesota Council on Foundations; she has been practicing journalism since the mid-1960s. She worked in upstate New York as a reporter and as a member of the editorial staff of Watt Publishing Co. in Illinois. Later she held positions with Washburn Child Guidance Center (Minneapolis) and the Current Newspapers (suburban Twin Cities).

SUSAN VAIL BERRESFORD, a native of New York City, studied American history at Radcliffe College, where she graduated *cum laude* in 1965. Ms. Berresford joined the Ford Foundation in 1970 as a project assistant. In 1980 she was named officer in charge of the Foundation's women's programs. Appointed vice president, U.S. and International Affairs Programs, in 1981, Ms. Berresford currently manages grants programs that have a total biennial budget of more than $300 million.

ROBERT O. BOTHWELL is executive director, National Committee for Responsive Philanthropy, Washington, D.C. He was formerly field representative for the U.S. Conference of Mayors, U.S. Office of Economic Opportunity (OEO), and Center for Study of Public Policy;

deputy director, OEO Community Action Program, Research and Development Division; and director, National Urban Coalition School Finance Reform Project.

BEA BRAGG is a free-lance writer, photographer, public relations consultant, and former news reporter in El Paso. Although she has primarily written and published nonfiction, she is looking forward, at 75, to publication of her first children's book of fiction.

BILL DOLL, a sociologist with a law degree, is a former theater critic and feature writer. He now runs his own business specializing in writing and research on social, cultural, and legal issues.

WENDY ELLYN is a free-lance writer based in Sebastopol, California. She has written for businesses and non-profit agencies and is published in various magazines, including *Bicycle Rider, Sierra Life, Executive Female,* and *Sonoma Business.* She lives in a 1901 farmhouse with a man and two cats.

LYN FARMER is president of Ampersand Associates, a Miami-based communications consulting firm. He writes copy for corporate brochures and annual reports and is a columnist for *The Miami Herald.* He also produces a weekly chamber music program for National Public Radio. Farmer was formerly director of cultural programing at the Voice of America in Washington, D.C.

DAVID C. HAMMACK, Associate Professor of History and Member of the Program Faculty of the Mandel Center for Nonprofit Organizations, Case Western Reserve University, taught at Princeton University, was a Resident Scholar at the Russell Sage Foundation, and has held a Guggenheim Fellowship. He is the author of *Power and Society: Greater New York at the Turn of the Century* (1982).

MIKE HEMBREE is a staff writer for *The Greenville News,* a morning daily published in Greenville, SC. He has worked at the newspaper for ten years and in the newspaper business for 20, has co-authored three books, and has won many state and national journalism awards.

JAMES A. JOSEPH is president of the Council on Foundations. He has taught at Yale and Claremont, directed several foundations, and served as Under Secretary of the Interior and vice president of Cummins Engine Company.

STEVE KEZERIAN, a journalist and editor, was for 35 years a public information officer for Yale University. Currently, he is a contributing editor for the Yale Alumni Magazine.

KENNETH LAFAVE, music editor of *The Kansas City Star*, has contributed to *The Los Angeles Times*, the *New York Daily News*, Reuters, the *Washington Times*, and elsewhere. Formerly a publicist for The New York Philharmonic, he is also a composer whose catalogue includes orchestral, chamber, and vocal music.

MARTIN C. LEHFELDT is the president of Lehfeldt and Associates, Inc., an Atlanta-based firm that for ten years has provided a range of fundraising, planning, evaluation, and editorial services to a wide variety of nonprofits. He was formerly a program officer of the Woodrow Wilson National Fellowship Foundation; Vice President for Development of Clark College; and Director of Development for the Atlanta University Center.

JENNIFER LEONARD is a writer and consultant specializing in community foundations. She has been a community foundation grants vice president, a grantsmanship trainer, a nonprofit lobbyist, and an adjunct professor of fundraising. Her articles on the nonprofit sector have appeared in the *Columbia Journalism Review, Foundation News*, and the *Los Angeles Times*.

RICHARD MAGAT, Visiting Fellow at The Foundation Center, formerly was president of the Edward W. Hazen Foundation and communications director at the Ford Foundation. Book editor of Foundation News, he has written or edited books and articles about philanthropy, including *Philanthropic Giving: Studies in Varieties and Goals* (Oxford University Press, 1989).

STEVEN A. MINTER is director of the nation's first community trust, the Cleveland Foundation. Before joining the Foundation in 1975 and then assuming directorship in 1984, he was director of the Cuyahoga County Welfare Department in Ohio and Commissioner of Public Welfare for the Commonwealth of Massachusetts. He also served as the first Under Secretary of the newly formed U.S. Department of Education (1980–1981).

BRUCE L. NEWMAN has been the Executive Director of The Chicago Community Trust since 1973. He served earlier for two years as Director of the Department of Urban Affairs for the State of Ohio and from 1965 through 1970 he was on the staff of the Cleveland Foundation.

MARIAM C. NOLAND is executive director of the Community Foundation for Southeastern Michigan, headquartered in Detroit and serving a metropolitan area with 4 million population. She has over 12 years experience in the community foundation field and is currently vice-chair of the Council of Michigan Foundations.

BEA QUIRK is a Charlotte-based free-lance writer who has been writing extensively about all aspects of life in the Queen City for a variety of national, regional, and local publications since 1981. She is the co-author of *The Insiders' Guide to Charlotte* and the author of *Charlotte: City at the Crossroads*.

KATHY SEAL is a freelance who has written for *Ms.*, the *Los Angeles Times, Los Angeles Magazine*, and numerous other publications. She was chair of the Los Angeles Coalition Against Plant Shutdown, worked for General Motors, and was active in the United Automobile Workers. She has published a novel.

MICHAEL SEGAL, a Cambridge-based freelance, has been writing about politics and government in Massachusetts for 12 years. He is co-author of *Dukakis: The Man Who Would Be President* (1988).

IRENE RASMUSSEN, a free-lance writer from Arizona, has worked with corporations, public agencies, and nonprofit organizations. She has served clients in several states as well as in Ethiopia, Mexico, Peru, and Bolivia. Her expertise is in nonprofit organizations and foundations.

MARION WOYVODICH is a free-lance writer in Seattle. Formerly a reporter for the Tacoma *News Tribune*, she focused on lifestyle and business issues.

PAUL YLVISAKER, a native Minnesotan, is former Dean and now Professor, Harvard Graduate School of Education. He was formerly Director of the Public Affairs Program of the Ford Foundation, Vice-President (Trustee) of the Boston Foundation, and currently serves on the Board of the Mary Reynolds Babcock Foundation and as Senior Consultant to the Council on Foundations.

Agility, Leadership, Myth, and Reality

An Introduction

Richard Magat

The world of individualistic competition is experienced every day; the world of harmonious unanimity is fully realized only in sporadic flashes of togetherness, glimpses of what might be if only people would cooperate and their purposes reinforce, rather than undercut, one another.

—*HABITS OF THE HEART,* ROBERT N. BELLAH et al., 1985

Anniversaries that mark the passage of many decades evoke images of venerable, if not hoary, institutions. But there is something odd about the impression cast by community foundations as the field turns 75 years of age. Many of the most thoughtful and active people engaged in community foundation work still regard the field as young. Certainly to outsiders like me, who have more than a passing interest, it *feels* young.

The reasons for this apparent contradiction of freshness against a backdrop of advanced age are not terribly mysterious. For one thing the field has developed in cycles. Some of the oldest foundations have responded and changed marvelously in the radically changed environment that James Joseph describes in Chapter 3. Others have not; in fact, some of them have atrophied or disappeared altogether. Still other community foundations that began during the first few decades of

1

this field played Rip Van Winkle, with the difference that they awoke from a long slumber to behave with youthful vigor and imagination. And, of course, the field is crowded with community foundations that are literally young. These are heirs to a tradition, and they show a certain respect toward the pioneers that Bruce Newman recalls in Chapter 4, but some of them are also adventurous—eager, if not impatient, to make their own marks. Full of ideas, now and then some of the newcomers violate the canon of politeness to dismiss, if not ridicule, the notions of their forbears.

So as the field observes this anniversary, the mood is less nostalgia and self-satisfaction than it is ferment and a willingness to acknowledge and grapple with issues and peer into a future that is as full of troublesome vistas as it is of happy prospects. And yet, optimism animates the souls of the men and women who people organized philanthropy. Problems will be identified, analyzed, and addressed. We should know better, but it is almost an article of faith in foundation philanthropy that all problems can be solved.

Even in a society that prizes individualism, community is valued as a framework for the development of individual potential and as a means of helping to assure individual well-being. Community is also supposed to be the crucible in which individual and group differences, even antagonisms, can be accommodated. In fact, according to the ideal, it is possible, from diversity, to forge cohesiveness and membership—call it citizenship—in a body whose common values and aspirations transcend unbridled self-interest. "In the most vibrant of communities, tolerance is superseded by affection and daily concern for the well-being of others," it was once observed by Dwight Allison, chair of the Boston Foundation and the Palm Beach Community Foundation.

The more fractured and troubled the present, the easier it is to romanticize the past. One of the fondest images of the American past is the cohesive community, its members cooperating to build a better future for succeeding generations, "one united people ... descended from the same ancestors, speaking the same language, professing the same religion ... very similar in their manners and customs," as John Jay wrote in the *Federalist Papers*. But literature, history, and social analysis are strewn with accounts of American life that dispel the impression of tranquil, cohesive, steadily evolving communities. Long before Independence, American communities were often rent by religious differences. The American Revolution itself reflected the special interests of a merchant class, sometimes harmonious with the interests of artisans and workers, sometimes not. The bonds of community were severely strained by differences and intolerance between patriots and Loyalists. As urban communities burgeoned in the nineteenth century, common interests were often overshadowed by industrial strife, and of course the nation/community itself was preserved only at frightening cost in the Civil War. The postbellum onrush of industrialization changed the face of rural and small-town America, and waves of immigration brought dramatic changes and conflict to urban communities. And so on into our own times. The Great Depression severely tested community stability. World War II restored a sense of common purpose, but the ideal of community suffered great shocks in the postwar period under the moral challenge of the civil rights movement and the corrosive domestic effects of the Vietnam War.

FIGURE 1. COMMUNITY FOUNDATION ASSETS: AVERAGE ANNUAL GROWTH RATE FOR PERIODS OF VARYING LENGTH, 1921–1987

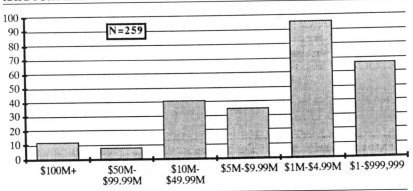

All along, writers, scholars, and journalists have examined communities with lenses that yielded either sober or fiery, dispassionate or outraged, portrayals of American communities—Sherwood Anderson's depiction of the dark corners of *Winesburg, Ohio,* Sinclair Lewis's scathing accounts of small-town parochialism, Thornton Wilder's shimmering recollection of *Our Town,* only begin to suggest the rich literary sensitivity to American community life. The muckrakers—Lincoln Steffens, Upton Sinclair, Jacob Riis, and others—exposed the running sores of poverty and corruption in scores of American cities. Social scientists have given us systematic, richly documented insights: W.E.B. Du Bois's *The Philadelphia Negro,* the Lynds' *Middletown,* Hollinghead's *Elmtown's Youth,* William Whyte's *Street-Corner Society* typify the rich bookshelf of scholarly interest in American communities.

Common Ground, J. Anthony Lukas's remarkable account of the effect on and reaction of Boston's several communities to such challenges as urban redevelopment and school desegregation is only the latest, though one of the most thorough, journalistic ventures into the heart of American communities.

This book about community foundations is neither a literary, scholarly, or journalistic venture. Nor is it a commemorative paean, despite its origins in the observance of the 75th anniversary of the field. To go one step further in a negative definition, *An Agile Servant* is not a primer or a handbook. The field was enhanced in 1977 by the publication of Eugene Struckhoff's *Handbook on Community Foundations: Their Formation, Development and Operations,* and technical literature about the field has expanded greatly since then. The expansion has been accelerated by the project from which this book arises, the National Agenda for Community Foundations. The products range from journal articles to competency manuals, to audiotapes to the remarkable *Lexicon,* a document that is as practical to present and future practitioners of community foundations as it is intimidating to interested outsiders like myself.

Having worked a long time in and around private foundations, I was prepared for *Lexicon* entries like "grant guidelines," "endowment," and "nonprofit organization." I even was familiar with some of the standard terminology of community foundations, e.g., "donor advised funds," and "distribution committee." But what to make of "ademption," "causa mortis transfers," "contingent legatee," "reversionary living trust," and "unitrust?" If one went no further than the *Lexicon,* it would be easy to assume that the field was run by bloodless accountants and lawyers; that a community foundation office was more likely to be equipped with rolltop desk and quilled inkwells than with computers. Fortunately, I have first-hand evidence that the field is full of humane, sophisticated, analytical—and interesting—men and women.

So what is this book? It is in large part—Part I—a dialogue among men and women deeply engaged in community foundation life. Along with a historian and a couple of concerned outsiders, contributors to Part I deal with issues and dilemmas of immediate moment that are likely to be at the forefront of the field for the 1990s and for several decades beyond. Part II, consisting of profiles of leadership in a wide cross section of community foundations, is intended to illuminate for present and future practitioners and donors the processes by which community foundations excel in their various functions.

It is a healthy sign that the field is willing to take a deep look at itself in public. There is some irony in the feeling—largely justified—

that community foundations are little known in their own communities. After all they serve these communities and reach out to them for funding. "Of all the threats to [an] institution, the most dangerous comes from within," A. Bartlett Giamatti, former president of Yale University wrote recently. "Not the least among them is the smugness that believes the institution's value is so self-evident that it no longer needs explication, its mission so manifest that it no longer requires definition and articulation." At least until the 1970s many private foundations had fallen into that error. If the same is true of community foundations, apparently it is far from pervasive. The hardest current evidence of this consciousness of the need for explication is the inclusion of "national awareness" as a major element in the National Agenda program and, to an extent, this book itself.

Scrutiny of financial practices by government is different from penetrating analysis of the basic rationale and programmatic operation of foundations. Very little such analysis existed until the last quarter-century. The most qualified outside critics were said to be constrained; organizations that benefited from foundation grants would not dream of slapping the hand that fed them, and scholars would not dare to jeopardize their chances of support from philanthropic coffers.

Stronger streams of analysis and criticism have begun to flow. Foundations themselves have started to shed the ethic of privacy, if not secretiveness. Consumer groups—from minorities and women to environmentalists and grassroots organizers—have begun to scrutinize foundation behavior and to lobby for a greater voice in and share of the enterprise. These stirrings have coincided with a greater diversity in the staffs of foundations and, to some extent, in governing boards. Finally, the scholarly community is bestirring itself to examine a sector of American life that is of the same order of magnitude, in assets, to say nothing of impact, as government and the for-profit sector. This new scholarly interest, beginning most prominently a little over ten years ago with the establishment of the Program on Non-Profit Organizations at Yale (PONPO) has been stimulated and encouraged by the principal professional organizations in the nonprofit world, Independent Sector (IS) and the Council on Foundations.

If research on philanthropy and voluntarism in general is thin, it is threadbare with respect to community foundations. For example, of 130 Working Papers that have emerged from PONPO at Yale, only one deals with community foundations. In Daphne N. Layton's *Philanthropy and Voluntarism: An Annotated Bibliography* (1987), only three of the 2,212 entries treat the subject. In a recent survey of scholars on future research needs in the sector conducted for the Independent Sector Research Committee, community foundations were listed as one of a half-dozen sparsely investigated priority areas.

A PERSONAL NOTE

Although I had worked in the foundation field for more than 30 years when I was asked to edit this book, my knowledge of community foundations was quite limited. Thus it has been an absorbing odyssey; it has also been astonishing to grasp the variety of operating styles, attitudes, and vision of community foundations. Some community foundations, for example, are run by men and women who are more comfortable with wealthy donors—present and potential—and the lawyers and bankers who advise them, than they are with the nonprofit organizations that look to foundations for help or partnerships. Some leaders in the field are so comfortable with nonprofit organizations, having in some cases worked for them, that they do not adjust readily to interaction with the wealthy. And it didn't take long to verify that what was true of private foundations was true also in the community foundation field: that there is no necessary correlation between size (of assets or community) and quality.

Had I known several years ago how complex this branch of philanthropy could be, I probably would not have ventured to provide the impetus and initial support for a new community foundation, the Greater Lawrence (Massachusetts) Community Foundation. It is a story worth telling briefly because it illustrates aspects discussed elsewhere in this book.

While President of the Edward W. Hazen Foundation, I persuaded the Board of Trustees to authorize a small subprogram in the advancement of philanthropy and voluntarism, with an emphasis on minorities. That program led, for example, to the initiation and initial funding of a major research project on black philanthropy at the Joint Center for Political Studies, a leading black think tank in Washington, D.C. I had heard that community foundations were not adequately responsive to minority needs (of course, the same complaint is heard about private foundations); I also learned that minority representation on the staffs and boards of community foundations was limited. My trustees agreed to let me look for a community with a substantial minority population that lacked a community foundation and to encourage the establishment of one with a significant minority role, even in its formative stages.

Anyone interested in labor history knows Lawrence, Massachusetts, as the scene of the Bread and Roses textile strike of 1912, in which the International Workers of the World (IWW), the "wobblies," organized immigrant workers to resist wage cuts for women and child workers. Lawrence officially advertises itself as "the birthplace of industrial democracy." In the summer of 1984 riots broke out there, principally between the Hispanic and French-Canadian communities.

With the advice of the Council on Foundations, I engaged two consultants: Douglas Jansson, Director of the Rhode Island Community Foundation, and Michael Borrero, former Executive Director of the National Puerto Rican Forum and adviser on the formation of the Puerto Rico Community Foundation. In due course, their feasibility study provided the go-ahead signal. Although Lawrence was on the way to recovery from the kind of economic depression characteristic of older industrial cities in the Northeast in the 1970s, Jansson and Borrero determined that the community proper lacked the wealth to sustain a community foundation. But the potential existed if the foundation's territory would expand to include three smaller but wealthier communities, Andover, North Andover, and Methuen. An organizing committee composed of hard-working task forces, worked for an entire year. Leadership was provided by Daniel J. Warner, Executive Editor of the Lawrence *Eagle-Tribune* and the local Stevens Foundations. The Hazen Foundation pledged $25,000 a year for three years toward administrative costs.

I was lucky, as was Lawrence. Community foundations have been started elsewhere without the experienced judgement of advisors like Jansson and Borrero and without the systematic planning of a broad-based, motivated group of citizens.

VALUE AND PROFESSIONALISM

In one sense past achievements by community foundations merely set the stage for exceedingly difficult new challenges. How can our communities withstand the devastation of an unprecedented epidemic of drugs and the wanton crime they bring with them? How can we forge common cause in an increasingly diverse American population? Money has accumulated massively in the accounts of America's community foundations, but as Dwight Allison reminds us, money "is not going to be the measure of [community foundations'] influence on the quality of American life. [T]he values which they recognize, nurture, and promulgate can have an impact which far surpasses the effect of their material resources. Community foundations stand on the threshold of a new vision—institutions which sustain and disseminate those social and civic virtues that make community life feasible and fulfilling."

Communities face new challenges from outside as well. They are often part of an international economy, with local plants owned by foreign commercial interests, to say nothing of hotels, office buildings, and golf courses. They are also part of an international environmental order. No place is immune from the massive threat against the natural world.

History seems to have turned full circle, for as historian Peter Dobkin Hall reminds us, civic leaders 75 years ago were ambivalent about larger forces that impinged on their localities. "Leaders in cities like Buffalo, Chicago, Cleveland, and Detroit ... admired and identified with the national prosperity [that] benefited their communities. On the other hand, they could not help resenting the extent to which the growth of the national economy was transforming their communities. Towns that were once relatively isolated and self-determined were becoming cities afflicted by the same problems of poverty, dependency, disease, and disorder characteristic of the great metropolises."

As much as community foundations have grown in this period, they are part of a philanthropic and voluntary environment in which change has been even greater. Despite the explosion of government into all human service, educational, and cultural realms, nonprofit organizations have expanded and diversified beyond anyone's imagination. Although volunteers remain an essential pillar of the enterprise, professionalism has developed in the management of both nonprofit organizations and the organized philanthropic sources that sustain them. The strategies and means of raising funds have become highly sophisticated and the competition for funds much keener. Community foundations themselves have had to become more entrepreneurial and aggressive in asset development.

Philanthropic and voluntary activity has come under government regulation, in part as a response to abuses, and more may be in the offing. Whatever the grounds, unquestioning public trust in presumably virtuous pursuits can no longer be taken for granted. Like so many cherished institutions in American life, philanthropy, too, must account for itself, peform tangibly in the public interest, and earn its protected status.

Largely in response to external threats, philanthropy in the 1950s began to organize in a remarkable array of intramural institutions. The motivations go beyond self-defense to include professional exchange and further development of the field. On the giving side we find national organizations, almost two dozen regional associations of grantmakers, a score of "affinity" groups of men and women who share programmatic interests ranging from health to the environment, or common backgrounds, such as the Association of Black Foundation Executives. Nonprofit organizations have formed their own groups; the National Committee for Responsive Philanthropy serves as a watchdog of the field.

The profusion of this machinery for cooperation should not cloud our memory of a habit of isolation that dominated the field through most of its history. Foundations not only regarded their affairs as private with respect to potential grant recipients, but also largely went their own way without much association with other foundations. Competition persists, some of it healthy, some not. As noted in Chapter 8, in a few communities, United Way and community foundations appear to be in competition, although often United Way has been responsible for starting community foundations.

Reflecting the field's habit of isolation, it was not until 30 years after the first community foundation was established that an organization of these institutions was born. It took another eight years, in 1957, before the National Committee on Foundations and Trusts for Community Welfare hired its first full-time staff director, the redoubtable Wilmer Shields Rich. In due course, with the admission of private foundations, the committee became the Council on Foundations.

Some members of the original group were worried that their interests would be pushed into the background by the admission of private foundations, especially the larger ones. Wilmer Rich's plan was designed to encourage large foundations to join at a relatively high level of dues but to prevent them from becoming a top-heavy force that could overwhelm smaller members. The interests of smaller members have not been engulfed, but private foundation members soon outnumbered community foundations.

So, not without some irony in view of the parentage of the organization, the National Agenda for Community Foundations arose in part from the desire of some community foundations for more services from the Council.

If the Council did not serve community foundations as well as some community foundations thought they should be served, it was not a case of malign neglect, and the Council responded to the sentiment. In 1984, James A. Joseph, president of the Council, proposed a special program for community foundations, outside the Council's regular budget. Under the leadership of Paul Verret, president of the Saint

Paul Foundation, then chairman of the Committee on Community Foundations (a national advisory group reporting to the Council's Board of Directors), that suggestion evolved into a plan for the concerted, multifaceted program that became the National Agenda.

The National Agenda also represented a bridge between two camps within the community foundation field—two dozen or so large community foundations and the much greater number of small and new ones. The former had begun to meet separately once a year; one of their major concerns was the need to reorganize their trust arrangements to enable them to meet the public support test imposed by the Tax Act of 1986. The smaller foundations were struggling to maintain themselves until they accumulated enough money to cover their operating costs and still have funds left for making grants.

The National Agenda was advertised principally as a self-help enterprise; particularly, some of the larger foundations viewed themselves as leaders of a national movement who would now make a concentrated effort to help their smaller colleagues. But the motivations certainly included greater understanding and visibility for the field as a whole, and the agenda for the Agenda has come to include one of the major interests of the smaller foundations—aggressive asset development.

The essay part of this book (Part I) begins with a historical overview of community foundations. It is accidental, but fitting nonetheless, that it was written by a member of the history faculty of a university in Cleveland, the birthplace of community foundations. As noted earlier, relatively few scholars have applied their talents to philanthropy and voluntarism, and David C. Hammack is no exception. However, in his widely acclaimed work on urban politics, *Power and Society: Greater New York at the Turn of the Century*, he observes that philanthropists were key players in urban economic and political decisions, and his book is full of examples of the part played in a great city by such nonprofit organizations as the Citizens' Union, settlement houses, and the Chamber of Commerce.

Hammack's chapter here on community foundations sets their development against the backdrop of transformations of the national charitable framework in the late nineteenth and early twentieth centuries. Major changes included separation of religious from secular purposes, a shift from control by a few donors to professional managers, and the development of federated charities. For community foundations that today may be timid about engaging in advocacy, he provides a reminder of the forthright exposition of community needs by the earliest community foundations. Hammack analyzes the developmental growth cycles of community foundations: flourishing in the Midwest and the Northwest between 1915 and 1935, slackening during the Great Depression, reviving in the wake of national pride stimulated by World War II, diminishing from the mid-1960s to the 1980s. Finally he suggests a future agenda for research on essentially unanswered questions about community foundations.

In Chapter 2, following Hammack's look at the past, Paul Ylvisaker glimpses into the future of community foundations. Ylvisaker is not a razzle-dazzle futurist; this courageous, grand man of organized philanthropy prefaces his forecasts of community foundations in the twenty-first century with a discussion of various "dimensions" along which the concept of community will be stretched—geography, diversity, fragmentation, values, and shared interests.

Ylvisaker's realism has been tested in many crucibles, yet he is optimistic about the ability of philanthropy to respond to changing conditions, for he believes it has already "emerged from a purely charitable preserve to become an essential social process—in effect, a set of private legislatures...." But he also envisions likely frictions and difficulties—community foundation competition with United Way and other institutions, and more public attention to and regulation of philanthropy in general.

In directly addressing the central theme of this volume in Chapter 3, James A. Joseph applies lessons of leadership he learned from work in government, business, higher education, and, especially, organized philanthropy. Returning like Hammack to the roots of the community foundation movement, Joseph points to an entrepreneurial model of leadership that evolved into a form that more resembles a special craft and a special calling. He views the esssential requirements of a leader as vitality, values, and vision. Applying these to community foundations, he dwells especially on values, because "community foundations by their nature stand for openness, public accountability, diversity ... and a commitment [to] the 'American creed.'" Joseph posits a typology of community foundation leaders that is thought-provoking in light of later discussions of the growth of foundations (Chapter 5) and grantmaking (Chapter 7). Finally, he makes observations on the evolution of community into a life among strangers; on the growing non-European demographics of American society; and the increasing pragmatic interplay of the governmental, commercial, and nonprofit sectors.

Would all ten pioneers cited in Chapter 4 by Bruce Newman (eight in detail), meet Joseph's criteria for leadership? Probably not entirely, because of the greatly changed circumstances over the years they span. They are all white, and with the exception of Wilmer Shields Rich, all males. But to a remarkable degree were both "asset-driven" and "needs-driven," two of Joseph's types. Given the origin of community foundations in the Midwest, it is not surprising that half of them hailed from that region, though the next largest group (three) were from the South, a region that came late to the field. They were a diverse lot—three lawyers, (Frederick Goff, Eugene Struckhoff, and Norman Sugarman), two social welfare workers (Frank Loomis and Wilmer Rich), two academic figures (Raymond Moley and James "Dolph" Norton), a publisher (Harrison Sayre), an advertising executive (Herb West), and a government official (John May).

To her examination of the birth and growth of community foundations (Chapter 5), Jennifer Leonard brings the twin vantage points of journalist and officer of a large community foundation. The essay is full of examples and, in one case, a literal illustration, an intriguing chart of stages of community foundation development by choice of mission. In one of the few ventures into whimsy in this long and serious book, Leonard describes the differences in community foundation growth rates by the paces of snails, tortoises, and hares. Glimpsing into the future, Leonard talks of such novel sources of growth as tax credits and corporate restitution funds, of the necessity of attracting minority donors, and of the delicacy of billion-dollar-range community foundations continuing on the fundraising trail.

It is logical but somewhat jarring to move from Leonard's tracery of the growth patterns of community foundations to the real voices of men and women who account for most of the growth—the donors (Chapter 6). The reasons for philanthropic giving are far from simple. A forthcoming bibliography of research on givers' motivations has 1,103 entries. Here we have the evidence of 13 men and women who have contributed to community foundations. Annual reports of community foundations are full of profiles of donors, often portrayed in roseate terms, sometimes, as in the case of memorial gifts, indicative of family tragedies as well as triumphs. The statements here are a bit different in that they emanate mainly from unrehearsed direct interviews. The speakers range from the truly wealthy to people of relatively modest means. Some are heirs, others self-made, in fields as disparate as accounting and skiing. What may strike the reader is an undercurrent of modesty and in several cases the inspiration of civic-minded parents. Several of the donors sit on community foundation boards, but others had never heard of a community foundation, and in one case the foundation had never heard of the giver of a substantial donation.

In Chapter 7, Mariam Noland conducts an analytical tour through the constituency, resource, and value context for grantmaking, and grantmaking strategies, methods, and styles. Any remaining shred of the simplistic view of grantmaking (an officer sits at a desk sorting applications in a love-thee, love-thee-not imitation of plucking daisy petals) are dispelled by Noland's account of the great array of choices available to program officers all along the way. Even more provocative are the grantmaking issues she takes up, beginning with whether community foundation grantmaking really differs from that of other funders. Finally, Noland springs the question that haunts every conscientious grantmaker in quiet predawn or midnight moments: "Can we ever really know what works?" The pragmatic answer will comfort some, but not all, which is probably healthy.

It is appropriate that Chapter 8, on collaboration, be written by an executive of a private foundation that has played a prominent role in joint ventures with community foundations. Given their fierce independence and even a tradition of isolation, foundations rarely dealt with one another until well into the post-World War II period. So what Susan Berresford describes as proliferating collaboration is extraordinary. Remarkable, too, is the variety of shapes collaboration has taken— among community foundations, between community and private foundations, and between community foundations and government in all branches. Despite the problems and perils of collaboration, she concludes that the pattern is here to stay and is likely to expand.

Little wonder that Steven Minter (Chapter 9) has a fascination for the essence of community foundations and for the essential differences between them and other grantmaking institutions. After all, he heads the community foundation where it all began. But his examination of their characteristics (including surprisingly loose legally prescribed characteristics) is only a means to an end. That end—perhaps the most controversial in this book—is Minter's strong plea for formal standards for community foundations. Minter rests his cases generally on the premise that if community foundations do not legislate for themselves, someone else will. Specifically, he views standards as helpful in sorting out issues of competition, geographic and otherwise, and of distancing legitimate community foundations from organizations that mislabel themselves and from community foundations that misbehave to the point of scandal. He proposes a careful approach to setting standards, allowing up to two years for the field to take its "first steps toward standards." But clearly he doesn't expect another seventy-five years to go by without standards.

In a meeting of the National Agenda's leadership subcommittee devoted to selecting cases (Chapters 11-26), Paul Ylvisaker asked whether the book would discuss failures as well as successes. This prompted me to reach out to critics outside community foundations, such as Pablo Eisenberg of the Center for Community Change, whose views are cited in Chapter 7, and Robert Bothwell, Executive Director of the National Committee for Responsive Philanthropy (NCRP). The result is Chapter 10, in which Bothwell depicts community foundations as virtually free of government regulation or public scrutiny, a breed apart from other foundations. Like Minter, Bothwell calls for standards of behavior by community foundations. Unlike Minter, he does not call for a process of codifying standards; he sets them forth straightaway— in accountability, accessibility, responsiveness, and fundraising. For handling grant proposals, Bothwell imagines a "seven-pile" system and recommends that community foundations pay more attention to item 7, "all other proposals, i.e., the unknown." He also outlines steps for casting the net more widely in attracting proposals. Bothwell is not oblivious to community foundation stringencies, including the public support test, though he suggests caution in how funds are raised. We can expect to hear more from him since the NCRP began its own study of community foundations in the fall of 1988 and is scheduled to report in 1989.

Part II of this volume, 16 case studies of leadership by community foundations, is intended to provide an insider's view of how things work at critical moments and on critical issues. The cases were selected for diversity in geography and size, categories of leadership, variety of subjects, and, to the extent that it is possible, replicability. The intent was to show present and future community foundation trustees, staff, and prospective donors (and, presumably grantseekers) how things are done. All this depended on candor. As we said in the guidelines for writers of these cases, "[They] should be lively, candid descriptions ... explicit and graphic, but not melodramatic. They should convey the actual dynamics of the situation, including difficulties and ambiguities as well as achievements...."

This was devoutly to be wished, but not altogether consummated. While we sought independent writers, we wanted them all to be familiar with the community; all but one are local residents, and a few had done some work for the foundations they wrote about. That does not necessarily compromise their objectivity; nor does it guarantee their independence. For another, CEOs of community foundations are no less protective of their institutions than executives of other types of organizations, so in a few cases executive directors were gun-shy about some parts of the first drafts.

The cases are grouped according to areas in which leadership was exercised, though clearly some cases could fit in more than one category.

As *conveners around community needs*, the work of four community foundations is discussed. The California Community Foundation (Chapter 11) enlisted banks, private foundations, government agencies, and an array of nonprofit organizations to tackle an issue arising from the Immigration Reform and Control Act of 1986—the costs illegal immigrants faced in the complex process of applying for amnesty. The issue that engaged the Dayton (Ohio) Foundation (Chapter 12) was the decay of the public schools following industrial decline and a bitter school desegregation struggle. The chosen instrument was the establishment of a Public Education Fund, one of a national network of such funds, for Dayton and the surrounding suburban county. The foundation knit together city and county school officials, the teachers union, and local businesses. The Dade Community Foundation (Chapter 13) took on the deep-seated, vexing issue of racial strife in the Miami, Florida, area. The foundation chose two programs for bridging the gaps between the county's black, Hispanic, and white communities. One helps inner-city teenagers set up businesses that operate in other ethnic neighborhoods as well as their own; in the other, the Miami Arts Bridge, arts organizations of all backgrounds share their talent with different ethnic audiences. Child care was the issue in Greenville, South Carolina, where 60 percent of all children under age six have mothers who work (Chapter 14). The Community Foundation of Greater Greenville collaborated with a church coalition human services support group, a community planning council, a university, the United Way, and local businesses in a comprehensive educational and referral effort. Despite delicate turf problems, the effort has succeeded.

Asset growth, analyzed at length in Chapter 5 and mentioned in many other places in this book, is illustrated in graphic actuality in cases concerning El Paso, Texas, Sonoma, California and Tacoma, Washington. In El Paso (Chapter 15), the community foundation takes literally the adage of personalized philanthropy and the principle that you have to ask to get. Some may regard such devices as the Giving Catalog, aggressive press relations, special occasion cards, and shopping mall tie-ins as faintly undignified, but it all works. When the foundation had to match a $500,000 Ford Foundation challenge grant, the money poured in not only from wealthy Hispanics and Anglos but also from elderly widows on Social Security who gave $1 to $5. In Tacoma (Chapter 16), the community foundation took the unusual step of building an endowment for administrative expenses before a grantmaking endowment. The impetus came from a local private foundation's challenge that members of the community foundation board match, dollar-for-dollar, a $270,000 grant—to be pledged in seven weeks. The board chairman struck boldly, he wrote figures he believed each of 12 board members could donate, and slipped them into envelopes. The shock treatment worked. The case study also describes one-on-one efforts with other individuals and companies to meet another provision of the grant, $540,000 for unrestricted endowment. In Sonoma (Chapter 17), a new executive director opened a path to new funds by gaining attention for the community foundation through a targeted effort on parent education at worksites. The effort drew funds from private foundations that had never before made grants in the area. The project was controversial and it required a juggling act to persuade several social agencies to cooperate.

Community foundations *help nonprofit organizations* in many ways besides writing checks. Under this rubric we have the cases of Atlanta and Cleveland (Chapters 18 and 19). Since the community foundation in metropolitan Atlanta has only a small proportion of its assets in unrestricted or field-of-interest funds, it helps the 600 nonprofit organizations in its region by sponsoring workshops on nonprofit management and fundraising skills and giving annual public recognition and cash awards to nonprofit groups that have improved their management practices or sustained good administration. Cleveland's work with one set of nonprofit organizations—arts groups—is far more complex and raises delicate issues of how far a community foundation should go in calling the tune. This intriguing study details the evolution of a coordinated approach to planning for the arts. Although the firmness of the foundation's guiding hand may be questioned, the results are impressive.

Closely related to the role of convener is the *catalytic leadership* a community foundation can exert on *critical issues*. The two examined here are Bridgeport, Connecticut, and Arizona (Chapters 20 and 21). Small, and living amidst geographically competing community foundations, the Bridgeport Area Foundation nonetheless demonstrated agile leadership on an extremely sensitive issue—teenage pregnancy and the volatile concomitants of birth control and abortion counseling. Over four years the community foundation obtained the formal collaboration of adolescent pregnancy coalitions—one Catholic, the other non-Catholic. The ingredients were not only money as a "carrot" (provided by a private foundation under a strict condition of collaboration), but painstaking consultation and negotiation and, above all, patience. In Arizona the issue was decidedly noncontroversial—the paucity of services for mentally ill children. A $500,000 Ford Foundation challenge grant obtained by the statewide community foundation was crucial. Of equal importance was its role in convening professionals in the mental health field, in working with a state-mandated mental health task force, and in acting as a partner in a complex legislative process that broke a logjam on state services and funds for children's mental health services.

Neighborhood development by community foundations in Boston, in Philadelphia, and in Charlotte, North Carolina (Chapters 22, 23, and 24) ranges from community organizations to the apparent luxury of beautification.

The Boston Foundation, in a marked shift from support of institutions close to the interests of its largely Brahmin donor base, branched out in the 1980s to launch a $10-million, five-year Poverty Impact Program. That was followed by a community organizing initiative, further underscoring the foundation's commitment to issues of poverty and race.

Philadelphia's community foundation has an older commitment to the underclass, reflecting, said one historian, "the good face of the power structure." In the 1980s the foundation adopted an "empowerment policy" that emphasizes advocacy over direct service, preference to smaller agencies, and direct participation by poor or minority people.

The Foundation for the Carolinas turned, with the help of a grant from the Charles Stewart Mott Foundation, to neighborhoods in Charlotte that had not shared that city's recent prosperous growth. The effort, involving a university on the one hand and, on the other, small grassroots groups, has had to overcome trepidation on its own "Who's Who" board and suspicion at the neighborhood level.

To call minorities and women *"new philanthropists"* is historically inaccurate but appropriate in the sense of new roles in organized philan-

thropy. In Kansas City, Missouri (Chapter 25), the Hall Family Foundations, concluding they were out of touch with the black and Hispanic
communities, stimulated the birth of funds run by and for those groups.
The local community foundation was a clear choice for handling administrative chores that would dilute the minority funds' concentration on grantmaking. Similarly, the Minneapolis Foundation (Chapter
26) was the vehicle for the new Minnesota Women's Fund—"a natural
fit," as one executive put it, though the process was complicated. Despite difficulties over lines of authority, fundraising goals, and organizational structure, it has grown to be one of the largest of the country's
40 women's funds and one of the few that is endowed and statewide.

Selecting 16 cases from a field of more than 300 is no way to win
friends, so on behalf of the National Agenda Leadership Committee
I want to underscore the obvious. Among the hundreds of community foundations not covered in this book are many excellent, agile
examples.

Visiting places that are not explicitly covered in these pages also
underscores the lesson not to leap to conclusions. Thus, if ever a
stereotype existed of an affluent community that needed social services
less than it needed another yacht, Palm Beach, Florida, would seem
to fill the bill. Yet as Shannon Sadler, Director of the Palm Beach County
Community Foundation has demonstrated, "the needs of migrant
workers, the elderly, victims of AIDS, the homeless, the handicapped,
the environment, the arts and education, have no boundaries." Nor,
after visiting the well-appointed offices of community foundations with
hundreds of millions of dollars in assets does one, against one's better
judgment, expect to find imaginative leadership in a small second-
floor office, equipped with used furniture, on a quiet main street in
Burlingame, California. Yet there one finds Bill Somerville's Peninsula
Community Foundation doing not only what a lot of other foundations do but also providing free office space for nonprofit officials between jobs, publishing handy tip sheets on raising funds from individuals and tapping corporations for cash and 38 nonmonetary
sources of support, drawing young adults into philanthropy, and in-
sisting that his staff answer the phone before it rings three tmes. One
sees a darker side too, as in being shown around East St. Louis, Illinois,
by Handy Lindsey, on loan from the Chicago Community Trust, in
a brave but (so far) vain effort to seed a community foundation in
a community of despair.

The Council on Foundations has published a broadside, "Common
Characteristics of Community Foundations." It is concise and useful.

But let us also praise the uncommon in the field, the variety, and the mood in the last several years in which the sleepiest of the lot, the most traditional, the most unconnected, can quickly evolve into vibrant instruments for service on the toughest community needs of the moment and for the longer run.

In that spirit, the last word falls to Martin Paley of San Francisco who, unhappily, no longer works in the field. They were written in response to one of the most interesting facets of the National Agenda, Alicia Philipps's Task Force on Future Needs of Community Foundations:

> I would hope that as the years unfold there will be no lessening of the spirit of adventure and exploration. . . . At all costs, the community foundation should avoid the tendency to become more formal, more bureaucratic and more distant. [And] if the community foundation sees itself as an active member of the philanthropic community rather than as a predestined leader, I think it will continue as a singularly important vehicle in sustaining community values, assisting in the resolution of current problems and fostering a sense of future.

New York, May 31, 1989

Part I: Essays

1

Community Foundations: The Delicate Question of Purpose

David C. Hammack

Frederick H. Goff's often-quoted rationale for the community foundation—that it is "an agency for making philanthropy more effective and for cutting off as much as is harmful of the dead past from the living present and the unborn future"—has an eminently sensible ring. As a careful student of the movement noted in 1961, Goff's "concept involved a partnership of expertness between the banks and citizen leaders," with bank trust departments managing the funds and "a committee of citizens selected by representative community leaders as being well versed in community needs and services" supervising the distribution of income and, where appropriate, principal, and holding the power, "if literal compliance with the donor's instructions became impossible, impracticable, unnecessary, or undesirable, so to amend the specifications for the use of funds that the donor's intent could still be carried out effectively."[1]

But on second thought, a community foundation seems a strange sort of institution. It differs in two striking respects from other philanthropic organizations that create endowments—such organizations as churches, schools, libraries, hospitals, museums, orchestras, and dance companies. By intent and definition, a community foundation has no single, fixed, active purpose. Nor are its leaders definitely to be drawn from a particular segment of the community: by intent, the archetypal distribution committee consists of people chosen for their knowledge of "community needs and services," not for their leadership in any particular religious group or profession or for their acceptability to previous members of the committee. Classically too, the members of a distribution committee are selected not by donors or their acquaintances, but by people who hold key posts in the courts and in such private institutions as chambers of commerce and universities, people whose qualifications and characteristics are certain to change from time to time. To put the point baldly, those who commit unrestricted funds to a community foundation agree to support purposes they cannot know, purposes that are certain to be changed in ways they cannot anticipate by a group of people whose identities and commitments are also certain to change. It was this very arrangement that Goff described as an instrument "for cutting off ... the dead past from the living present."

Since contributors to community foundations are very much alive when they make their donations or write their wills, they must have reason to believe that the foundation's purposes will, in fact, be purposes they approve. To judge from the ups and downs of 75 years of history, potential contributors have accepted the community foundation rationale much more readily at some times and places than at others. As a result, community foundations have expanded (if we measure their size in total assets, valued in constant dollars) with particular

FIGURE 1. COMMUNITY FOUNDATION ASSETS: AVERAGE ANNUAL GROWTH RATE FOR PERIODS OF VARYING LENGTH, 1921–1987

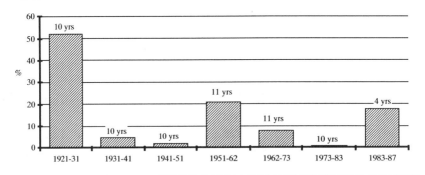

Sources: *Community Trusts in the United States and Canada,* issued by the Trust Company Division, American Bankers Association, 1931. Frank D. Loomis, *Community Trusts of America, 1914–1950* (Chicago: National Committee on Foundations and Trusts for Community Welfare, 1950). *Community Foundations in the United States and Canada, 1914–1961,* prepared by Wilmer Shields Rich (New York: National Council on Community Foundations, Inc., 1961).

vigor in the Midwest and the Northeast in two distinct periods: the 1920s and the 1950s and 1960s.

More recently, community foundations have shown considerable vigor in the 1980s, both in their original regions and also in parts of the West and the South (see Table 1 below and Figure 2 of Chapter 2). Looking back, we can identify clear purposes and the social conditions that account for community foundation growth. Perhaps we can also discern some of the leading purposes that are guiding the community foundation movement at present.

TABLE 1. COMMUNITY FOUNDATION ASSETS, 1921–1987

Year	Current assets ($ million)	Assets in 1967 ($ million)	Period growth rate in 1967 (%)	Average annual growth rate in period (%)	Assets of NY, Chicago, Boston, San Francisco, Marin, & Cleveland as % all assets
1921	7	13	–	–	76
1931	37	81	523	52	58
1941	54	122	51	5	42
1951	110	141	16	2	45
1962	425	469	233	21	45
1973	1,200	902	92	8	48
1983	2,800	966	9	1	50
1987	4,719	1,675	73	18	44

Sources: *Community Trusts in the United States and Canada,* issued by the Trust Company Division, American Bankers Association, 1931; Frank D. Loomis, *Community Trusts of America, 1914–1950* (Chicago: National Committee on Foundations and Trusts for Community Welfare, 1950); *Community Foundations in the United States and Canada, 1914–1961,* prepared by Wilmer Shields Rich (New York: National Council on Community Foundations, Inc., 1961); Frederick Bartenstein, III, and Charles W. Ingler, "Community Foundations Growth Analysis," unpublished working document, The Dayton Foundation, June 1985; Joanne Scanlan, Council on Foundations, 1989.

ORIGINS OF THE COMMUNITY FOUNDATION

A clue to the success of the community foundation movement in the 1920s can be found in the circumstances of the creation of the pioneer community foundation in Cleveland, Ohio, in 1914. The Cleveland Foundation was only one of several new organizations that provided a new framework for philanthropic and nonprofit activity between 1903 and 1919. Nineteenth-century philanthropy generally involved small organizations affiliated with particular religious groups; in nearly every case, these organizations were personally controlled by small numbers of wealthy sponsors. Twentieth-century philanthropy increasingly distinguished religious from secular purposes; provided greater scope for professional control of medical, educational, and social services; and developed funding and coordinating agencies that served the metropolitan community as a whole. Cleveland took the lead in this national transformation of the charitable framework.[2]

The critical first step in the creation of Cleveland's new philanthropic framework was a decision on the part of Protestant leaders to separate religion from most charitable activity, and to establish a new organization, the Federated Churches of Greater Cleveland (1911; now the Interchurch Council of Greater Cleveland) to coordinate fundraising and specifically religious charitable activities for most Protestant denominations. The Jewish Community Federation, established in 1903, provided a partial example for the Federated Churches; the Catholic Charities Corporation, dating in preliminary form to 1910, formally organized in 1919, followed.

Once the separate religious associations were in place, the Cleveland Chamber of Commerce took the lead in creating a new Federation for Charity and Philanthropy (1913). Designed to evaluate and monitor the nonreligious activities of charities in the metropolitan area and to conduct annual community chest-type drives to raise operating funds for them, the Federation for Charity and Philanthropy emphasized professionalism and businesslike management rather than religious commitment. In effect, the charity federation played the role of a private government, carrying out both the annual fundraising and supervisory functions now carried out by United Way, and the planning and coordination functions of many welfare councils. To the distress of those who believed that "any system of charity which ignores the transforming power which the Gospel brings to the needy ones is false"[3]— but to the relief of Catholics and Jews who also wished to participate in community-wide charitable activities—the federation's leaders emphasized secular virtues: businesslike efficiency and professional expertise.

The Cleveland Foundation fit very well into the new governing framework for private charity. As defined by Goff, president of the Cleveland Trust Company, it was to be a private, nonsectarian organization with public purposes. In keeping with the defining purpose of flexibility, and with the new emphasis on interfaith cooperation based on a separation of charitable work from religious work, the funds were also to be used "for such other charitable purposes as will best make for the mental, moral, and physical improvement of the inhabitants of the City of Cleveland as now or hereafter constituted, regardless of race, color or creed."[4]

Goff was determined that his new organization should serve two special purposes. One had to do with the kinds of funds involved:

the community foundation was to accumulate and manage permanent charitable endowments, rather than to raise annual operating funds. The community foundation's second distinctive purpose had to do with leadership. The great new foundations—Russell Sage Foundation (1907), Carnegie Corporation (1911), Rockefeller Foundation (1913)—sought to understand the causes of human misfortune and social dysfunction through scientific, medical, and social research. Having identified the causes, the great foundations intended to lead— to find and promote, among both private and public agencies, new social policies that would put the results of disciplined inquiry into effect.[5]

Goff himself had been an attorney for John D. Rockefeller and he had read the account of *Seven Great Foundations* by Leonard C. Ayres of the Russell Sage Foundation; he fully understood the ways in which a foundation might play a leading part in defining needs.[6]

To assure that the Cleveland Foundation would indeed carry out its public purposes and contribute effectively to the new coordination of philanthropy, Goff acceded to the suggestions of a Cleveland journalist—and of his own wife—and worked out a way to secure public representation on what would later be known as the distribution committee. This would consist of five people, two selected by the Cleveland Trust Company, and one each chosen by the mayor of Cleveland, the senior judge of the United States District Court, and the senior probate judge of Cuyahoga County.[7]

Having defined most of the legal and institutional arrangements that would characterize community foundations, Goff moved quickly to make the Cleveland Foundation creditable to the public and attractive to donors by arranging for several ambitious "surveys." Using Cleveland Trust Company funds and his own, he brought to Cleveland as survey director Allen T. Burns, who had for five years directed the effort of a local civic committee to carry out the recommendations of the Russell Sage Foundation's famous Pittsburgh Survey, a study of living and working conditions in the steel district. Under Burns and, later, Raymond Moley, a Western Reserve University political science professor who would go on to become a member of Franklin D. Roosevelt's brain trust, the Cleveland Foundation sponsored a remarkable series of studies of relief agencies, public schools, recreation, and criminal justice. Conducted with the cooperation of such other agencies as the charity federation, the public school system, and the bar association, these studies were carried out by such nationally distinguished experts as Sherman C. Kingsley, director of the Elizabeth McCormick Memorial Fund of Chicago; Leonard C. Ayres, head of the Russell Sage Foundation's Education Department; and Harvard law professors Roscoe Pound and Felix Frankfurter.

The "fundamental purpose" of the surveys, as Moley put it, was "to make the public want certain conditions changed." Change itself, he added, would come when "democratic institutions," both private and public, "be they schools or settlement houses or courts," recognized that the public demanded it.[8]

TRUST COMPANIES AND CHAMBERS OF COMMERCE: INITIAL SUCCESS IN THE MIDWEST AND NORTHEAST, 1915-1935

The community foundation spread quickly from its Cleveland origin in the years between 1914 and 1929. Two regions proved most receptive: the Midwest, where community foundations fit effectively into the civic culture, and the Northeast, where nonprofit organizations already played such important roles. Trust companies, which at the time provided valued investment management and advising services to many people who held large estates, took the lead in promoting community foundations everywhere; to assist them, the Trust Division of the American Bankers Association established in 1920 a Committee on Community Trusts.

Community foundations fit particularly well into the civic culture of many cities in the greater midwestern region that reaches from Buffalo to Minneapolis to St. Louis, and whose influence extends south to Dallas and Atlanta and west to Denver. In the years between 1900 and 1929 this culture found vigorous expression in the activities of chambers of commerce. As in Cleveland, many chambers of commerce in this region took the lead in setting up both federated fundraising campaigns and community foundations, thus subordinating social agencies to a central community chest. Historian Peter Dobkin Hall has shown that, by 1922, there were active community foundations and charitable federations in many midwestern cities, and nowhere else in the United States.[9]

Community foundations in many midwestern cities also emulated Cleveland's example by sponsoring forthright surveys, as they were called, of disputed social problems. In Chicago, Norman Wait Harris and his son, Albert Wadsworth Harris, of the Harris Trust and Savings Bank, set up a community trust in 1915, underwrote its early expenses, and endowed it with their own funds. To attract attention and support, they launched a systematic study of "Americanization Services in Chicago," a matter of great controversy at the time. This study gained a good deal of local attention and led, between 1918 and 1922, to surveys

TABLE 2. COMMUNITY TRUSTS WITH ASSETS GREATER THAN $100,000 IN 1930
BY REGION AND DATE OF ORIGIN

Region/City	Year formed	Assets ($1,000)			
		1930	1949	1960	1987
Midwest					
Cleveland, OH	1914	3,000	11,100	26,000	459,051
Chicago, IL	1915	5,100	10,800	31,000	278,024
Detroit, MI	1915	200	300	600	*
Milwaukee,WI	1915	700	300	1,100	61,737
Minneapolis, MN	1915	200	1,900	4,600	106,322
Indianapolis, IN	1916	1,900	3,200	8,100	44,712
Youngstown, OH	1918	700	800	2,200	32,396
Dayton, OH	1921	300	300	700	20,532
Grand Rapids, MI	1922	100	400	4,100	38,334
Northeast					
Boston, MA	1915	4,800	8,700	36,600	194,375
Cambridge, MA	1916	200	400	600	2,826
Williamsport, MA	1916	200	700	1,100	16,881
Philadelphia, PA	1918	600	1,500	3,800	60,865
Buffalo, NY	1920	1,000	1,600	4,800	24,001
New York, NY	1920	8,700	18,700	30,100	545,076
Hartford, CT	1925	100	1,700	11,600	133,393
New Haven, CT	1927	100	1,700	9,000	73,510
South					
Winston-Salem, NC	1919	400	3,700	9,700	42,165
Tulsa, OK	1919	100	20	200	1,024
West					
Los Angeles, CA	1915	300	4,300	8,700	69,961
Denver, CO	1925	1,000	200	—	19,021
Canada					
Winnipeg, Manitoba	1921	2.3	3.0	5.2	NA

*Defunct after 1985, assets of about $1 million turned over to the Community Foundation of Southeastern Michigan.

of other contemporary problems, ranging from housing for young working women, to prenatal care, to the deplorable conditions in the Cook County Jail.[10] In 1930 the Buffalo Foundation still maintained a Bureau of Studies and Social Statistics. Similarly, the Dayton Foundation was, in 1930, devoting much of its income of just over $16,000 to "Research in Civic Affairs" through the Dayton Research Foundation and the Community Chest.[11]

In the Northeast, Connecticut and New York revised their laws in the mid-1920s to encourage community foundations, and these states, together with Massachusetts, proved fertile ground for the new institution.[12] But here the appeal had less to do with a comprehensive restructuring of philanthropic activity. In many northeastern cities, as William P. Gest, chairman of the board of the Fidelity–Philadelphia Trust Company put it in 1927, the community foundation was seen simply as "the mechanical side of individual philanthropy . . . a mechanism of conservation and distribution of charitable funds."[13]

For its first three decades the New York Community Trust provided the most striking example of the "mechanical" quality that Gest emphasized, a quality that might more accurately be described as that of a utility or common carrier providing efficient service to many donors but eschewing a leading role in the general reorganization of philanthropy. Although the New York Community Trust hired Frederick Goff's special assistant, Ralph Hayes, as its first director in 1923, it put its emphasis on the accumulation of distinct funds devoted to a specific purpose—on the creation of what it called "a community of funds, a community of trusts"—and it did not limit itself to funds designed to serve the New York region. One of the first funds that Hayes and his distribution committee attracted, the Moritz and Charlotte Warburg Memorial Fund, was established as early as 1925 to provide scholarships at the Hebrew University in Jerusalem. In 1931, the New York Community Trust accepted its first donor-advised fund, $50,000 from William S. Barstow, who determined himself how the fund's income was to be spent each year until his death more than ten years later. The New York Community trust also influenced many other community foundations, and further developed the community foundation idea as a utility, by adopting from the start the Multiple Trust Plan arrangement, first employed in Indianapolis, of inviting several banks to serve as trustees.

The northeastern community foundations also eschewed the midwestern practice of conducting independent surveys of social and civic problems. In Hartford, Connecticut, for example, the distribution committee formally decided "that it should *not* act in a research or demonstration capacity, but should appropriate funds to already established institutions," enabling them to conduct research or provide services they could not otherwise afford.[14]

As they gathered large resources, however, many of the northeastern foundations found themselves in the thick of debates over the policies that controlled both government and private agencies. The Hartford Foundation supported surveys carried out by the Council of Social Agencies. And by 1930 the Permanent Charity Fund of Boston was appropriating over $200,000 to 117 different private organizations, and taking pride in the leverage it was able to wield over their operating procedures. "One of the most valuable results" of its work, it reported to the American Bankers Association, "has been the strengthening of the trend toward closer association and cooperation between the charitable organizations of Boston and its vicinity." Each of the organizations to which the Fund contributed was required to "consider itself in relation to the whole work of the community, and to adopt "a uniform accounting system."[15]

Despite regional differences, community foundations throughout the United States attracted funds from two groups of donors: well-known business leaders and obscure citizens who identified with the community. Established business leaders played a key role in starting the foundations, defining their purposes, and lending them credibility. Some, like Goff in Cleveland, the Harris family in Chicago, John H. Patterson of Dayton's National Cash Register Corporation, and James Longley of the Boston Safe Deposit and Trust Co., provided significant initial endowments to foundations they started. Others, like the Warburgs in New York and "Wheat King" James A. Patten of Chicago, sought both to use a community foundation's facilities and to lend support to a local institution.

These established leaders sought to define a sense of community: a considerable number of obscure citizens responded with contributions and bequests. One of the first was Alphonse P. Pettis, who had made a small fortune through investments in Indianapolis. He heard about the Indianapolis Foundation many years later, during his retirement on the French Riviera, and he left it an entirely unexpected $300,000 for the benefit of a city in which he had never lived. Every community foundation also received modest contributions: in the 1930s the Hartford Foundation for Public Giving received a typical legacy of this sort, $13,220 from Clara M. Goodman, a public school teacher.[16]

To judge from the paucity of references in the literature, however, smaller contributions were never sufficiently numerous to give community foundations the resounding vote of public approval and support that their leaders might have wished. As Loomis of the Chicago Community Trust observed in 1949, the "glowing expectancy of large and easy money which seems to have animated many of the early Community Trusts [was] seldom realized. Three or four of the early Trusts were fortunate in having substantial funds turned over to them for administration soon after they were organized." But, he added, "most of the Community Trusts which have achieved any success at all soon found they would have to settle down to hard work, to diligent, patient, intelligent promotion of the community trust idea on its own merits.[17]

POSTWAR GROWTH: COMMUNITY FOUNDATIONS AND COMMUNITY CHESTS, 1945–1965

The Great Depression brought the community foundation movement nearly to a halt. The "Crash" reduced many fortunes, and the economic uncertainty that followed may well have discouraged wealthy people from parting with their money. But the depression also reduced confidence in the banks. In 1933, the terrible year of the "bank holiday," the Committee on Community Trusts of the Trust Division of the American Bankers Association ceased to function. Banks appeared to be less secure, and bankers were no longer so self-assured and respected as leaders of civic and charitable affairs. Popular sentiment, and perhaps the sentiment of some people wealthy enough to contribute to community foundations, saw many private organizations as failures and shifted in favor of action by government. As Wilmer Shields Rich pointed out, "by far the outstanding characteristic of these ... years was the lapse into inactivity of a number of community foundations," including those of Louisville, New Orleans, Cincinnati, Houston, Washington, D.C., and Spokane, as well as many in smaller cities.[18] At least 91 community foundations had been started between 1914 and 1939; only 66 remained in operation in 1949, and only 35 controlled the $200,000 in assets needed to earn, at 5 percent, the minimum of $10,000 to pay for a full-time staff person and an office.[19]

The community foundation movement did revive after World War II, but when it did so, it was directed not by banks and trust companies, but by "leaders in community planning." The name of the new umbrella organization for the movement, the National Committee on Foundations and Trusts for Community Welfare, reflected the change. The new promoters often preferred the charitable corporation form (already adopted, largely for tax purposes, in Boston and several other cities) rather than the bank trust agreement; and in some cases they also broke with earlier practice by making their boards self-perpetuating. They also preferred the multiple trustee plan, so as to give all banks providing trust services a reason to encourage donors. The corporate form placed general control in the hands of a citizen committee, subordinating the trust functions carried out by banks.[20]

Postwar community foundation leaders also emphasized a version of the purpose stressed before 1929, the creation of a strengthened framework for private charity, a framework responsive to business and professional leadership and independent of government. More specifically, several spokesmen insisted that their main purpose was to strengthen the local Community Chest. The community chest movement that had developed in middle-sized and large cities in the Midwest, West, and parts of the South in the 1920s had not been ready for the challenge of the depression, and in many places community chests were only weakly established by the late 1940s. After the war, community chest advocates sought to take advantage of revived patriotic and community feeling to put more community chests on a stable footing.

In the West and the South, postwar community chest promoters sought to cope with new problems, and to respond to new opportunities created by rapid urbanization during the war. Everywhere, the leaders of private social welfare organizations were looking for ways to cope with uncertainties about the scope of continuing federal and state activity in the social welfare field. Everywhere, too, private social welfare, medical, and related organizations were pressed to respond to the new situation presented by the historic labor agreements that settled the great strikes of the postwar years. Under these agreements, the company unions and corporate welfare plans provided by many manufacturing and some retail corporations, and some of the welfare activities historically provided by independent unions, were ended. Workers in manufacturing won a very large increase in fringe benefits and vacation time: henceforth they would be able to pay for more medical services, able to make more use of recreational facilities—and more able to contribute to community chest campaigns.[21] In many manufacturing centers, community chests would be called on to support the diagnostic, rehabilitative, and recreational services formerly provided by corporate welfare programs. Everywhere, they would need new resources—often capital resources for new buildings and equipment— to support new activities and to persuade old agencies to accept new missions or consolidations. Community foundations promised the community chest movement stability, legitimacy, and access to a significant source of capital.

The statement of purpose for the community foundation movement offered in 1950 by Edward L. Ryerson, who had been the founding president of the Community Fund of Chicago (a limited community chest organized to coordinate private fundraising during the depression), makes sense in this context. "Community planning for health and welfare, in recent years, has been largely the work of local community chests and councils, and it has been restricted largely to current financing of current needs," Ryerson wrote. "Community planning for social welfare will never be well-rounded or comprehensive until it includes planning for capital gifts and bequests. These are likely to affect the character, the stability and the adaptability of many of our community services over long periods of time."[22]

Accounts of many community foundations in the 1940s and 1950s emphasize their support of community chests. According to Loomis, those in "Boston, Buffalo and Chicago ... had an important part in the development of the local Council of Social Agencies and the local Community Chest." The relationship was reversed in Dallas, Colorado Springs, Norfolk, Newark, Syracuse, New Britain, Bridgeport, Flint, Fort Wayne, Columbus, and Madison, where Community Chest leaders took the initiative in starting or reviving community foundations.[23]

The fullest analysis of community foundation giving patterns in the 1950s concluded that more than half of their grants were going for the operating expenses of social agencies. In 1953 the Indianapolis Foundation played a major role in financing a $2-million building for the United Fund and 35 member agencies. And according to one historian, "in its early days, most of [the New Haven Foundation's] income went almost automatically to established agencies ... the Community Chest regularly received a large contribution." Between 1931 and 1947 the Cleveland Foundation made an annual grant from the Coulby Fund to the community chest.[24]

The close alliance between community foundations and community chests was by no means universal. The San Francisco Foundation, for example, took the position from the time of its creation in 1949 that it would not contribute to federated fundraising campaigns. Like the Philadelphia and Pittsburgh foundations, it took the view that if it made such contributions it would be "abandoning its responsibility to make the best possible distribution of the undesignated funds at its disposal."[25] These community foundations promoted themselves as custodians of capital funds for the changing capital needs of their communities, not for operating needs of ongoing organizations.

Everywhere, contributions to community foundations may well have been stimulated by more general factors. Notable among these was surely the general revival of national pride stimulated by the American experience in World War II. Characterized by the "we've got to do this together" spirit that broke down some of the barriers between Protestants, Catholics, and Jews during the war, this new national pride encouraged a more inclusive sense of community and may well have been behind an increase in the number of smaller contributions to community foundations. There was also a spillover sense of local community pride, especially in towns— in the West and the South as well as in the Midwest and the Northeast—where many people had been deeply engaged in the war effort. And there was the strong postwar suspicion of government and a growing commitment to voluntarism, exemplified by the fringe-benefit clauses of the new labor contracts and the concomitant development of Blue Cross rather than a national health service.

Whatever the explanation, community foundations did grow vigorously in assets between 1945 and 1965. Despite scattered new interest in the South and the West, the Midwest and the Northeast continued not only to sustain the largest number of established community foundations, but to produce the largest numbers of new ones. The result, by 1960, was the general adoption in the larger and wealthier cities of the United States outside the South, of the community chest and the community foundation as central elements in the framework of private agencies for the control of community life.

COMMUNITY FOUNDATIONS SINCE THE MID-1960s: NEW COMMUNITIES, NEW PURPOSES

After expanding vigorously from the end of World War II to the mid-1960s, the total assets of community foundations, measured in constant dollars, failed to grow much at all for 15 years. Why? And why have those assets grown again—at nearly the pace of the postwar years— in the 1980s? The answers seem to have to do with the abrupt changes in the sense of community Paul Ylvisaker describes elsewhere in this volume—and with changing notions of community foundation purposes.

In the mid-1960s several of the largest community foundations played a direct part in challenging the sense of community that had prevailed since World War II. Much of that sense was expressed in what now reads as a very dated statement of the qualities to be desired in a community foundation director. This statement, by the leader of a large community trust in the late 1940s, was intended as advice for the use of community foundation boards across the country. Implicitly, it also described the nature of the community such a director would serve.

"The community trust executive," the statement began, "should preferably be a *man* (although one of us was a woman who in time became a great social leader in her community) who is a *college graduate* and who is 'native' to the community to be served." It went on to explain each of the desired qualities. "Men," it noted, "have better entree ... in the numerous areas in which the community trust executive works—such as the banking and legal professions, the courts, the universities, and the social agencies." College training was necessary, "because he will eventually have to turn to the university for help." And the executive should be " 'native' to the community in the sense that he is well-acquainted, well known, and believes in its heritage, present and future." Jews had played important roles in community foundations in Connecticut, New York, San Francisco, and elsewhere; nevertheless, the statement was couched in the language of Protestant discourse: "Since a community trust exists to improve the community, the director must have an abiding faith in it."[26]

Chicago's Frank Loomis added that while "mere professionalism" was to be avoided, a "community trust executive must have an aptitude for welfare work, a 'feel' for it ... ability to understand and appreciate [and evaluate] the teachers, the preachers, the nurses and physicians, the social workers."[27] Loomis expected these criteria to be applied by trustees selected without regard to "political, partisan, or sectarian considerations." Trustees should be "men and women highly respected for their character, intelligence, and good judgement ... in community welfare work"; they would ordinarily include former "presidents or vice presidents of the Community Chest, or chairmen of its Budget Committee, or ... of the Welfare Council or of one of the large private charities." The trustees, in turn, would be selected by such public officials as the mayor, a judge of the United States District Court, and the judge of a probate court; and by such "semi-public" officials as "the president of a local college or university, the president of the Welfare Council or Community Chest, the president of the Chamber of Commerce or the Bar Association."[28]

The civil rights and women's movements challenged the racial, gender, class, and religious-group assumptions that defined the sense of community for Loomis and other community foundation leaders in the late 1940s. Remarkably, executives and boards at several of the larger, firmly established community foundations quickly "got the message" and changed direction.

These community foundations were able to change because they were large and well-established in four ways: they had significant unrestricted endowments, independence (of a kind never available to a community chest or a welfare council) from both donors and grantees, professional and imaginative staffs, and strong leadership from their boards. They were also strongly encouraged by the Ford Foundation, especially by Public Affairs Program director Paul Ylvisaker. Ylvisaker was seeking ways "to move out of safe and sane hospital, university and similar do-nothing grants ... to begin getting after the more gutsy urban problems." He thought that perhaps "Ford block grants to local foundations [could] ... address the tough problems ... get other philanthropists involved ... and gain the large-scale leverage necessary for getting this country to wake up to social change."

The Kansas City Association of Trusts and Foundations (organized in 1949 to manage four separate trust funds; reorganized as the Kansas City Community Foundation in 1986) enjoyed all the advantages that permitted a sharp change, and it was perhaps the first to move in the new direction. With assets of about $12 million in 1961, a forceful director, Homer C. Wadsworth, and a $1.25 million grant from Ylvisaker's Ford program, the Kansas City organization moved boldly, about 1960, into "community-action style philanthropy," some of which involved work with the public schools, even as it also pressed separate initiatives to reorganize health care and increase opportunities for higher education.[29]

In Cleveland, a Ford Foundation evaluator would later write, such key business and civic leaders as Kent Smith and Harold Clark had become "dissatisfied with the course of philanthropy," and in particular with the Cleveland Foundation. In their view the oldest community foundation had become "embedded in a routine pattern of responding to unimaginative requests from a standard list of institutional grantees ... a pattern that was ... less and less responsive to the real and changing needs of the Cleveland community." Encouraged by the availability of the very considerable assets of the newly available Hanna Trust and by conversations with Ylvisaker and Henry Heald, then president of the Ford Foundation, Smith and Clark developed a plan to shake things up. As journalist Diana Tittle reconstructs it, their plan called for a new "Greater Cleveland Associated Foundation," to be sponsored by, but somewhat separate from, the Cleveland Foundation and four other local foundations, and to be financed and endorsed by the Ford Foundation. The purposes assigned to the Associated Foundation harkened back to the Cleveland Foundation's early surveys and anticipated the work that several other community foundations would undertake in the later 1960s and the 1970s:

to encourage research on and solutions of community social welfare problems ... ;

to establish priorities for community action thereon;

to make grants for research, pilot, experimental and other projects toward the solutions of such problems;

to make professional staff services available for ... trusts and foundations ... operating ... under difficult circumstances, without professional aid.

Dolph Norton, a young public administration professor whom Kent Smith and Case Institute of Technology president T. Keith Glennan had brought to Cleveland to work in what proved to be an unsuccessful campaign to secure metropolitan-area government, became the head of the new Associated Foundation. Deeply concerned that "the metropolis has no regularized democratic procedures for choosing its goals and bringing the community's resources to bear in achieving them," Norton thought the foundation might, in part, play the role of a regional government.[30]

In practice, Norton and Smith used the Greater Cleveland Associated Foundation to bring the region's business leaders into contact—for the first time—with leaders of the black community, and to provide leadership and resources for aggressive efforts to confront segregated and inadequate public education and employment opportunities, juvenile delinquency, and other intractable urban problems. Several years later Norton also successfully encouraged the Ford Foundation to support a voter registration program in Cleveland's black neighborhoods (part of a national voter registration effort by the Ford Foundation, this action drew severe criticism and restrictive legislation in Congress). When votes from those neighborhoods helped elect Carl Stokes, the city's first black mayor, in 1967, the Greater Cleveland Associated Foundation underwrote Stokes's effort to develop a program. The foundation provided a one-year grant of $68,000 to enable him to employ a public relations consultant. It also worked, with varying degrees of success, to encourage diverse business, neighborhood, and institutional groups to define economic and physical redevelopment plans for the city.[31]

The more active community foundation programs pioneered in Kansas City and Cleveland soon found counterparts elsewhere. Bruce Newman, who went on from an internship at the Greater Cleveland Associated Foundation to become director of the Chicago Community Trust, later asserted that Dolph Norton had "opened up the very closed world" of the community foundation by getting "out in the community, talking with people." Quite independently, John R. May of the San Francisco Foundation was also "out in the community" in the mid-1960s, as Newman shows in his sketch of May in Chapter 4. By the early 1970s, May later recalled, "an overwhelming proportion" of San Francisco Foundation grants were going "to support efforts to try to equalize opportunity in every way."[32]

At the other end of the country, between 1961 and 1964 the Permanent Charity Fund of Boston (now the Boston Foundation) invested over $500,000 in Action for Boston Community Development, which later became the city's official antipoverty agency, and related efforts. In San Francisco and Boston, as in Kansas City and Cleveland, community foundations were pursuing a new purpose, that of enlarging the sense of public—and government—responsibility.

The new sense of community at these and other foundations was soon reflected in staff policies as well. When Dolph Norton left the Cleveland Foundation in 1973, Barbara Rawson, his administrative assistant, became the foundation's acting director—one of the first women to hold such a post. By the mid-1980s black administrators held important positions in several community foundations. Two of them, one man and one woman, head two of the largest—those in Cleveland and Boston. In her first annual report, Boston's Anna Faith Jones announced a $10 million, five-year commitment to "a new assault on poverty"[33] (see Chapter 22).

FEDERAL REGULATION AND METROPOLITAN REGIONS: COMMUNITY FOUNDATIONS SINCE 1969

The new community purposes advanced by the more active community foundations—and by the Ford Foundation and several major private foundations—after 1960 provoked criticism as well as praise, and some of the criticism contributed to the stagnation in asset growth between about 1965 and 1980 shown in Table 1. (The failure of the stock market to keep pace with inflation during these same years—and the deflating effect of inflation on the value of bonds—also accounted for some of the asset stagnation.) Some potential donors certainly rejected the newly inclusive definitions of community advanced by the Cleveland, Boston, Kansas City, San Francisco, and other community foundations. Less affluent whites, members of European ethnic groups and of labor unions, and Catholics perceived, not incorrectly, that they were only marginal to community-building activities that emphasized relations between blacks (or women) and business leaders: they added protests of their own.

FIGURE 2. COMMUNITY FOUNDATION ASSET GROWTH: 1921–1987

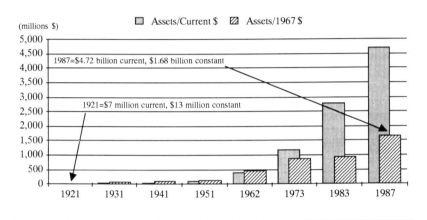

FIGURE 3. COMMUNITY FOUNDATION ASSET GROWTH: 1981–1987

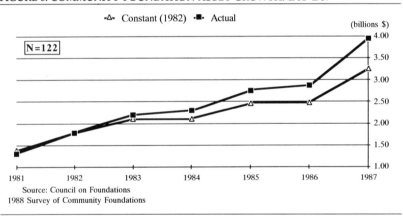

Source: Council on Foundations 1988 Survey of Community Foundations.

Several congressmen responded to these and other currents by challenging the Ford Foundation's support for voter registration drives in black communities and the efforts of many foundations, including several community foundations, to develop and promote new policies to address poverty and inequality. Wright Patman and other congressional critics also objected to the self-dealing and other abuses of many family foundations. These concerns led to the passage of the Tax Reform Act of 1969, with extensive new provisions for foundations of all kinds. Although the Act treated community foundations relatively well, its passage failed to settle many questions. Treasury officials found the entire foundation field baffling, and they did not issue the rules and regulations required by the Act until 1976. There followed a period of negotiation and adjustment as Norman A. Sugarman and other community foundation leaders worked to modify the new rules in a process well described by Newman in his chapter (4) on "pioneers."[34] It is not surprising that donations to community foundations lagged during this period of uncertainty.

When the new federal tax rules were established in late 1976, community foundations emerged with significant new advantages. As shown in Chapters 4 and 5, the regulations encouraged the wealthy to give to community foundations, with their more accountable boards and often more adequate professional staffs, rather than to set up private family foundations. Under the tax code, community foundations offered greater deductions to donors, were burdened with fewer limitations on their operations, and, after a few years of additional negotiations, were relieved of the excise tax placed on other foundations.[35]

As Susan Berresford shows in Chapter 8, several large national foundations moved to reinforce the new federal encouragement of community foundations. Four community foundation missions, singled out by the Charles Stewart Mott Foundation, impressed these national foundations:

- Developing a permanent, unrestricted endowment.
- Responding to emerging, changing community needs.
- Providing a vehicle and a service for donors with varied interests.
- Serving as resource, broker, and catalyst in the community.

These are the general agenda-setting, decision-making functions Paul Ylvisaker has in mind when he describes community foundations elsewhere in this volume as "private legislatures." They are also the functions pioneered in Cleveland through surveys and demonstration projects to provide, through a private organization, a kind of leadership unavailable through metropolitan government.[36]

The development of community foundations, encouraged by federal government regulations and by national foundations alike, has apparently been effective. Certainly, community leaders in many cities were impressed by the arguments for community foundations. Businessman Robert H. Levi, for example, became convinced that "you can't sit back and say a city the size of Baltimore is going to survive as a first-class city without a community foundation—without that tool to work with," and joined the board of the Greater Baltimore Foundation.[37] Although most community foundations continued to place the greatest value on the unrestricted endowment, many moved aggressively to attract money that might previously have gone into family foundations by emphasizing "donor-advised funds" and "special interest funds" through which donors (and sometimes their heirs) might continue to influence the use of their money. As Table 1 shows, community foundation assets grew as rapidly in the 1980s as they did in the 1950s.

The newer cities of the South and West have, at last, become large enough and wealthy enough to support effective community foundations. In most of them, donors have been persuaded that community foundations play an essential part among the controlling institutions of private charity. The Midwest and Northeast, however, continue

FIGURE 4. ASSETS OF SIX LARGEST COMMUNITY FOUNDATIONS*
AS % OF ALL ASSETS

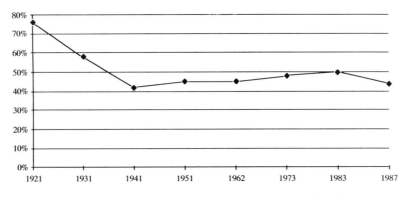

*Boston, Chicago, Cleveland, Marin, New York, San Francisco

Sources: Frederick Bartenstein III and Charles W. Ingler, "Community Foundation Growth Analysis," unpublished working document, TheDayton Foundation, June 1985; Joanne Scanlan, Council on Foundations, 1989.

to provide the most fertile ground; established foundations in those regions have continued to grow, new ones have appeared, and community foundation assets per capita remain much higher than in most places in the South and West.[38] As total assets grew the largest community foundations held their own. New York, Cleveland, Chicago, and Boston, joined in the 1970s by San Francisco and in the 1980s by the Marin Community Foundation, created by the Buck Trust, held between 45 and 50 percent of all community foundation assets throughout the period from 1941 on. Finally, and still more striking, is the emergence of multiple community foundations in many metropolitan regions, especially in the already well-developed Midwest and Northeast (see Table 3).

All this points to one last observation: community foundations, like other private—and public—governing organizations in the United States, have become so numerous and diverse that it is impossible to pin them down to particular organizational forms or animating purposes. Community foundations are divided according to size, region, relationship with the local United Way, and local tradition. They also compete with one another, with operating agencies, and in some places with other coordinating organizations like United Way and the Jewish federations for endowment funds, including funds intended to be used in flexible ways.

Similar patterns operate in other spheres of American life, in the public sector as well as among other "private legislatures" and "private governments." Several chambers of commerce operate simultaneously in many large cities: a large, general chamber often dominated by banks and retail firms, large and small; an elite general chamber comprised of the 50 or so largest corporations in a metropolitan region; many neighborhood and suburban chambers serving local retailers; and a variety of industrial and professional associations. Nor is it any easier to draw boundaries around municipal governments: certain Cleveland residents, for example, live within the boundaries of the school district of Shaker Heights, an adjacent suburb; Shaker Heights residents pay a Cleveland department for water and sewer services; residents of many municipalities use the trolleys and buses of the Regional Transit Authority and the Metropolitan Parks; and the police employed by the private housekeeping organization for most of the city's cultural institutions, University Circle, Inc., have arrest powers within Cleveland's city limits.

The purposes of community foundations are bound to continue to proliferate. But in the increasingly fragmented context of the great metropolitan regions that now house nearly four-fifths of the American population, well-endowed and effectively led community foundations may be able to shape many social, cultural, and economic development policies. Under Herbert West, president for the last 22 years, the New York Community Trust, for example, took on growing responsibility for community leadership in response to New York City's fiscal, energy, and substance abuse crises, encouraged the development

TABLE 3. FIFTY LARGEST METROPOLITAN REGIONS, BY POPULATION, 1986,
WITH SELECTED COMMUNITY FOUNDATIONS SIZE AND RANK, 1987

Rank	Region	Population (1,000)	Foundation	Assets ($1,000)	Rank	Founding Date
1	NY–NJ–Long Island	17,968	(NY Com. Trust)	545,076	1	1923
			(Westchester)	1,520		1975
			(Long Island)			1978
			(Com. Fdn. NJ)	4,157		1979
			(Plainfield, NJ)	3,603		1920
			(Westfield, NJ)	1,502		1975
	–Connecticut		(Bridgeport, CT) (Berkshire–Taconic Fdn.)	6,011		1967
			(Fairfield, CT)	878		1982
			(Greenwich, CT)	705		1955
			(New Canaan, CT)	1,900		1977
	–New Haven	512	(New Haven, CT)	73,510	13	1928
			(Branford, CT)			1981
			(Guilford, CT)			1975
			(Waterbury, CT)	5,354		1924
			(Meriden, CT)	2,600		1932
2	LA–Anaheim– Riverside	13,075	(California)	69,961	14	1915
			(Riverside)	6,268		1941
			(Pasadena)	3,215		1953
			(Glendale)	1,200		1956
	–Ventura		(Ventura)	103		1987
	–Santa Barbara	339	(Santa Barbara)	31,536	28	1928
3	Chicago–Gary– Kenosha	8,116	(Chicago Com. Trust)	278,024	4	1915
			(Aurora)	7,162		1948
			(Evanston)	149		1986
			(Oak Pk–Riverforest)			1959
			(Kenosha)			1926
4	SF–Oakland– San Jose	5,878	(San Francisco)	164,144	6	1948
			(Marin)	448,972	3	1986
			(East Bay)	6,962		1928
			(Peninsula)	14,289	47	1964
			(Santa Clara)	7,160		1954
			(Santa Cruz)	2,119		1982
			(Sonoma)			1986
5	Phila–Wilm– Trenton	5,833	(Philadelphia)	60,865	19	1918
			(Delaware)	50		1986
6	Detroit–Ann Arbor	4,601	(SE Mich)	15,081	45	1984
			(Ann Arbor)	2,820		1963
7	Boston–Lowell	3,705	(Boston)	194,375	5	1915
			(Old Colony)	2,790		1955
			(Cornerstone)			1953
			(Perpetual)	1,788		1932
			(Cambridge)	2,826		1916
	–Nashua, NH		(New Hampshire)	33,830	26	1962
	–Worcester	408	(Worcester)	10,048	61	1975

TABLE 3. FIFTY LARGEST METROPOLITAN REGIONS, BY POPULATION, 1986,
WITH SELECTED COMMUNITY FOUNDATIONS SIZE AND RANK, 1987 (cont.)

Rank	Region	Population (1,000)	Foundation	Assets ($1,000)	Rank	Founding Date
8	Dallas–Fort Worth	3,655	(Texas)	157,964	7	1953
			(Dallas)	12,344	53	1929
			(Tarrant Cty.)	14,808	46	1980
			(Navarro)	7,053		1938
			(Waxahachie)	450		1970
9	Houston–Galveston	3,634	(Houston)	—		—
10	Washington, D.C.	3,563	(C.F. of Greater Wash.)	9,253	62	1973
			(N. Virginia)	250		1978
			(Columbia, Md.)	792		1969
11	Miami–Ft. Lauderdale	2,912	(Dade Cty.)	12,182	55	1967
			(Broward Cty.)	996		1984
			(Palm Beach Ct)	3,309		1972
12	Cleveland–Akron–Lorain	2,766	(Cleveland)	459,051	2	1914
			(Bratenahl)			
			(Akron)	9,214	63	1955
			(Stark Cty.)	23,371	35	1964
			(Lorain Cty.)	8,395	69	1980
			(Lake Cty.)			1932
	–Canton	400	(Canton)	9,000	64	1963
	–Wooster		(Wayne Cty.)	435		
	–Mansfield		(Richland Cty.)	15,245	43	1945
13	Atlanta	2,561	(Metro. Atl.)	68,020	15	1951
			(Atlanta Fdn.)	6,416		1921
			(Gwinnett)			1986
14	St. Louis	2,438	(St. Louis)	6,686		1915
15	Pittsburgh	2,316	(Pittsburgh)	108,690	10	1945
16	Minneapolis–St. Paul	2,295	(Minneapolis)	106,322	11	1915
			(St. Paul)	104,132	12	1940
			(Minnesota)	8,025	72	1949
17	Seattle–Tacoma	2,285	(Seattle)	31,394	29	1946
			(Tacoma)	4,952		1977
			(Stanwood–Camano)	69		1961
			(Spokane)			
18	Baltimore	2,280	(Baltimore)	11,252	58	1972
19	San Diego	2,201	(San Diego)	29,802	31	1975
20	Tampa–St. Petersburg	1,914	—	—		—
21	Phoenix	1,900	(Arizona)	12,298	54	1978
22	Denver–Boulder	1,847	(Denver Fdn.)	19,021	39	1925
23	Cincinnati–OH–IN–KY	1,690	(Greater Cin.)	61,835	16	1963
			(Hamilton City)	8,386	70	1951
24	Milwaukee	1,552	(Milwaukee Fdn.)	61,737	17	1915
25	Kansas City, MO–KS	1,518	(Greater K.C.)	27,764	32	1978
26	Portland–Vancouver WA	1,364	(Oregon)	41,151	23	1973
			(Clark City, WA)	1,040		
27	New Orleans	1,334	(Greater New Orleans)	5,151		1924
28	Norfolk–Va. Beach	1,310	(Norfolk)	26,061	33	1950

TABLE 3. FIFTY LARGEST METROPOLITAN REGIONS, BY POPULATION, 1986, WITH SELECTED COMMUNITY FOUNDATIONS SIZE AND RANK, 1987 (cont.)

Rank	Region	Population (1,000)	Foundation	Assets ($1,000)	Rank	Founding Date
29	Columbus, OH	1,299	(Columbus)	119,000	9	1943
			(Columbus Youth)			
			(Mt. Vernon)	6,714		1944
			(Licking Cty.)			1956
30	Sacramento	1,291	(Sacramento Reg.)	2,755		1983
31	San Antonio	1,276	(San Antonio Area)	13,696	50	1964
32	Indianapolis	1,213	(Indianapolis)	44,712	21	1916
33	Buffalo–Niagara	1,182	(Buffalo)	24,000	34	1919
34	Providence–Pawtucket	1,108	(Rhode Island)	59,000	20	1916
35	Charlotte–Gastonia	1,065	(Carolinas)	35,753	25	1925
			(Gaston Cty.)	2,353		1978
36	Hartford–New Britain	1,044	(Hartford)	133,393	8	1925
			(New Britain)	1,700		1941
38	Oklahoma City	983	(Oklahoma Cty.)	29,900	30	1969
39	Rochester, NY	980	(Rochester Area)	11,351	57	1983
40	Louisville	963	(Louisville)	5,827		1916
41	Memphis	960	(Greater Memphis)	18,339	40	1969
42	Dayton	934	(Dayton)	20,532	38	1921
			(Springfield)	2,500		1948
			(Troy)	9,000	64	1924
43	Nashville	931	—	—	—	—
44	Birmingham	911	(Greater Birmingham)	14,017	48	1959
45	Greensboro–Winston-Salem	900	(Fdn. of Greater Greensboro)	2,427		1983
			(Winston-Salem)	42,165	22	1919
46	Orlando	898	(Winter Park Com. Trust)	2,043		1951
47	Jacksonville, FL	853	(Greater Jacksonville)	3,897		1964
48	Albany–Schenectady–Troy	844	(Mohawk–Hudson)	1,028		1968
			(Cooperstown)	50		1960
			(Corning)			1972
49	Honolulu	817	(Hawaii)	8,785	65	1916
50	Richmond–Petersburg	810	(Greater Richmond)	3,515		1968

Source: David Hammack, *Statistical Abstract of the U.S., 1988.*

of the Tri-State United Way, and supported the formation of community foundations in three suburban areas. As private organizations with quasi-public boards, strongly public purposes, and expansive territories, community foundations may be particularly well designed for such a role in metropolitan regions where no central city houses a large portion of the total population.

As they become more important, community foundations will certainly attract more attention. At present, we have only a few impressionistic efforts to evaluate their impact; only three or four community foundations have yet been the subject of extensive histories. Hence this initial overview of their history can only raise some basic questions: To what extent do community foundations attract endowment funds that might otherwise go to individual agencies? What is the effect of reserving a portion of a community's capital for demonstrations, projects, start-up costs of new organizations, rather than making it available for the difficult-to-finance operating expenses of ongoing agencies—particularly universities, museums, and other educational and cultural institutions? Do metropolitan areas with large community foundations have larger numbers of inadequately funded small research and social service organizations? Or do community foundations increase the tendency to encourage small organizations to merge into larger ones? How widespread are the trends toward more professional management and toward boards that are more representative of the entire community? How general is the apparent shift from support for the capital and operating needs of existing social welfare organizations to investment in active antipoverty programs, inner-city or downtown or regional economic development initiatives, and humanities and the arts? The research agenda will lengthen as community foundations grow.

NOTES

1. *Community Foundations in the United States and Canada, 1914-1961,* prepared by Wilmer Shields Rich (New York: National Council on Community Foundations, Inc., 1961), pp. 8–9.

2. David C. Hammack, "Philanthropy," in *The Encyclopedia of Cleveland History,* edited by David D. Van Tassel and John Graowski (Bloomington: Indiana University Press, 1987), pp. 764–768. An excellent detailed study of the origins of one of these key institutions, the Federation for Charity and Philanthropy, is Brian Ross, "The New Philanthropy: The Reorganization of Charity in Turn of the Century Cleveland" (unpublished Ph.D. dissertation, Case Western Reserve University, 1989).

3. Christian League for the Promotion of Purity, *The Search Light,,* July, 1908, quoted in Ross, "The Reorganization of Charity," ch. V, p. 201.

4. Resolution of Trust of the Cleveland Trust Company, January 2, 1914, quoted in Nathaniel R. Howard, *Trust for All Time: The Story of the Cleveland Foundation and the Community Trust Movement* (Cleveland: The Cleveland Foundation, 1963), pp. 11–12.

5. Barry D. Karl and Stanley N. Katz, "The American Private Philanthropic Foundation and the Public Sphere, 1890-1930," *Minerva* 19 (1981), pp. 236–270; David C. Hammack, "The Russell Sage Foundation," in *Foundations,* edited by Harold M. Keele and Joseph C. Kiger, (Greenwood Press, 1984), pp. 373–380.

6. Rich, *Community Foundations in the United States and Canada, 1914-1961,* p. 9.

7. The best account of the Cleveland Foundation is Diana Tittle, "A History of the Cleveland Foundation," an authorized and unpublished manuscript history in preparation in 1989, ch. II, p. 9. Commenting on Goff's 1913 proposal for the Cleveland foundation, a Rockefeller attorney and Rockefeller Foundation trustee asserted that he had "been greatly interested in the idea which seems to be widely prevalent in Cleveland of getting together in the matter of philanthropic activities of the city. This has already expressed itself in the Cleveland Federation for Charity and Philanthropy ... and the same idea seems to underlie the plan which you have suggested" for a community foundation. Letter, Starr J. Murphy to Frederick H. Goff, December 24, 1913, Cleveland Foundation Papers, Western Reserve Historical Society, quoted in Tittle, "The Cleveland Foundation," p. 13. Murphy's suggestion "that instead of ... the legal form of a trust for charitable uses it would be better to have a corporation organized for the purposes stated" anticipates later developments in the community foundation movement. *See also* Howard, *Trust for All Time,* pp. 7–9.

8. Raymond Moley, *A Review of the Surveys of the Cleveland Foundation* (Cleveland: The Cleveland Foundation, 1923), p. 4–7; Howard, *Trust For All Time,* pp. 30–33.

9. Peter Dobkin Hall, "The Community Foundation in America, 1914-1987," in Richard Magat, ed., *Philanthropic Giving* (New York: Oxford University Press, 1989, pp. 180–199.

10. Frank Denman Loomis, *The Chicago Community Trust: A History of its Development, 1915-1962* (Chicago: Chicago Community Trust, 1962), pp. 4–12.

11. *Community Trusts in the United States and Canada,* issued by the Trust Company Division, American Bankers Association, 1931, pp. 24–26.

12. Glenn Weaver, *Hartford Foundation for Public Giving: The First Fifty Years* (Hartford: Hartford Foundation for Public Giving, 1975), pp. 13–14; *The Story of the New York Community Trust—The First 50 Years* (New York: The New York Community Trust, 1974), pp. 11–12.

13. "The Modernization of Charity: An Explanation of Philadelphia Foundation," by William P. Gest, 1927 (Philadelphia: Fidelity-Philadelphia Trust Company, 1945), p. 6.

14. Weaver, *Hartford Foundation for Public Giving: The First Fifty Years,* pp. 15–18.

15. *Community Trusts in the United States and Canada,* issued by the Trust Company Division, American Bankers Association, 1931, p. 24.

16. Howard, *Trust for All Time*, p. 18; Loomis, *The Chicago Community Trust*, pp. 30–82; Weaver, *Hartford Foundation for Public Giving: The First Fifty Years*, pp. 19–20.

17. Frank D. Loomis, *Community Trusts of America, 1914–1950* (Chicago: National Committee on Foundations and Trusts for Community Welfare, 1950), p. 8.

18. Wilmer Shields Rich, *Community Foundations in the United States and Canada, 1914–1961*, p. 12.

19. Loomis, *Community Trusts of America, 1914–1950*, pp. 8–9.

20. Rich, *Community Foundations in the United States and Canada, 1914–1961*, p. 12.

21. For a penetrating discussion of the difficulties faced by community chests, see the excellent study of Indianapolis, John R. Seeley *et al.*, *Community Chest* (Glencoe, Illinois: The Free Press, 1957).

22. Loomis, *Community Trusts of America, 1914–1950*, pp. 3, 7.

23. Loomis, *Community Trusts of America, 1914–1950*, pp. 17, 19–23.

24. Rich, *Community Foundations in the United States and Canada, 1914–1961*, pp. 45, 48; Howard, *Trust for All Time*, p. 92; Thomas J. Farnham, "The New Haven Foundation," in Harold M. Keele and Joseph C. Kiger, eds., *Foundations* (Greenwood Press, 1984), p. 309; Tittle, "A History of the Cleveland Foundation," ch. 2.

25. Rich, *Community Foundations in the United States and Canada, 1914–1961*, p. 45.

26. Quoted in Loomis, *Community Trusts of America*, p. 27.

27. Loomis, *Community Trusts of America*, p. 27.

28. Loomis, *Community Trusts of America*, p. 25–26.

29. Tittle, "A History of the Cleveland Foundation," ch. V.

30. Ibid., ch. V.

31. Ibid., ch. VII.

32. Gabrielle Morris, interview with John Rickard May, "Building a Community Foundation," Bay Area Foundation History, Regional Oral History Office, The Bancroft Library, University of California, Berkeley, 1976, pp. 111, 114–15, 133.

33. Permanent Charity Fund of Boston, *Annual Report* for 1975, p. 6; The Boston Foundation, *Annual Report* for 1985, p. 3.

34. John A. Edie, "Congress and Foundations: Historical Summary," in Teresa Odendahl, ed., *America's Wealthy and the Future of Foundations* (New York: The Foundation Center, 1987), pp. 47–64; Jack Shakely, "Community Foundations," *Grantsmanship Center News*, March–April 1976, pp. 30–48.

35. John A. Edie, "Congress and Foundations," pp. 54–55; Council on Foundations, "The Public Support Test," Final Report of the Subcommittee on Legislation and Regulations, Committee on Community Foundations, April 1982.

36. Charles Stewart Mott Foundation, "Community Foundations: A Growing Force in Philanthropy," special section of the foundation's *Annual Report* for 1985, pp. 10–14. Lois Roisman provides another good overview of community foundation activities in "The Community Foundation Connection," *Foundation News*, March–April 1982, pp. 2–7.

37. Charles Stewart Mott Foundation, "Community Foundations: A Growing Force in Philanthropy," pp. 23–24.

38. Individual bequests still play a large part in the fate of particular community foundations. It may well be mere chance that accounts for these variations—for the failure of large community foundations to emerge in Detroit and St. Louis, Baltimore and Washington, despite the examples of nearby Cleveland and Chicago, New York and Boston—and for the fact that of the fifty largest metropolitan regions, only Washington D.C., Louisville, St. Louis, Houston, Tampa, New Orleans, Sacramento, Salt Lake City, and Honolulu had failed to develop a community foundation with assets of $10 million or more in 1987. Overall, there is a fairly close correlation between the rank of a metropolitan region in population, and the rank in assets of its largest community foun-

dation. For the fullest current discussion of the recent history of asset growth of private foundations, a history that parallels that of community foundations, see Odendahl, *America's Wealthy and the Future of Foundations.*

2

Community and Community Foundations in the Next Century

Paul N. Ylvisaker

Community is a word of elastic meaning; its capacity to stretch has been challenged over the last century and will be tested even more dramatically during the next. The changing dimensions are not only geographical but include forces of diversity, social fragmentation, values, and shared interests.

THE GEOGRAPHIC DIMENSION

The attraction of the local is so powerful that "grass-roots philanthropy" will never lose its appeal, even as the territorial concept of community constantly expands.

The geographic stretching of community is actually a constant process, simultaneously moving in opposite directions: downward, to the individual neighborhood, and outward, to embrace the entire world and eventually (certainly with environmental concern) all of space. These polarities are magnetic in their attractions; one can draw from them almost a general rule: the more global the foundation, the more it is attracted to the local; the more local the grantmaker, the stronger the urge to reach outward.

What are the driving forces? There seem to be at least four. First is the expanding reality of what we call community. The stable environment we once knew as our neighborhood has dissolved into a fluid urban environment that melds imperceptibly at its edges into a region, a nation, and the world. Physical definitions are almost totally elusive, except as we mark them by imposed feelings of belongingness: Minneapolis–St. Paul are most clearly identified by who roots for the Twins and the Vikings; Boston, by the viewing area of the Celtics, the Red Sox, and the Patriots; New York and Los Angeles, by their televised and otherwise-stereotyped images and life-styles.

In this flowing world of indistinct boundaries, and with modern philanthropy assigned the task of finding generic solutions to root causes mostly lying beyond any local jurisdiction, it is hard to resist the drive toward enlarging territories.

The second and equally powerful force for expansion is financial: the greater potential of a larger territory for fundraising and asset building. This has undoubtedly prompted much of the recent movement toward regional and state-wide community foundations, now accounting for over 10 percent of the total number and rising. The outward movement of the Spokane Inland Northwest Community Foundation is but one example.

A third generating force—the vacuum that usually exists in the coverage of community foundations in adjacent, more rural, areas and regions beyond metropolitan boundaries. Nature abhors vacuums and so do many human-made institutions. It is almost inevitable that existing community foundations would reach out to supply the missing philanthropic service.

It is a short step from such a lack to the fourth motivation for geographical expansion: the social necessity represented by community foundations—a bonding and leavening influence in modern society that only a private agency with flexible resources and public credibility can provide. Modern philanthropy has evolved as America's contribution to the theory and practice of constitutional democracy in an age when complexity and the demand for shared power have outstripped the capacity of governments to handle social problems on their own. Gradually, foundations have emerged from their purely charitable preserve to become an essential and recognized social process—in effect, a set of private legislatures allowing an autonomous determination and implementation of public needs and agendas.

Community foundations are the localized expression of what modern philanthropy has become and has to offer; and as such, they are coming to be everywhere in demand.

✓ THE DIMENSION OF DIVERSITY

Two great social movements have vastly expanded modern concepts of community, both in the United States and worldwide: migration and liberation.

World War II marked the explosive release of these two forces. Self-determination became the rallying cry of colonies everywhere; within a decade it was echoed within industrialized nations as well—dramatically evidenced by the civil rights and women's liberation movements in the United States.

The war had also released another genie—the power to see a global world, over which there could be human movement on a massive scale. The result is the modern "community," an incredible potpourri of human beings drawn or forced from all kinds of cultures and places—as in London and Los Angeles speaking 100 or more languages—everywhere motivated by an intense desire for self-direction and survival. It is that kind of community—diverse and individualistic—to which community foundations are now trying to adapt.

But a cultural lag is evident. Boards and staff only minimally reflect their community's burgeoning diversity. And the distance remains (in some cases is growing) between a status quo perception of a homogeneous citizenry that once may have been, and the heterogeneous, self-determining mixture that has fast become the community of present and future reality.

THE DIMENSION OF FRAGMENTATION

Two other forces are tugging at the very notion of community: individualization and polarization. The rugged individualism that flourished on the frontier and gave the private sector the enviable strength and autonomy it now has, has inexorably extended itself into a ruling maxim: "Get government off my back and let me be."

That elaborating syndrome has become, as de Tocqueville put it, "a habit of the heart"; and while it has extended the range of human freedom, it has also created a pervasive climate of individual isolation and aloneness—poignantly documented by Robert Bellah and his associates in *Habits of the Heart.* Elemental social institutions—family, church, neighborhood—have all been eroded by this atomizing force; the "community" has become more of an ideal to be arduously fabricated than a reality to be assumed and counted upon. Simultaneously, the social cohesion that the concept of community calls up is further jeopardized by the recurrent tendency toward stratification. America's middle class, long the bulwark of its stable communities and its politics of equilibrium, is being magnetized in two opposing directions, the richer and the poorer, while at the same time it is being atomized.

THE DIMENSION OF VALUES

Some jagged fangs of adverse change and reaction are gnawing at that sense of a community of values, the noble truths of the Declaration of Independence and the Constitution, the common aspirations of successive waves of immigrants, the dominance of Judeo-Christian heritage, and the accumulating bonds of an achieving economy and national pride. One scarring bite has come with the rise of religious fundamentalism both here and abroad—an unyielding insistence on value uniformity, an unwillingness to tolerate diversity, a readiness to impose rather than arbitrate social solutions. Another has come from an ominous source wholly alien to accepted values—one to which there is no apparent bridge. Generically, it is known as "the criminal element," a counter-culture built on a combination of violence and greed. The international drug cartels with their own treasuries and armed forces are one variant; the emerging "corporate" street gangs of central cities like Detroit, with bulging bank accounts and armament of their own, are domestic equivalents. So are those now known as "white-collar" criminals, as well as those who take from the community without giving in return. All challenge the presumptions of community, and if not contained could lead to an era of global hegemony of warlords.

THE DIMENSION OF SHARED INTERESTS

If neighbor no longer knows or interacts with neighbor, bonds are increasingly being formed with kindred, if distant, spirits. We reach out and touch them, by telephone, rapid travel, satellite, computer, fax, and every other medium of modern technology. In so many ways, the more distant, the closer; the closer, the more distant.

As one travels outward along this dimension, homogeneity displaces heterogeneity; we select our "neighbors," and it becomes easier to live in this community than in that of our actual residence.

Community foundations live with this depersonalized residue; the question is, to what extent have they, or will they, or can they adapt to it or make something more of it? And will another form of community foundation emerge that fits and flows along this elusive dimension—community foundations of common interest rather than common place?

THE ESSENTIAL ROLE AND CHALLENGE OF COMMUNITY FOUNDATIONS

Whatever territory they select, and whichever dimensions they move along, the essential role that community foundations play is that of making a community more of a community: to strengthen its sense of itself as a community, to help forge ties that bind, to assist in overcoming divisiveness while releasing the powers of diversity, to reap the benefits of self-reliance while tempering the excesses of self-centeredness and escapism into isolating worlds beyond the humanizing discipline of personal interaction.

Community foundations have the distinguishing responsibility of supplying what philanthropy has to offer within a defined territory—however much that territory may enlarge and one's conception of community may expand. Their distinguishing structure—sometimes more, sometimes less—adds the burden and discipline of accountability.

FIGURE 1. COMMUNITY FOUNDATIONS: ASSETS PER CAPITA POPULATION BY STATE

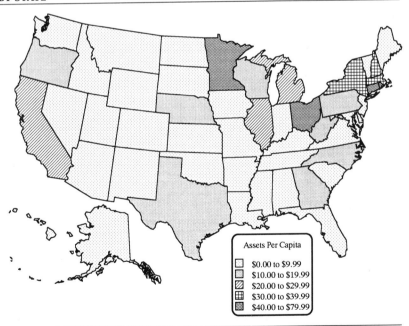

Over half of some 310 community foundations are concentrated in nine states: California (20), Ohio (29), Michigan (27), New York (22), North Carolina (14), Connecticut (14), Florida (10), Pennsylvania (14), and Wisconsin (9).

Source: Nonprofit Services Group, Inc. Washington, DC.

What About That Future and Their Likely Adaptation to It?

1. *Community Foundations will continue to be the fastest-growing sector of the foundation world.* The reasons are several. The most important is the role that philanthropy plays in an evolving and complicating society—a role now coming to be recognized even in the controlled economies and politics of the socialist world. Philanthropy symbolizes and releases the social energies that are only available when expressed spontaneously and autonomously.

Furthermore, the potential represented by community foundations is available to only a selected number of localities. Table 1 shows the geographic distribution of these foundations, now totaling over 300. They are not evenly spread, nor do they cover all the metropolitan areas and cities of a size that could benefit from such philanthropic resources. Greater proliferation and coverage can be expected. This will occur as the notion catches on that the generic concept of community foundations is relevant at different scales, from neighborhoods to regions and states—and for diversifying purposes and constituencies.

TABLE 1. COMMUNITY FOUNDATIONS: NUMBERS, ASSETS, AND GRANTS BY REGION

Region No.	Region Name	States	Number of Community Foundations	Assets (U.S. $)	Grants (U.S. $)
1	Pacific	AK, CA HI, OR, WA	34	905,485,481	45,788,952
2	Mountain	AZ, NM, CO, UT, NV, ID, MT, WY	12	44,030,495	2,222,137
3	West North Central	ND, SD, NE KS, MN, IA, MO	29 19	293,596,956	16,910,149
4	West South Central	TX, OK, AR, LA IL, IN, OH, WI, MI	87	298,356,270	25,903,350
5	East North Central	MS, TN, KY, AL	9	1,421,001,631	101,346,544
6	East South Central	WV, VA, MD, DE,	58	63,736,120	862,840
7	Middle Atlantic	PA, NJ, NY, DC		939,438,984	62,848,826
8	South Atlantic	NC, SC, GA FL, PR	33	228,481,500	29,336,065
9	New England	CT, RI, MA VT, NH, ME	28	524,821,859	30,857,245
		Totals	309	4,718,953,055	316,076,108

Another reason for continued, and probably accelerating, growth is the greater compatibility of community foundations with the democratic tradition of this and other modernized and modernizing nations. Congress, in the historic Tax Reform Act of 1969, recognized this distinctiveness by giving preferred status to these and other nonprofit institutions precisely because of their "public-ness." They were separated out from "private foundations," reflecting congressional respect for their greater accountability to the general public, their heavier reliance on public contributions and the discipline involved, and the assurance they give (with few exceptions) of governance less insulated from public influence than the closed and self-perpetuating boards of private foundations. For all these reasons, one can safely predict the continued and accelerating growth of community foundations well into the next century.

2. There will also be a proliferation of "kinds" of community foundations in the foreseeable future. One can expect not only differing scales of operation, from neighborhood to region and state, but also differential adaptations in form and style to diversifying constituencies, needs, and cultures.

This trend is already evident. In Washington, D.C., Cleveland, and Boston, secondary school students have been organized to become "philanthropists" in their neighboring communities, first analyzing and ranking in priority the needs of those communities and then raising monies to dispense, along with the obligation to monitor and evaluate.

In that mode, neighborhoods—set in motion by what seems to be a new round of combating poverty, and imbued with the growing tradition of assertiveness and self-reliance—are likely to preempt the generic concept of community foundations, raising funds they will independently disburse. Not only neighborhoods but also communities of like-minded citizens of similar origin are operating independently. Prototypes can be found in the Haymarket Fund and similar funds being organized as public charities, systematically raising funds for distribution, and having an attachment to defined localities. Ethnic equivalents are also likely to appear and multiply, converting their historic analogues—the mutual aid societies—into modern counterparts of community foundations.

Similarly, those intent on solving such particular problems as drug addiction and crime in their locales may well develop focused grantmaking agencies, borrowing the community foundation format.

3. Community foundations, along with their kindred variants, will become more explicit and assertive about their generic philanthropic function. In the social context of the next century, either community foundations will live up to their philanthropic responsibilities or they will wither and be discarded. It will not be an easy century. Globally, the pressures of exploding and impoverishing populations, together with a depleting and deteriorating environment, will demand a level of human creativity and a readiness for social change beyond anything yet exhibited by this or any other nation. The signs and beginnings are already in place. The nonprofits, already squeezed by government cutbacks, are besieged by accumulating social needs, as are their counterparts in the governmental sector. Mayors, long diffident toward the world of private giving, are now explicit in their rhetoric, and in their planning, about the essential role of private donations if city halls are to achieve any progress and partnership in their efforts at civic improvement and unity. So are their colleagues at the state and national levels—governors calling for public-private alliances in educational reform, President Bush evoking the helping spirit of "a thousand points of light."

Community foundations will find this demanding environment their world of everyday reality—the more so as formal institutions, dealing uncertainly with the restive tradition of shared power, will experience more and more roadblocks in their attempts to proceed multilaterally through consensus or unilaterally through authority.

A promising segment of local philanthropy gives evidence of being ready; one can see it conspicuously in the creative talent and programming of the very large community foundations, but also in the more diminutive ones that have discovered the many nonmonetary ways in which "small can be effective."

4. *But all will not be sweetness, growth, and enlightenment.* Undoubtedly some community foundations will fall by the wayside. One type of casualty will be those that fail to reach critical mass of funding and growth potential in the communities they serve.

There will also be casualties of competition. There are already somnolent community foundations that have not responded to developing trends and urgencies, yielding the initiative, and sometimes turf and survival to more farsighted and assertive private foundations and other funders. Another source of competition stems from the large versus the small, usually the case in major urban and metropolitan areas where a centralized community foundation enjoys a territorial and fundraising advantage over smaller nearby colleagues.

Competition also exists in the relationship between some community foundations and the United Way. Both are in the fundraising business, with similar interests in community betterment. The boundary marker of current funding, as against endowment funding, does indeed differentiate the two but tends, in the heat of practice, to crumble under obliterating traffic from both directions.

The prospect of philanthropy stepping out front and acting more assertively is a likely reason for other local friction. This might occur as conventional charities lose some of their advantage in funding patterns of some community foundations that favor less traditional or more grass-roots organizations, and equally with new agencies and programs vying aggressively for a bigger share of the funding pie.

Lastly, community foundations will face the probability of a plethora of new grantmakers adopting the same format and even the label. There are, after all, no restrictions on how many community foundations can operate in the same geographic area. Boston, for instance, has three community foundations within the metropolitan area and another two within hailing distance. Each bears the name of a different municipality, but there is definite overlap in the areas they serve. Another variant is the ethnic community fund.

5. *Philanthropy in general, community foundations included, will be inviting targets for public attention and increased regulation.* Foundations—fortunately and unfortunately—have been surprisingly insulated from informed and consistent public scrutiny. But with philanthropy entering a period of increasing social significance, one can expect a more intense focusing of public attention on what foundations are doing and how they are doing it. The notoriety of the Buck Trust case in Marin County, California, may exaggerate what philanthropic life in the future may be like, but it foreshadows some of the turbulence that lies ahead.* Certainly the wakening interest of the press, of scholars and educators, and of state attorneys general and legislatures are omens of an environment to come.

Community foundations, because of their "public-ness," are in a better position than private foundations to endure in this environment and to retain their cherished attributes of independence and flexibility. Their increasing exposure to the public eye, however, will make certain of their characteristics (such as slowness to respond and initiate, and insulation from the social diversity of their communities) more vulnerable to criticism and to appeals for more public control.

---

* In a 1986 settlement, a judge removed from the San Francisco Foundation the $400-million-plus Buck Trust. The deceased donor had earmarked the funds for use in Marin County, and the San Francisco Foundation tried unsuccessfully to modify the restriction.

6. *Giving in the United States is likely to rise. If indeed it does, community foundations will be among the principal beneficiaries.* While there are conflicting trends, the greater probability is that private giving in this country will grow significantly. The mood favors what is voluntary rather than compulsory; and as social needs expand, giving of time and money is likely to follow.

Individual giving is also becoming more cautious, more pragmatic, more favorable to what is known and close at hand. That is much to the advantage of community enterprises and foundations. Their further edge is that they afford larger givers favored tax status, smaller givers the efficiencies of combining lesser gifts into larger endeavors.

Giving may never reach Independent Sector's 5 percent goal of persuading more Americans to volunteer five or more hours per week and to give more than 5 percent of their income to charitable causes, and clearly will never match the rising level of public need. Nonetheless predictable gains will substantially assist community foundations in fulfilling the role the coming century will assign them.

7. *The community foundation model is adaptable in other countries as well, and is likely to spread internationally.* Interest in community foundations has been expressed by a number of non-Americans; it seems compatible with a variety of cultures. Its "naturalness" and its affinity with the long tradition of mutual aid societies are congruent with experience everywhere, not least the emerging formation of private foundations within the Soviet Union. That the notion of community foundations is already taking hold in Japan, Britain, Canada, and elsewhere is further confirmation of the adaptability of the format.

CONCLUSION

Futures are hard to predict, and likely scenarios can diverge widely, depending upon a bewildering variety of forces and the volatility of their interplay. What has been written here flows from a relatively optimistic reading of social tea leaves. It does not take much of a Pollyanna, however, to conclude from the record of community foundations over the past 75 years that, as a class, they have performed effectively and have become an increasingly vital force on the American scene. Nor is it a flight from reality to see their flowering, along with philanthropy in general, as a fundamental social process needed for the flexibility, independence, and creativity they represent.

Whether they are as strategically positioned as this essay suggests, or as prepared as they might be to realize their potential, may be arguable. What is beyond question, one might reasonably conclude, is the logic that has brought them into being and embedded them as habits of the American heart.

3

Leadership in Community Foundations

James A. Joseph

In 1914, Frederick Goff, a banker in Cleveland, Ohio, developed a cooperative model of philanthropy that gathered together a mix of charitable funds under one umbrella. In describing the new foundation, he wrote, "Men of great wealth have in the past created private foundations, but no way has been provided by which even greater foundations may be created out of the contributions of many citizens." From the outset, he sought to appeal to "men and women of moderate means whose surplus (after caring for children and relatives) would not be great enough to endow a chair or a charity."

Leadership for the first community foundations was provided by civic-minded bankers. But as these foundations began to grow and flourish, bankers began to play less of a community leadership role and more of a management support role.

The leaders of community foundations were now more likely to be from other sectors of the community—wealthy donors, civic activists, service providers and other nonprofit institutions. The emphasis was on leaders who could invest the charitable dollar the way investment managers invest the investment dollar—for maximum return. Leading a community foundation came to be viewed as both a special craft and a special calling. As a craft, it required cognitive skills and knowledge that enhance the capacity for effectiveness. As a calling it required affective qualities of empathy, judgment and wisdom. It was important to be able to master the varied forms and techniques of asset development as well as to understand and evaluate community needs.

LEADERSHIP REQUIREMENTS

Three words describe what seem to be the essential elements of community foundation leadership: vitality, values and vision. The first of these, *vitality*, is the ability to activate power in others, the capacity to influence the will of another. Effective leaders create the space and provide the support that enable good people to do great things.

In an information society, the power to persuade or prod, to motivate or inspire, is one of the most fundamental elements of leadership. But a person of true leadership power is one who, as part of his or her persuasive powers, is able to win acceptance for substantial views of his own or those he represents. Martin Luther King, Jr., knew, and voiced, what his constituency wanted to hear, but he guided them into accepting his strategy for achieving their objectives. Franklin Roosevelt knew, and voiced, what many of the people wanted to hear, but he persuaded them to accept his solution to their problems. The community foundation leader, on the other hand, must be skilled in the delicate art of supporting the views and strategies of others, while ensuring that they further the objectives of the foundation and its donors.

There is much emphasis on the leader as communicator. But communication by community foundations is more than simply gaining access to the press, publishing a report, or identifying people who embody the aspirations of the donor. It is the lifeblood of the community foundation idea, ensuring that all stakeholders are informed of, and involved in, the foundation's vision for the community.

Effective community foundation leaders also need to be able to affirm and practice the very special *values* that are unique to community foundations. Values provide moral authority and public appeal. Community foundations by their nature stand for a broad set of principles: openness, public accountability and diversity are the most obvious, but community foundations receive their special status because of a higher degree of public responsibility.

Among the values presumed to be included in this commitment is what we generally call the "American creed": a belief in the essential dignity of the individual, in the importance of private initiative, in the fundamental equality of all men and women, and in certain inalienable rights to justice and fairness.

These are not simply values to be affirmed, but a leadership ethic that applies to the day-to-day operation of the foundation as well. The leaders of community foundations, board or staff, work within an institutional framework and share a responsibility to bring to the internal operations of the organization the same qualities of humaneness and caring that are brought to the community role. It is both an irony and a seeming contradiction that some men and women who champion social needs and appear to feel social pain treat those whom they employ with inhuman disregard and reckless abandon.

Vitality and values need to be accompanied by *vision*: the capacity to see connections, the ability to focus on the future, to understand it, interpret it, and to help shape it in ways that are fulfilling. Within their organizations, visionary leaders are planners, people who think before they act. They are also managers who know how to separate the passion of the moral self that leads to subjective advocacy from the dispassion of the professional self that requires objective analysis.

Some observers argue that good managers are rational people whose goal is to maintain order and to improve on the status quo while leaders are creative people, agents of change who must sometimes introduce chaos. The community foundation leader who can master both roles is both an organizational asset and a community resource.

Scientific management tended to separate thinking from doing, those who were planners from those who executed plans, those who set policies from those who implemented them. Community foundations will need to integrate these as two sides of the same coin. The disciplines most clearly associated with professionalism have been those that sought to impart knowledge-specific skills like finance and accounting. But the disciplines associated with the foundation professional in the years ahead will be those of ethics, civics, psychology and even demography.

LEADERSHIP TYPOLOGY

Some community foundation leaders are asset-driven, some needs-driven and others program-driven. The best leaders, however, are those who have mastered each of these elements.

Asset-driven leaders often subordinate other foundation objectives to the building of assets. They focus primarily on the donor community, spending much of their time on "donor relations," "donor services," or "donor development." Two-thirds of the more than 300 community foundations in the United States have assets of $1 million or less. But since 1969 all community foundations have been required to meet a "public support test," making it necessary for some of the larger ones to actively seek gifts as well. The day-to-day relations of asset-driven leaders are primarily with wealthy individuals, wealthy families, advisors to the wealthy, and prominent businessmen.

Program-driven leaders are often committed primarily to managing existing funds and relationships. One community foundation described this approach as "digesting the game we've shot." The emphasis is on grantmaking programs. Few grant or staff resources are available to meet major initiatives outside of the program priorities designated by the foundation's donors or by an earlier board. The public relations activities of a program-driven community foundation emphasize grants to established programs rather than to evolving community needs or new funds and donors.

Needs-driven leaders focus on the community's current needs rather than on building assets or managing existing programs. The foundation's board and staff build up expertise in these areas, and the public relations emphasis is on meeting a social need rather than on the donors' largesse or legacy. The board and staff are representative of the community mosaic in race, ethnicity and backgrounds.

Some community foundation leaders might look at this typology and argue that they do not see their faces in the mirror. That is because the best community foundations are a combination of some or all of the above rather than a stereotype of any one in isolation.

WHO ARE THE LEADERS?

The present leaders of community foundations come from a variety of backgrounds and experiences. A 1989 survey by the Council on Foundations found that more than 50 percent of the staff officers who responded came to their assignments (president/director/CEO) from other positions in the nonprofit sector. Seventeen percent came from colleges and universities and 14 percent from government agencies.

Board and Distribution Committee leaders, on the other hand, are more likely to be in business or law; of those responding, about 40 percent and about 20 percent, respectively. Both staff officers and board chairs tended to be heavily involved in community activities, with the United Way the most frequently mentioned.

We come now to two pivotal questions: 1) Who can best lead a community foundation at any given time? and 2) How can community foundations aggressively attract and retain leaders who have the experience, insight, and skills to meet coming challenges? The leadership of a community foundation may come from any one of several "stakeholders": donors, their descendants and grant recipients; governing bodies and trustee banks; executive and program staffs; and a wide variety of publics.

Donors

Community foundations are dealing more and more with larger numbers of living donors. This provides opportunity for active relations with the foundations. Even where the donor's charitable interest may not initially coincide with the foundation's assessment of community needs, both parties may profit from a more active donor engagement. Many donors have insights, experiences, and networks that can be as useful to the community as the funds they provide. It would be a mistake to isolate rather than involve them.

Governing Body

They may simply set policy, hire the CEO and exercise the fiduciary requirements of trusteeship, or they may provide leadership in developing assets, identifying and analyzing community needs, or in providing vision. They get into trouble when they seek to micro-manage the foundation, but their leadership is essential in many other areas.

By charter or trust instrument, many community foundations reserve governing body seats for a person holding a particular office or representing a particular organization; this can include United Way officials, county commissioners, judges and community representatives. The notion that governors are primarily responsible to the donors—and only secondarily society—is increasingly under attack. It would seem to be in the self-interest of both groups to insure that a wide spectrum of experiences and views are represented in their deliberations about needs and priorities. Yet this is not the present case, since 92 percent of all community and public foundation board members are white, 6 percent are African-American, 1 percent Hispanic, and 1 percent reported as "other," most likely Asian.

Staffs

The opportunity for leadership lies most clearly with professional staff. But though the spotlight focuses on the CEO, other staff, by virtue of their program knowledge or experience, can be effective leaders as well.

Donees

In making a grant, a foundation not only acquires a new stakeholder in its own organization, it becomes a stakeholder in a new organization as well. It has a stake in the effectiveness and efficiency of the donee, but it also has a resource that can help inform members of the foundation's board and staff about community needs. Donees are seldom thought of as leaders, or potential leaders, in a community foundation, but their experiences and insights can inform and enrich the grantmaking process in myriad ways.

Others

The media, the banking community, advisors to the wealthy, and even community groups not receiving grants may also be regarded as stakeholders of a community foundation.

THE COMING CHALLENGE

Peter Dobkin Hall, a Yale historian, has argued that the earliest community foundations "seemed to have had their greatest appeal to inland cities with strong, elite-dominated, reformist political cultures." Both community foundations and communities have changed in many important ways since then.

The first change is conceptual. In his book, *The Company of Strangers,* Parker Palmer argues that the basis of a community is no longer the intimacy of friends, but the capacity of strangers to share a common territory, common resources, common problems—without in many cases ever becoming friends.

We romanticize the good old days when frontier neighbors came together to build one another's barns. We lament the decline of this sense of neighborliness and solidarity, but public life now and in the future is destined to be a life among strangers, "strangers with whom we are interdependent whether we like it or not."

The new strangers with whom our lot is cast are the millions of new immigrants from Latin America, Africa, Indochina, and the Caribbean. Along with Native Americans and African Americans, Hispanics, and Asians who arrived here earlier, they are now widely dispersed in unlikely and sometimes unreceptive communities. Together, they are the non-European minorities who will soon constitute the majority of American society.

Thus, the second major challenge facing community foundation leadership is demographic. The first community foundations were dealing primarily with the descendants of Europe whose notions of *noblesse oblige* and stewardship permeated institutional and communal life. In the years since, we have seen the decline of European dominance in the world and we expect a declining influence of the descendants of Europe at home.

Some Americans are especially concerned about the potential impact of these changes on educational institutions—how best to deal with cultural pluralism in our colleges and what cultural adjustments will be required in our schools. But very little attention has been given to the implications for the tradition of private generosity and public benevolence that has characterized American communities. Is there likely to be a greater dependence on government, a greater social role for the public sector, or will the historic pragmatism that has seen us use both public and private resources to promote the general welfare continue?

A third new challenge is functional. In 1914, to speak of a cooperative society was to speak of the roles of three clearly delineated sectors—a public or governmental sector driven by the ballot, a private or business sector driven by profits, and a third or voluntary sector driven by compassion. The notion of a cooperative society is now more ambiguous, with each sector performing functions once thought to be reserved for the other.

Three major implications of these changes deserve attention if the social transformations of the future are to facilitate rather than stifle the community foundation movement:

1. *Promoting pluralism in philanthropy.* The practice of inclusiveness on the demand side of philanthropy could lead to a new pluralism on the supply side. Those newly accumulating wealth who have seen members of their community benefit from community foundation activities and participate in foundation decisions are more likely to choose the community foundation as a vehicle for their own giving. Moreover, the more minority groups are respected by the majority as benevolent communities in their own right rather than as simply the recipients of charity, the more likely the minority groups are to use their new wealth to continue the legacy that has been the genius of our democracy.

Some community foundations are actively promoting equity and diversity in their own organizations and among those who receive their grants. First, a number of grants are specifically designed to promote diversity and increase access to services for historically disadvantaged groups. Second, the foundation seeks broad representation on its own board and staff, believing that without such diversity, the foundation's ability to achieve diversity in its own grant program would be seriously constrained. Finally, the foundation encourages diversity in the boards, staff, and service populations of the organizations receiving its grants.

Pluralism is thus affirmed by some community foundation leaders as both a civic value that is implicit in the public character of the foundation and an enlightened self-interest.

2. *A new pragmatism in cooperation among the governmental, business, and voluntary sectors.* At the beginning of the 1980s, the emphasis on private sector initiatives was often used as a code word for government abandonment. A new pragmatism regards the debate about the social role of government as really a debate about the nature of the social contract between a community and its citizens.

Cooperation among all sectors is consistent with the long American tradition of using private and public institutions, profit and nonprofit organizations, to promote the general welfare. But the new partnerships must recognize the unique strengths of each partner rather than a relationship in which a senior partner dictates the terms to a junior partner; partnerships that recognize that government is consensus-driven while philanthropy is free to be compassion-driven, taking risks that government often cannot take or the public might not want it to take.

3. *Sustaining community and philanthropy.* The psychiatrist, M. Scott Peck, argues in his book, *The Different Drum,* that we may build community by accident, through crisis, or by design. The problem with stumbling into community is that we will not know how to sustain it. The problem with the sense of community that comes through crisis is that once the crisis is over, so—virtually always—is the sense of community. But creating community by design enables people to learn and sustain the process. Effective leadership in community foundations will require a subset of values that emphasize connectedness, the interdependence even of strangers; commitment, the staying capacity to grapple with a problem until a solution is in hand; compassion, the transformation of consciousness that moves one from passive altruism to active engagement; and communication, the recognition that community and communication derive from the same root word and we cannot have one without the other.

The encounter between grantmakers and a community is all too often like one between a bank and a borrower. For all the potential present in the meeting, a fundamental human connection is not always made. Funds may change hands, but they are not often likely to cause a full participation in the underlying concerns of the two parties to the transaction.

Dollars make poor social cement. They can only create the conditions that may bring a community together. They do not of themselves constitute an effective bond. A relationship may be instituted by cash, but it is in coming together around a true community need that an enduring connection is likely to be made. It may be the need of some group within the community—rather than the whole community—but a sense of community develops when the association and the transaction bring together a significant portion of the community in a way that creates community-wide ownership of that need. When what was "their problem" becomes "our problem," a mere association is transformed into a community.

This model of community-building has universal applicability. Civic leaders in many countries now see community foundations as a way for people in a community to pool resources to address their own community needs. It contributes to a sense of community and civic pride, while responding to the desire to solve local problems locally. Whether the movement that began in 1914 can seize this moment for further growth and maturity depends on the ability of community foundations to recruit and retain men and women with the vitality, values, and vision that have characterized the leadership of the past.

4

Pioneers of the Community Foundation Movement

Bruce L. Newman

In the mid-1960s, as assistant director of the Cleveland Foundation, I was lucky enough to play a principal role in the creation of a free medical clinic where young drug users could get sorely needed health and counseling services. I went to visit the clinic one day shortly after it opened, feeling no small amount of pride at having accomplished such an undertaking.

It occurred to me, as I glanced over the freshly painted walls and the new carpeting, that this was what community foundation work was all about. The satisfaction of seeing such a clinic get off the ground is something few people in other walks of life ever experience, some-

I wish to acknowledge the assistance of the many people across the country who sent material for this chapter to me or who discussed the subjects over the phone; of Barbara Denemark Long of the Chicago Community Trust, who did the research; and of Dr. Bruce Hatton Boyer of Chicago, who helped put the material into its final form.

thing that was not diminished by the fact that no one there seemed to know who I was.

In the intervening years that visit has become something of a measuring rod for me. Those of us who have the good fortune to work for community foundations know that, every once in a while, we are somewhat more successful in one of our programs than at other times. We are buoyed through our failures not by memories of past praise but simply by the knowledge that what we have helped create has benefited our entire community.

For many, doing our job well is enough, but a few people—a handful, really—have gone beyond this. In every instance they not only provided substantial service to their communities but also made substantial contributions to the community foundation field as well.

These people are our pioneers, and I have selected eight of them to celebrate here, and had space permitted I would certainly add Harrison Sayre, who established the Columbus Foundation, devoted much of his life to promotion of community foundations, and was the first head of the National Council on Community Foundations; and Raymond Moley who, while better known as part of Franklin Roosevelt's "brain trust," perfected the idea of surveys of community problems as the first executive director of the Cleveland Foundation. Others might select a different group, but in looking back these stand out in my mind as the ones who most shaped the field in which we now work.

THE PIONEER

> GOFF FREDERICK H. (1858-1923). *Lawyer, banker, and civic leader; born Dec. 15, 1858, in Blackbury, Illinois; later moved to Cleveland, Ohio, where his father became a prominent coal dealer; attended Cleveland public schools and graduated from University of Michigan in 1881 with a Ph.D. degree; admitted to Ohio Bar 1883 or 1884; partner in a succession of Cleveland law firms, working primarily in corporate law; became president of the Cleveland Trust Company on June 8, 1908, where he remained until his death; also, Mayor of Glenville, Ohio, trustee of the Community Fund of Cleveland, Hirman House, and Western Reserve University.*

Clearly, no discussion of pioneers in community foundation work could begin except with Frederick Goff. He invented the community foundation in 1914; from his imagination have come more than 300 foundations.

Of those who have acknowledged our debt to Goff, Ralph Hayes, his colleague who later founded the New York Community Trust following the Cleveland example, said it best:

> ... [Goff] not only fashioned the concept of the first community foundation, but he blue-printed it, put it in operation, supported it personally, expounded its utility, rallied its uncertain friends, nursed it through infancy, shared it freely with all who wanted it and left it at last the vibrant project it has proved itself to be.

Even Goff would be amazed at the growth of the movement he started. He had great hopes for his idea, no doubt, but he was pragmatic enough to realize the obstacles it faced. Indeed, he is reported to have said concerning the first seven years of slow growth at the Cleveland Foundation, "Oh, give it time! If it's a good idea, it'll grow and if it isn't, it won't. We're not trying to push it aggressively. It'll grow because I'm convinced it's sound."

But Goff's greatest contribution was, in my opinion, his firm belief in the need for community action. He was the first to see the need for an endowment based on geography. He was also the first to expound the idea that the wealth of a community belonged to all of its people, not just to a chosen few:

> We are, after all, only trustees of the wealth we possess. ... Without the community and its resources ... there would be little wealth for anyone. The community where a man has lived and worked has a real claim to a portion of the results of a successful life. ... If it be known that a generous measure of the wealth one accumulates is ultimately to be devoted to community use, it may be deemed honorable ... for men who prefer struggle and achievement to idleness and leisure to continue the pursuit of wealth.

Even today this doctrine would be challenged by some; in 1913 it was radical beyond description. Yet Goff lived by it, in the trust he started and in his own life. Harrison Sayre, the founder of the Columbus Foundation, reported Goff as believing "that a man owed his wife, his widow, and his children such help as he could give them to enable them to live in the style to which he had accustomed them. ... It's up to them to take care of *their* children." Goff believed that, after providing for his immediate family, a man ought to provide for his community. Indeed, his grandchildren were reportedly quite upset when he put this practice into his will—that part of his estate reverted to the Cleveland Foundation after the death of his wife and children.

ORGANIZING THE MOVEMENT

LOOMIS, FRANK D. (1880–1969). *Foundation administrator, social welfare organization leader. Born December 4, 1880, Bowling Green, Ohio. Attended Ohio Wesleyan University, A.B. 1904, and Union Theological Seminary, N.Y. Executive Secretary, Children's Aid Association, Indianapolis, 1909–1917. Secretary and Executive Director, the Chicago Community Trust, 1919–1949. Secretary, National Committee on Foundations and Trusts for Community Welfare, 1949–1957, as first staff person. Co-founder, The Community Fund of Chicago, Executive Secretary 1930–1938, and the Welfare Council of Metropolitan Chicago. Member, Illinois State Board of Welfare Commissioners; Citizens Board, University of Chicago.*

In dedicating the second edition of his *Community Foundations in the United States and Canada, 1914–1961* to Frank D. Loomis, Harrison Sayre described Loomis as "the dean of community trust executives, and prime actuator and founder of the national movement to help community foundations."

Loomis would perhaps have disagreed, for he eschewed self-promotion in favor of directing his energies into those arenas he thought essential for social betterment. As a result, his was a nearly invisible hand in many of the institutions we take for granted today. This quiet, deeply religious man—he always said that he had learned the spirit of giving in his church—seems an unlikely person to have spearheaded with what his successor at the Chicago Community Trust called "missionary zeal," the national movement of community foundations. Yet his work in this area led directly to the formation of the Council on Foundations.

When he retired as executive director of the Chicago Community Trust in 1949, after thirty years of unstinting service, he wrote in a long farewell letter to the social service agencies he had come to know so well:

> The road from the community trust to your door is a two-way road. The possibilities of the Community Trust for support and encouragement have scarcely yet been tapped. I am confident that the Community Trust both here and over the United States will become one of the great services of our time—a voluntary dedication to health and welfare.

In reporting his retirement, *Community*, the bulletin of the United Way of America's predecessor, Community Chests and Councils of America, wrote:

Mr. Loomis last fall made a suggestion ... that a national committee be organized to assist in the development and guidance of the Community Trust movement *in its relation to general community planning for social welfare* (emphasis added).

The article went on to note the creation of just such a committee, with 15 members representing that organization, the National Social Welfare Assembly, and several community foundations.

Loomis served as secretary of this committee, the National Committee on Foundations and Trusts for Community Welfare, which was chaired by Edward L. Ryerson, a prominent steel executive in Chicago who also served for years on the Executive Committee of the Chicago Community Trust. The committee operated under Loomis's hand out of the Chicago Trust's offices. Eventually the committee incorporated itself in 1957 in New York as the National Council on Community Foundations. In 1964, it changed its name once again to its present form, the Council on Foundations, Inc.

Both Loomis and Ryerson were involved with the United Fund movement that began in the 1920s and was greatly expanded in the 1950s, and both are credited with having helped to form the Chicago Community Fund, the predecessor to the local United Way. Loomis also worked closely with Ralph Blanchard, who, from the 1920s, played an important leadership role in the Community Chests and Councils of America.

Loomis clearly saw that the welfare movement needed overall planning if it were ever to dream of having an impact on the social problems of the day. He, Ryerson, Blanchard, and others believed strongly in the need for coordination between Community Chests (and their successor United Funds), such local research and planning mechanisms as each community may possess, and the local community foundation. Loomis knew that the national committee had a vital role to play in developing the relationship between community foundations and other local civic welfare organizations.

Loomis continued to work on the national movement even after his retirement from the Chicago Community Trust at the age of 70. And although his role in the national committee was limited by then, it was his voice as early as the 1930s that gave clarity and force to the need for such a movement. It was for that foresight, that vision, that Harrison Sayre correctly labeled Frank Loomis as the "prime actuator" of the national movement.

Rich, Wilmer Shields (1903–1979). *Social worker, association executive, editor. Born January 22, 1903, in Natchez, Mississippi. Educated at Tulane University (Sophie Newcomb College), A.B., and Bryn Mawr (Social Work School), M.A. Served as Executive Secretary of the Council of Social Agencies, New Orleans, 1929–1942. Headed the Office of Civilian Defense, Community Service Division, in Washington, overseeing home-front morale and voluntarism during World War II, 1942–1945. As Director of the American Foundations Information Service (1948–1954), produced first edition of* The Foundation Directory *(1955). Executive Director of the National Council on Community Foundations, 1957–1968. In addition, served as consultant to Community Chests and Councils, Inc., and was active in the Junior League of America.*

Eccentric. All business. Spicy. Refined. An introvert. Sharp-tongued. Feared. Splendid. Difficult to work for. Lovely.

Contradictory as they may be, all these words have been used to describe Wilmer Shields Rich, the lady who in 1957 became the first full-time executive director of the National Council on Community Foundations. By the time she retired in 1968, the Council had done far more than simply change its name to the Council on Foundations— it had grown to include 334 foundations of all sizes and types.

Henry Smith, a veteran of 37 years with the United Way of America, who worked closely with Rich, remembers her this way:

> She felt she had a mission to accomplish in life and nothing should stand in the way of her work. She was dedicated and never slowed down. She had single-mindedness and was not like most people—she felt she had been put on earth to accomplish certain things and so had no time for fun and seemed very alone.

Like Eleanor Roosevelt, with whom Rich had worked during World War II and who visited the Community Chest offices several times in her pursuit of projects, Rich "had a quick walk and was not pretty, but when you looked into her face, you saw there was a particular beauty about her," Smith remembers.

Rich knew from the outset that she faced obstacles in the foundation world, not the least of which was its dominance by men. Richard Oman, former executive director of the Columbus Foundation, tells of meeting Rich at his first national foundation meeting in 1956:

She was a lovely, lovely woman. She was so small, like an aunt or a surrogate mother to me. She was the only woman there and all of us husky men wanted to hug her. [But] she had a bone disease, very brittle bones and if you got within two feet of her, she'd start. I can still hear her, "Get away from me, Dick Oman, get away from me! Don't you touch me!"

Yet according to Diana Cullen, who worked with Rich at the Council on Foundations:

Wilmer never minded when people addressed her in correspondence as a man.... She was a good little lady from the South, and she used to say that the organization would never really be respected until it was run by a man. It wasn't that she didn't have respect for herself as a woman, but at the time, hers was the practical attitude.

Whatever her motives, it worked. Homer Wadsworth, the former director of the Cleveland Foundation, said of Rich at annual meetings of the Council, "God help anybody who didn't belong there—especially grantseekers. Wilmer had a steady, penetrating gaze that could wither a man who towered a foot above her."

There is disagreement about whether Rich wanted to admit other foundations to the national committee and make it the broad-based association it is today. Indeed, she wrote in *Community Foundations in the United States and Canada, 1914-1961*: "In keeping with the pattern of local community foundations to hold overhead to a minimum, there is no plan to build a large national organization." Smith and Edward Thomson, former counsel at the Council on Foundations, both agree that she liked the coziness of the small group and hoped to keep it limited to community foundations because, in Thomson's words, "they believed in philanthropy in the community, not the world."

On the other hand, Lindsay Kimball of the Rockefeller Foundation remembers Rich having "a dream of a national association of all types and sizes of foundations.... Some of us thought the community foundation group filled a vacuum but many large foundations stood aloof." He went on:

[The national foundations] felt they had their own eyes and ears for trends and national developments. Our argument was that they had a duty beyond their individual interests to protect the whole field of which they were a part. The other side of the coin was that many community foundations felt they had little in common with large foundations.

Yet under the direction of Wilmer Shields Rich the council did grow and it did change. By the early 1960s it had opened its door to all foundations and Rich was actively pursuing a broader membership. Whether the change was good or bad became a moot point, as Harrison Sayre dryly commented—"I feel very much like the Bedouin who had invited the camel into the tent and now can't get back into the tent himself."

Under Rich's direction, the foundation movement as a whole grew, and the community foundation movement grew with it. Community foundations throughout the country today are a testament to her dedication that "giving will prove more effective because the 'dead hand' of charity will have been transformed into a warm, living hand, always extended to those causes which merit help and will use such help wisely and well in enlightened service to the community."

SPREADING THE WORD

STRUCKHOFF, EUGENE C. (1920–   ). *Lawyer, association and founda-tion executive. Born November 14, 1920, in St. Louis, Missouri. Educated at Colby College, B.A. magna cum laude, 1946, and Harvard University, LL.B., 1949. Admitted to the New Hampshire Bar, 1949, and to the U.S. Supreme Court Bar, 1970. Joined law firm of Orr and Reno in Concord, New Hampshire, 1949; Partner, 1955–1971. Served the Council on Founda-tions as Vice-President, 1971–1978, President, 1979–1981, and consultant, 1981–present. Executive Director of the Baltimore Community Founda-tion, 1982–1989. Also Executive Secretary of the Spaulding-Potter Charitable Trusts, Concord, New Hampshire, 1959–1972; National Chair, Citizens Scholarship Foundations of America, 1962–1968; Trustee, University of New Hampshire, 1964–1967; founding member of the Associated Founda-tion of Greater Boston; and author,* The Handbook For Community Foundations: Their Formation, Development and Operation *(1977).*

No one spread the word like Eugene C. "Struck" Struckhoff. There is hardly a community foundation in the country that he has not influenced in some way, that he has not coddled, shaped, pushed, prodded or helped nurture into existence. Over and over one hears from community foundation people in large cities and small towns, that "Struck was instrumental in our founding."

Though a well-educated lawyer, Struck's success was due in no small measure to his down-to-earth approach to foundation-making. He is a quintessential Yankee, possessed of a single-mindedness in his love for community foundation work that is infectious. Charles Rooks, the

executive director of the Fred Meyer Charitable Trust, describes him
well:

> Struck hit it off really well with some people, especially in areas where lat-
> ent hostility to the Eastern establishment existed. He [came across] as in-
> tense, folksy, small-town and not the sophisticated, big-city person that
> they had expected.

Even though he was a sophisticated Easterner, Struck's manner, according to Rooks "said to smaller cities and those far from New York, 'I'm
really just a little New Hampshire boy.'"

His practical, straight-ahead approach to things led him to create
the *Handbook for Community Foundations*, the essential text by which
countless foundations have been started. In it, he eschewed high-level
talk of goals—presumably on the assumption that such goals were
already in place or a community would not be starting a foundation
to begin with—for a step-by-step guide on how to make a community foundation prosper. Even now, a dozen years after the *The Handbook*'s publication, "It is such a bible that it has still not been replaced,"
observes Herb West, former president of the New York Community
Trust. Struck's own words in the preface display the temperament
of the author well:

> As author, my opinions on many topics are stated or show through. Al-
> though I had the advantage of wise counsel from an advisory committee of
> four skilled practitioners of the community foundation art, its members did
> not require the statement of their preference or dissents. I am therefore re-
> sponsible for errors, skewed viewpoints, omissions and other deficiencies.

Struck joined the Council on Foundations in 1971 with duties as
a regional planner, and he traveled widely, promulgating his love of
the community foundation movement, and he became president in
1979.

Since 1981 he has traveled across the country to assist in establishing
new community foundations under the auspices of the Council. He
also provides direct assistance to struggling community foundations
as a senior consultant working with six other Council leaders who
have spent the past three years as apprentices to the master.

MASTERS OF THE CONCEPT

NORTON, JAMES A. "DOLPH" (1922–   ). *Political scientist, educator, public
policy administrator. Born May 28, 1922, in Haynesville, Louisiana. Attended Louisiana Polytechnic Institute, 1939–1942. Louisiana State Uni-*

versity, B.A., 1945; M.A., 1946. Harvard University, M.A., 1949; Ph.D.,
1950. Taught at several southern universities and lectured at Harvard School
of Public Health, 1946–1956. Taught at Western Reserve University and
Case Institute of Technology, 1959–1962. Served as President of the Greater
Cleveland Associated Foundation, 1962–73; Executive Director, the
Cleveland Foundation, 1968–1973. Chancellor of the Ohio Board of Regents,
1973–1978. Over the past decade has worked as a university professor
and administrator in Ohio and Virginia. Currently Interim President, Hiram
College, where he has served as a Trustee since 1979. Civic roles include
Chairperson, Economic Research Committee of the Ohio Department of
Development, 1965–1969, and Trustee, National Municipal League, 1975.

"Dolph Norton made the modern community foundation. He had to forge the administrative systems that are now taken for granted. He invented the role a community foundation plays, which now goes beyond grant requests." This estimation by historian Diana Tittle sums up Dolph's contribution to our field admirably.

I worked for Dolph Norton for five years—actually, I didn't work for him, I worked with him. He was the consummate team player, a teacher who led his staff to expand their inquiries until they bore fruit. Someone once said that if you went to Dolph with a dumb idea, after he finished talking with you about it, it was well on its way to becoming a good idea. That is the way this man is.

Dolph pioneered internships in foundations, a radical idea in 1965. I was working for a law firm in Cleveland when he hired me as a one-year intern at the Greater Cleveland Associated Foundation (GCAF). Dolph used the internship to bring people of different backgrounds and disciplines into the foundation world for a year, to help open up what was then perceived as a closed, passive world.

The GCAF was started in December 1962 under the auspices of the Cleveland Foundation, using a five-year $1.25 million matching grant from the Ford Foundation. Dolph was its director. Its official purpose was to:

> encourage research on and solution of community problems; to establish
> priorities for community action; to make grants for research, pilot, experi-
> mental and other projects toward the solution of such problems; and to en-
> courage wise use of philanthropic funds.

And when it merged with the Cleveland Foundation in 1967, Dolph brought those same pioneering ways of working into the community foundation world proper.

Today, because of Dolph Norton's vision, the mission statement of the GCAF could describe any community foundation. He believed that the community foundation was the proper entity to lead the way in solving problems, that it was proper to bring people together under its auspices in the search for new solutions. He saw that it was appropriate to take calculated risks, to experiment. He envisioned a foundation that was open and available to the public and believed it was important to bring diversity inside the foundation to help it with its work. He also saw that such measures had a price, that it was fitting for a foundation to spend money on its administration as a way of ensuring high-level work.

Dolph possesses an infinite capacity for work, says Barbara Rawson, former assistant and acting director of the Cleveland Foundation and Dolph's close friend. He was always thinking about ways to use the foundation's human and financial resources more effectively. For example, one day he showed me a *New York Times* article about something in New York called the Vera Institute of Justice. It wasn't long before I was on a plane to New York, charged with finding out more about this organization dedicated to influencing the criminal justice system. When I returned, one thing led to another and in a short time the Cleveland Foundation had its own Vera-type program. This was Dolph's way: he was a master at seeing opportunity, convincing others, and using the foundation's resources to bring the opportunity to fruition.

Dolph brought the modern administrative world to the community foundation movement. Barbara Rawson puts it well:

> He came at a time when most community foundations felt that all money should be expended for grants—no administrative money was needed. . . . He made that attitude ripe for change. He fostered an *esprit* among staff and the Distribution Committee. . . . His genius as a pioneer was to get the trustees to think through a problem and its solutions using the problem as the catalyst for initiatives creating solutions.

WEST, HERBERT B. (1916–   ). *Advertising executive, foundation executive. Born April 19, 1916, in Birmingham, Alabama. Birmingham-Southern College, A.B., 1936. Writer, Vice-President, and Account Supervisor for Batten, Barton, Durstine & Osborn, Inc., New York, 1936–1966. President and Member, Distribution Committee of the New York Community Trust, 1967–1989. President of Community Funds, Inc., 1967–1989. President, The James Foundation, 1968–1989. Chairman, Board of Trustees and Executive Committee, Foundation Center, 1975–1981. Member, Board of Welfare*

Research, Inc., 1972– and Chairman, 1978–1984. Member, Board and Executive Committee, National Charities Information Bureau, 1978–. Member, Board of New York University Medical Center, 1973–, and Executive Committee, 1979–1984. Board Member, Council on Foundations, 1980–1987, Vice-Chair, 1984–1987; Chair, Data-Gathering Committee of the Committee on Community Foundations. Chair, Joint Committee on United Way/Community Foundation Cooperation, 1987–.

Everyone in the foundation community uses at least one of Herb West's ideas. For example, many community foundations have a central investment fund into which income is deposited awaiting payment to grantees, so that they can earn interest on the income. Many have brochures describing our foundations and their missions. Many honor individual donors with special publications. Many put out a collection of "How to Use the Foundation" brochures. Many even have communication specialists on their staffs. Many have separate funds established to represent neighboring communities. Many have special corporate funds. The list goes on and on.

Herb West is the community foundation field's marketer. Dolph Norton has indicated that one of Herb West's major contributions to the field is his emphasis on service to donors and potential donors: "He is a strong exponent of that. He understands what donors want and sees that the Trust provides it." He delights in thinking up new ideas. As Lorie Slutsky, his successor as president of the New York Community Trust, describes him:

> In spite of all of his years doing this, Herb has a youthful approach. He has the most youthful, creative, energetic mind of anyone I've ever worked with. And the quickest. He comes in every day thinking about what he can do next. He gets off the train—he has an hour's ride—and comes in with 3 × 5 index cards in his pocket, pulls them out and says, "Let me tell you about this ... " and starts in on a new idea he came up with on the way in.

Personally, I think Herb carries those 3 × 5 cards everywhere, even on the airplane going to another community foundation meeting. Anyone who has ever attended a meeting of community foundations with Herb can recall hearing, after the discussion of some issue has gone on for a while, Herb's distinctive " YES! Let me tell you what we're doing in New York about this problem." And participants will also recall writing furiously to capture Herb's innovative approach to what should be done!

As committed as all of us in the community foundation movement are to Herb West, he is committed to us. He never turns us down, he is always ready to help. Lorie Slutsky says of him:

> People don't know about the many hours he spends meeting with some small community foundations and others in philanthropy. He doesn't have to do that. But he sits with these foundations and listens to their problems as if they were his own.

Norton adds that Herb is "a very gentle person, always friendly, always persistent—not stubborn, just unwavering." Herb came to the community foundation world from advertising. He clearly spent some hours doing research in the public library before making that career change. Of course, he was helped by 30 years he had already spent doing volunteer work for the United Community Funds and Councils of America, the predecessor of the United Way.

And he obviously chose well. Slutsky observes, "For him, the Trust is his passion." And all of us are glad it is.

OF COUNSEL

SUGARMAN, NORMAN A. (1916–1986). *Lawyer. Born September 12, 1916, Cleveland, Ohio. Educated Cleveland public schools, Western Reserve University, A.B., 1938; J.D., 1940. Spent early years (1940–1943; 1945–1954) Internal Revenue Service, Attorney, Office of Chief Counsel; Special Assistant to Chief Counsel; Assistant Head, Management Staff; and Assistant Commissioner supervising technical tax work. Partner, Baker & Hostetler, 1954–1986, in Cleveland until 1977. Moved to Washington to help establish firm's office there. Special Counsel on community foundation matters to the Council on Foundations, 1971–1975. Member, Advisory Council to the Committee on Private Philanthropy and Public Need, 1975. General Counsel to the Jewish Federation of Cleveland, 1971–1975, and Member of the Council of Jewish Federations. Trustee, Dyke College, Case Western Reserve University. Editor of the* Federal Bar Journal. *Co-author of* Tax-exempt Charitable Organizations, *2nd edition, 1983, the seminal work in its field.*

There was a time when anyone who had a legal question about community foundations didn't dither around; he or she just called Norman Sugarman. Sugarman was the attorney for many community foundations and for the Council on Foundations on community foundation matters. Many credit him with defining and interpreting in the 1970s to the Joint Committee on Internal Revenue Taxation of the U.S. Congress the case for community foundations. More than anyone else, he was responsible for seeing that the final regulations distinguished between public and private support, and between private foundations and community foundations.

"The community foundation world can be eternally grateful for his having been Deputy Commissioner of the I.R.S.," says Eugene Struckhoff. Sugarman worked hard to keep the I.R.S. from issuing final regulations until they contained provisions that would allow community foundations to prosper.

Working closely with Dolph Norton and Herb West, another of his accomplishments was to steer the Joint Committee's chief counsel into clarifying and preserving the vehicle of the advised fund that most community foundations enjoy today.

But Sugarman was more than an outstanding lawyer. He was a leader in civic and charitable affairs as special advisor, board member, and enthusiastic supporter. Edward Thomson, counsel to the Council on Foundations, remembers him particularly liking community foundations because he saw parallels and relationships between them and the Jewish philanthropic organizations in which he was so active. The parallels are most evident in his work on advised funds, which are popular with both groups.

His recognition of the effects of the 1969 Tax Reform Act led him to predict—quite accurately—in a 1975 paper he prepared for the Filer Commission (the Commission on Private Philanthropy and Public Needs) that the role of the community foundations would mushroom in the coming years. And it was his judicious temperament that made him warn community foundations to be prepared to justify their privileges as public charities and "to build adequate staffs, to fulfill the need for broad-based participation, and to provide leadership in support for private philanthropy." In this way, he said, community foundations could "encourage greater participation by the involvement of more citizens in foundation efforts."

A SIGNIFICANT CONSCIENCE

MAY, JOHN R. (1909–1988). *Foundation executive. Born July 9, 1909, Denver, Colorado. Raised in Berkeley, California, where he attended public schools. B.A. in political science, Stanford University, 1931. A top official in the U.S. Office of Price Administration during World War II. Served in the U.S. Navy, 1942–1946. Executive Director, the San Francisco Foundation, 1948–1974. Founding Board Member, National Committee on Community Foundations and Trusts for Social Welfare (later Council on Foundations),*

1949–1977. Founder, Northern California Grantmakers. Consultant to the William and Flora Hewlitt Foundation and the Columbia Foundation.

In January 1948, John May got a letter from an old San Francisco friend, Frank Sloss, an attorney and a trustee of the Rosenberg Foundation. Sloss reported a "new enterprise now being founded here, known as the Community Trust. If that leaves your mind blank, think nothing of it; mine was even blanker." It seemed to Sloss that this "farrago" of an organization would need in addition to the "big shots," a director:

> Obviously, as of now, such a job, compared with what you now have, is financially uninviting, to say the least. But there might be compensating advantages, one being that the work might appear to have more social significance than vacuum cleaners (I say that with all due respect), and another being that it's in San Francisco. . . . How about it?

Well, May took the job so unenticingly described by his friend, as he said many years later in his life, "practically not knowing what the word philanthropy meant." He learned quickly and well, for May over the next 26 years had much to say about community foundations, as a strongest supporter and an astute critic.

He was an ethical man who was very direct. Ruth Chance, a dear friend who was for years the executive director of the Rosenberg Foundation, said of him:

> He would stand out anywhere. He was an unusual man. A man of wit, intelligence and, above all, character. . . . He had a high sense, a principled sense, that philanthropy requires of one who works in this field.

She confirmed he was sometimes "crotchety," the way others found him "opinionated," "a curmudgeon," and "outspoken." But wisdom informed his manner and bespoke a deep concern not just for the things that we do in the community foundation field, but for the way in which we do them. He was, in a field of honest and honorable men and women, our most honorable standard-bearer.

May was also present at the creation of the Council on Foundations, serving with Frank Loomis on a small organizing committee in 1949. He also served as a board member of the Council for 28 years, the longest term of service in the Council's history.

His observations so reflect our concerns as community foundation people even today that it is fitting to conclude this chapter with his words:

> —I think a foundation is entitled to do risky things. If everything it does is successful, it is not taking enough chances.

—Perhaps the Congress has overlooked its opportunity to differentiate between the foundation which is in reality the founder's conduit for his gifts ... to charities of his choice and the foundation that diligently (even if mistakenly) seeks the path to a life of better quality and more promise for all. Surely the latter merits more favorable tax treatment than the former.

—Let me venture to touch briefly on that uncomfortable subject—representative board composition. I am confident that a foundation's ability to do its job is crippled if some—or any— of its board members are representative of anybody except the foundation's whole constituency. Let's, however, move faster toward governance by boards which are more reflective of the communities we serve. Let us seek a wider range of viewpoints, and still avoid "spokesmen."

—Must we cling so tenaciously to the concept of perpetuity? No human enterprise has yet achieved it. It appears clear to me that we should be less concerned about the remote future than about today and tomorrow.... Let us adopt a generous "pay-out" and serve our chartered ends better today, trusting that—if foundations justify their existence—there will be more of them to meet the needs of the far-off future.

—The only thing you've got to put into something is money, perhaps a little advice now and again.... What the person on the other side of the table contributes is vastly more important. It's everything else: organization, skill, quality. All you do is put in that little bit at the end of the process....

5

Creating Community Capital: Birth and Growth of Community Foundations

Jennifer Leonard

. . . a growing and a becoming is the character of perfection . . .

—*MATTHEW ARNOLD*

Community foundations have formed to build hospitals, to give equipment, to bring dead trusts to life. In so doing, they have chosen ways to grow, deciding what money to seek and from whom. Many, but not all, succeed in raising the kind of discretionary "community capital" that affords them freedom to visualize, to respond, to counsel, and to contribute.

Community capital grows through the synergy of donor, recipient, and community. The history of community foundations suggests that a mission balancing the needs of these constituencies will lead to steady growth and maximum flexibility. But most community foundations initially favor one or two. These multiple interpretations of the community foundation role have spawned disparate fundraising strategies and rates of growth.

Money is both the means *and* the end for community foundations. But if we grow for growth's sake, we shrink to opportunistic fundraisers;

if we give over control to donors, we can issue checkbooks and wait for the I.R.S. to call. Yet if we give without growth, we may as well be private foundations.

In planning asset-development strategies, community foundations should reexamine their mission, with an eye toward a balanced and fully realized future. Given fortune and foresight, each can raise community capital, a growing reserve earmarked for the common good.

A PINCH OF ECONOMY, A DASH OF TAX REFORM

Bankers begat the first generation of community foundations, modeled after Cleveland colleague Frederick Goff's inventive plan to remove the "dead hand" from doomed bequests. Through this new vehicle to manage charitable endowments, banks hoped to attract wealthy clients and increase fee income, while reducing legal and trust department costs. Bank sponsors typically structured distribution committees to include their own appointees and referred prospective donors to trust officers acting as part-time staff. The community foundation focused on giving away the income in grants; the banks kept firm control of the assets.

Then came the Depression. Those of Goff's community foundations that had thrived in the Roaring Twenties hung on for the duration. Others, stillborn or sickly from the start, came to a standstill as personal income shrank. The Great Depression offered the first evidence that community foundations need a healthy economy to flourish.

With war and its aftermath, America prospered. So did foundations (see Chapter 1). But the debilitating Tax Reform Act of 1969 sharply reduced the rate of birth of private foundations, leaving community foundations the beneficiaries. More than 100 community foundations first saw light in the 1960s and 1970s. In the 1980s (at least 62 births through 1988), this proliferation has been restrained only by the diminishing availability of territory to conquer.

With banks no longer the central community institutions of pre-Depression days, most new community foundations formed as freestanding nonprofit corporations. In this second generation of community foundations, their structure as public charities becomes more apparent, their stakeholders increasingly diverse, and their roles beyond bequest management more evident.

Second-generation founders have included donors, attorneys and bankers; corporations, foundations, United Ways, Junior Leagues, chambers of commerce, city councils, and even other community foundations.

FIGURE 1. COMMUNITY FOUNDATIONS: ASSETS AND GRANTS 1975–1987

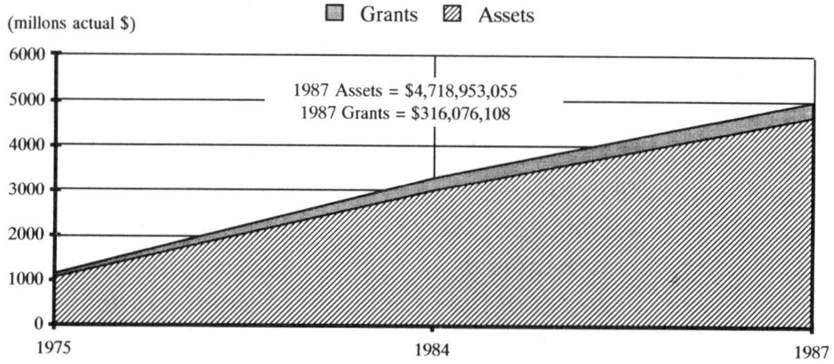

(millons actual $)   ☐ Grants   ▨ Assets

1987 Assets = $4,718,953,055
1987 Grants = $316,076,108

Source: Council on Foundations.

COUNTDOWN TO COMMUNITY FOUNDATION

New and revitalizing community foundations need three key elements to thrive: a driving force of personality, credibility with the wealthy, and the right territory.

PERSONALITY AND PERSONNEL

There lies in the history of successful community foundations an undeniable relationship between the charisma, articulateness, and perseverance of certain trustees and executives, and the community's embrace of the concept (see Chapter 4). Reserved or flamboyant, down-home or elitist, all seem to share leadership qualities required to propel a newborn community foundation toward adolescence.

The importance of personality lies in the very abstruseness of the community foundation idea, one of the most difficult notions to convey that ever challenged a public speaker. Community foundations lack a common definition (see Chapter 9). Overcoming this language barrier requires impressive command of metaphor and persuasion, as well as a willingness to wear out many pairs of shoes marketing the foundation's virtues to bank trust officers, estate lawyers, and the wealthy.

Many Goff-generation foundations languished because they lacked a forceful personality. Unless a distribution committee volunteer took on the role (and some did, with great success), most community foundation marketing was assigned to trust officers, who tend to be passive salespeople for charity. Other banks hired part-time outsiders. Rhode Island Community Foundation director Douglas Jansson tells the story of a Brown University English professor who once staffed that community foundation in addition to his teaching responsibilities and a command position in the National Guard. "It was like watching an artist at work," someone once told Jansson, "as he switched roles from talking about English grades, to dealing with grants, to chewing out some decorated officer." Yet this approach remains common among foundations with assets under $15 million, 80 percent of which reported part-time or no staff as recently as 1984.

But attitudes are changing. Second-generation community foundations invest far more frequently in staff, recognizing that money must be spent to be made. More than one in four community foundations with assets under $100,000—presumably new second-generation foundations—retain a full-time paid chief executive officer. By 1988, two-thirds of all community foundations surveyed by the Council on Foundations reported a full-time paid director, compared to one in four only 13 years before.

Seed money to staff new community foundations has been donated by banks and service groups, by local and national foundations, by corporations and wealthy donors, and by small donors contributing to operating funds. The number of community foundations reporting administrative endowments doubled to 23.9 percent between 1984 and 1988. While staffing is no guarantee of a forceful personality, it does allow for full-time attention to matters other than proposal review, especially developing new gifts.

CREDIBILITY WITH THE WEALTHY

In Goff's day, banks were well positioned to encourage wealthy patrons to use the new endowment vehicle. The granddaughter of the Philadelphia Foundation's founding banker, William P. Gest, used to stop by the desks of trust officers each December to remind them to recommend the community foundation to clients. Credibility with prospective donors was enhanced when founding distribution committee members wrote the community foundation into their own wills.

But as succeeding generations of civic leaders replaced the founders, distribution committee posts were increasingly regarded as honorary. Fewer members felt obliged to give personally, considering development the bank's responsibility. At the same time, these banks were facing increased competition from other banks and from nonbank financial services. Single-bank community foundations were losing potential donors who patronized other banks, some of which started competing community foundations. By the 1970s, as inflation eroded the value of cash, some prospective donors began to mistrust banks as overly conservative.

Diminishing credibility with the rich, during an era of exploding wealth and, later, special advantages for post-Tax Reform Act (1969) growth, forced a number of Goff-generation community foundations to reexamine their structure. Spurred by other banks and by donors, they demanded multiple-bank trustee relationships, which broadened credibility with the wealthy. Many formed what could be called "corporate twins," parallel incorporated charities that allowed them to direct investments and serve donors leery of banks.

Without the crutch of bank trust departments as sole asset conveyors, second-generation community foundations recognize that board credibility is their only starting currency. They form larger boards and charge members with the public charity credo to give, get, or get off. The *ad hoc* committee that planned California's five-year-old Sonoma County Foundation represents a typical combination of wealth, access to wealth, and civic credibility: a community volunteer, the head of the volunteer center, the telephone company manager, a retired Superior Court judge, the staff director of United Way, an attorney, the head of the largest accounting firm, and four wealthy people (see Chapter 17).

The importance of credibility with the wealthy helps explain the generally poor performance of community foundations started by government entities. They are less likely to have independence from political machinery, which makes them suspect with wealthy taxpayers; are less likely to recruit people based on their wealth or credibility than on a more political form of equity; and may look as if the government is seeking an alternative revenue-raising mechanism.

TERRITORY: WHAT'S IN A NAME?

Banks set the territory served by first-generation community foundations: generally contiguous areas headquartered where the bank was. These community foundations never crossed state lines because their banks could not, even when only an invisible political boundary separated wealthier portions of metropolitan areas like St. Louis and Philadelphia from their needier cores in East St. Louis and Camden.

With the greater freedoms of corporate status, second-generation foundations may choose large regions, states, or even multiple states to achieve an adequate base of wealth and population. A Council of Michigan Foundations study of community foundations serving smaller populations shows that the smaller the community, the fewer the assets.

The exceptions, such as Michigan's Fremont and Kalamazoo, generally enjoy special relationships with wealthy donors (here, the Gerber and Upjohn Companies, respectively).

A state or large region can be difficult to organize. Small towns offer the advantages of a coherent leadership structure, easily identifiable donor prospects, and cheap, effective promotional avenues. As a result, a number of community foundations have chosen to organize locally to get off the ground, and *then* expanded. In doing so, most found that they had to change their name to appear inclusive of the new territory. Examples include Dutchess County (formerly Poughkeepsie), Mohawk-Hudson (Albany), Greater Triangle (Durham), and Peninsula (San Mateo). As geographic scope expands, community foundations can maintain contact with local donors and grantees through regional committees.

Where a community foundation actively cultivates its territory, competition is unlikely to flower. Community foundations have coexisted geographically with quiescent colleagues (in Boston, Atlanta, Los Angeles), have encircled another's territory (Minnesota, Arizona, Texas, the Carolinas), have inhibited new formations through expansion (New York City), and have even given up territory in favor of another foundation (Los Angeles, California). But it is rare for two active and growing community foundations to proceed in parallel for very long.

GROWTH: THE RAW MATERIALS

As innovative practitioners in the field have demonstrated, community foundation fundraising opportunities are virtually unlimited.

Gifts from living donors appear to have overtaken bequests as the largest single source of community foundation income, according to a 1988 Council on Foundations survey. Most community foundations accept donor-advised funds, and some have successfully marketed donor-directed funds, which afford donors more control during their lifetimes but become unrestricted at death. Marketing efforts to reach living donors with certain kinds of wealth, such as closely held stock, are becoming common. Some community foundations have become skilled at soliciting more flexible current gifts to unrestricted, administrative, and "community priority" funds for the arts, women, or other fields of interest.

More sophisticated cultivation of estate lawyers, financial planners, and other intermediaries who advise prospective donors has kept community foundation bequest income high, as well as providing an avenue to identify wealthy donors with charitable and tax motives to make substantial lifetime gifts. Testamentary bequests remain more common than complicated planned gifts.

Income from private foundation terminations, which peaked following the Tax Reform Act of 1969, still continues as banks look to cut administrative expenses. Transfers of free-standing private foundations have been facilitated through increased use of the 509(a)(2) supporting organization device, which allows terminating foundations' directors a continued measure of control.

The growing availability of grant support for community foundations has turned grantmakers into grantees (see Chapter 8). Beyond grants, waxing government confidence in community foundations is evidenced by turnovers of mishandled charitable assets and corporate penalty payments. Corporations have created community foundation funds in operating locations and to replace local giving following corporate takeovers. Some, for tax reasons, have bypassed their own corporate foundations to give appreciated assets to community foundations.

Nonprofit endowments make up an increasing proportion of community foundation income, as do activities in which the community foundation holds more temporary funds for a variety of community drives.

THE INTERPLAY OF MISSION AND GROWTH

Discussions among community foundations today often entail a decorous show-and-tell of asset development. The details reveal diverse fundraising styles of pass-through or permanent, living donors or dead, slow growth or harried. Yet whether community foundations survive or thrive concerns less the specific tools by which they hope to prosper than the mission that drives these choices.

Differences of asset strategy commonly contrast community foundations favoring a donor service role with those committed to grantmaking. But Dayton Foundation director Frederick Bartenstein III suggests a third leg to steady the stool—commitment to the community at large. Few community foundations have examined how their implicit preference for any of these three roles guides the way they ask for and accumulate money.

The *grants-oriented* community foundation emphasizes unrestricted funds over designated, grantmaking over donor services, and unabashedly requires living donors to contribute toward discretionary funds. The *donor-oriented* foundation actively courts living contributors, allows paydown from principal, and tinkers little with donor desires.

The *community-oriented* foundation raises permanent charitable capital for the future, invests in the personnel and project costs of leadership, and proves a flexible fiduciary in collaborative efforts.

No community foundation is purely any one of these types; many embrace them all in some fashion. Nonetheless, these roles are predictive of growth patterns. Below is a proposed taxonomy of models for growth. Before examining it, it may be helpful to review several current issues in asset development.

- *Unrestricted or Designated?* Should community foundations encourage donors' designations of charitable beneficiaries, or should they urge creation of more flexible unrestricted and broad field-of-interest funds?

- *Pass-through or Permanent?* Should community foundations manage temporary funds to gain visibility and administrative underwriting, or should they focus on the development of long-term capital?

- *Donor Advisors?* Should community foundations actively solicit and serve living donors, or should they impose restrictions that favor growth of unrestricted endowment?

Table 1 suggests how community foundations orient themselves to these issues based on their embrace of one or more of the three basic elements of mission: grantmaking, donor services, and community leadership.

DISCUSSION: MODELS FOR GROWTH

Grantmaking

Typically first-generation foundations in which the bank trust relationship separated grantmaking from fundraising, include many unstaffed foundations in small communities. At their best, they can strengthen the nonprofit community and demonstrate innovative grantmaking. But because of this model's passive approach to fundraising, many fail to achieve the assets necessary to thrive or to distinguish their giving from that of individual donors or private foundations.

Donor Services

Aggressive recruitment of living donors offers a jackrabbit way to start a foundation or revitalize one with some history of grantmaking and asset management. But with a majority of funds designated, advised,

TABLE 1. COMMUNITY FOUNDATION ASSET DEVELOPMENT BY CHOICE OF MISSION

	Stage I: Characteristic of new, revitalizing, and first-generation foundations			Stage II: Characteristic of maturing foundations			Stage III: Mature
	Grantmaking	Donor services	Community leadership	Community leadership & grantmaking	Grantmaking & donor services	Community leadership & donor services	Community leadership, grant-making & donor services
Unrestricted/ designated funds	Prefers unrestricted; may suggest broader terms	Allows donor to choose; tends to draw designated	Actively seeks unrestricted	Prefers unrestricted; agency endowments OK	Accommodates donor but seeks flexibility; suggests options	Suggests unrestricted; accepts all	Promotes unrestricted; accepts others
Permanent/ Pass-through	Prefers permanent but may seek program grants	Allows donor to choose	Seeks permanent though may hold community-wide temporary funds; may require pass-through to benefit endowment	Prefers permanent; may require pass-through to benefit endowment	Accepts both	Accepts both; may request that pass-through benefit endowment	Accepts both but limits pass-through
Advised funds	If accepts, may restrict payout from principal; tries to influence grants	Actively encourages, including funds from companies, foundations, supporting organizations	Does not actively encourage; requires benefit to unrestricted endowment	Does not encourage; restricts payout and heritability of advisor role	Actively encourages, then educates about grantmaking	Encourages, especially endowments with broad purposes	Encourages but restricts principal payout and heritability of advisor role
Growth rate	Slow	Rapid	Moderate	Moderate	Rapid	Moderate to rapid	Moderate to rapid
Principal marketing targets	Attorneys, bankers, financial planners ("intermediaries")	Diverse	Living donors, intermediaries, other grant-makers	Living donors, intermediaries, other grant-makers	Diverse	Diverse	Diverse
Administrative costs	Low unless offers technical assistance	Moderate to high	Can be high relative to assets	Depends on project costs	High	Moderate to high	High
Visibility	Grantees	Attorneys, bankers, financial planners	Community leaders	Community leaders/grantees	Intermediaries/ grantees	Intermediaries/ community	Widespread

or pass-through, even a large community foundation can find itself unable to build much long-term capital or respond independently to emerging needs.

Community Leadership

By facilitating projects, managing prominent fund drives (e.g., for an arts center or library books), and promoting unrestricted gifts for the community's future, many second-generation foundations achieve community acceptance before they have many donors or grantees. However, since these activities can rob valuable staff and volunteer time better spent on asset development, successful foundations generally transit quickly to a model that incorporates more attention to grants and/or donors.

Grantmaking and Community Leadership

These complementary roles each emphasize the growth of long-term unrestricted capital. The Mott Foundation Technical Assistance (now Council on Foundations On-Site Consulting) Program and the Ford/ MacArthur Leadership Program for Community Foundations promote this model for new and growing foundations. Because of their modest growth rate, these community foundations often seek grants and current gifts to supplement administrative, grantmaking, and endowment funds. Established community foundations can implement this model more easily than newer foundations, whose desire to grow may occasionally outweigh their ideals.

Grantmaking and Donor Services

These service-oriented community foundations can be innovative grantmakers, while attracting a wide variety of donors. Rapid growth helps compensate for the model's lower proportion of long-term unrestricted capital. These community foundations can capture donors, then encourage them to make smarter grant decisions, improving the overall quality of philanthropic spending.

Donor Services and Community Leadership

The least internally consistent model incorporates flexible service to donors with a desire for long-term unrestricted capital. These foundations often start with a community orientation, then grow quickly through donor services. They are more likely to attract community campaigns and advised funds than unrestricted endowment, but can compensate for their own limited flexibility by leading other funders toward mutual goals.

Grantmaking, Donor Services, and Community Leadership

The most influential and independent community foundations accommodate all three competing roles and grow in a balanced, purposeful manner. Some newer community foundations that have recruited experienced staff have been able to grow this way almost from the beginning, but this is a long-term goal for most. Over the long run, a strategy that balances grantmaking, donor services, and community leadership promises the greatest contribution to the community in managing, expanding, and expending charitable capital.

Growing community foundations tend to progress toward more diverse roles and thus more diverse fundraising strategies, as depicted in Table 1 by stages I, II, and III. Given a core of unrestricted endowment, a community-oriented foundation can respond more flexibly to donor desires. Conversely, with a sufficient asset base, a donor-oriented foundation can dare to restrict living donors, correcting shortages in discretionary funds. And while, historically, most grants-oriented foundations have grown least, there are numerous examples in which they successfully added roles in donor and/or community services and grew almost exponentially.

Given this increasing diversification of mission, stage III community foundations should become more common in the next century, finally ensuring the perpetuity the field has promoted for its first 75 years.

SNAILS, TORTOISES, AND HARES

One might divide the rough differences between community foundation growth rates into three paces—snails, tortoises, and hares. The *snails* rarely travel fast enough to get out of the road before being run over. Their timing may be wrong, their leadership disorganized, their asset strategy nonexistent, or they may be overly reliant on sleepy banks. Snails generally have been first-generation foundations of the grantmaking type, but there are more modern examples as well. Of the Gannett Foundation's generally successful efforts to seed 30 new or revitalizing community foundations in its operating locations, one never managed to add to Gannett's initial $25,000 grant.

Slow growth costs many snails their tax status as community foundations, and with it incentives for new donors. Most snail assets rest

quietly in banks; a committee may make grants from the small investment income, but inflation erodes its value. When a snail's community gets lucky, a new organizing group will come along to resurrect
the community foundation concept. In 1986, the two-year-old
Community Foundation for Southeastern Michigan absorbed the
Detroit Community Trust, which had accumulated assets of only $1
million since 1915; by early 1989, the new group had already raised
$18 million in permanent assets.

Tortoises and hares, however, each have a chance at the finish line.
Just as Aesop told us, *tortoises* travel slowly but steadily. They include
modestly successful first-generation foundations as well as many
second-generation foundations that have chosen a community orientation. Even some of the largest community foundations travel at a tortoise
rate, although their feet are larger and they cover more ground with
each step than the green turtle newborns. This generally reflects a
distrust for pass-through and donor-advised funds—the most common sources of rapid growth—and a firm commitment to unrestricted
endowment.

Most tortoises in larger cities—generally first-generation foundations—have revitalized to push their assets up to a point commensurate
with their communities' needs, populations, and wealth. This
transformation from green turtle to Galapagos tortoise has occurred
rapidly and not always with balance, a problem that afflicts the hares
as well.

Hares start fast and keep running. If, to follow Aesop's analogy, they
stop on the way, it is generally to tend to the burgeoning demands
of living donors or complicated pass-through funds. Generally of a
donor orientation, hares tend to be lean on unrestricted funds and
some never become accomplished at asking for them. In the long run,
these hares probably should take some lessons from the tortoises if
they intend to have resources to meet future community needs.

THE QUEST FOR THE TAKE-OFF POINT

The issue of fundraising pace came to the fore in the 1980s with Eugene
Struckhoff's theory of a "take-off" point for community foundations.
Struckhoff traced the asset history of a sample of foundations to show
that most grew well, even rapidly, after attaining $5 million in assets.
At that point, postulates Struckhoff, a community foundation could
generate fees for staffing, convince donors of its permanence, obtain
reduced investment fees, and demonstrate unique capabilities in
grantmaking and community service.

Struckhoff—who has personally midwifed and foster parented more than 100 emerging community foundations—encouraged experimentation with his "take-off" theory in the Mott/On-Site Consulting Program, which has forever changed the growth patterns of second-generation community foundations. Instead of lying quiescent for years, as did a majority of Goff-generation foundations, community foundations in what can rightfully be called the Struckhoff generation are taught to race for take-off, using a combination of challenge grant support and direct solicitation of wealthy potential donors for unrestricted endowment.

"Take-off" has been misinterpreted, however, in two fundamental ways: that assets will grow automatically (and rapidly) after it is reached, and that there is a magic number common to all communities. A number of foundations with rapid growth after "take-off" are hares, whose assets grew rather indiscriminately. Yet the preparation of the Mott/On-Site community foundations is to move like hares at first but with a tortoise's purposefulness, eschewing easy targets like donor-advised funds in preference for unrestricted endowment. This is a prescription for more modest growth once the challenge grants fade away.

"Take-off" might instead be regarded as the point at which a community foundation reaches the economies of scale that give it greater utility than a private foundation. Just as donors with less than $5 million or $10 million can be persuaded to establish a fund rather than a private foundation, so can a community foundation with those assets point to economies in administration, investment, and grantmaking. Inflation will continue to push up the point at which these economies apply, and with it the "take-off" number.

The issue of economies of scale also applies to larger communities, where "take-off" is probably at a higher point. To adequately serve a Detroit or Miami requires quite a bit more than the staff that can be bought with fees from a $5 million corpus. Because of the huge needy populations they will serve, these foundations have attracted enormous seed funding from a few early, big donors, but this exposure does not automatically win them community acceptance. Selling the community foundation idea has always been harder in large communities, and success still depends on spreading a lot of personality around and constantly proving one's credibility.

WHAT WE WILL BE WHEN WE GROW UP?

Future growth seems assured. Ever more sophisticated fundraising techniques are being shared and applied more quickly. Improved donor cultivation is turning donor/advisor families into permanent contributors. Community foundations have become more willing to work with government, more skilled at serving national foundations and corporations, and smarter about turning that support into local visibility.

Community foundations have learned to work together to build assets. Michigan community foundations lobbied successfully in Lansing to get their donors a 50 percent tax credit. Community foundations in New York, Maryland, and other states have successfully sought joint awards of corporate restitution funds. California community foundations have lobbied to manage all escheated (abandoned and unclaimed) funds in the state. And community foundations have begun to collaborate in reaching donors who maintain multiple households.

Community foundations will continue to compete for endowment gifts with campaigns for such causes as public education, art centers, hospitals, universities, and United Way. Other nonprofits are also discovering the marketing potential of donor-advised funds, including Jewish philanthropies in New York and Los Angeles and the United Negro College Fund. Such competition will heighten community foundation efforts to strengthen, staff, and diversify development activities. Special projects and community-wide drives will be used more and more as marketing tools, gathering attention rarely paid to individual grants by the press or public.

Community foundations should also focus on managing the assets they already have. The next few decades will probably see some innovative attempts to commingle assets among community foundations or to follow the California Community Foundation's example in moving bank trust assets under direct corporate control, but the experiments should be based on better research regarding comparative investment performance.

Nipping at our heels will be the public support test, the federal mandate to raise funds from broad enough sources to retain public charity status. Ironically, although the community foundation's endowment-building focus distinguishes it from most other public charities, the public support test encourages community foundations to raise more small gifts than large, and penalizes those with growing endowment income by proportionately raising the current gift requirement. Most community foundations, especially the largest, worry about meeting the test in future years.

Neither the government nor community foundations know yet whether, or when, a community foundation may reach an optimum size at which it can fulfill its community role without growing. Several community foundations may reach $1 billion by the end of the century. Is it rude to raise funds for a billion-dollar organization? Should community foundations (presuming no change in the public support test) at some point simply become private foundations, and focus on community leadership and grantmaking? Probably not, since community foundations raise funds for communities, not for their own organizations. In large cities, even income on $1 billion pales beside needs.

More to the point may be the position of influence such a mega-foundation may hold. The Marin Community Foundation, born from San Francisco's Buck Trust with $430 million, has a challenging task in meeting its support test. But probably more of a headache is the assumption by the Marin County Board of Supervisors that the community foundation is so large it should take on some of the burdens of government. While the Marin Community Foundation and other private funders naturally rebuff the contention, it does raise a question as to whether large community foundations exercise their influence on behalf of the entire community.

Community foundations, despite their charge to respond to diverse community needs, tend to be run by the few for the many. Larger community foundations even have smaller boards, on the average, than the less well-endowed. As they reach a position of major influence in their communities, what measures should community foundations take to ensure their own accountability?

And, if the position is taken that community donors set a foundation's agenda along with the appointed board, who are the donors? Movements to create separate funds for minority communities (see Chapter 25) reflect the development of wealth in demographic groups that have not been adequately served as donors. This gap needs to be addressed if community foundations are to remain responsive to the America of tomorrow; it may become crucial if they are to retain favorable tax treatment as they grow ever larger and more visible in the twenty-first century.

6

Why Donors Give:
Thirteen Views

HELEN ROGERS, the first woman executive in an advertising agency in Oakland, California, won the national Advertising Woman of the Year award in 1975. She has also won several awards from local and regional groups for contributions to community services. She has donated $20,000 to the East Bay Community Foundation in Oakland and has pledged an additional $5,000 annually through her lifetime.

HELEN ROGERS: I was born in Oakland and I'm unabashedly loyal to this city, which has given me such wonderful opportunities and in which I've lived all but a handful of my 80-plus years. I'm quite sold on the East Bay Community Foundation. It's a local organization, and I'm very much in favor of patronizing local community fund raisers. And I'd rather spend my money where it goes directly to help people, as the foundation grants do. I particularly like the arts, education, and youth groups the foundation works with, and I think I know a little about community organizations because I've been a board member or otherwise involved in the Children's Fairyland, the Easter Seal Society, Junior Achievement, Campfire Girls, Booth Memorial Hospital, Oakland City College, and others.

I've tried to give my civic work the same energy I applied to my profession. When possible I've combined the two—for example, in designing advertising campaigns for volunteer organizations. Once I ran a campaign to collect $650,000 in Betty Crocker coupons to purchase medical equipment for the Easter Seal Society.

Now that I've retired, I choose my projects carefully. They include the Oakland Youth Chorus, the Oakland Museum, and the Oakland Heritage Alliance, which also happens to be supported by the East Bay Community Foundation. The management and financial operating style of the foundation appeals to me, because I've always tried to be prudent and knowledgeable about affairs of the pocketbook. Finally, the foundation meets another test I've always worked by: if you find someone whose work you admire and appreciate, stick with them.

ROBERT W. BOOTH, 74, is the retired president of radio station WTAG and part owner of the *Worcester Telegram & Gazette*. In 1988, he set up a $10-million fund in the Greater Worcester (Massachusetts) Community Foundation in memory of George F. Booth, his father. The gift doubled the foundation's assets. After donations totaling $800,000 over a period of five years to the Worcester Historical Museum, the First Unitarian Church, and the Worcester Art Museum, in 1993 the funds will become discretionary.

ROBERT W. BOOTH: My father was widely known as "Mr. Worcester" because of all the civic work he did. For example, he founded the city's parks and playground system and helped set up the Community Chest, now the United Way of Central Massachusetts. So it was only natural for me to leave most of my money for the benefit of the community. Also, Dad was a very outgoing person who knew a great many people. I hope that this fund will make it possible for people who didn't know him to learn of him and of his concern for the community.

The money came mainly from the sale of the newspapers. I'm a bachelor and, after providing annually for several nieces and nephews, I decided I really didn't need all that money. At my age, I had no desire for a castle in Spain, a townhouse in London, or whatever. It was a problem knowing what to do with it. My lawyer pointed out that if I didn't take some steps the government would take a horrendous part of it when I died. So he outlined several options, including the establishment of a private foundation. I had respect for the Greater Worcester Community Foundation, and the more I learned about it, the more I liked it. It would have been very foolish to have set up my own foundation and duplicate the administrative details that the community foundation was already handling well. Frankly, too, it relieves me of meeting after meeting with organizations that wanted money from me. One organization that was conducting a capital campaign tried to make an end run around the community foundation by placing one of my nieces on their board and asking her to solicit from me. She told them, "Absolutely not," and advised them to go to the community foundation. They then asked if she felt a former business associate should solicit me. She again said she thought it would be a mistake and that I would resent it. She was quite right.

I hope others will also take advantage of the flexibility and permanence the foundation provides for putting their gifts to use for Worcester so that the foundation can become an even greater source of good for the community.

Over the years I've learned something of needs in the community, as a trustee of the Orchestral Society, the American Antiquarian Society, with service for the Worcester Redevelopment Authority, the Art Museum, and other organizations. The structure of the Greater Worcester Community Foundation, however, constitutes a set of eyes into community needs greater than any single person's.

JUAN LOUMIET is a partner in the Miami law firm of Greenberg, Traurig, Hoffman, Lipoff, Rosen & Quentel. For nearly a decade the firm has been making annual contributions through a named, advised fund of the Dade Community Foundation. Each year the 40+ partners pool a percentage of their income and earmark the combined total of $150,000–$200,000 for support of a wide variety of educational, social service, and cultural agencies. When Juan Loumiet became a partner, the Cuban-born graduate of the University of Miami Law School welcomed the opportunity to become an active participant in this form of philanthropy.

JUAN LOUMIET: Not surprisingly, the Greenberg Traurig Philanthropy Fund directs much of its support to organizations in which individual partners are especially interested, but the informal review process also includes consideration of requests from groups that have no ties to the firm. Keep in mind, though, that this approach isn't designed to replace other forms of giving. For example, although I am a member of the Dade Community Foundation board, I also am a strong supporter and heavy-duty solicitor for United Way, for my church, and also for the archdiocese. But what I especially like about the community foundation kind of pooled giving is the ability it gives us to make major lead gifts to projects that need this kind of support.

There are those who say that we're not adding to the foundation's permanent endowment. But I think this approach does a lot to heighten awareness among individuals who have access to other potential donors about a foundation that is growing into maturity.

Actually, I guess our fund is moving in the direction of establishing support in perpetuity. For example, the foundation recently joined forces with a developer to sponsor the grand opening of an urban mall. All of the proceeds were to be used to create something called the Miracle Fund. That's a permanent endowment whose income will be used for support of some of the community's smaller and less visible arts organizations. My partners and I decided to make a five-year capital pledge to this endowment.

I like this approach so much that I'm working hard now to encourage the partners of [another Miami professional firm] to do exactly what we're doing, and they seem to be interested.

I especially value the foundation's ability to react quickly to needs that come up in the middle of the year. And I also appreciate its flexibility, which makes it accessible to many different kinds of needs. Don't get me wrong. Our United Way, for example, is a very creative organization, but it's not set up to be able to have the same quick response time as the foundation.

I'm looking forward to staying involved as a member of the Board of Governors. I think the board includes just the right mix of people to be effective in the multi-ethnic environment of this community. The members reflect the wide range of people here—spanning the older and more established names to those who represent Miami's current growth and diversity. Since coming here in 1971 I've seen Miami change tremendously in its ethnic makeup. As a member of one of the largest ethnic groups here, I am concerned about ethnic understanding. I would like the community to appreciate the value of the differences and learn how to integrate them into a working coalition. That's why I think the foundation's intercultural initiative (see Chapter 13) is so important. The numbers—and not just the amounts—of contributions are increasing, and I want to encourage that pattern. Over time I also want to promote the expansion of our permanent endowment. I can also envision us channeling some of our money into other leadership activities of the foundation that may include more than just grantmaking.

DR. GEORGE H. HITCHINGS, 83, winner of the Nobel Prize for Medicine in 1988, contributed the entire $130,000 prize money to the George and Beverly Hitchings Fund, an unrestricted endowment of the Greater Triangle Community Foundation, Durham, N.C. Dr. Hitchings, former vice-president for research of Burroughs Wellcome Co., was a founder of the community foundation in 1983.

GEORGE H. HITCHINGS: I have had a wonderful life and have been rewarded many times over by meeting people and parents whose children have been saved by drugs that have come out of my program. My current life is devoted one-third to philanthropy and two-thirds to science. Despite all the scientific honors and the scientific chapters in print, I think one of the most prideful things I've done is get the Greater Triangle Community Foundation (then called the Greater Durham) off the ground. Several community leaders met in the Burroughs Wellcome auditorium, chose electors, and those electors selected a board of directors and officers. Later I found and gave Shannon St. John, the present executive director, a real hard sell about the concept of the community foundation, and she decided that that was what she wanted to do the rest of her life.

On my eightieth birthday my dear relatives and friends did me the most appropriate honor in establishing in the community foundation the fund in my name and my wife's. It has grown. Money poured in when my wife died and continues to come in. People are sometimes surprised when a scientist is active in local community affairs, because they think he or she is single-minded, hunched over a microscope constantly, even in the old stereotype, absentminded about everything but the pursuit of knowledge. But I have never found any conflict between my research and my community interests, and apparently one hasn't suffered for the other. Along with the long years of basic research in biochemistry and of endless trial and error in chemotherapy, I managed to find time for the United Way, the Durham YWCA, American Red Cross and Cancer Center, the Durham Symphony, and many other causes, even the Chamber of Commerce and the Tobaccoland Kiwanis.

When I received the Nobel award, I disclosed a little secret that's worth sharing here. My sister, Dora, told me that when I was baptized, my father held me up and dedicated my life to the service of mankind. She was kind enough to say she thought my father would have been pleased with what has happened, and I am sure he would include my work on behalf of the community foundation.

People have asked me why I gave the Nobel award fund to a community charity rather than to research. Well, research and science are relatively well funded, but a lot of "people things" need it more. Not that many scientific endeavors aren't also "people things," but you know what I mean.

So far the Hitchings endowment has provided scholarships to help needy children attend summer classes, a program to help people who suffer from both mental illness and substance abuse, and speech therapy for mentally retarded preschoolers. But the terms of the endowment are very broad. The proceeds can be used for anything from the arts to human services, and I am confident that the foundation's board, for uncounted years to come, will target it toward the most promising projects in the community.

MRS. JEAN SCHULZ is chairperson of the board of the Sonoma Community Foundation, in Santa Rosa, California. She and her husband, Charles Schulz, creator of the comic strip "Peanuts," have given the foundation a gift lead trust that provides $50,000 a year for 15 years toward administrative expenses.

JEAN SCHULZ: My optimism of thirty years ago has proved naive. When I finished college then I thought that solutions to the problems all around us were at hand. I thought that through education and public awareness we would put these good ideas to work. In the 1960s I saw Head Start as a wonderful idea, catching children at a very young age to make up for any barriers that would block them from opportunities more advantaged children had. But education now seems worse than then. I also thought that terrible traffic problems and pollution would be handled by carpooling and mass transit, by people becoming aware of the problems and cooperatively changing their behavior to solve them.

I'm a lot less certain about all that now. People seem too concerned with their own lives to spend a little energy worrying and doing something about the fallout of social problems if it means changing comfortable patterns. I'm really saddened by the young people who appear completely unaware of the larger implications of their actions. The problems we hear about daily have the potential to destroy the happy lives we've constructed for ourselves. It behooves us all to care about people we don't even know and situations that seem remote.

I think that by working for the foundation I am doing something, in however small a way. It can be wonderfully rewarding, but it is frustrating sometimes. After all, people have their own agendas and don't necessarily grab on to my idea of supporting the foundation. But just at the point where I've concluded that people are tired of hearing from me, someone will say, "The foundation is a great idea," and that's a shot in the arm.

Given that problems seem so entrenched, I believe that we need an entrenched, secure body of permanent funds to help address them. That's why the concept of community foundations appealed so to me. I had worked many years as a volunteer for the League of Women Voters, so I knew what sustained attention to certain issues can do.

I was glad to serve on the committee that set up the Sonoma Foundation. My husband is not a committee person or an activist. He understands why I spend all the time I do on the foundation, and he's very impressed with what's being accomplished and glad that we are spending our money this way. We wanted to be sure that the foundation began with a solid base. So our gift served two purposes—one, to assure future donors that the foundation will survive; two, assurance that their gifts will be applied entirely to projects and programs rather than to operating expenses.

This is definitely deferred gratification. I truly believe that if my grandchildren stay in Sonoma County, they will know it's a better place because a core of people began something 30–40 years ago.

GEORGE F. REDMOND, an attorney with the Milwaukee firm of von Breisen & Powell, has advised several donors who have used the community foundation (the Milwaukee Foundation) as a vehicle for philanthropic giving. One of them, Mrs. Dorothy Shaw, by the time of her death in 1980, established funds that account for some $8 million of the foundation's $72 million in assets.

GEORGE F. REDMOND: My clients and I have felt that the use of a community foundation would provide flexibility of administration and avoid possible

IRS-related problems or complications, as well as provide centralized administration.

When I notified the foundation of these funds they had simply not been aware of Mrs. Shaw, though her late husband had left $10,000 to the foundation a long time ago (1950) for support of the University of Wisconsin law school. She had been quiet and not very active in community affairs, but she had been very wise in investing the money her husband left her.

Mrs. Shaw established two funds. One provides scholarships and other financial assistance to students at her husband's alma mater, over $100,000 a year. The role of the Milwaukee Foundation goes beyond simple monitoring. Its staff works closely with the Law School, periodically reviewing the use of the funds and their impact in helping the school attract top students and carrying out the donor's desire to maintain and improve the quality of the school. The students are always aware of the source of their financial assistance.

Another fund, the principal of which now amounts to more than $6 million, carries out the donor's desire to fund research in biochemistry, biological science, and cancer at the University of Wisconsin–Madison and the University of Wisconsin–Milwaukee.

As a young woman Mrs. Shaw had worked with an organization that dealt with tuberculosis, and she lost two sisters, to whom she had been very close, to cancer. I think that explains her interest in the medical research capacity of these two branches of the University of Wisconsin. The funds could have been left outright to the universities, and I am sure they would have been put to good use. But the way the foundation has shaped this fund, it has turned into an instrument for producing top-rank scientists.

In consultation with a committee of distinguished, nationally recognized scholars, the foundation has established a number of imaginative programs at the two universities to carry out these purposes. Since the fund was established six years ago, it has used more than $3.5 million to strengthen and stimulate research. In one innovative program, the foundation brings in leading researchers from throughout the country to select nominees for Shaw Scientists awards. The awards are generous— $35,000 a year for five years of unrestricted support to pursue research of the young scientists' choosing in whatever way they wish. They are extraordinary resources for young developing researchers. It would not surprise us if we were thereby producing some Nobel laureates of the future.

Another cluster of grants from that fund has played a key role in development of the Center of Great Lakes Studies, an environmental center of excellence at the University of Wisconsin–Milwaukee. Among other things, two distinguished professorships and a visiting scientist program have been initiated as part of this program.

In short, the foundation is an excellent vehicle in situations in which people wish to make contributions of any size, from modest to large, for the public interest. The foundation offers the possibility for the individual either to create a designated fund with a donor name, identify a special purpose, or make meaningful additions to existing funds and programs. The foundation provides ongoing review and evaluation of these programs so as to be able to mold and shape them in a manner to best carry out the donor's wishes.

PENNY PITOU, twice an Olympic ski medalist, and her husband, Milo Pike, a businessman, made a $1 million gift to the New Hampshire Charitable Fund. The gift came in the form of stock that appreciated from $2 to more than $30 per share.

PENNY PITOU: Milo and I each came from financially underprivileged backgrounds, so we are particularly thrilled to be able to make this donation. This gift speaks to the hope in the American system where good ideas, persistent hard work, and perhaps a little luck can provide comfortable wealth.

I remember very vividly having only $1 a week to spend for lunch at Stowe, Vermont, when I was trying out for the Olympics in 1955 at the age of seventeen. Now Stowe is a very cold place, and you need to eat well in order to feel warmth and energy from the food. But because I had only 20 cents a day to spend on lunch, I would go to the Octagon, which is the top of the mountain, and I would buy myself a hot dog, and I would eat a whole box of saltine crackers loaded with relish and mustard and anything else they had there in order to fill me up. I never could afford anything to drink. I still don't drink coffee or hot chocolate or any juices when I ski, because I programmed myself very young since I had no money.

It's the most wonderful feeling to be able to give back to people—to society—a little bit of my good luck. If it hadn't been for the local people in my hometown of Laconia and Gilford, New Hampshire, who raised $400 in 1955, I never would have been able to afford to go to the Junior National in Whitefish, Montana. There and in North Conway, Vermont, I accumulated the points that enabled me to make the Olympic team the next year. That was the beginning.

At that time, I made a solemn pledge that if I could ever repay the kindnesses that gave me a boost, I would. In my life I have always tried to make a difference in anything I've ever done. I consider that growing as a person. Being able to be a part of this gift has enabled me to continue the growth process. And it's a thrill to have been able to live up to a solemn pledge a young, idealistic girl made so many years ago.

Milo is a quiet man who prefers his donations to be made anonymously, but this gift is one he hopes will encourage others who have become wealthy to contribute to local foundations so their good work will be passed on from generation to generation. It's his way of ensuring that "new" money works in the same way as "old" money.

This gift is the dream of a young girl come true, the dream of a woman fulfilled. To know that the work I've done will live after me and that people who need help will be able to better face their future is an experience that I wish I could share with everyone. I know Milo also has deep feelings about helping others.

Being able to decide where the income from our gift will go is also a good feeling since in that way we can directly affect areas of community life that we feel are important to the overall well-being.

V. I. MINAHAN retired in 1984 as president and CEO of Post Corporation, a newspaper, broadcasting, and printing firm headquartered in Appleton, Wisconsin. He is a member of the board of the Community Foundation for the Fox Valley Region, to which he has donated $150,000.

V. I. MINAHAN: When Walter Rugland first told me of his ambition to start a community foundation for the Fox Valley Region, my first reaction was, "Oh, no, not another organization which will compete for the charitable dollar with everyone else." But as Walter explained how a community foundation works, and especially when I realized that the majority of money contributed to a community foundation comes from bequests, I became an enthusiastic supporter.

Besides, there was Walter, a citizen of our community who commands absolute trust, who is recognized as a visionary, but a positive one. He was the retired chairman and CEO of the Aid Association for Lutherans, the world's largest fraternal insurance firm. To honor him, the association established the Rugland Award for outstanding contributions to philanthropy, and he was the first recipient. He used the $5,000 award to finance a feasibility study for the Fox Valley Regional Community Foundation. I think his interest in the subject had been stimulated by a son of his who lives in Hartford, and who had sent him material about the Hartford Foundation for Giving.

In any case, I realized that I knew many people—some of considerable means and some of very modest means—who loved this region and would like very much to leave something to "their community" but simply did not know how to do it. I realized that the flexibility of a community foundation, whose various funds— all the way from designated to unrestricted— offered donors many options to do exactly what donors wanted to do.

My own first donation to the Community Foundation for the Fox Valley Region was to set up a designated fund for Lawrence University in Appleton. Once again, the flexibility of the community foundation impressed me. For if I gave the money directly to the university, how would I know that 50 years after my death, or 100 years, the university would still be deserving of this gift? (Some universities have simply gone out of business, or moved away from their original home.) By placing the funds in the community foundation, I knew that many years from now a group of civic leaders would be responsible for seeing to it that my original gift was used according to my original intent.

Later, I made gifts to the foundation for a local museum endowment fund, and to the foundation's own Administrative Endowment Fund.

RICHARD H. AUSTIN, Secretary of State for the State of Michigan for the last 19 years, had been a local and national leader of the United Way when he became one of the founders of the Community Foundation for Southeastern Michigan. He has contributed $1,500 to the foundation.

RICHARD H. AUSTIN: I was raised in a poor family—my father died from injuries suffered in a Pennsylvania coal mine when I was age eleven—so I think I have a special sensitivity to family needs in a community, like southeastern Michigan, that has come upon hard times and has seen severe cyclical unemployment. It is the automotive capital of the U.S., if not the world, but because of the sharp up-and-down spiral of our economy, a community foundation is especially necessary.

On the economic downswing, charitable organizations have a very tough time raising money. Consequently, we founders felt the need for a more permanent vehicle for private philanthropic support. The problem in the Detroit area is not a lack of generosity; people give generously to annual drives. I came to this conclusion as a participant in annual solicitations for various organizations. However, before creation of the community foundation, there was no organized effort to generate a permanent source of funding.

Why was I invited to join the founders? Perhaps because of thirty years as a certified public accountant I was particularly sensitive to budget problems of nonprofit organizations, having worked as a volunteer in United Way's budget review process. It also helped to work on the inside of nonprofit organizations, such as the Boy Scouts, YMCA, YWCA, Urban League, Homemaker Agency, and hospitals.

In its short history, I think the Community Foundation for Southeastern Michigan has done remarkably well. Its assets are nearing $20 million. It has become a major source of support for New Detroit, an urban coalition formed after the race riots of the late 1960s. Key board members took leadership roles in persuading the Michigan Sate Legislature to allocate a tax credit for contributions to community foundations in Michigan. Although I certainly can't take credit for initiating the proposal, I was pleased to call on some legislators to encourage them to vote favorably.

Our community foundation makes special efforts to reach out to organizations that are deeply imbedded in the community and to donors of all income levels. We've received checks ranging from $1 million to $100.

We're proud of all of them, but the small gifts help to keep the spirit alive in a city that can easily be dispirited. That's one reason why I'm optimistic about the Detroit area in the long run. The community foundation itself is a sign of that optimism, in my view, and if Detroit as a whole turns around in a fundamental way, it will have been due in no small part to the foundation.

MARY VAN EVERA is the granddaughter of a Duluth, Minnesota lawyer, Chester A. Congdon, who played an active part in the opening and development of the Mesabi Iron Range. Through the Duluth–Superior Area Community Foundation, Ms. Van Evera established the Global Awareness Fund and contributed $145,000.

MARY VAN EVERA: I have been active in trying to advance world peace and justice since the early 1960s. My political and educational activities have included membership in the League of Women Voters; Sane/Freeze; and I'm Board Chair of the World Policy Institute, a national public policy think-tank. I believe it is terribly important for Americans to understand the shrinking world they share—the danger to the environment, population pressures, and economic interdependence. We need to know other peoples' cultures as well as our political and social systems.

Although I had worked on these matters nationally, I also wanted to focus on them in my own community. Setting up a private trust would have been a pain, but I had an opportunity to create the Global Awareness Fund with two $50,000 contributions from two family charitable trusts. A friend, Kay Slack, who was president of the Duluth–Superior Area Community Foundation, showed me how the foundation would be a useful vehicle for this purpose.

I'm very enthusiastic about the foundation's flexibility and its geographic spread—nine counties—reaching even to Northland College, 80 miles away. We helped Northland College acquire materials for its Peace Center to complement one of its academic majors, Studies in Conflict and Peacemaking.

We have a wonderful advisory committee; in effect the community itself monitors the Global Awareness Fund. The foundation's professional staff support is strong and has made it possible to attract and initiate projects I couldn't possibly have conceived of myself. I love the process—the development of cases and applications that we're attracting. Grants from the Fund have ranged from $7,000 down to $250.

The Fund has been a catalyst in making things happen—a visit by William Sloane Coffin with our local Sane/Freeze group, the establishment of a Peace and Justice Center at St. Scholastica College, and an exciting series of mini-grants (up to $250 each) for schoolteachers—and with easy application procedures. In one case the funds made it possible for a teacher to mount an exhibit showing how the Ojibway Indians and the Mayans of Mexico used similar musical instruments; then the kids made replicas and learned to play them and appreciate them. A physics teacher used an oscilloscope for a radiation demonstration that was the trigger for his pupils to write essays on value-free discoveries that have potentially destructive possibilities.

The Global Awareness Fund was the first fund to help establish our Soviet Sister City relationship with Petrozavodsk, in Karelia, U.S.S.R. Now, students, teachers, and the general community are embarked on regular exchange visits and there is widespread interest in learning the Russian language. Our Fund has already attracted another donor and stimulated the establishment of the Our World Fund, which provides $5,000 a year for educational travel for both students and teachers, including trips to Petrozavodsk.

The people who, more than 20 years ago, established the original trusts which formed our Global Awareness Fund, were globally sensitive and concerned. I know they would be pleased that their funds, in the framework of the Community Foundation, will be used indefinitely into the future to serve contemporary needs as they change.

WILLIAM E. SIMON is president of the Community Foundation of New Jersey and a former U.S. Secretary of the Treasury. He has donated $100,000 to the foundation.

WILLIAM E. SIMON: I am a lifelong resident of New Jersey, and am excited to see so many things happening here to make the Garden State one of the leading economic areas in the country. To be such a leader requires sound educational opportunity and an environment that is not only conducive to enjoyable living, but challenges the best in us too.

I have long believed that citizens owe something back to their community, whether it be time or money or both. The government cannot and should not take full responsibility for people's lives. It is private enterprise, both in business and human services, that sparks the most innovative and valuable ideas that move us forward.

Thus, when I first learned about the Community Foundation of New Jersey from a friend, I was delighted to know there existed a vehicle that all citizens could use to make New Jersey an even better place to live. The Community Foundation's potential was enormous.

By starting my own named fund for urban scholarships at the foundation, I felt I could accomplish several things. First and foremost, I could further one of my deepest interests—the education of children in our urban areas. We must try to place within the reach of every child of God a ladder upon which he or she may rise, and I hope that through my scholarships, the foundation and I can help youngsters climb a few rungs. Second, I wanted my own children to be involved in this work, and by starting a donor-advised fund I ensured that they, too, in partnership with the professional and experienced staff of the foundation, could help needy and worthy candidates in a process which will continue long after I'm gone. Finally, I hoped that by making a commitment myself, I could point the way for others to do the same.

Initial donors to a young community foundation make a statement of faith both in its work and in the willingness of others to give. I wanted to make such a statement and help to build a framework that would ensure that people of modest means could also be philanthropists, thus strengthening private sector responses to human need. This seems to me a most worthy goal, and one that my family and I are delighted to support.

THEKLA R. SHACKELFORD, an educational consultant, is a member and former chair of the Governing Committee of the Columbus Foundation. She also is a founder of the "I Know I Can" program, which guarantees every high school graduate in Columbus a college education. She and her husband have contributed $343,000 to the foundation.

THEKLA R. SHACKELFORD: I opened my Donor Advised Fund in the Columbus Foundation in 1977. Having this kind of fund has enabled me to plan my charitable giving. Consequently I can maximize the effect of the money I distribute among the various charities I support each year.

In a year when, for tax purposes, it makes sense to give away more than usual, I load money into my fund. Then when those years come along when I don't have as much to give away, I can continue to support my favorite causes at a sustained level.

Another advantage has been the access it gives me to foundation staff. I am able to gain insight into some of the organizations that approach me for contributions, and I regard the information I get from the foundation as being expert in nature. No other organization in Columbus has comparable across-the-board experience with the nonprofit sector. Health, education, the arts, social services, conservation, civic affairs—no matter where an organization fits in the fabric of community life—the staff of the foundation knows it or knows how to get information about it for me.

Of course, by participating in the Columbus Foundation I am helping to support the development of an important permanent endowment for this community. The foundation plays a vital role in Columbus now, and that role will only grow as the years go on. When I first became a member of the Governing Committee, in 1980, my father—who had been involved in the Columbus Foundation from its beginning in 1943—talked to me very inspiringly and seriously about my responsibility for helping the assets of the foundation grow.

I've been an enthusiastic salesperson for the foundation ever since. Columbus has been good to me and my family; I want it to be a place where my grandchildren can live and prosper as well.

Lou Fockele of Gainesville, Georgia, represents the third generation of a family with printer's ink in its veins. His grandfather and father operated country newspapers in Kansas, and Lou ran a daily and two weeklies in Florida until he took over the operation of the Gainesville *Times* some 40 years ago. In 1981, when the newspaper was sold, Lou and his wife, Jean, took a portion from their share of the proceeds and established a fund with the Metropolitan Atlanta Community Foundation and played an important part in establishing the Gainesville Community Foundation, in which they have created a similar fund. Their contributions total $3.3 million.

> Lou Fockele: In our family we'd just be grateful when we got a regular pay-check for work adequately rewarding in itself. Jean and I were committed to the principles of stewardship, of course—giving to our church and all the other programs that are part of the normal warp and woof of any small community. But then, when we got to the point of selling what we thought was a small business, we discovered that some other people thought it was worth one helluva lot more than we ever dreamed possible. All of a sudden we were faced with some interesting decisions.
>
> The next thing we knew, we were sitting down with some attorneys in Atlanta to discuss how to handle this windfall. One of them, Ben White, knew that we had an interest in putting back some of what we'd been given into the community. He brought up the subject of using the Metro-politan Atlanta Community Foundation as a vehicle. We didn't know a thing about the organization, but the more we learned, the more we liked the idea.
>
> I need to say, incidentally, that we've always resisted making decisions based on the tax implications, but Ben showed us that the tax consequen-ces of being able to park our money in a donor-advised fund were a lot more attractive than trying to figure out how to give it all away in one tax year. Besides, we didn't know with any precision at that time just how we wanted to direct our giving, so we liked the possibilities in this approach. In our dreamy-eyed state, it sounded pretty good, and that's what we did.
>
> Since then we've had a couple of more windfalls, but we've concluded that we didn't want to establish yet another little private foundation to memorialize ourselves into all eternity. We don't want to become the head-line in a story like the ones about the little old ladies who leave everything to their cats—the last cat dies and then what? Furthermore, wills are not necessarily satisfactory instruments for the disposition of significant funds.
>
> We're going to give our children—as designees—some suggested guide-lines, but to us it makes sense to let the Atlanta and Gainesville community foundations be the instruments for disposition of the income from these

funds. Needs change over time, and we don't want to impose unnecessary restrictions upon our "heirs and assigns."

I've become a real missionary for community foundations. I'm not a very patient guy, so of course I'm totally dissatisfied with the results in Gainesville so far. We're located in a historically poor area in which there are pockets of real old money but no tradition of philanthropy, but I guess I'll have to admit that we're making some progress.

We are attracted to the community foundation concept by its very nature: continuity, flexibility, sensitivity to community needs. Their existence enables us to elevate our giving decisions to a new and more exciting plateau. We determine the "how-much" from time to time. With that behind us, then we have the fun of recommending to the foundations specific distributions of the money—whether income or principal.

We've expressed some of our gratitude to the community foundation for being there to help us when we needed it with unrestricted commitments to both of the foundations as well. To my way of "pick-'em-up, put-'em-down" country sort of thinking, this kind of giving—philanthropy is really too high-falutin' a word—makes a lot of sense.

7

Grants: Giving Life to the Public Trust

Mariam C. Noland

Community foundations enjoy a special double trust: a promise to respect and honor thousands of generous benefactors while advancing new visions for communities. Grantmaking, the tangible result of caring stewardship, is the most visible product of these "public trusts," as community foundations often describe themselves. Yet community foundation grantmaking has been little studied. Data collection has focused more on current management practices and asset growth than on funding patterns.

We do know that community foundation grantmaking represents an increasing portion of total philanthropic giving. For the over 300 community foundations in the United States, the Council on Foundations estimates that in 1987, grants totaled in excess of $316.1 million, an increase of 10.8 percent since 1984.

Grantmaking patterns vary widely, reflecting both the asset size of foundations and the creativity used in tailoring grantmaking to local needs. Smaller community foundations face special challenges, but the record shows that community impact is not directly related to the size of grant budgets. In a 1988 survey of small community foundations in three states, the Council of Michigan Foundations found that smaller community foundations believe that their very lack of resources requires creativity, innovation, and cooperation in grantmaking.

What is the context within which community foundations distribute funds? What are common grantmaking strategies and methods? What issues should be considered in developing grantmaking programs, and what does the future hold for our "public trusts"?

THE CONTEXT OF COMMUNITY FOUNDATION GRANTMAKING

Despite their great diversity, community foundations share a common set of factors that influence grantmaking. Each foundation must consider its constituencies, resources, and chosen leadership roles in crafting funding processes and programs.

Constituencies

Community. "The community" embodies a complex, ever-changing array of organizations, interests, needs, and opportunities. The responsible and successful community foundation views itself as a part of that community, within which it hopes to exercise some leadership and influence. And community foundation grantmaking also depends on the skills, creative energy, and commitment that can be derived from or stimulated within the community.

Given this interdependence, community foundations must weigh the interests advanced by governmental and politically related organizations, advocacy organizations, well-established major charities, individuals who are disenfranchised from traditional systems, and many other local players. Successful community foundations often have achieved the role of valued partner, working closely with individuals and groups, yet retaining a position of trust with all.

Donors. The multiplicity of funds created by caring individuals and organizations carry with them threads of intent that weave a diverse mosaic of charitable purposes. Traditionally, the majority of gifts have been received through bequests, their donors' interests reflected in testamentary language interpreted over the years. Community foundations must remain vigilant to those donor concerns, yet exercise judgment to take current circumstances into account to assure the most effective use of the funds.

In recent years, community foundations have sought and attracted a sharply increased number of living donors. This new constituency challenges community foundations to encourage the active involvement of the donors in the giving process. Yet serving these new donors can demand foundation staff time and energy beyond that commensurate with the donors' contributions. The foundation must manage the tension of offering a service to living donors without overlooking the continuing development and distribution of less restricted funds.

Trustees, Staff, and Advisors. Volunteer trustees, distribution committee members, and professional staff contribute a multiplicity of perspectives, expertise and interests to form the collective judgment needed to make grant decisions that assure that community ideals override personal concerns. Many community foundations also seek diverse community knowledge and insight through advisory committees convened for needs assessments, program planning, and grant recommendations.

Since community foundations (or their appointing authorities) usually select trustees who have already demonstrated charitable concern for the community, conflicts of interest can arise when grants are considered for organizations in which trustees are actively involved. Many community foundations handle this by requiring trustee disclosure of community activities and, increasingly, by defining limits on grant discussion and decision-making in cases of apparent conflict of interest. Staff, too, can be subject to such rules.

Resources

The permanence of unrestricted funds and the freedom to choose grantmaking directions enable the community foundation to take risks and stimulate initiatives.

The community foundation is one of few institutional givers in the community that can afford to take a long-term view of community betterment.

The flexibility of permanent endowments also challenges trustees and staff to look hard at the toughest issues and problems. Yet prudence dictates that foundations, especially those with limited assets, be realistic about the scale of resources they can provide over time and look for opportunities to intervene strategically.

Other Functions

The grantmaking program can help support other responsibilities that community foundations often assume. Thus if a community foundation chooses to act as a convenor or a catalyst for change, to manage projects or provide services to donors, grantmaking can complement and enhance those roles. In turn, all of these functions can facilitate effective grantmaking.

Values

Finally, the values inherent in community foundations exert a central influence on the grant program. While some commentators have suggested that the community foundation be a neutral player in its community, it is not an organization devoid of values.

James A. Joseph, president of the Council on Foundations, suggests that "community foundations are an embodiment and reflection of the Constitutional values we now celebrate.... Positioned as they are to see their communities in a holistic way, community foundations are uniquely prepared to turn problems into opportunities and to channel the public debate in such a way that those issues which could tear a community apart, end up bringing it together."

Ethicist Michael Josephson argues that organized philanthropy has a responsibility, along with others that share a public trust, to observe the highest standards of ethical conduct. These include honesty, integrity, promise keeping, fidelity/loyalty, fairness, caring and respect for others, responsible citizenship, pursuit of excellence, accountability, and safeguarding the public trust.

GRANTMAKING STRATEGIES AND METHODS

Given the diversity of communities and community foundations, no one "right formula" exists for effective grantmaking. Indeed, many in the field delight in inventing new and even better ways to design programs and make grants.

Grantmaking Strategies

Many of the strategies common to community foundations resemble those used by other types of grantmakers. Used in a wide variety of programmatic areas, these strategies provide assistance in looking at alternative types of program interventions:

- Develop and strengthen institutions.
- Enhance individual skills and capacities.
- Improve systems and services.
- Improve information and understanding.
- Focus attention on issues.

- Build and strengthen community.

Developing and Strengthening Institutions. To enhance the capacities or abilities of organizations to carry out their purposes, grants can be made to provide general support, to strengthen particular functions of the organization, or to help an organization develop new efforts. Support might also be given to help start new organizations to address unmet needs. Community foundation grants to strengthen organizations have supported expansion, planning, fundraising, marketing, reorganization, staff training, executive recruitment, and various forms of technical assistance (see Chapters 18 and 19).

Community foundations have also found it appropriate to house Foundation Center funding libraries that are open to the public without charge, and to sponsor workshops for nonprofit organizations on grantsmanship, public relations, group purchasing, accounting, insurance planning, and computerization. Many community foundations routinely provide individualized technical assistance for applicants and grantees, or finance their access to independent management support organizations.

Enhancing Individual Skills. Since the quality of life in each community depends on the work of skilled individuals, community foundations seek to improve skills through the support of education, training, and remediation programs for all ages. While grants are usually made to organizations that provide the training, individuals may be supported directly through scholarships or other awards.

Community foundations in recent years have developed many programs to improve the quality of public education, including school-to-work transition programs, model curricular projects, and teacher training programs (see Chapter 12). Because of the emphasis on individuals, small grants can leverage larger impact.

Improving Systems and Services. Most services are provided through a complex combination of public and private agencies. For example, some community foundations have funded activities to improve child-care or juvenile-justice systems. In other cases, grants support experimentation with new ways to deliver services or stimulate collaborative efforts, often involving cooperation between the public and private sectors (see Chapter 21). Support may also focus on governance and control issues or on how services are financed.

Improving Information and Understanding. Community foundations often are asked to support research and data collection on broad public policy issues. In addition, many use field-of-interest fund income to help underwrite scientific or other academic research.

In the public policy area, community foundations have funded research into issues as varied as court congestion, the quality of life in minority communities, child-care supply and demand, and local giving and volunteering.

Focusing Attention on Issues. Efforts to promote a specific set of issues, viewpoints, or actions might include public media campaigns or support for the organizing activities of a wide variety of advocacy organizations. Many of the recent efforts to prevent the spread of AIDS or to safeguard the environment exemplify this strategy.

Appropriately, community foundations have often taken steps to stimulate public awareness of philanthropy. Community foundations have funded and even managed local campaigns in Independent Sector's "Give Five" effort to increase giving and volunteering.

Building and Sustaining Communities. Inherent in the mission of community foundations is outreach to, and strengthening of, all segments within the service area. Thus they support efforts to solve basic community problems, programs that help bridge traditional differences, and programs that encourage institutions to work collectively toward common goals (see Chapter 13). In the future, community foundations may find this strategy particularly appropriate as communities continue to struggle with basic issues of justice and equal rights for all citizens and to absorb new waves of immigrants.

Methods

Community foundations also display a complex and highly diverse set of methods in grantmaking. Different from the steps and techniques used in reviewing grant requests, they are the range of program components used in a grantmaking program. They fall into these categories: styles of operation, types of grant, and forms of allocation.

Grantmaking Styles. In grantmaking, the manner in which community foundations relate to applicants, grantees, other funders, and the community varies widely. Figure 1 illustrates this array of grantmaking styles by posing a continuum between opposites or extremes of each of these relationships.

FIGURE 1. GRANTMAKING STYLES

REACTIVE
Responds solely to proposals from community; open to any type of request

HIGHLY PRESCRIPTIVE
Funds within foundation-determined program areas

HANDS-OFF
Leaves project management to grantee

PROJECT MANAGER
Actively oversees grantee programs or develops and runs own

BANKER
Supports proven organizations and activities with probability for success; prefers no risks

VENTURE CAPITALIST
Supports new or unproven efforts and accepts possibility of failure

INDEPENDENT
Likes to be sole supporter of programs

COLLABORATIVE
Leverages own and grantee resources through joint funding

MINIMAL GRANTEE CONTACT
No active or ongoing involvement with applicants or grantees

CONTINUOUS GRANTEE CONTACT
Assists grantees through staff, trustee, or technical support

LIMITED COMMUNITY INVOLVEMENT
Board sets all priorities and makes all grant decisions

DIRECT COMMUNITY INVOLVEMENT
Solicits external advice on needs, priorities, and/or grants

BASIC TRACKING
Accepts grantee assurances of level of success

FORMAL EVALUATION
Requires extensive reviews of funded programs

Choices regarding styles of operation tend to shape the community foundation's reputation. For example, a funder may help grantees, or favor established agencies, or prefer to work with other foundations. However, the styles of most community foundations tend to range between the opposites depicted in Figure 1.

Types of Grants. Community foundations use a variety of types of grants. Just as grantmaking styles can be understood by looking at extremes, types of grants can be arrayed between opposites. For example consider those shown in Figure 2.

FIGURE 2. TYPES OF GRANTS

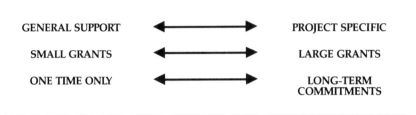

1. *General Support to Program Specific.* Grantmakers who prefer program-specific grants point out that they simplify evaluation and provide greater identification for the grantmaker with a given project. But general support may be an organization's greatest need at a given period, and the community foundation may be the only source capable of a timely response.

2. *Small Grants to Large Grants.* The size of grant amounts reported by community foundations in 1987 varied from a few dollars to $3 million. Rather than solely a function of asset size, grant amounts may also reflect a foundation's strategies and other interests. The Philadelphia Foundation, for example, with annual grant disbursements of almost $4 million, keeps a majority of its grants in the $5,000 to $25,000 range so that more grassroots organizations may be served (see Chapter 23).

3. *One-Time-Only to Long-Term Commitments.* One-time grants can appeal equally to the reactive funder who wishes to remain flexible as new proposals arrive, or to the venture capitalist, who wants to put money in only at the beginning of a project.

Long-term commitments can be made either to agencies or in programmatic areas. Since long-term commitments substantially affect the flexibility of the foundation's total resources, they tend to be made by community foundations that have narrowed their areas of interest and favor the "prescriptive" style of grantmaking.

Forms of Allocation. While grants and scholarships continue to be the most common forms of financial assistance available from community foundations, a variety of other vehicles appear to be gaining popularity.

Program-related investments (PRIs) are loans, financed from assets or income, that assist projects related to the foundation's own charitable purposes. They have been used successfully by community foundations for predevelopment planning in housing programs, for mortgage capital, for family immigration costs (see Chapter 11), and for assistance to nonprofits with the cost of energy-conserving renovations. The community foundation in Carlsbad, New Mexico, for example, solved a local physician shortage by providing relocation loans to medical practitioners.

Loans and PRIs recycle a foundation's funds, since they are generally repaid. They can also lead to new types of relations with community organizations, particularly in areas like housing and economic development.

Monetary awards can be used as part of a community foundation's strategy to focus attention on an issue, such as race relations or civic leadership. Qualities and accomplishments celebrated in these awards include leadership in neighborhood development, a history of community service, organizational initiative in response to a significant contemporary problem, and improving human relations.

Money need not even change hands for the community foundation to accomplish some purposes. Community foundations have begun to use their financial strength to back nonprofit organizations through such mechanisms as loan guarantees.

While being mindful of constituents, combining all these funding strategies and methods into a total grantmaking program is a major challenge for foundation leaders. Some community foundations have developed underlying principles of grantmaking that help provide a way to organize and communicate their basic operating philosophies and to provide a useful rationale for individual decisions on grants. The Community Foundation of Southeastern Michigan's, for example, are:

- Identify creative, innovative solutions to community problems and take risks to stimulate and initiate innovation.
- Focus on the long-term perspective of community betterment, yet respond with flexibility to immediate needs.
- Address emerging needs not yet being adequately addressed by government or nonprofit organizations.
- Be available to all nonprofit organizations regardless of their programmatic and service area.

- Make investments in activities where the scale of foundation resources is likely to have an impact on the proposed activity.
- Provide leverage to attract support from other foundations as well as new or additional financial resources to serve the people.
- Provide positive visibility for the foundation.
- Recognize the necessity and desirability to fund exceptional opportunities that are outside of the foundation's defined programmatic areas.

ISSUES IN DEVELOPING FUNDING PROGRAMS

Several key issues challenge our understanding not only of grantmaking program possibilities but also of the values that should guide our stewardship.

Is community foundation grantmaking really different from that of other funders? Understanding where we stand *vis-a-vis* other funders may help us choose more appropriate funding opportunities, make us more effective collaborators, and help communicate the realities of community foundation strengths and limitations to our constituents.

Community foundations provide financial grants just as other funders do, but we differ in purpose, structure, and tradition. Our geographical commitment requires that the foundation be concerned about the needs and potential of all community residents. This direct tie means that community foundations live with their successes and failures. Unlike other private funders, they cannot distance themselves entirely from community opinion; their grants are never abstract experiments.

As public charities, we enjoy increased flexibility over private foundations under the law—through the ability to distribute funds to individuals, unincorporated groups, or even for-profit operations without incurring the obligation of expenditure responsibility. Free of the private foundation payout requirement that requires minimum annual payments to charities, community foundations are free to time the distribution of resources to best meet needs and seize opportunities.

Pablo Eisenberg, president of the Center for Community Change, suggests that community foundations could be even more responsive. "I think the issue is whether a community foundation is actually serving the needs of the total community," he says. "In so many cases, community foundations have acted more or less like an establishment foundation that puts all its money into safe projects—the arts, culture, higher education, health, traditional social services—and has really neglected poor people, neighborhoods, low-income housing, all those tough issues. Not that they should exclusively focus on them, but at least there should be a fair share, since those comprise a really high percentage of the community's real problems." True, we could do better.

Perhaps the most striking difference between community foundations and other funders lies in their mission to serve the needs of multiple community donors and to encompass overall needs.

Are community foundations inherently "middle-of-the-road? Many of the advantages of community foundations facilitate risk-taking: a permanent and flexible source of funds, independent governing bodies, and freedom from the vagaries of political or familial pressures.

Yet because they are responsible to multiple constituencies, they cannot move totally independent of prevailing community norms. Often, this dictates that program initiatives move somewhat more cautiously and slowly than might be ideal.

Particularly important, and perhaps more so in the last decade, is the desire and need for community foundations to secure additional financial support, to attract and retain donors. Community foundations have therefore become unusually sensitive to public opinion and the interests of prospective donors. Community foundations that position themselves to be seen as either highly conservative or extremely liberal should recognize that their attractiveness will be limited to certain constituents.

Since most community foundations believe it is important to provide leadership, it may be wise to:

- Choose carefully the issues to pursue.
- Make sure the foundation has the ability to perform.
- Look for opportunities where some success is likely.
- Find ways to involve others.
- Be willing to adjust and shift course.
- Take a very long-term program perspective.
- Never forget all the donors who made the foundation possible.
- Be prudent.

Are grantmaking and fundraising related? One may argue that as a public trust the only consideration in grantmaking should be the public benefit.

But the pure, externally driven public trust model is not possible, or perhaps even desirable. First, since donors are important constituents of community foundations, it is prudent to consider the many factors that influence donors. The challenge is to match that intent with current opportunities for the public good.

The *cy pres* doctrine supposedly solves this "dead hand" problem by allowing community foundations to vary the purposes of funds where the original intent cannot be carried out because it is impossible, impractical, or unnecessary. In practice, few funds are varied unless the circumstances are extreme, for example, an organization going out of business or a disease cured. The chilling effect of the Buck Trust case in San Francisco has led community foundation lawyers and legally minded trustees to question any variance in which such absolute circumstances cannot be proven.

The charitable concerns of past donors may be a significant restraint on community foundations' future flexibility. They can minimize the problem for tomorrow's leadership by actively encouraging prospective donors to include flexible funds as part, if not all, of their bequests.

Second, the community foundation, in order to maintain its public charity status, must continually secure new contributions. Surveys indicate that people give because they feel they are giving to a worthy cause. Thus community foundations recognize this when they use their grantmaking records as marketing tools in annual reports and newsletters. Some community foundations have also raised money by soliciting gifts for field-of-interest funds in such areas as small arts organizations, women's programs, and Hispanic issues.

However, if the drive to raise funds leads to shying away from higher risk, unpopular, or more controversial grantmaking, it brings into serious question our independence and public responsibility. Accepting the premise that grantmaking and fundraising are related, community foundations should remain clear about their ultimate charitable missions and the values reflected by their grantmaking decisions. Yet the community foundation also must meet changing needs never envisioned by these donors.

Should community foundations strike a balance between their own strategic initiatives and unsolicited requests from the community? Many larger community foundations seek more and more to focus grantmaking on selected community issues as a way to increase impact.

The issue is whether community foundations have a responsibility to select areas of philanthropic interest or whether they have become too prescriptive and less reflective of community interests. One solution is to ensure that the selected areas do, in fact, represent the real needs of the community.

Many new ideas are first discovered when they come "over the transom," as unsolicited proposals from brand-new agencies. With too much money locked into their own strategies, community foundations risk losing out on such opportunities.

Does our grantmaking program help or hinder? One of the principles of good grantmaking is "do no harm." Grants may fail, or be put to poor use, but they should not leave a nonprofit organization in worse straits than when it entered the relationship.

Because a grant will sometimes change the recipient agency, grant requests must occasionally be denied not because the program is worthless, but because it would imbalance the agency or comes at the wrong time in the organization's history. This argues for a close understanding of the community foundation's nonprofit clientele and frank exchanges about their internal condition. This interchange has spurred the development of nongrant assistance to nonprofits: workshops, technical assistance, training, and other forms of help.

Can we ever really know what works? Community foundations have set out on tasks that draw them directly into complex issues. Objectives like "changing communities" or "improving the public welfare" are difficult to measure. Nor is it realistic to conceive of scientifically controlled experiments to evaluate the long-term impact of hundreds of grants. Therefore, it is likely that boards and staffs will never really have the satisfaction of knowing—with certainty—what their work has achieved.

Yet grantmaking evaluations can provide important assistance in setting grantmaking priorities, improving individual grant decisions, and gauging the effectiveness of the foundation as a grantmaking organization. The following questions might be asked:

- Is there clarity of grantmaking purpose and philosophy?
- Is the foundation using the most effective grantmaking strategies to meet needs?
- Has the foundation selected the right issues to receive support in relation to public needs and opportunities?
- Do the other activities of the foundation enhance the effectiveness of the grantmaking program?

- Does the foundation grantmaking program ensure decisions that encourage charitable activities of high quality and effectiveness?
- Does the grantmaking process effectively put into practice the ethical values the foundation espouses?

Some foundations use programmatic reviews to share information with grant recipients and thus to provide technical assistance to funded projects.

SOME THOUGHTS ON FUTURE TRENDS

Several predictable trends will directly affect community foundation grantmaking. First, available public funds will fall increasingly short in meeting basic human needs, and the issues won't get any simpler. While community foundation resources will continue to grow, demand for those dollars will increase. This will accelerate the development of new methods to leverage foundation resources.

For example, direct grants may become less the norm and give way to more sophisticated financing arrangements. Community foundations may exercise more leadership as convenors and information providers. They may help their communities to become more competitive in a growing national and international market for limited charitable resources.

A second clear trend will be for additional collaboration in grantmaking with other funders, as detailed in Chapter 8.

It is also likely that community foundations will continue to work more closely with the public sector. Key examples already exist, such as the partnerships of community foundations and states to promote energy conservation.

Another trend will be an increase in the range of relations with living donors. Many younger and more active living donors will have specific interests, which will result in limiting, at least in the short term, the growth of unrestricted grantmaking resources. These donors will also want to be involved more in setting funding priorities and in the grants process.

Community foundations probably will join in a variety of arrangements to share access to technical expertise on selected topics and other skills necessary for effective grantmaking. For example, 14 small community foundations in Michigan share a staff person. Thereby they gain access to expert staff at almost no cost. In other cases, private foundations will share staff with community foundations on projects of joint interest.

It is also likely that community foundations will continue to grow in their role as local outreach arms for national funders, such as corporations or private foundations.

Living the public trust, community foundations face an awesome task in grantmaking—to spend carefully but creatively, to honor donors while exercising independent judgment, to move inexorably forward with fairness and accountability to all.

8

Collaboration: Models, Benefits, and Tensions

Susan V. Berresford

Collaborative efforts among community foundations themselves and between community foundations and others have proliferated.

When there are several community foundations in one area, they sometimes find reasons to be allies or partners. Another factor, surely, is the increasing recognition that our society's problems are exceedingly complex and require attention from multiple actors, for example, regional environmental issues, either ground water or air pollution, require effort in many communities.

Collaboration also stems from the transfer of substantial power from the federal government to states and localities in the last decade. National donors and government policymakers must pursue their work in combination with local actors if they seek local impact. Collaborative agreements help to test ideas and to promote successes in multiple localities.

A third factor quickening the collaborative impulse is the recognition that need far outstrips resources in many fields and that greater efficiency will help make the best use of limited funds. Often, the consolidation of back-up functions, data management, and fundraising by several community foundations seems to offer administrative savings that can be turned into grant dollars. Similarly, small community foundations may benefit greatly in their early growth stages from reliance on the professional grantmaking and administrative experience of their more established colleagues.

Another impetus may be the legendary mobility of Americans. We move frequently, and many Americans feel obliged or privileged to contribute to social needs wherever we are. Some community foundations that have identified patterns of mobility into their areas (for vacation and retirement) have developed collaborative arrangements with their counterparts where the donors originally resided. Moreover, as wealthy donors' children establish themselves or go to schools in new places, the donor impulse may range more widely than it has in the past if community foundations are alert to the opportunities.

Finally, our complex society needs more effective participatory structures—organizations and processes in which people with differing backgrounds work together on important common problems. All too often our communities are segregated, the opportunities for discussion of crucial problems limited, and the formation of powerful and diverse alliances and understanding thereby constrained. Community foundations seem to offer the potential for a community-oriented, diverse, and flexible participatory structure.

WHAT DO THE COLLABORATIVES LOOK LIKE?

The collaborative efforts of recent years are remarkably varied. They can be divided into two broad categories: collaboratives where program goals are dominant and those related to process or operations.

Process Collaboratives

In a number of areas, several community foundations have affiliate relationships. These are often the result of the emergence of small community "funds" near a larger, more established community foundation and both the large and small entity find advantages in affiliation. For example, the New York Community Trust, with $500 million in assets, has affiliates in Long Island, Westchester and the Berkshire-Taconic area. A recent survey of some 80 community foundations chosen to represent a range of geography and size indicates that slightly over 11 percent have some sort of affiliate or satellite arrangement.

The North Dakota Community Foundation (NDCF) offers a striking example of the affiliation approach in its relations with small-scale endowments in eighteen communities across the state. Each "mini-endowment" community was required to raise $25,000, which the NDCF supplemented with $5,000. NDCF makes every effort to invest each local area's funds in local financial institutions, and each fund has a local advisory committee selected by community residents. This impressive geographic reach is the result of early seed grants provided to North Dakota from the Otto Bremer Foundation, the Charles Stewart Mott Foundation, and corporate and individual donors.

The affiliation approach provides a speedy start-up for new community foundations, enabling them to avoid legal and procedural problems. If the smaller funds grew very slowly they would not be able to afford the degree of back-up service, and in some cases professional staffing, on their own that they enjoy as affiliates. However, once an affiliate grows to significant size, it may prefer to control all of its operations and thus seek independent status.

A group of community foundations known as the California Consortium exemplifies the service-link models. The consortium worked with Apple Computer in 1988 to develop a common plan under which Apple donated 50 MacIntosh computers, printers, modems, and older peripheral equipment. The Consortium's executive committee then allocated the equipment to 48 community foundations across the country, principally those with less than $2 million in assets. The community foundations received a year's free access to Apple's corporate worldwide telecommunications network, Apple Link, and Microsoft software packages.

By far the most ambitious process collaboration among community foundations and others is the National Agenda project, as described in the preface. One of its most striking features is the care the project has taken to bring together the needs and interests of large and small, old and new, emerging and established community foundations.

Program Collaborations

Three models here illustrate the range of activities they cover: collaborations with national donors, with corporations, and with government.

1. Community Foundations and Private Foundations. The Charles Stewart Mott Foundation has worked since 1979 to strengthen community foundations' capacities to engage a broad cross section of Americans in philanthropy and to help the foundations contribute to strong communities. Its first effort was designed to fortify small, struggling community foundations with grants for administrative costs, projects, and endowments with matching requirements. Seven community foundations received a total of $1.4 million.

Following that program, between 1982 and 1986, the Mott Foundation supported a program of technical assistance for community foundations at the start-up stage and for others in need of revitalization.
Under this additional program, the Council on Foundations received
$460,000 to coordinate and provide technical assistance, and Mott
granted $740,000 to 17 community foundations that received the
technical assistance. The 17 community foundations received intensive technical assistance, 19 others received more limited service, 37
were involved in staff exchanges, and more than 80 sought and used
materials produced by the project. The Mott Foundation renewed the
program in 1987 for another two years.

Mott has also begun a neighborhood program to support mini-grants
for emerging groups in low-income neighborhoods (see, for example,
the experience of the Foundations for the Carolinas, Chapter 24).

The Mott Foundation's partnerships with community foundations
show elements that recur in other associations with national donors.
First is the step-like program development process. Second is the
attractiveness of combining, in one program, attention to the grantmaking, endowment building, and administrative functions of the community foundations. Third is the focus on the emerging and revitalizing community foundations and the prospect that many of them could
become as effective and significant as the major community foundations.

Another example of national/community foundation partnerships is
the Ford Foundation's work. The program began with two separate
efforts. One, undertaken with Carnegie Corporation and the Rockefeller
and MacArthur Foundations, was to help create a community foundation in Puerto Rico. This initiative grew from national donors' realiza-
tion that effective grantmaking on the island was difficult to achieve
from afar and that an opportunity existed to create and help fund
an island-based and controlled community foundation. The notion
involved mainland donors granting approximately $4 million, with a
two-to-one matching requirement. In late 1988, the Puerto Rico
Community Foundation met its first phase fundraising goal of $12
million.

The Ford Foundation's second effort involved collaboration with community foundations in programs to address teen parenthood. Replica-
tion of a successful intervention with teen mothers and the design
of new programs to reach teen fathers were the focus of efforts
undertaken in collaboration with a group of 16 community foundations. Funding totaled close to $1.5 million over three years. The

partnership provided that, in general, community foundations would cover basic operating costs of the local programs and Ford would cover unified evaluation, communication, and exchange of experience. The effort was not problem-free. There were misunderstandings about how costs would be shared between the foundations, how the local projects would be supported after the collaboration, and how to share press attention nationally and affect the local press. Despite these tensions, the collaboration produced a set of effective service projects.

In part as a result of the positive results from the local foundations' work, the Ford Foundation began an asset-building/leadership development program for community foundations with assets of less than $10 million. The program involved challenge grants of approximately $500,000 each, awarded through a competitive process, for staffing and five-year program strategies that held promise of establishing the foundations' identities and attracting new undesignated endowment funds. Eight community foundations received grants in the first round in 1986 and, with MacArthur Foundation participating, nineteen in the second in 1988. An advisory group composed of experienced grantmakers helped select the original eight partners and design a second round of awards.

Ford's interest reflects the fact that the effectiveness of national donors rests on the quality of information they receive, the capacity of local areas and regions to maintain innovations that work in the pilot phase, and on the existence of trusted institutions that bring competitive and contending parties together to solve problems. One element of the Ford/community foundation partnerships involved encouraging racial, gender, and occupational diversity in the decision-making bodies of community foundations.

A number of other national donors, such as the Gannett and Kettering foundations, have extensive and imaginative programs related to community foundations.

2. Community Foundations and Corporations. Both large and small corporations have worked with community foundations in addition to or in place of a regular corporate giving program. In some instances the collaboration is for a specific purpose such as grants to local arts organizations, and in others it is for a broad array of philanthropic work. Despite the leveling off of corporate contributions programs overall, this sector seems to represent a growth field for community foundations. In fact, the mechanism offered by community foundations may be increasingly attractive to corporations as mergers occur and staffs are reduced.

Among the many examples of the range of corporate partnerships, the Kalamazoo Foundation has several advised funds from corporate sources including a law firm, major manufacturing firms, and a newspaper. Its largest allocation from a corporate source is $10 million from the Upjohn Corporation for improvements in the county's infrastructure over five years.

The San Diego Community Foundation is targeting small corporations with up to 20 or 30 employees, branch offices of large corporations, and decent numbers of mid-sized to small businesses. It offers them such services as review of needs in a field, proposal screening, or grant monitoring.

3. Community Foundations and Government. Community foundations have ties to government at the legislative, executive, and judicial levels. For example, courts sometimes turn to community foundations to be part of case settlements or decisions in which restitution funds are created. Thus, in Pittsburgh, the community foundation was chosen by the Pennsylvania Public Utility Commission to administer a $1.5 million fund resulting from utility overcharges by a local lighting company. The funds are to be used for economic development of the Monongahela Valley. And in New York, a $15 million restitution settlement with Exxon Corporation channeled the funds to community foundations to help nonprofit agencies improve the energy efficiency of their facilities. More than 30 community foundations in Ohio and Michigan were involved in a similar project. The Arizona Community Foundation provides another set of examples of program partnerships with government (see Chapter 21).

A very unusual example of government funding for a community foundation occurred in South Dakota. The foundation received a $2 million challenge grant from the 3M Company, which stimulated the Governor to reallocate an unused $1 million set-aside fund (formerly earmarked for a supercollider project). Both houses of the state legislature then voted an additional $1 million to make the match. The earnings of the fund are designated for economic development.

ISSUES ARISING FROM COLLABORATION?

It's Hard to Do

The leadership of each institutional partner must be convinced that the need for the collaboration is clear, the timing right, and the roles appropriate to each organization's special capacities. Getting agreement to move ahead within a reasonable period requires meshing of widely varying decision processes and board meeting schedules. Moving ahead on a commonly agreed upon program can require suspension of practices that have been sacrosanct, such as restriction of grants to one year, or a policy of no renewals, or focus on a tightly defined geographic area, or a governmental practice of operating through requests for proposals. Potential partners may grow impatient, other priorities crowd the agenda, leadership changes, and suddenly the collaborative effort loses steam.

Collaborations between national donors and local community foundations carry their own tensions. Some community foundation staff seem to feel that their national colleagues owe them something since community foundations are such experts on the local terrain. Perhaps the only debt they want paid is a fair measure of respect and consultation before intrusion on their home ground. National foundations sometimes feel locally oriented staffs are shortsighted when they fail to see the value of joining a multi-site project that could affect policy widely. A little less arrogance on both sides would go a long way, and each needs to speak of the other with care.

Finally, if the collaboration yields good results, comes the question of whether credit for success and media attention is appropriately shared. What the press thinks important may differ substantially from the views of the collaborative partners.

These difficulties can be reduced or avoided if staff and leaders of organizations involved in the collaboration counter them aggressively. Oversight bodies ought to be formed at the outset to pick up signs of trouble and to suggest remedies.

WHAT PART OF THE COMMUNITY DO COMMUNITY FOUNDATIONS BRING TO A COLLABORATION?

The assumption that community foundations are attuned to community needs, directed by respected community residents, supported by community members, and devoted to building a sense of community attracts other organizations into partnership with them. When several community foundations collaborate in fundraising, they do so in the belief that their appeal will be more powerful by virtue of greater geographic and programmatic coverage. But in some areas the reality is farther from the ideal than we would like, and that harsh fact can ultimately undermine the rationale for collaboration, and possibly the broad credibility of community foundations.

First, who supports community foundations? Few of the large community foundations seek funds as aggressively from community members with very modest means as they do from the wealthy, corporations, and private foundations. Surprisingly few of the small community foundations even target the young, upwardly mobile population for participation. One exception, the Peninsula Community Foundation, in Burlingame, California, has established the Catalyst Fund: A Young Adult Philanthropic Effort, through which men and women in their 20s and 30s make grants.

Nearly total reliance on the wealthy cuts the foundation off from people who may be closest to some of the problems the community foundation wants to address and who may therefore have both insight and time to contribute. The active engagement and supporting voice of donors of varying backgrounds can also be programmatically and politically valuable. If, for example, a program partnership involves grants for a controversial problem, the community foundation will be able to act with greatest confidence if its donors span class, race, and neighborhood.

The El Paso Community Foundation seems to be particularly creative in involving varying types of donors in its work across ethnic, income, and neighborhod lines (see Chapter 15).

Next, who controls community foundation policy and grantmaking? The pattern frequently shows overrepresentation of male civic leaders from the wealthy white community. What would change with more diverse leadership is unclear; but the failure to draw significant leadership from ethnic and racial communities and women surely undercuts the community foundation's local credibility.

And finally, what is the scope of community foundation programs? Small community foundations are naturally limited in what they can cover with available funds. Even large community foundations must beware of scattering their work so widely that it has no cumulative effect. But again, the credibility of community foundations as "retail grantmakers" or as effective magnets of major donations must rest on their breadth of vision and knowledge (see Chapter 7).

In sum, the credibility and attractiveness of community foundations as a special kind of partner in programming, fundraising, and leadership on crucial issues derive from their status as a vehicle for community initiative, not as a creation of community elites, however well intentioned and well directed.

WHOSE AGENDA IS PRIMARY?

Another problem arises when the community foundation's agenda seems to be distorted by the collaborative project. After agreeing with its partners on a shared effort, the community foundation may later find that the project's demands exceeded what was expected, blurred the community foundation's identity, or brought on unexpected controversy.

One such example can develop when national foundations or corporations want to work through a group of community foundations to test a specific program intervention. The national partner may have a very clear plan that it asks the community foundation to implement and for which it provides funding. As the program begins operation, the community foundation staff may believe that the program strategy should be adjusted, but the donor insists that the original model be followed. It is possible that the national donor's rigidity could thus undermine both foundations' reputations as responsive and professional funders.

Agenda confusion may also arise in cooperative efforts between United Way and community foundations. In some parts of the country relations have become badly strained. In a number of places, however, United Ways help fund the normal core operating costs of social service agencies, and community foundations support new projects and experimentation. Their funding sources also often differ. In more and more communities, however, United Way and the community foundation are joining in support of innovative programs—for example, in funding producers of affordable housing. And often now, United Ways are exploring endowment building, sometimes with the community foundation holding the endowment.

Confusion over agenda can also be seen in some of the affiliate/satellite relationships. Leaders of satellite funds generally prefer to direct all their grants to their own geographic area, whereas leaders of the "umbrella" community foundation may seek at least some satellite dollars for multi-community or regional projects. If ultimately the satellite attracts only modest amounts of new money to its area and shares none of it with the "parent," the larger community foundation may not see much value in continuing the relationship.

CAN COMMUNITY FOUNDATIONS HAVE A LOUDER VOICE?

In instances where community foundations join in supporting common programs across regions, they are likely to amass experience that should reach a national audience. The same probably holds true for work that community foundations do independently. Community foundations could jointly seek or construct public forums in which the lessons from their work are presented to policymakers. If thrusting themselves into public policy discussions seems too bold, several community foundations could surely link effective grantees that share a common goal—advocates for low-income housing, for example—and help them become part of the policy debate. Otherwise some nonprofits might resent the community foundations upstaging them. Moreover, community foundations could offer another voice from the community, to add to those of elected and appointed officials and to those of citizens and organizations already participating in public debate.

The models of collaborative response of community foundations to undiminished social need, mobility patterns, and complex local community disputes or problems is varied—be they networks, umbrella agreements, partnerships, dependencies, or experimental efforts—and will continue to proliferate and vary even further.

But their efforts to address challenges in their own field will have a strong influence on whether community foundations continue to be attractive to donors and potential collaborators. Problems such as diversity, focus, agenda, breadth of community ties, and characteristics such as risk-taking capacity are key to the future.

9

The Search for Standards: Why Community Foundations Are Different

Steven A. Minter

What assurance is there that each of the institutions calling itself a "community foundation" is worthy of the public's trust and support? The answer is none.

So I believe that the time has come to develop "industry standards" for community foundations—outlining the characteristics that, taken together, distinguish us from other funding organizations such as private foundations and the United Way—and to use that set of standards as the basis for some form of accreditation or self-regulation.

Why should we go beyond the "Principles and Practices for Effective Grantmaking" to which members of the Council on Foundations subscribe? Quite simply because we ask more of the *public* than do other types of foundations. We and our donors enjoy the maximum tax benefits that our society bestows. We ask the public to entrust to us its money and, increasingly, a critical leadership role in civic life.

Whatever standards may be set should not be immutable, because community foundations are, after all, predicated upon the certainty of change. The process will require a light hand, for community foundations must themselves remain free to innovate. But they should recognize our obligation to be exemplars of our core values. The process of building consensus must itself reflect these values of representativeness by including community foundations of all sizes, developmental stages, geographic regions, and programmatic emphases.

WHY NOW?

The enormous growth of the community foundation movement raises the very real possibility of competition among foundations whose service areas abut or overlap. Industry standards would be helpful in devising a process for resolution of disputes arising from competition.

Further, it is almost inevitable that an organization calling itself a community foundation will become involved in a public scandal. In all likelihood we could not stop anyone from using the name, and accreditation would not prevent incompetence or abuse, any more than a license to practice medicine guarantees a physician's competence. But a rigorous accreditation process *would* allow us to distance ourselves from disreputable organizations and to articulate to the public what we expect of community foundations.

Significant pressure for a definition or standards comes from community foundations themselves. Demand on the Council on Foundations to provide training opportunities for members of our staffs and governing bodies is tremendous. Yet training on any significant scale presupposes some common understanding about a community foundation's functions, sound practices, board–staff relations, and job descriptions.

Finally, many professionals in our field anticipate that in time it will be necessary for community foundations to seek from the Congress or the Treasury Department an exemption from the public fundraising requirement for public charities. This task will be far easier if as a field we have developed and tested standards that protect the public interest—if we can, in short, say how we are different and why we should be accorded special treatment. But even if the public-support test endures, standards would permit us to embrace foundations that cannot or do not wish to meet the public-support test but are in all other respects recognizable as community foundations.

THE FORMAL/LEGAL FRAMEWORK

The law is not particularly helpful in guiding us toward an operating definition. Except for a passing reference in the 1940s, federal statutes have never even mentioned community foundations! Until the enactment of the Tax Reform Act of 1969, there was no major distinction between private foundations and public charities.

In fact, a community foundation is defined more by its own governing instrument than by any laws. The laws and regulations concerning tax exemptions and deductibility of gifts may *influence* the form of community foundations, but they do not *dictate* it.

The "Cleveland Plan," the basis for the Cleveland Foundation's governing instrument, embodied certain key elements: (1) separation of investments (managed by the trustee bank) from charitable disbursements (authorized by a distribution committee); (2) a distribution committee appointed in part by public authorities; (3) formation of an open-ended, permanent endowment; (4) service to a well-defined geographic area; and (5) public disclosure of operations and grantmaking.

Although most of the community foundations established in the two decades after 1914 followed the Cleveland Plan closely, slight variations in form began to appear almost immediately. For example, the Indianapolis Foundation, established in 1916, pioneered the multiple trusteeship concept, with several banks receiving and administering funds on its behalf. Likewise, the corporate form (as distinct from the trust form) had emerged by 1920, according to Council on Foundations documents, and gained tremendously in popularity after the Great Depression made banks less likely sponsors of community trusts. Today the vast majority of community foundations are incorporated or, in the case of those in trust form, have corporate affiliates that may receive nontrust gifts and engage in other legal transactions not available to pure trusts.

Federal tax policy shaped the next major formal innovations in the field. The 1969 Tax Reform Act made it less attractive, from a tax standpoint, for individuals or families to establish and operate private foundations, but made it possible for such funds to become supporting organizations or component funds of community foundations or other public charities so long as they were controlled by the governing body of the parent public charity. The Act stimulated the creation of supporting organizations within community foundations and donor-advised funds.

The 1969 Act and its implementing regulations also augmented the preexisting public-support test for public charities, further distinguishing community foundations from private foundations. Most community foundations qualify as public charities, thereby allowing their donors maximum tax deductions, and they prize that status as a symbol of their public nature. As such, these community foundations, like United Ways and Jewish community federations, must derive one-third of their new funds over a given four-year period from government sources and/or a representative number of donors, or they must meet a "facts and circumstances" test that sets a 10 percent minimum on such donor and imposes additional minimum requirements as to the board's composition and authority, public accountability, and mechanisms for attracting new funds.

Community foundations organized in trust form must also meet the so-called entity test embodied in additional Treasury regulations adopted in 1976-1977 concerning treatment of component funds. It will be a surprise to many in the field that a community foundation organized solely in corporate form—that is, one that is not an aggregation of trust funds—and that satisfies the public-support test need not comply with this set of regulations in order to be tax-exempt. Nonetheless, these regulations are useful in that they contain general language meant to define community foundations. In brief, these regulations lay out four structural elements necessary to qualify a community foundation in trust form as a single entity for tax purposes: (1) a name conveying the concept of a capital or endowment fund to support charitable activities in the community or area served; (2) a common governing instrument to which all funds of the foundation are subject; (3) a common governing body with certain specified powers; and (4) periodic common financial reports.

Even where the laws and regulations are relatively prescriptive, I believe that they represent only minimum standards and that we should aspire to more.

On the basis of my experience, reading, and discussions with colleagues, I offer eight hallmarks that, taken in combination, add up to the beginnings of a definition: service to a geographic area of natural cohesion, permanence, flexibility, commitment to diversity (reflected, among other ways, in limited terms of service for board members), public accountability, independence, multiple donors, and breadth of programmatic activities.

Let us examine some of the more difficult issues that will inevitably arise in the quest for common standards.

Geography

Customarily set up to serve cities, community foundations have grown along with metropolitan areas and, in some cases, now serve portions of two or more states. Some, such as the Arkansas and New Hampshire community foundations, serve entire states that are low in wealth, sparsely populated, or geographically compact. But this adaptability is beginning to pose some problems. How should we mediate the conflicts that are certain to arise from overlapping, particularly in the area of asset development? What are acceptable criteria for a foundation's geographic reach? And under what conditions should the Council on Foundations encourage mergers or the formation of new community foundations?

Changing notions of "community," too, are posing challenges, as Paul Ylvisaker details in Chapter 2. For example, if a community foundation's purpose is to benefit people in its area, does that suggest involvement in global issues with local impact, such as arms control or the environment?

Donor Relations

Services to donors have expanded and now may include holding endowment for nonprofit organizations such as museums and the United Way; managing corporate giving programs; receiving the assets of private foundations; acting as fiscal agent for projects involving community-wide collaborations; and providing vehicles for living donors who wish to retain some involvement in disbursement decisions.

Community foundations of all sizes are seeking more living donors, and some younger community foundations have little or no permanent endowment. Since permanence and flexibility are usually considered hallmarks of community foundations, should standards for community foundations encourage the creation of permanent endowment, or even set percentage goals?

A second area of concerns is donor control over donor-advised funds. The 1977 Treasury regulations require that the community foundation's governing body, and not the donor, have final authority over disbursements. In practice, governing boards rarely override donor recommendations. But it seems prudent to develop standards for staff and governing body review of donor-recommended grants to ensure that they are consistent with the foundation's own mission.

Scope of Program Activities

This is the area in which community foundations probably are most readily distinguished from the United Way, Jewish community federations, and other public charities.

First, community foundations are dedicated to the broadest possible charitable purposes within their service areas. Also, community foundations have often created new organizations to meet emerging needs. United Way, Jewish Federations, Catholic Charities, and like organizations, in contrast, were formed as federations and continue to distribute funds to member service agencies.

Second, in disbursing discretionary funds not subject to donor recommendation, community foundations generally eschew operating support in favor of project grants that seek to address the underlying causes of community problems or to support research. and demonstration projects.

Third, their public nature demands that community foundations be prepared to play multiple roles in their communities—as neutral convenors around important local issues, as catalysts to influence public policy or private investment, as partners with other funders, as coalition builders seeking to mobilize community resources around critical issues.

Public or Private

The Council on Foundations estimates that some 80 percent of all private foundations concentrate their grantmaking within a defined geographic area. If there is validity to the growing concern about the public-support test, we may begin to see some established community foundations lose their public charity status. Some think the effect of this would be disastrous, particularly for younger foundations seeking to earn their place in the community, but others believe it would amount to no more than a relatively small expense in the form of the 2 percent excise tax on investment income. Whichever is the case, I can see no reason to exclude these foundations from the accredited ranks of community foundations.

A FIRST STEP TOWARD STANDARDS

It seems clear that if our profession does not act to reach some common standards, someone else will.

I propose that a process be inaugurated within the next two years, under the auspices of the Council on Foundations, to reach some consensus around standards for community foundations. Community foundations of all ages, sizes, legal forms, geographic regions, and programmatic emphases should be represented in this process. A small but representative working group should report periodically to a larger and even more diverse advisory committee, with reports to the entire membership at predetermined intervals.

Professionals and volunteers in our field have much experience and wisdom to bring to this process. Although there is no single source of ideas and information, it might be useful to begin with what might be called the "body of literature" in the field: applicable federal and state laws and regulations and legal memoranda interpreting them; Council on Foundations guidelines for all members; the Council's "Common Characteristics of Community Foundations," the revealing work of the Community Foundation Fiscal and Administrative Officers' group on accounting standards; common practices developed by affinity groups in grantmaking fields; and the governing documents, mission statements, and operating philosophies of a variety of community foundations.

This project should produce a detailed framework from which the following may be developed:

- A set of model policies and practices—covering governance, geographic focus, asset development/donor relations, and program practices.

- A procedure for site visits and formative evaluations by accrediting teams.

- A process for resolving territorial disputes.

- Criteria for Council on Foundations technical assistance to community foundations and standardized function descriptions to inform the Council's staff training for member foundations.

- An acceptable definition of a community foundation that could form the basis of a new and more detailed "facts and circumstances" test should an attempt be made to exempt community foundations from or otherwise modify the fundraising requirement of the public support test.

- The development of a network of accredited community foundations that could have reciprocal relations in grantmaking and donor relations.

To say the least, this effort will not be without controversy, but I hope my colleagues will consider it worth the struggle to establish standards with some meaning. At the age of 75, the community foundation movement still has to explain every day what it is all about. By developing, enforcing, and publicizing standards, we can enable our public to "know it when they see it."

10

Are They Worthy of the Name? A Critic's View

Robert O. Bothwell

Community foundations need more public scrutiny. They are favored by the tax laws, and are little monitored by federal and state authorities. Yet they have enormous and rapidly growing wealth, with increasing power to do good or evil. What standards must community foundations meet? Which ones should apply? This essay addresses these questions in four sections: public accountability, accessibility, responsiveness, and fundraising.

Community foundations are a breed apart from other foundations. While often looking like private foundations, sounding like them, and acting like them, community foundations do not have to live under the important restrictions that the Tax Reform Act of 1969 imposed on private foundations. Yet, while they have the favorable "publicly supported" status of public charities, giving them significant tax and operational advantages over private foundations, community foundations are also creatures part from public charities.

Community foundations control $4.7 billion in assets. They made $360 million in grants in 1987. In some localities they are giants. And in other places they are big players in the nonprofit world. Often they act as the "Good Housekeeping Seal of Approval" for local charities, giving credibility and access to money to some nonprofits, denying it to others.

But who monitors these special creatures? When reading between the lines of the I.R.S.'s testimony before Congress in 1983, the first serious hearings on foundations since 1969, it is clear the I.R.S. has put little effort into monitoring *any* foundations. State government monitoring of community foundations is invisible, except in isolated cases.

So how the quality of our lives is affected by community foundations essentially is of no concern to government. It remains for citizen activists and foundation activists who want to improve their communities to assess how well their community foundations are doing and to determine what steps can be taken to rechannel inadequate community foundation activities.

PUBLIC ACCOUNTABILITY

Foremost is the formal interaction between community foundations and the public. This involves required reporting to the I.R.S., periodic printed reports to the public, public meetings, and governing board issues.

Required Public Reporting

All community foundations are required by law to file annual tax returns with the I.R.S. (forms 990 for community foundations and other public charities). While containing essential financial data and important information on the officers, governing board and top staff, form 990 requires little information on grants made to organizations (e.g., the recipient's name and address and the amount of grant are all that are required), and no information on grant purposes, limitations on grantmaking, grant application procedures or submission deadlines, all of which are required in the I.R.S. tax return private foundations must file (form 990-PF).

Nor does the 990 require information on a community foundation's statement of program and funding interests, indications of amounts available the next year for each program area, policies on length of funding, proposal evaluation procedures, key governing board policies (such as conflict of interest policy), investment policy, report on percentage rate of return on investments, nor an independent audit report. While none of this is required of private foundations either, this information is critical to grantseekers and an informed public.

Voluntary Public Reporting

Thus, it is clear that a community foundation worthy of the name should voluntarily publish information that goes beyond form 990 if it is going to communicate effectively to grantseekers and the public.

Why is this necessary? I remember a former Council on Foundations chairman asking this question. He said that when he was president of a college everyone knew who had money available for grants, that no foundation reports were necessary to communicate this crucial information. He was right—the old-boy network worked fine, for old boys. But the many additional segments of the public that community foundations should reach aren't necessarily tied into old-boy networks. They need to learn of grant opportunities in other ways.

A 1980 study by the National Committee for Responsive Philanthropy, *Foundations and Public Information: Sunshine or Shadow?*, carefully evaluated the annual reports and other information routinely provided to the public by 208 of the country's largest foundations, including the 30 largest community foundations. No community foundations scored "excellent," and only 60 percent published "adequate" information on program priorities, grant application and evaluation procedures, grants made, financial and governance information. However, only 10 percent failed to publish anything at all. Has the public reporting of community foundations improved since 1980? Probably, but certainly a new look is needed.

Even very good foundation annual reports tend to focus on the past rather than the future. Grantseekers want to know a foundation's plans, commitments, even intentions. They want to know about changes in grant program priorities, shifts in how much might be committed to each program area, and expectations about payout changes. Such future-oriented reports would help community foundations as well. Prospective donors to community foundations might also want a glimpse into the future if they are being asked to endow that future.

Public Meetings

Public accountability also means public meetings, advertised widely beforehand, to discuss community foundations' grant program priorities, where the foundations explain future directions, and the public has an unfettered opportunity to raise questions or offer facts or opinions about those directions. How many community foundations have held such public meetings? On a regular basis? Very few.

Do community foundations simply want to keep their decisionmakers cloistered, keep their decision-making private, focus just on the few segments of the public represented around the solid mahogany board room tables? Community foundations worthy of the name should deliberate carefully before choosing to avoid the sunshine.

Representative Governing Body

A fourth aspect of public accountability involves the governing body. I.R.S. regulations say that community foundations will have but one "governing body or distribution committee" with power over distributions, whether the foundation be in a trust or corporate form. The regulations call for a "representative governing body" that "represents the broad interests of the public *rather than the personal or private interests of a limited number of donors*" (emphasis added). Public officials, their appointees, subject experts, and "community leaders" are to comprise such a governing body, the community leaders being "clergymen, educators, civic leaders, or other such persons representing *a broad cross section of the views and interests of the community*" (emphasis added).

In this day and age this group must include the various racial/ethnic minorities and women. According to the most recent Council on Foundations research (*1988 Foundation Management Report*), only 8 percent of community foundation board members are minorities, and 29 percent are women. These percentages, very similar to those for independent, private foundations, have been increasing slightly over the years. Nevertheless, community foundations worthy of the name should have substantially better representation of minorities and women.

Others also should be included to ensure a "broad cross-section of the views and interests of the community." What about the disabled, an important part of every community often ignored, who continue to have difficulty leading normal lives because of access barriers? How about people under 40, or under 30, in order to assure the new generations' input? What about representation of gay and lesbian activists? The politics of sexual orientation may not be everybody's cup of tea, but these activists speak for substantial segments of our local populations.

In developing a diverse governing body it is important to keep in mind that one minority person or one woman is not enough. One person alone is rarely a successful spokesperson for a group's interests. Intimidation, even if unintentional, is likely, no matter how talented or experienced the individual.

The composition of many governing boards is dictated by a community foundation's trust or corporate documents. Appointments are made by predetermined public officials and private organizations (e.g., the local Chamber of Commerce or a major private university). Yet such appointments do not necessarily lead to boards representing "the broad interests of the public," as the I.R.S. regulations require. All too often these appointments go to a community's elite. Union leaders, respected teachers, successful public interest activists, and effective grassroots leaders, for example, are rarely appointed.

Community foundation chairs and staff can do much to increase board diversity by nominating diverse people for mayors, judges, and the like to consider when making their appointments. But changing the appointing orders is also possible, even if difficult. And existing boards often have (or can be given) the power to elect additional board members.

ACCESSIBILITY BY ALL GRANTSEEKERS

Proposals On Hand

Sometimes I imagine myself at a community foundation desk with a stack of proposals. Since there are so many more than can be funded, each must be reviewed conscientiously. But before starting the reviews, I sort the proposals into seven piles:

1. Proposals my boss has said are top priority.

2. Submissions by people I know personally or professionally.

3. Current community foundation grantee proposals.

4. Prior community foundation grantee proposals.

5. Submissions by people vouched for by people I know personally or professionally.

6. Proposals from people or organizations with good public reputations that don't fit any category above.

7. All other proposals—i.e., the unknown!

Now, being human, I expect I'd just go through the proposals in the above order, leaving the "unknown" pile to last. In fact, considering proposal volume these days, I wonder if the dust would ever be disturbed on pile 7. Isn't this reality? Just a bit?

Unless a foundation has a firm and explicit commitment either to giving all proposals equal treatment or to giving proposals from "unknowns" special treatment, why wouldn't a program officer leave pile 7 until last? Yet as foundations with public charity status, it is especially important for community foundations to demonstrate greater accessibility than private foundations to all grantseekers, not just those who are established or well connected.

One East Coast community foundation head says he finds greater innovation in pile 7, and, when taking adequate time to evaluate unknowns' proposals, frequently discovers excellent organizational capacities. Domestic violence shelters were often started by young, new organizations, not by the long-established YWCAs. Discovery and action on new environmental hazards usually is the work of grass-roots citizen groups before the larger, established, national environmental organizations take them on.

Proposal Solicitation

Of course, the foregoing is but one aspect of accessibility. Another aspect is whether or not any proposals are coming in from organizations that are not now or never were grantees. Every community foundation should have a basic classification system to tell the origins of incoming proposals:

A. Current grantee

B. Prior grantee

C. Never a grantee

The third category should be further subdivided:

C1. Affluent zip codes

C2. Non-affluent zip codes

Or, subjectively:

C1. Mainline organizations

C2. Non-mainline organizations

The point of using these categories, or more sophisticated ones, is to be able to determine if a community foundation needs to beef up its outreach to various segments of the public. If few or no proposals are coming in from category C, particularly C2, then the community foundation should take steps to discover why.

A recent National Puerto Rican Coalition study found that half of the Puerto Rican organizations in nine U.S. cities where Puerto Ricans are concentrated received no community foundation funding in 1987. Had they ever received funds? Had they ever submitted proposals? Were any of the nine community foundations aware of these organizations' existence as additional resources in the generally poverty stricken Puerto Rican communities?

Discovering why proposals are not coming in from some sections of the public is not difficult. A community foundation should seek out some of the "never a grantee" organizations and conduct focus groups to discuss why. One important benefit of this process might be an awakening of a community foundation to the existence of organizations and leaders who are additional community resources. In fact the whole process could be systematized, and called "Talent Scouts." Professional sports have used talent scouts for years. Their focus groups are called "tryout camps."

When Jim Joseph, president of the Council on Foundations, headed the Cummins Engine Foundation in the early 1970s, talent scouting is precisely what he and his colleagues did. They scoured America's cities and backwoods for black leaders upon whom they loaded leadership development grants.

Hiring staff with five to ten or more years of nonprofit experience in poor neighborhoods is another way for community foundations to be more sensitive in seeking out new grantees among the disenfranchised.

Face-to-Face Meetings

Most important in having a truly accessible community foundation are face-to-face meetings between grantseekers and community foundation staff and trustees. As the old saw goes, foundations fund people. No face-to-face meeting, no grant. The National Committee for Responsive Philanthropy has been soliciting funds for 13 years now. I can count on one hand the number of grants larger than $1000 that NCRP has received with no meeting. Grantseekers must be sized up before they can become potential grantees.

Several years ago, seeking a reality check, I asked a friendly major foundation program officer how many brand new people, previously unknown, he had met with in recent months. He reported that at least 25 percent of his meetings were with new people. I was shocked. If the foundation world were really so open and accessible, why was the NCRP even in business? The next week, however, he called to change his report. He had carefully checked his calendar and discovered that fewer than 10 percent of his meetings were with new people.

Since meeting with people one knows is often routine, and meeting with new people special, it's easy for our perceptions to be distorted. Community foundations should institute regular procedures to guard against perpetuation of the old-boy network, or if that is already less influential, to guard against establishment of a replacement yuppie network. Standard operating procedures could be set for foundation staff periodically to review their calendars against the seven categories of grantseekers, or at least categories A, B, and C.

A community foundation might even set a goal that everyone who wants one will have a hearing on his or her proposed ideas, at least once a year. Clear goals have a way of getting an organization in motion.

RESPONSIVENESS

A community foundation's responsiveness may be viewed in several ways. Is the foundation responsive to its donors' gifts, bequests, legacies, etc.? Is it responsive to its governing body's policies? Is it responsive to I.R.S. regulations, for being one entity, publicly supported, etc.?

But basically the definition of "responsiveness" of concern here involves grantmaking. Is a community foundation's grantmaking responsive to all segments of the community? The I.R.S. doesn't require this, but the concept of a community foundation should demand that it be responsive to the diversity in its city, metropolitan area, state, or region.

The Inversion Commitment

Is it enough for a community foundation to be at least as responsive to the poor, the disadvantaged, and the disenfranchised, as to all other community sectors? No.

It is important to the peacefulness and civility of a society not to be torn apart by festering differences, but constantly to seek to eliminate, reduce or bridge those differences. Community foundations might want to embrace this proposition as their primary mission. Thus they could consider, since 50 percent of our national income goes to only 25 percent of the people, that they commit at least 50 percent of their grants to benefit that 25 percent of our population with the lowest income. Call it the Inversion Commitment.

Income, of course, is only one measure of our differences in society. Religious and cultural differences also set us more apart at times than income differences. But income translates into life's important basics: food and shelter, education and opportunity.

Otherwise Disadvantaged and Disenfranchised

There are, of course, many others deserving attention outside the 25 percent low-income segment. Community foundations should devote disproportionate shares of their remaining grant resources to benefit the nonpoor disadvantaged and disenfranchised. They include racial/ethnic minorities, women, the disabled, and others who the courts have determined have experienced systematic discrimination. Also, citizens seeking redress or prevention of public or private institutional wrongs, if their financial resources are dwarfed by their adversaries' spending (e.g., citizens fighting a toxic waste dump placement, or opposing bank redlining policies), should be targeted for assistance.

Providing grants for the poor, disadvantaged, and disenfranchised involves tough decisions. It might mean not supporting a new theater, a private university, or advanced medical equipment for a hospital. More community foundations than now do may have to undertake research and conduct community discussions about their localities' most pressing needs in order to make these tough decisions.

Implementing responsiveness on this order also will take different operational approaches than grantmaking to mainline arts, cultural, educational, and medical institutions. Dealing with elite representatives of the symphony and university is different from dealing with representatives of the poor, disadvantaged, and disenfranchised. The first impulse is to get the latter to understand and conform to doing business the way the community foundation always has done business. But generally that will not work, and the result will be frustration and even anger on both sides. The better approach is for the community foundation to set up new operational procedures to implement the Inversion Commitment.

WHAT ABOUT FUNDRAISING?

What good is a publicly accountable, thoroughly accessible, progressively responsive community foundation if it has little money to give away? Growth must also be an important community foundation goal.

But note that this subject is approached as the cart following the horse. It is more important, first, to develop a clear mission and effective ways to implement the mission, then to plan fundraising. Fundraising, thus, is more purposeful, and can be more effective.

The 10% Public Support Test

Community foundations, in order not to become private foundations, must raise at least 10 percent of their total support from the public (and must also meet other "facts and circumstances" tests about their public character). This test propels community foundations to raise money and grow. It forces interaction with more of the public.

The downside of the public support test, however, is that community foundations generally seek their 10 percent public support from their communities' most affluent citizens. This skews the dialogue about what the community foundation should be doing. The opera, symphony, theater, prestigious private university, affluent neighborhood hospi-tal—any or all could become foci of the fundraising instead of those who need help the most. But community foundations can minimize the skew by being forthright about having an Inversion Commitment—a primary mission to assist the poor, the disadvantaged, and disenfranchised.

Types of Funds

Various types of funds can be raised: unrestricted/discretionary, field of interest, designated to specific organizations, and donor-advised funds.

One view of fundraising for community foundations holds that it is first necessary to get donors "into the tent" in whatever way possible, even if that is through advised funds. Get donors acquainted with the community foundation, its mission, its staff, its way of doing business; then, after they have developed confidence in the institution, get them to write unrestricted gifts to the foundation into their wills.

Other veteran community foundation leaders say that too many community foundations have "lost control" pursuing such a policy. Their focus is on growth, and more growth leads to much decision-making by donor advisers and less by governing boards. Grantmaking strategy becomes the inevitable casualty.

Some community foundations have become donors' lackeys, doing whatever they desire. Donor-advised funds become the rule in their fundraising; unrestricted monies are minimal. Other community foundations have sought to raise funds with their mission uppermost. Unrestricted, discretionary funds become the target, designated and donor-advised funds discouraged unless fitting the mission. While they may raise less this way, these community foundations may, nevertheless, raise more monies to implement their primary mission.

CONCLUSION

Community foundations are a breed apart from other foundations. They are favored by tax laws, and they have to meet less stringent rules than private foundations. They have great and growing wealth with expanding capacity to do good or evil. They clearly need much greater public scrutiny than federal and state authorities have provided.

Citizen activists and community foundation activists may choose to accept the standards for public accountability, accessibility, responsiveness, and fundraising suggested here or devise other standards. But if community foundations are to be worthy of the name, by serving *well* the poor, the disadvantaged, and the disenfranchised of their localities, as well as their donors and their upper-class concerns, then the activists have to activate.

Part II: Cases

11

California: The Fund for New Americans

Kathy Seal

The attitude toward Mexican immigrants in Southern California has long been schizophrenic. When faced with labor shortages, the community welcomed immigrants with open arms. Later, economic hardship ushered in waves of racism and cries to deport the people called "wetbacks" (because so many crossed the border by swimming the Rio Grande).

Mexicans helped build American railroads and pick crops in the burgeoning Imperial and San Joaquin valleys. They were particularly welcome while American men were off fighting World War I. But with the Great Depression and the influx of Dust Bowl Americans to California, federal immigration officials launched a massive "repatriation" campaign, eventually deporting about 500,000 people—more than half of them U.S. citizens of Mexican origin.

World War II labor shortages spawned the Bracero Program, which allowed Mexican farmworkers to enter the United States legally as temporary "guest workers." At the height of a second deportation campaign, "Operation Wetback," in 1954, federal officials expelled more than 1 million people of Mexican origin.

In recent decades, the U.S. government has refrained from nationwide deportation campaigns. But factory raids and border patrol beef-ups are frequent, and in 1976 Congress cut immigration quotas and slashed legal Mexican immigration from 40,000 to 20,000 per year.

Limiting the flow of legal immigration from Mexico, however, flies in the face of the need for labor to fuel the region's booming economy. In the last 15 years, Southern California's gross regional product has almost doubled, to $355 billion.

Pushed by poor economic and political conditions in their own countries and pulled by the burgeoning opportunities in California, about 235,000 undocumented aliens enter the United States every year. Demographers using 1980 U.S. census data estimate that there were 2.1 million undocumented persons in the United States in 1980, 55 percent of whom emigrated from Mexico.

In the early 1980s, several factors converged to produce a new chorus of cries to stop illegal immigration. U.S. unemployment climbed to nearly 10 percent. Political and economic instability in their countries sent Mariel Cubans, and Haitian, Salvadoran, and Guatemalan refugees to U.S. shores. When added to an influx of Mexicans impoverished by successive peso devaluations and hundreds of thousands of Indochinese resettled in the United States at the end of the Vietnam War, "American consciousness of immigration peaked," explains Linda Wong, an attorney and longtime immigration activist who then was an official of the Mexican American Legal Defense and Education Fund (MALDEF). That the latest immigrants were all people of color sparked racial fears.

In such an atmosphere Congress passed the Immigration Reform and Control Act (IRCA) in 1986. Designed primarily to close U.S. borders to illegal immigration, IRCA allotted $841 million over two years to increase the U.S. Border Patrol and other Immigration and Naturalization Service (INS) enforcement. Also for the first time it imposed sanctions, including fines, on employers who knowingly hire undocumented workers. But to make the bill palatable to liberals, its conservative sponsors included a provision for "amnesty"—granting of legal resident status for immigrants who had resided continuously in the United States since 1982. (This amnesty section passed the House by only seven votes.) There were also special amnesty provisions for seasonal agricultural workers. Since most Asian immigrants had entered legally and those from Central America came largely after 1982, in southern California the amnesty provision chiefly affected Mexican immigrants.

THE "TYPEWRITER FOUNDATION"

The California Community Foundation (CCF) had been tracking the progress of IRCA. Founded in 1915 by Joseph Sartori, a Los Angeles banker and friend of Cleveland Foundation founder Frederick Goff, CCF was the second community foundation in the nation. For many years the foundation made small grants for capital projects and equipment purchases, soon acquiring the nickname—at least among local nonprofits—of "the typewriter foundation."

That changed radically in 1980 when Sidney Brody, then chairman of the CCF board of governors, read an article by Jack Shakely, at that time Director of Communications for the Council on Foundations. Shakely's article criticized CCF for making unimaginative grants, aimed only at well-established organizations. Because of this policy, argued Shakely, CCF had managed in 65 years to build assets of only $17 million. Community foundations like San Francisco's, on the other hand, had blossomed by nurturing innovative projects, often with seed money, and by basing its grants on investigations of community needs, not just an organization's credentials. Brody invited Shakely to Los Angeles, introduced him to the five CCF board members, and then brought him on as executive director. Shakely now had the opportunity to "put his money where his mouth was."

A former Peace Corps volunteer in Costa Rica, Shakely spoke Spanish and in 1979 had helped generate a Council on Foundations position on giving to Hispanics. At CCF he hosted a series of meetings between private foundations and corporate funders and members of the Los Angeles Hispanic community. In 1984 CCF helped set up a fund to assist predominantly Hispanic artists. The foundation also helped start a medical clinic for Central American refugees and a fund that gives grants to community and free medical clinics in Hispanic neighborhoods.

As Congress considered the new immigration law, Shakely and other CCF staff were aware of studies projecting that 60 percent of California's population in 2010 will be ethnic minorities, two-thirds of them of Hispanic origin. They knew that the illegal immigration status of millions of these Hispanics already in the United States prevented them from receiving adequate health care, for example. Thus when IRCA passed, Shakely knew that the foundation faced an opportunity that "was extremely important and that [probably] wouldn't happen again."

"We felt it was an area in which we could have an enormous impact, fitting our mission of helping Los Angeles grow and change," explains Jennifer Leonard, then a CCF vice-president.

With the approval of the CCF 15-member board of governors, staff convened briefings with local immigration advocates, social service providers, school districts, and INS staff. Many participants in these meetings were opposed to and dismayed by IRCA. They felt it ignored the Central American civil wars and other political factors propelling people over the borders, and that the employer sanctions would aggravate discrimination against people who look or speak like illegal immigrants. ("Which in fact has happened," points out Wong.)

Nonetheless, the CCF staff decided to "support the best spirit of the act rather than its less popular provisions," remembers Leonard. Briefing participants clarified the needs created by the law—one of which was acquiring the money to pay filing and processing fees.

Then, says Leonard, "one morning Jack woke up and read an *L.A. Times* story highlighting that amnesty applicants were facing fees of up to $420 for a family." Unlike private foundations, community foundations can readily give or loan money to individuals; Shakely felt that CCF could make a unique contribution by helping individuals meet these costs. With IRCA frequently in the news, such a program could reap the side benefit of positive publicity for the foundation.

Others, including *La Opinion,* the major Spanish-language daily in Los Angeles, and the local Coalition for Humane Immigration Rights had already announced education efforts. Shakely decided that CCF should initiate a revolving loan fund to help families apply for amnesty. "We didn't have much money, so I was looking for a way to leverage it," he explains. If a conventional lender would administer the loans, he thought, the new immigrants could leapfrog into the American mainstream and emerge from amnesty with a credit record. Finally, the idea was a perfect candidate for a program-related investment (PRI): lending money, below market rates if necessary, from a foundation's assets to a charitable cause—a concept to which his board had been previously unreceptive. (Although a PRI yields less than a commercial investment, it permits a foundation to recycle its funds instead of spending them in an outright grant.)

Shakely and Leonard began meeting with banks and foundations to bring them on board. They approached the Ford Foundation, which had already decided to put $2 million toward IRCA-related projects. But the Ford Foundation said it preferred a traditional route—helping agencies form coalitions for immigration advocacy and educate the public about IRCA—and doubted that "we would ever find a traditional lender to play ball with us," recalls Leonard.

But the Ford Foundation didn't realize that Security Pacific Bank had founded CCF and administered the foundation until 1981. Furthermore, the bank's president, Bob Smith, had hired Shakely in 1980, and the two had become friends. "After I proposed the loan fund to him [in April 1987]," says Shakely, "he called me back on his car phone in half an hour and said, 'Let's do it.'" That Security Pacific already had a "soft loan" program for displaced homemakers helped pave the way.

The proposal was that CCF would deposit funds with Security Pacific, which in turn would train nonprofit agencies to fill out credit requests along with amnesty applications.

Shakely discussed his idea with a number of the board members individually. Then, armed with promised cooperation from the bank, Shakely presented the proposal for a "Fund for New Americans" to the CCF Board May 4, 1987. The meeting was somewhat chaotic, since a film crew was taping it for a documentary for The Foundation Center. But the discussion went smoothly. The board discussed at length some agencies' views that the money should be given to the immigrants, not loaned. Shakely argued strongly that loans would carry more dignity. "Loans would say, 'We believe in you, and welcome you to America, but there is no free lunch,' " he argued.

THE BOARD WEIGHS RISKS

Shakely described the program in detail without using the word "PRI." He stressed the need to move quickly. Board members were nervous about the size of their commitment: Shakely was asking for $500,000, and the largest previous CCF grant had been $150,000. Some board members questioned whether the loans would be repaid, but members Ignation Lozano and Bruce Corwin parried that Mexican immigrants had one of the lowest default rates in the country; there were snide comparisons to Beverly Hills borrowers being a higher-risk group. Finally Shakely pointed out that applicants would be highly motivated to repay the loan, at least during the six months of waiting to hear about their applications, because a bad credit report could lead the INS to reject their amnesty application. At that time, about 20 percent of amnesty applicants were expected to be rejected.

The board voted unanimously to put $500,000 into the loan fund. It would be up to staff to raise the remainder; at that time Shakely thought the fund should have $4 million for the 300,000 people (60,000 families) he estimated could qualify for amnesty in Southern California.

CCF staff then went into a "blitzkrieg fundraising mode," with Shakely and Leonard contacting local private foundations they thought could act quickly: the one-year period for amnesty applications began May 5. Shakely suspected that the Conrad N. Hilton Foundation, which had close ties to Catholic Charities, a major agency assisting amnesty applicants, would be interested; in two weeks, the Hilton and James Irvine Foundations handed over $500,000. The Irvine Foundation asked that its portion be recycled into CCF grants when the loans were repaid. The Ralph Parsons Foundation, intrigued with the idea of a PRI, gave $250,000.

But raising funds was merely the first hurdle; larger challenges lay ahead. Staff were faced with structuring a loan program for immigrants who for years had been living "underground" for self-protection, staying away from mainstream institutions. "Little by little we worked out these funny problems of applying bank processes to a group that had avoided becoming known to credit agencies," says Leonard. Security Pacific agreed to accept applicants without Social Security numbers or credit histories, to process the loans at cost and accept a loss—estimated at about $200,000. Loan forms were translated into Spanish. The Fund for New Americans would offer a family loan package of $425 to cover INS and processing fees for one adult and one child. Requiring families to pay for one spouse on their own would make them appreciate the value of the loan more, Shakely felt. At 10 percent interest, the loans would be repayable in 24 monthly installments of about $20.

Six nonprofit agencies agreed initially to handle loan forms along with amnesty applications. Responding to the agencies' needs for staffing and equipment, CCF allotted them $75,000 in enabling grants. During June, Security Pacific and CCF trained nonprofit staff in loan processing, and on Friday, July 3, a well-attended press conference presented the Fund for New Americans to the public. The following Monday, a deluge of phone calls swept over the six nonprofit agencies.

But something was not right. By August 1, immigrants had submitted only 40 loan applications, and only six loans had been granted. By September, the program had expanded to nine agencies with 121 sites, but only 64 loans had gone through. The Fund for New Americans was nowhere near approaching its goal of making 3,000–6,000 loans.

Clifford Lum, CCF's operations manager, was appointed project manager, charged with ferreting out the fund's problems and setting it on the right track. He began with marketing, for which the nonprofit agencies had no budget. He brought in Spanish-speaking loan counselors to talk on Hispanic radio stations, contacted newspapers (many of which ran free ads), and sent out information packages to executive directors of United Way agencies.

Out in the field, Lum discovered numerous cultural and administrative problems. Mexican immigrants customarily borrowed money from their own families; for some, applying for a loan was shameful. Some nonprofit staffers felt uncomfortable asking for financial data. Many of these staff people, hired temporarily for the amnesty program, were college students or homemakers who themselves had never taken out a loan or bought on credit. "Usually only about a quarter of them had credit cards," recalls Lum.

In addition, many immigrants who did apply were not qualifying for the package. Screening criteria were too stringent; many were making too much or too little money to qualify. Seasonal or day laborers couldn't prove current employment. Security Pacific was also turning down applicants whose debts took 70 percent of their income; to scrap that rule, Shakely wrote a letter to the bank absolving them of their fiduciary responsibility. Finally, a large number of the applicants were single adults who didn't fit the one child/one adult package.

Lum and Sue Trujillo, a Spanish-speaking operations manager in Security Pacific's loan-processing center, set about training and retraining the agency workers processing the loans. Staff from 26 new agencies were trained and those from five of the initial six Los Angeles-based agencies were retrained. Lum talked to both program heads and those helping immigrants fill out their applications. He now wonders whether his own Chinese-American background (Lum does not speak Spanish) hindered him, linguistically and culturally, from getting across to the largely Hispanic agency personnel. But he persistently visited every agency, explaining and reexplaining the loan process.

"The ones who grasped the idea of how loans operate ... were able to sell the loan program very well," says Lum.

Lum's investigation also led him to recommend easing the loan requirement and creating new loan packages.

It took a little arm-twisting at Security Pacific, but by November 3 all income criteria were dropped and the Fund for New Americans began offering two new loan packages, one for single adults and the other for two adults. Later the number of packages would expand to eight.

After these adjustments in November, the program began to take off. The number of loans approved began doubling each month. In January, however the *Los Angeles Times* ran an article on the fund which began, "'Jack Shakely has a million dollars he is trying to give away, but he can't find many takers." Lum, who'd been with CCF a year and was in the thick of battle in the trenches, was momentarily devastated. Shakely felt the article was fair, and that the publicity would help. Sure enough, although staff had to weather some worried phone calls from board members, the article brought more applicants into Catholic Charities, which was mentioned in the article, and several new agencies signed up for the program. Other nonprofits that had signed up became more active.

Then in the last two months of the program—April and May— loans zoomed to 412 and 619, respectively. In the last 30 days of the year-long amnesty program, applicants swamped the INS and the loan fund. Since Security Pacific took two weeks to process loans, CCF set up shop in its own offices. The foundation assigned two Spanish-speaking employees and hired a temporary worker to help fill out applications, and sent checks daily by messenger to agencies handling amnesty processing. "It was absolutely crazy," remembers Lum. "We were here till 10 p.m. . . . we didn't have manpower." CCF processed more than 500 loans in the last five days of the program. Had the program lasted another six weeks, estimates Lum, the Fund for New Americans could have made another 800 loans. As it was, the fund issued 1,606 loans, totaling $538,400.

LESSONS FROM A NEW VENTURE

Since loans and operating expenses totalled $573,000, the fund had $600,000 left over, of which it paid back $350,000 to the Hilton Foundation immediately. The remainder, along with CCF and Irvine Foundation monies received from the loan repayments, went for a new phase of the program. Phase II grants funded English-as-a-Second-Language and citizenship training classes, also needed by amnesty applicants.

Was the Fund for New Americans a success? "It was a real good idea," says Lavinia Limon, whose International Institute processed 143 loans at eight sites. "Most of the applicants were working poor, and for them to pull together that money would have been impossible. . . . We know some of those people wouldn't have applied [for amnesty] without that financial help."

The final number of loans made was good, concludes Leonard, "but nothing like the thousands we'd hoped to make." One problem, admits Shakely, was failure to perceive a psychological nicety: not realizing how many people would wait until the last minute to sign up.

On the other hand, only about 1.7 million people sought amnesty in California, far fewer than the 3 or 4 million some had anticipated. Limon feels that more financial support to the nonprofits would have resulted in more loans. "At least one quarter of the people who called [us] didn't get adequate service," she says.

Wong credits CCF for soliciting feedback before launching the project, but criticizes the foundation for not asking the organizations' opinions on priorities. "The foundation came up with the idea of a loan fund on its own," she says. Rather than a loan fund, Wong would have preferred strengthening the service network for undocumented immigrants and increasing education on IRCA. "Many people didn't apply on a timely basis," she says. "They didn't understand the eligibility criteria." Also, many immigrants were not adequately informed after the INS changed some small but significant regulations in midcourse.

Some immigration activists in Los Angeles also criticized the Fund for New Americans for not addressing United States support for oppressive regimes in the region. The fund "was a politically safe way for CCF [and other foundations] to help in the amnesty effort," says one activist. "It distanced them from the real issues: they didn't have to give money to an organization fighting U.S. policy in Central America."

Interestingly, far fewer immigrants defaulted on the loans than the 20 percent Shakely had predicted. The default rate was only about 10 percent, partly because the INS approval rate was higher than anticipated. Shakely says his faith that new Americans would be trustworthy has been reinforced time and again. "People ride a bus 45 minutes to hand us a $20 installment on repayment. That's impressive," he says.

For CCF, the Fund for New Americans was a bold leap forward. Shakely is proud of the speed of CCF's response and the flexibility of its board, which allowed so many mid-course revisions, and its willingness to risk doing something no other foundation had done. It was the largest project in the foundation's history; previous grants had averaged $12,000; the largest had been $150,000. The Fund for New Americans paved the way for CCF to fund a Community AIDS Project to the tune of $500,000, matched by the Ford Foundation.

The fund also broke ground for future use of PRIs. The Los Angeles Emergency Loan Fund, a consortium of banks and foundations that Shakely chairs, offered "bridge loans" in 1989 to several youth services agencies awaiting reimbursement by federal government sources.

The largest collaborative project CCF had undertaken, the Fund for New Americans represented a major broadening of the philanthropic community into the immigration arena. "In the past, foundations were very reluctant to allocate any resources toward immigration because of the controversial nature of the issue," says Wong. "To have CCF become a new player in the immigration field was in and of itself a significant gain for immigrants and refugees in general."

12

Dayton: The Quality
of Schools

Mark Bernstein

In the spring of 1989, a vice-president from a Dayton bank sat at a dinner honoring area teachers who had each received a $500 grant to carry out some special classroom project.

The executive had only recently been designated the bank's envoy to education, so he was coming in cold. Education, he thought, was a six- or seven-figure problem, requiring solutions on the order of over-hauling the methods of school financing or restructuring the tax base.

"What can you accomplish with $500?" he asked the other non-educator at the table. He soon found out.

All were teachers of the learning disabled. One told of how she had used the grant to establish a bicycle repair shop, where her students gained self-esteem by repairing the bikes of their fellow students. A second teacher helped high school-age students gain employment skills by opening and operating a bookstore in the school cafeteria.

For the teachers, it was the chance to show that in public education—chronically short of discretionary dollars—small funds can achieve measurable ends.

For the bank vice president, it was a chance to scale down his assumptions about the needs of public education to a level at which his institution could usefully participate.

And for the other non-teacher at the table, Fred Bartenstein, director of the Dayton Foundation, it was the chance to play the foundation's customary role—intermediary between community groups.

Among its other activities, the Dayton Foundation serves as the administrative home of the Dayton–Montgomery County Public Education Fund. Since 1985, the fund has underwritten hundreds of grants to educators and provided a forum for presenting education-related concerns to the community. In serving education, the fund has also contributed to the rapid development of the Dayton Foundation itself.

DAYTON'S BEST-KEPT SECRET

In 1984, the Dayton Foundation was best known for its obscurity. As "Dayton's best-kept secret," it granted the limited earnings of its $4 million endowment to a variety of civic works. In so doing, the foundation was carrying on the interests—though hardly the style—of John H. Patterson, founder of the National Cash Register Company (NCR), who in 1921, with $250,000 in personal and family donations, led the effort to create the foundation.

Patterson helped secure for Dayton its tradition of innovation. It was in Dayton that the Wright Brothers, working essentially from scratch, devised the entire field of aerodynamics. It was in Dayton that Charles Kettering invented the self-starter, the single most important step to the popularization of the motorcar.

Dayton capitalized on such work to become a prospering manufacturing town. The city's tone was set by the thousands of relatively well-paid workers at its two premier employers—NCR and General Motors.

Manufacturing was the muscle, and the city atrophied as factory operatives gave way to computer technicians. First, in the 1960s, NCR shifted from mechanical to electronic equipment, moved production elsewhere, and closed out 20,000 local jobs. Second, with the 1970s, Dayton rode the insecure ups and downs of the auto industry, the dispiriting pattern of layoff, recall, and doubt.

Economic and psychological setbacks distracted attention from community concerns, most notably from the public schools. During the 1970s, the Dayton city schools had been mired in a seemingly irresolvable conflict over busing to achieve racial integration. Dayton is a heavily segregated city—the West Side is predominantly black, the East Side is heavily Appalachian—and the schools became the major point of racial contact, and conflicts, within the city. The issue saw a divided school board embroiled in lawsuits, a community leadership providing a hesitant and uncertain response, and apprehensive parents swelling the flight to the suburbs.

Busing overshadowed but did not eliminate other problems. City school enrollment was plunging—from 55,500 in 1970 to 30,100 in 1984. Teachers were demoralized—27 percent of city teachers, 21 percent county-wide, said they would not again choose teaching as a career. Parents were losing faith; in one survey, 57 percent of city school parents said they would send their children to private or parochial schools if they could afford it.

A VEHICLE FOR PARTICIPATION

In 1983 three factors would begin to reverse this decline, creating, among other things, the Dayton–Montgomery County Public Education Fund as an instrument for improving education.

First, having bottomed out, the regional economy began to improve.

Second, with court-ordered desegregation an accomplished fact, the Dayton school district began emerging from the acrimony the battle had caused. In June 1983, local voters approved $13 million in new school taxes, the first increase in seven years, allowing the district to pay off loans and resume such basic expenditures as textbook purchases. That levy had been strongly supported by the business community, a sign that local leadership was ready to reinvolve itself in the schools.

The third factor was that Fred Smith decided it was time to *do* something with the Dayton Foundation. Smith, retired chairman of Huffy Corporation, a manufacturer of bicycles and other consumer products, had been chairman of the foundation's board since 1978. In that time, he had come to regard its operations as sleepy at best. Smith prevailed on the board to hire, as a one-time experiment, a professional director. Smith's choice was Fred Bartenstein, who had recently completed six years as administrative assistant to Dayton's city manager and shared Smith's desire to create "a private sector organization that could honcho community concerns."

These elements, then, were ready to be assembled:

- A recovering business community was looking for a vehicle for directing support to the public schools.
- The region's largest school district was looking for the means to channel that support.
- A newly aggressive community foundation was looking for a useful task to take on.

These strands met in Smith's office on February 14, 1984. The meeting was prompted by a request to the foundation from a city high school that wanted dollars to carry out a computer project. Bartenstein contacted Susan Sibbing, the president of the Dayton school board, to ask how that proposal meshed with the school district's plans. Sibbing suggested that perhaps they'd better talk.

To that meeting, Sibbing brought Leonard Roberts, general manager of GM's Inland Division and a longtime supporter of public education, to meet with Bartenstein and Smith, the foundation president. The schools had needs, Sibbing said, but no funds to meet them. The business community was offering help, but those efforts were uncoordinated and piecemeal. "Everybody wants to save us," she said, "but they don't talk to us."

Sibbing proposed a Public Education Fund as a means for the community to channel its efforts. She had read that the Ford Foundation was seeding such efforts through challenge grants from the national Public Education Fund, based in Pittsburgh.

All picked up on the idea. Smith pointed out that administering the program through the Dayton Foundation would give it a neutral home base and staff support. Sibbing urged that it be a county-wide program, to promote regionalism and prevent presenting the Dayton schools as the area's stepchild. Smith argued that contributions go directly to operations, rather than to an endowment. This would assure donors that money was being put to immediate use.

This conversation presaged the basic framework of the Dayton–Montgomery County Public Education Fund—it would be a vehicle for channeling community interest in education; it would operate through the Dayton Foundation; it would include both city and suburbs; and it would not seek to establish a permanent endowment.

A WAY OF GETTING SOMETHING DONE

In 1985, all events were running in favor of establishing a local Public Education Fund. Major studies, among them "A Nation at Risk," were calling attention to "a rising tide of mediocrity" in the nation's schools. At a local economic summit in Dayton, business leaders concluded that greater attention had to be paid to K–12 education.

In this climate, Arnold Rosenfeld, editor of the *Dayton Daily News*, and David Ponitz, president of Sinclair Community College, invited 15 civic leaders to meet with a representative of the national Public

Education Fund. Rosenfeld turned to Bartenstein: Would the Dayton Foundation prepare a concept paper on the idea?

Soon thereafter, Bartenstein sponsored what he calls his "Noah's Ark" meeting—two teachers, two business leaders, two administrators, etc. These he asked to set down whatever ideas they had for improving the public schools. Dozens of ideas emerged; when Bartenstein pushed for consensus, three stood out:

- A program of small incentive grants and awards to educators.
- An effort to improve marketing of the Dayton schools.
- Establishment of community forums "to keep education high on the civic agenda."

The February 14 meeting had established the purpose and framework for the fund; the "Noah's Ark" meeting set its basic program.

Events moved rapidly. Dennis Shere, publisher of Dayton Newspapers, Incorporated, signed on as chairman of the fund's governing body (appointed by the foundation, this board operates with considerable latitude). Shere recalls, "I thought of this project not as the answer to all the problems, but as a way of getting something done. We could act without spending tremendous amounts of money; it would have an immediate impact; and we could act without being perceived as threatening to the schools."

The fund, Shere adds, "was not a hard sell. I raised $120,000 with four phone calls and follow-up letters."

Meanwhile, Sarah Harris—a noted local educator and past president of the Dayton Urban League—prepared a grant submission to the national Public Education Fund. Her proposal sought $100,000 over three years, a figure granted in its entirety, provided local matching requirements were met.

Matching proved no problem. Fund organizers broadened their solicitation, in all securing $440,000 from local sources to cover three years of operations.

A WINDOW ON WHAT'S HAPPENING IN THE SCHOOLS

Harris soon left the fund to take a position in private industry. In her place, fund directors hired Gail Levin to a half-time directorship. Levin, who had served as Dayton's first city councilwoman, was community relations director for WHIO-TV, the city's CBS affiliate.

Levin's first task, she recalls, was "to make sure the stakeholders in the concept felt comfortable. Primarily, you market first to the people you affect most—in this case, the teachers. If they don't buy in, forget it."

The program offers teachers up to $500 for classroom projects that could not be accomplished with existing school resources. Such programs are popular with local Public Education Funds. Gerri Kay, executive director of the Public Education Fund Network, reports that all but a few of the 57 affiliated funds operate some variant of the teacher grants program. The reasons, she says, are many—program success rate is high, dollars go directly to the classroom, the grants build visibility and credibility and give the fund "a window into what's happening in the schools."

Dayton organizers stress an additional reason—the need to build teacher morale through recognition and the chance to do something special. "Teachers are generally demoralized," Shere points out. "They're in the trenches, but recognition generally goes to those in private enterprise."

Through 1987-1988, 345 grants totaling $163,327 were made, with 238 new proposals submitted for 1988-1989. Program red tape is minimal. The grant application, both sides of a single 8½ × 11 sheet, asks the teacher for basic professional information and paragraph-length descriptions of the proposed project and the hoped-for results. Further, teachers incur no out-of-pocket expenses; the grant check, made payable directly to the teacher, is presented before the project's starting date. "To teachers who've been dipping into their own pockets for years for money for classroom projects, this is terrific," says Sue Elling, a former teacher, program officer at the Dayton Foundation and Junior League president who succeeded Levin as fund director in 1987.

Many teachers use grant projects as a basis for seeking further support from community organizations, thus extending the project's classroom impact and creating another tie with the community. The fund itself is now working to increase the program's payoff, organizing seminars at which teachers who have developed particularly successful projects will pass them on to their peers.

MARKETING AND COMMUNICATIONS

As the grants program was becoming established, the fund moved ahead on its other two program agendas—marketing the schools and providing a forum for discussion of education.

Marketing projects included the following:

- A basic information brochure on the Dayton schools, distributed to area realtors and at the schools.
- A multimedia slide presentation on the strengths of the Dayton schools.
- Grants to 37 schools to promote school-parent involvement.

The marketing program has been less successful than the grants effort. The effect of the publicity work was hard to gauge, and the programs for parents did more to identify the reasons for low parent involvement—the demands of single parenting, or the parent's own bad school experiences, among them—than to increase that involvement.

In its communications efforts, the fund has sponsored forums to help focus community attention on education. At one, Owen Butler, retired chairman of Procter & Gamble and chair of the education task force for the national Committee on Economic Development, spoke to business leaders. At a second, Ohio Governor Richard Celeste led a "town meeting" on education for a mixed student, teacher, and business audience.

More generally, Dayton Foundation director Fred Bartenstein says, the fund provides "the only regional forum for the discussion of education." For example, when the State of Ohio passed legislation to permit school districts to annex adjacent territory, this posed a potentially divisive city/suburb question. The fund brought in a professional mediator and sponsored a series of meetings at which city and suburban school representatives sorted out criteria for annexation.

PROGRAM EXPANSION

In 1985, the fund expanded its incentive grants and awards to educators by taking over the administration of a local grants program that disbursed money for projects initiated by school principals.

In 1986, it began administering an "Excellence in Teaching" program. This program annually awards $1,000 to each of ten area teachers, and recognizes them at a luncheon sponsored by the 300-member downtown Dayton Rotary Club. The program is funded by Dayton Newspapers, Incorporated, and Dayton Power & Light. Unlike the grants program, this effort prompted controversy. Shere recalls it as "a real minefield. The teachers union was apprehensive, seeing it as a potential first step to merit pay. And the administration was apprehensive, because it put outsiders within the reward structure." Levin helped smooth the way. She junked her tentative set of award criteria, replacing it with one developed by teacher representatives. The awards have been recognized as a substantial accomplishment.

The programs of grants and awards have limited goals—challenge creativity, boost morale, add curricular variety. Now, the Dayton–Montgomery County Public Education Fund is looking to more systemic changes—specifically, to an improvement in county-wide mathematics instruction.

The impetus came in early 1988 from Charlie Joiner, president of a high-technology division of the Mead Corporation. Joiner and other Mead executives were concerned about the quality of mathematics instruction in American schools. They came to the fund looking for a way to connect that concern with the schools.

With Sue Elling coordinating, the group began exploring the Mathematics Collaborative, a national effort to tie business to mathematics teaching. Both city and county superintendents, and their respective math coordinators, joined the effort. Mead and the Dayton-based Engineering and Science Foundation have committed funds for the local match to grant requests now pending with major national grantmaking organizations.

Elling sees the convening of schools and community leaders to focus on a particular educational concern as a model the fund is likely to pursue in the future.

WE ALL KNEW WHO LUNCHED WITH WHOM

In assessing the history of a movement like the Dayton–Montgomery County Public Education Fund, it is easy to sacrifice people to process. The fund had a number of advantages at its founding—a recovering business community and a recovering school district were seeking ways to collaborate, against a general backdrop of increased concern for education. Their need for an intermediary matched the Dayton Foundation's desire for a project that would bring it more actively into the community's life.

At the same time, this model overlooks the shared characteristics of those responsible for initiating the effort: that is, all were well-placed and knowledgeable in the community. As president of the Dayton school board, Susan Sibbing brought all but instant cooperation from the schools, something other public education funds have had to work hard to achieve. Sarah Harris, who drew up the grant proposal, was one of the community's best known educators. Fred Smith, foundation board chairman, and Leonard Roberts of GM were well-established business and civic leaders; Dennis Shere's enthusiastic support brought with it favorable attention from the region's largest newspaper. And Fred Bartenstein, the foundation director, had nearly a decade of experience in various municipal and civic affairs.

As Gail Levin puts it, "Not only did we all know who lunched with whom, we had also all pretty much lunched with each other. Many of us had worked together in previous projects." That familiarity made it possible, for example, for Levin to say on one occasion to Shere, "Look, Dennis, I'm an old lady [she isn't] and I'm used to doing things my own way," and have the newspaper publisher ungrudgingly agree.

But a smooth start is not necessarily the best formula for long-term success, a point made by Gerri Kay of the national Public Education Fund network. The Dayton Fund's affiliation with the Dayton Foundation, she says, provided important initial strengths. "The real advantage," she says, "is the instant credibility gained through the relationship with the community foundation. That helps in attracting board members and contributions, and in lending staff. Otherwise, there's always the question, 'But who's going to do the work?' "

Over the long term, however, she says, that relationship presents problems of identity and autonomy, problems the Dayton funds and the community foundation are now facing.

An anecdote points up how far things have changed. In the fund's first year, director Levin wanted it to have its own logo, to help establish its public identity. Bartenstein opposed this; the foundation at that time needed all the public presence it could get, he reasoned, and could not afford to lose credit for any of the favorable publicity the fund was generating.

Both the fund and the foundation have grown. In 1984, when the Dayton–Montgomery County Public Education Fund was established, the Dayton Foundation had assets of $5 million. In 1989, after an aggressive program of consolidating small local endowments into the foundation, its assets stand at $24 million, and officials speak of a possible $100 million endowment by the turn of the century.

For the foundation, growth has meant both possibilities and complications—the latter, principally, of how best to manage its varied roles of local grants-giver, instigator, convener, broker, and program administrator. As one response, the foundation, under its recently adopted strategic plan, proposes to administer no program beyond an initial five years. At that point, Bartenstein says, if the program isn't ready to stand alone, it should be phased out.

The Public Education Fund's current charter with the foundation runs until 1991–1992; beyond then, it will likely have to go independent or seek a new affiliation. Fund director Elling points to a second concern, that the fund can become too program-bound, its broader mission lost in the administrative details of the programs it operates. The fund, she stresses, does not exist to operate specific programs. Rather, it should be the means whereby the community can connect with the schools in ways that promote education.

Bartenstein shares Elling's view. He cites three specific achievements that came in part from the more optimistic, cooperative atmosphere the fund has helped create.

First, in June 1988, Dayton voters—by a substantial margin— approved both an extension of the 1983 tax increase and $9.5 million in new taxes.

Second, Dayton has been selected as one of five school districts nationally to participate in the Annie E. Casey Foundation's "New Futures Initiative," which will spend $21 million in Dayton over five years to coordinate services to youth at risk.

Third, Dayton was able to hire and retain a nationally known school superintendent, in part, Bartenstein says, because the fund could offer the newcomer immediate access to the region's leadership.

In assessing the fund, Elling observes that a decade ago, "the community was bailing out of education as fast as it could. Now, the question isn't 'Why should we help?' but 'Where?' and 'How?' Our task is to provide the answers to those questions— 'where' and 'how' the community can most effectively support public education."

13

Miami: Overcoming Intercultural Isolation

Lyn Farmer

In Miami, Florida, where the "sun and fun" reputation thinly covers a racially strife-torn community, the Dade Community Foundation has set in motion an effort to bridge cultural and ethnic barriers by developing leadership and self-respect at the grassroots level. What makes the effort unusual is the foundation's innovative way of reaching into the community—from teen entrepreneurs to cross-cultural arts programs, to special neighborhood funding to build skills and enhance communication.

Dade County has a population of nearly 2 million people, spread over a land area about the size of the state of Delaware. Despite the tourist's image of Miami as a city of brilliant colors, sandy beaches, and tropical exoticism, the city faces the same serious problems confronting any urban center, shaped by an ethnic makeup that shifts with each new political upheaval in the Caribbean, Central America, or South America. Describing Miami's troubles in paradise, Ruth Shack, president of the Dade Community Foundation, says, "the major problem affecting [this] community is the pervasive feeling of cultural alienation and lack of effective mechanisms for building a cohesive community."

Called by some "the capital of South America" and considered by others a rough pioneer town, Miami is a city built on wealth that has been largely imported from elsewhere. Retirees brought their savings from the industrial Northeast and the middle American rust belt, in many cases without giving up their ties to other regions.

At the turn of the century, Miami was nothing but a small outpost without the transportation necessary to bring it into the twentieth century. In the 1920s, the railroad came to South Florida, and after World War II, many servicemen who had been stationed there returned to settle in the sunshine.

In the 1950s, Miami was considered a sleepy Southern town made up mostly of retirees and "snowbirds," wealthy northerners who came south for the winter. For decades it was marketed to the rest of America as the city that had nothing but sun and fun. Unspoken in all this advertising was the understanding that Miami was actually more northern than southern in feel, and that ethnically it was primarily white and middle class.

In 1960, that was true: 80 percent of the population was white Anglo, and some 20 percent was black. That has changed dramatically. Today, Miami is 44 percent Hispanic, a multi-lingual city notable for its international character and ethnic tensions.

Miami is where the American dream of a "melting pot" is being redefined. Some characterize this new mix as a "beef stew" becoming a "salad bowl." To Shack, "It is a TV dinner with three compartments, each separate from the other. Our mission is to break down the barriers between the groups and enjoy the special character of a truly international, Hispanically flavored city." Miami is now what many large urban centers may be in the future—as a foundation statement put it, "a post-industrial society which is both service oriented and international. While other cities have managed to assimilate and acculturate immigrants in one generation, in Dade County that process has almost stopped. The new immigrant populations—Cubans, Haitians, Central Americans, South Americans and Caribbeans—have built distinct communities separate from the traditional North American and black communities."

The events that changed the city are clear: in the early 1960s, waves of Cuban refugees crossed 90 miles of water to escape Castro's revolution and, quietly at first but with increasing force, began creating a revolution of their own in South Florida.

In the 1950s, Miami was popular as a convention center; in the 1960s, that reputation gave way to ethnic fears as the city became a refugee center. The 1970s saw a period of assimilation, as the Cuban community became a powerful force in the city's growing financial community. But, as the pre-Castro Cuban professional elite increasingly settled in Florida and prospered, many black residents felt bypassed, just as deprived as ever. The bubble burst with a vengeance in 1980 in Liberty City, one of Miami's many black neighborhoods. This city within the city blew up in a frenzy of civil disorder and racial tension. Even after the riots were quelled, racial hatred and fear continued. Not long afterward, tensions rose again as Castro expelled more than 100,000 people, the Marielitos; most ended up on South Florida's shores, provoking what writer T. D. Allman called "a kind of chronic, slow-motion, law-and-order riot on the city." Then, boatload after boatload of Haitians, trying to escape the horrors of their own country, ended up in Florida.

The sudden influx of immigrants, Florida's lax gun laws, and overworked police forces threatened to tear the city's social fabric. As ethnic groups remained in enclaves, Dade County became an area "without a common community vision or outlook characterized by the perpetuation of prejudice, discrimination, stereotyping, scapegoating and racism." It was that problem the Dade Community Foundation has set out to address.

EVOLUTION OF A FOUNDATION

In one sense, this is a story of David and Goliath. The Dade Community Foundation was neither large nor particularly powerful when it set its goal on building a more cohesive Miami. In 1967, the Greater Miami United Way had a small endowment of about $50,000 managed by a group of volunteers. William Rubin, then an executive with the retailer Jordan Marsh and a member of the United Way board, convinced his colleagues that the charity was in no position to maintain and manage an endowment. So a separate fund was established, governed by its own board drawn equally from United Way and the community at large. This fledgling Dade Community Foundation took out a full-page advertisement in *The Miami Herald* to announce its mission, but, as a volunteer organization, its profile remained low and funds accumulated very slowly. Over a period of years, the foundation separated entirely from the United Way and organized its own board. It was not until 1977, though, that it was able to rent an office and hire a full-time executive director.

During its first decade of existence, the Dade Community Foundation trust funds increased to only $350,000. In 1978, it could award only some $50,000 in grants—small, but enough to gain visibility in the community. By 1981, however, the foundation had grown to embrace 80 individual funds, and $3 million in assets. Four years later, it reached $5 million.

At the end of 1988, its assets were in excess of $12 million. Many board members attribute the growth in large part to Ruth Shack, a former Dade County Commissioner who was hired to direct the foundation in 1986. For many years, Shack had been active in Dade County social, civic, and political circles, working closely with the many neighborhoods that make up the county-wide government.

One of the Dade Community Foundation's founding governors, Harry Hood Bassett, wrote in the 1987 annual report that Shack gave the foundation "impetus, visibility and prominence." Alvah Chapman, chairman of Knight-Ridder, publisher of *The Miami Herald,* wrote in the same report: "It is a sign of maturity when a community can claim the resources of a successful foundation."

Chapman's sense that the Dade Community Foundation was maturing stirred the board's interest in hiring Shack. Chapman and a number of other board members had been pushing the foundation toward greater involvement in Miami's ethnically diverse community. In Shack, they saw an activist who could both help increase assets and position the foundation as a major force in bridging the community's ethnic differences.

Shortly after Shack was hired, the possibility arose for obtaining a Ford Foundation challenge grant to supplement the foundation's own assets in furthering that community involvement. The Ford Foundation was ready to commit $100,000 a year for five years for a project important to the community if the Dade Community Foundation could raise $1 million for its endowment in two years. "We used this whole process of pursuing the Ford money as an exercise to challenge us, to make us grow, to stretch our abilities," she says. "We had all the drive and capability, we just didn't have the resources."

Shack responded by convening a group of civic leaders and activists. It included Maurice Ferre, a businessman and former Mayor of Miami (1973–1985); Carrie Meek, a black state senator with a strong base in Overtown, a black ghetto; José Astigarraga, a young attorney well-regarded as a leader in the emerging generation of Cuban Americans; Sandy Lindsay, a program specialist on the United Way staff with a good grasp of where problems in the community are concentrated; and JoAnne Bander, a consultant with long experience in community social services.

As Bander recalls, at that meeting "It was clear from the beginning that whatever we proposed to Ford had to be something extremely important to the community. I think Ruth, because of her background in county politics as well as social programs, believed we must look at the complicated, multi-ethnic, multi-cultural system in Dade County. That was almost a given in her own process of developing a concept of what a community foundation must be. Her approach was a classic advisory system approach, a concept that you need to develop a broad base of support. She convened a broadly based group of people active in the community (and she knows *everyone*) and, in essence, dropped the problem in their laps. She said, 'We have an unparalleled opportunity to bring additional resources into this community. What do you feel is our main problem?'

"We looked at all sorts of problems that face the community—teen pregnancy, illiteracy, unemployment, the sort of problems that face any community," says Bander. Many of the people attending that meeting say it was former Mayor Ferre who gently turned the talk away from a discussion of broadly based urban issues to an issue that was both specific to Miami, and still crucial to solving social problems in general.

CONNECTING THE COMMUNITIES

"What we decided," says Ferre, "was not to focus on a disadvantaged group like blacks or Hispanics or Haitians. We believed that none of Miami's ethnic groups could prosper individually until they could cooperate and prosper together."

The project they eventually proposed dealt with upward mobility in the free-enterprise system. "It's a lot more than just poverty," says Ferre. "We needed a social program that wasn't limited to teenage pregnant women, or situations like that, but that would really have a long-term impact on the community. In other words, it's better for Miamians to gather together to define and try to seek solutions to problems according to our own priorities. We choose what needs to be done."

Everyone was aware that the Dade Community Foundation had limited resources to carry out projects, but also understood that the purpose of the Ford Foundation money was to make it bigger and stronger. JoAnne Bander noted that "they had been working on projects to develop community leadership through clever approaches at mixing money together, and bringing groups together, but there came a point when big bucks were needed to make an impact." The foundation decided on the theme of building a cohesive Miami.

The Ford Foundation awarded a five-year challenge grant of $500,000 in January 1987. The community foundation was ready with a one-year initiative called *Miamians Working Together*. It was a very straightforward program. They set out to fund existing organizations with teen programs, or teen businesses, in their own communities, not so much concerned about what businesses were set up as whether they were feasible. However, the Dade Community Foundation was determined that, whatever the business was, it would take teens from their ethnic enclave into the broader community. For example, a group from the Belafonte-Tacolcy Community Center had a mobile ice cream business. It wasn't enough for them to sell only in their home neighborhood in Liberty City. Instead, they went out to street fairs and gatherings throughout the community, taking a group of inner-city black kids out into the broader community. Another group designed multi-lingual greeting cards and sold them on the courthouse steps, at businesses, at fairs ... places very far out of their home territory. A third group designed a guide to Dade County and published it in Spanish, English, and Creole.

The community foundation made it clear to these groups that it would provide one-year grants, that its assumption was that most of the businesses would be successful so they would have retained earnings to keep going. It did not plan on continuing to fund the projects after the initial year.

Ruth Shack says this approach is not the only way they could have handled the project. "If I had known enough at the time, we would have given them no-cost loans instead of grants. I think that would have better engendered the entrepreneurial spirit in the youth—let them pay us back from the profits over a long period the way other businesses borrow and repay."

Still, the entrepreneurial spirit did grow, and the teen projects began to prosper (albeit on a limited scale). In all, the Dade Community Foundation helped 12 teen groups go into business in all parts of Miami, but didn't feel that that sufficiently fulfilled the goals of the program. "So we brought all the teens together at Florida International University's Multi-lingual, Multi-cultural Center to run cross-cultural training sessions," says Shack. "For example, Terri Zubizarreta is owner of the largest Hispanic woman-owned ad agency in the area. Zubizarreta told the teens how to market to the Hispanic people, how to attract Hispanic attention. We had the president of the Chamber of Commerce in Little Haiti come in to tell them what they needed to know to do business in Haitian neighborhoods.

"We've continued quarterly training sessions with the kids: it allows them to meet one another, learn what they're doing right and wrong, do deals and talk over projects together. They studied business skills, but they also studied each other's culture. It was all done very simply: we had one day where we had lunch at a Cuban restaurant; another day they got together in Miami Beach where they held the meeting in a synagogue and ate kosher deli for lunch."

The Dade Community Foundation had said in its grant proposal that it also intended to work closely with a number of established groups in the city, drawing them into the cross-cultural process. Two that figured prominently in the first year were the Cuban National Planning Council's Leadership Training Program and Leadership Miami, a multi-ethnic, multi-racial leadership development program of the Greater Miami Chamber of Commerce. Both groups work to identify individuals with leadership potential, and then train and educate them across ethnic and racial lines.

"While the leadership program had accomplished its goals," says Shack,"we thought a pool of talent had been developed that still wasn't being used to its fullest. To get even more out of that pool, we involved them in the creation of a mentor program that assembled a group of about 50 dynamic young leaders from the ranks of those multi-ethnic leadership programs and matched them cross-culturally with each of the agencies to which we'd given grants. We didn't want to control the process—we only encouraged them to work together in whatever way was comfortable for both parties."

The durability of some of the first year's projects came as a surprise to a number of participants."It's hard to keep a group together when you're not putting new money in," say Bander, now program consultant to the foundation."There's attrition in any program. The initial goal of the foundation was reached by just getting the teen entrepreneur groups up and running for the one year, but there's a longer-term benefit that we hope for as well. Some of the agencies to which we awarded grants have ongoing programming now, which in turn will provide excellent training for their participants and organizers, and that's very exciting to us."

Eight community foundations were awarded challenge grants by the Ford Foundation and given two years to raise the matching funds. To meet the challenge, other foundations created structured campaigns to increase assets, but the Dade Community Foundation used enhanced visibility as a fundraising tool. It believed that being successful at projects and garnering good will and favorable publicity would prompt a level of support and involvement a direct campaign could not inspire. It would reach sectors that do not normally react to traditional fundraising measures. Thus far, this indirect approach is working: in the first year, enough money was raised to meet the entire challenge though little was said publicly about fundraising progress.

"What we purposely *are not doing,*" Shack wrote an evaluator,"is announcing that these funds fulfill our Ford Challenge Grant. Our goal is to keep the pressure on and to raise the match several times!" The Dade Community Foundation apportioned the grant funds at a rate of $100,000 for each of the program's five years. The proposed budget earmarked 75 percent of that amount for grants, drawing on $25,000 each year for all administrative costs.

Each year, discretionary and general field-of-interest endowments of the Dade Community Foundation generate income used as the foundation's own project money. In 1988, the amount was about $250,000. The president annually recommends to the board areas where the money should be dispensed after an evaluation of grant requests received from the community. To strengthen the foundation's leadership effort, for the past two years the Dade Community Foundation has used its own income for similar projects."It has been made clear to the community that the Dade Community Foundation is particularly interested in cross-cultural programs to promote a more cohesive Miami," says Shack.

The intercultural message has become primary in all Dade Community Foundation business—it is brought up at all meetings, and it now sparks initiatives that extend beyond those funded directly with Ford Foundation money. The board composition has changed from an old Miami look to reflect the demographics of new Miami. The staff has also become ethnically diverse. In addition, groups with which the foundation deals now view the organization as having a focus and an area of great expertise. People come to the foundation looking not just for money, but for advice, which of course was one of the intentions of the program to begin with, enhancing the Dade Community Foundation image as well at its size.

YEAR TWO: THE ARTS AS A BRIDGE

"We approached year two with a commitment to continue the training of these young entrepreneurs, though we had no intention of continuing to fund their businesses—that was for the kids to do," says Shack."We reconvened the advisory group, added some different voices and asked the same questions again: how do we get our cross-cultural message across given the resources we have?"

The advisory panel now recommended that they work through established arts organizations, with a preference for emerging minority groups. Dubbing the second year of the project *Miami Arts Bridge*, the foundation gave the groups a very specific challenge, different from what most people think of when they hear "cross-cultural." The challenge posed to the city's arts groups was to create a cultural program with a specific, ethnically based cultural message, and tell the Dade Community Foundation how they would share it with differing ethnic audiences. The foundation wanted the arts organizations to share cultural values in a way that would help educate one group about another's value system.

Ballet Flamenco La Rosa, a Hispanic ensemble and Freddick Bratcher and Company, a black contemporary dance troupe, proposed a performance as a combined ensemble. The two groups started a discussion at a request-for-proposal conference held by the foundation, to which all arts groups were invited, and ended up making a joint proposal. "That isn't so much proactive on our part as it is an outgrowth of our creating a forum," says Bander. "The very act of our offer created a bridge between two groups that might otherwise never have gotten together."

An important lesson learned by the foundation concerned the way networks are formed. In the quarterly meetings with teens, the Dade Community Foundation found that many of the advisors would form a network of adults from different cultural and ethnic backgrounds who had never worked together before. Similar structures evolved with the arts groups as well, says Bander. "Once we'd made our funding decisions, we convened a meeting of the recipients among the arts groups to tell them what they could expect. They immediately sought an opportunity to get together and have their own workshop. They were so enthusiastic about the project that on their own they devised a tri-lingual brochure on all their programs, listing every group and event in English, Spanish and Creole. The group members raised their own funds for the brochure, and technical support was provided through a grant from the foundation to Business Volunteers for the Arts, an organization that trains and places lawyers, accountants and marketing professionals as volunteers in arts and cultural groups. The short-term result was the Dade Community Foundation fostered a

number of successful programs; the longer-term benefit was the creation of new networks."

One of the participants in the arts bridge meeting was Mitchell
Kaplan, owner of Books & Books, a popular "corner bookstore" in
Coral Gables and a board member of the annual Miami International
Book Fair. The program he came up with began as an effort to highlight
local authors who often get lost among the national authors and stars
at the Book Fair. "I got the distinct impression the foundation wasn't
interested in forming committees to study things, and they didn't want
to give out 'seed money,' " Kaplan recalls. "They wanted to create
and sponsor programs that would do something finite to contribute
to the community. What the community did from there on was out
of the foundation's hands. I thought that was fantastic."

Kaplan says that the most important role the foundation played
was not so much one of funding but of inspiration. "They got us
thinking about what *might* be done. We had been kicking around some
ideas, but didn't have the money to put some of our hopes into practice.
With money from the grant, though, some of our ideas became much
more feasible. So we came up with the program and then they supported
the effort." With foundation encouragement, the Book Fair created a
special program called *Write In Our Midst.* Instead of giving a series
of lectures or programs at the main Book Fair venue in downtown
Miami, the Book Fair organizers took the program into the community.

"We further developed our concept by staging events in nontraditional locations: bringing Hispanic authors into the black community,
Haitian authors into Anglo areas and so on, trying to enhance that
sense of cultural cross-fertilization," Kaplan says. "We had four
presentations in the series, underwritten by a $5,000 grant from the
Dade Community Foundation and augmented by funds we raised:
one in North Dade, one in Overtown, one in Little Havana and one
in Coral Gables. We fully intend to do it again in 1989."

Miami Arts Bridge enjoyed considerable success within the community: events were staged, and people came. On one level, that was
really all the Dade Community Foundation expected from its grants.
As Shack says, measuring success is not always easy: "We made a
decision not to do a lot of counting. We're measuring success in terms
of whether a group did what they said they'd do. Did the production go on? Was the location indeed in a different neighborhood? Was
the event reasonably well attended? Did we get a report back that
it was a cross-cultural audience? We're getting very positive messages

back, but we expected that because we were very careful about what we funded. We chose vehicles we felt had a high likelihood of success. If a group didn't bring the right project, we didn't fund it. This is just careful grantmaking. And what we feel happening is a change in the groups' comfort level with what they're doing."

The foundation intentionally kept paperwork and oversight to a minimum to give the groups—and the foundation—enough freedom to succeed or fail. "We could have created elaborate and extensive requirements, like long preliminary evaluations, post-project reviews and quarterly reports, but that alone would have used up huge amounts of the Ford money which then would not have been available for work in the community," she says. "We opted instead to fund groups to do programs that we, from our experience, felt would be good risks. The yardstick for these projects often did not measure 'quality' first, but more a sense of 'would it make a difference to the community?' The joint dance presentation, for example, did not have to be the greatest artistic success. The very fact these groups were working together is, from our point of view, a triumph.

"We also made it clear that we hoped that boards of organizations we supported would become ethnically diverse, then their staffs, and finally that diversity would spread to the clientele they serve. As a foundation we have the luxury of saying to groups, 'If you're going to be responsive it can't be tokenism.' A business or social service agency can't be out there spending money alone in the black or Latin community. To have true involvement, people who live there have to be making some of the decisions as well."

"We're now developing the concept of devoting the last three years of the Ford Foundation initiative to finding, empowering and training leadership at the grassroots level," says Shack."We think Dade County sorely needs this. Certainly from my political background I saw it, and in the civic sector it's pretty apparent. We go to the same people over and over again to do what needs to be done. I'm not talking about the young leadership level from corporations. We want to reach to the neighborhoods themselves, to help people have access to their due, and to begin to build a sense of neighborhood pride in Dade County.

"We know that once one goes into neighborhoods there is no turning back—there's nothing worse than raising expectations then dashing hopes. Another advantage to the foundation stems from these projects: our assets grow, our visibility grows, and our technical ability grows. Testing our limits in funding cross-cultural initiatives means more risky grantmaking to institutions less proven than we've gone with before, something that tests our abilities at identifying risk, at evaluating emerging groups."

Two years into the project, the Dade Community Foundation has an excellent image with the media, an enhanced reputation in the community and with national foundations thinking of funding a project here, growing assets, and a reputation in the business sector as a tough group of innovators who get things done, galvanizes the community across ethnic lines, and is a good financial partner. The prospect is a healthier community and a thriving community foundation that succeeds not only at raising major resources but local consciousness.

14

Greenville: Early Intervention for Children

Mike Hembree

Events that would lead to one of the biggest projects in the 32-year history of the Community Foundation of Greater Greenville began in the summer of 1984 in the South Carolina Fire Marshal's office.

The Fire Marshal notified South Carolina child care centers in July of the department's intent to enforce new fire code regulations for infant care facilities beginning July 1, 1985. The ramifications of that notification, and other problems that were beginning to emerge, ultimately would attract the Greenville foundation into a complicated and wide-ranging initiative involving one of the big issues of the 1980s and beyond: child care.

The new fire regulations, which were designed to make South Carolina's codes consistent with those in most other states, emphasized improved exit access for rooms in which infants from birth to 24 months were kept. A direct exit door to the outside was required for every ten infants housed. For example, rooms with doors that opened only into hallways would not qualify as acceptable.

The situation presented problems for some low-income child care centers, most of which had little money for additions or renovations that might be required.

At the same time a serious shortage of child care providers for children of infant and toddler age had developed. Dr. Jean James, a former public school teacher and college professor who was working with the Piedmont Council for the Prevention of Child Abuse, saw the problem all too clearly. "The council had a respite program whereby parents who were at risk for abusing their children could seek counseling, jobs or whatever. The child could have some child care paid by the council," she said. "I was having difficulty locating enough care for infants and toddlers, and I had taken the problem to the Community Planning Council."

Council leaders decided to call a meeting of 38 community leaders in August 1985. The group included many in the human services field. Although the fire code and infant care problems had prompted the meeting, the discussion broadened to include numerous other child care difficulties.

"What emerged," James said, "was that we really needed some mechanism of coordination, an agency that could serve as a catalyst to address the issues related to the child care problem and to go on from there to use resources we already had in the community and to generate additional ones if needed."

The Community Planning Council and United Ministries, a Greenville human services support group, agreed to collaborate on a study of the Greenville child care situation. United Ministries is an organization formed by Greenville-area churches to provide various forms of aid to needy people. It is supported by financial contributions from churches, foundations, individuals, the United Way, and the federal government.

About a year later, the child care issue became one of paramount concern for the Community Foundation of Greater Greenville. In late summer 1986, a subcommittee of the foundation's board of directors conducted a survey of various community problems in preparation for applying for a Ford Foundation grant. It looked into teenage pregnancy, illiteracy, and substance abuse. All were jeopardizing the quality of life in the area served by the foundation, but none overshadowed the issue the foundation ultimately selected as its target: child care.

Foundation and community officials decided that the seed of many of the county's other problems could be found in child care difficulties. Improving child care in the infant-through-preschool years might well undercut such problems as drug abuse, illiteracy, and teenage pregnancy in the future.

A recent extensive examination of the county's child care situation had pointed out in hard figures what all too many mothers and fathers could verify from their own experiences: there was a major problem coordinating parents' child care needs with available resources, too little was being done to assure that the needs of children in child care circumstances were being met, there was a severe shortage of infant–toddler care, and there were very few support services for child care providers.

The foundation took a closer look at these and other imposing community problems because of the possibility of securing a $500,000 grant from the Ford Foundation. Twenty-eight foundations across the country applied for the grants, which Ford Foundation officials had designated for use in response to significant community problems with local foundations as the vehicles.

The Greenville child care study showed that the area had many of the same difficulties caused by the child care dilemma in most parts of the United States. As the work force continues to absorb more women, the dynamics of the American home continue to change, and the children usually are left in the middle. With both parents working, the answer to, "Who's minding the children?" all too often has been "whoever happens to be available." Often, no one is.

The problem has grown in Greenville as the city and its surrounding area have grown in recent years. Located in the northwestern part of South Carolina on the fringe of the Southern Appalachian Mountains, Greenville has a three-county Metropolitan Statistical Area population of more than 600,000. Long known as a leader in the textile industry, Greenville has broadened its industrial scope in the last quarter-century to include such firms as Michelin Tire, 3-M, and Digital Electronics. One hundred and twenty new industrial firms have moved into the area in the past 15 years, contributing to a population growth of 25 percent. The area retains strong agricultural ties but also has significant representation in the manufacturing, construction, wholesale and retail sales, and financial fields.

About 82 percent of the county's population is white, and most of the rest are black. Greenville's per capita income has been first on the state's list of 46 counties in recent years. About 11 percent of the county's residents live on income considered below the poverty level.

More than 45 percent of the area's total employment is female, and about 60 percent of all children under age six have mothers who work. More than 12 percent of the 111,400 households in Greenville County are headed by women.

According to a report in 1988 by the United States Conference of Mayors, about 45 percent of the national need for licensed child care goes unmet. In Greenville, the numbers came down to these: about 11,000 available child care "slots" for 13,274 children under age 13 who needed child care, with most child care centers maintaining waiting lists. The impact has affected parents at all income levels.

Some parents impose on relatives who might be reluctant; others take their children to work and leave them in cars or on workplace grounds; others leave their children at home with older siblings or with neighborhood children and hope for the best. Child care problems often lead to a mother (or father) quitting a job, financial strain because of a significant drop in family income, and placing the "blame" on the child or children for circumstances they cannot control.

Numbers are not the only problem. In too many cases—in Greenville and elsewhere—existing child care situations are of poor quality. Some centers are too small and ill-equipped to provide the bright, pleasant atmosphere beneficial to children. Some center employees are poorly trained, if at all. Many salaries are dismally low, and turnover is high.

The majority of corporations and businesses have only begun to accept the fact that child care is an issue that could have a serious negative impact on their operations. In Greenville, the child care study found no full-fledged, on-site corporate child care centers and little evidence of companies taking a serious approach toward dealing with the issue. Yet parents with small children frequently miss work because of illnesses, school problems, or failure of babysitters and other child care providers to produce reliable services. Employee absenteeism decreases productivity, increases overtime pay and use of temporary employees, and contributes to other corporate headaches.

A few months after presenting its child care plans to the Ford Foundation, the Greenville community foundation became the smallest of eight chosen to receive Ford Leadership grants. All the others went to larger cities, including Miami, Detroit, and Phoenix.

Study and Action

The foundation had been established in 1956 after area business and community leaders observed the success of nearby community foundations, particularly in neighboring Spartanburg County. The Greenville foundation operated without a paid staff for its first 20 years, relying on volunteers and business and civic leaders to handle grant request reviews, awarding of funds and general operations.

The foundation had an initial endowment of $5,100, and that had grown to only $356,709 by 1971. Despite limited funds, the foundation contributed substantially to the community's growth and welfare. It furnished money to help establish the Greenville Urban League, the Greenville Blood Assurance Plan, the Greenville Council on Aging, the Senior Citizens Center, the Metropolitan Arts Council, Volunteer Greenville, the Community Food Bank, the Textile Museum, and Junior Achievement.

The foundation also totally funded county-wide immunization of children against polio, measles, tetanus, and other diseases.

Beginning in the mid–1970s, the foundation's endowment swelled, boosted by the acquisition of resources from several private foundations and the implementation of a "founders society" program that generated $1 million in new funds by seeking $25,000 contributions from prominent civic leaders. The endowment topped $2.4 million as the foundation moved into the 1980s. The organization had a major impact on the cultural life of the area by purchasing land for the construction of Heritage Green, a center that includes a museum, a library, and a theater.

The foundation hired its first executive director in 1981 and moved toward participating in larger projects. Subsequently, the foundation played a significant role in the development of Greenville Commons, a downtown complex that includes a luxury hotel, convention center, parking garage, and an office building.

The foundation marshaled its forces in 1986 to raise $1 million in matching funds to qualify for the $500,000 Ford Foundation grant. Given two years to raise the money, the foundation obtained $1,086,410 in contributions and pledges in only nine months, with gifts ranging from $20 to $100,000.

Much of the groundwork for the child care improvement made possible by the Ford Foundation grant had been done during the Community Planning Council–United Ministries study and the succeeding months. The study involved research by a team of more than 50 volunteers organized into six areas: licensing, infant–toddler care, alternative types of child care, low-income child care, coordination of child care, and barriers to quality child care.

Participants included human services professionals, business people, child care providers, government officials, and school system officials.

The study benefited from a survey coordinated by the Education Department at nearby Furman University. "A Survey of Barriers to the Provision of Quality Day Care Services in the Greenville

Metropolitan Area" included interviews by Furman graduate students of personnel at child care centers.

The overall child care study was completed in April 1986. Among the key findings were the following:

- Poor coordination between parents' child care needs and available resources.

- A lack of accountability of child care centers about their services and operations.

- Corporate sponsorship of child care in the county was practically nonexistent.

- The problems of low-income child care programs, such as the need for additional staff training and subsidies for child care costs, needed to be addressed.

- Infant–toddler care was more difficult to obtain than care for older preschool children.

In response, the study group recommended:

- A centralized child care program to provide resource and referral services for parents seeking child care, educational and technical assistance to providers, consultation on child care to business and the community, and advocacy on behalf of quality care for Greenville's children.

- Upgrading of licensing, educational, and accrediting standards for child care providers.

- A variety of alternative types of child care, such as after-school enrichment programs, corporate-sponsored programs, sick child care, and care for children with special needs.

- Additional infant–toddler programs.

- Subsidies for low-income child care.

United Ministries officials decided to devote staff time to pursuing the report's recommendations and to search for funding to finance some of the suggested programs. Its orientation toward human service programs and its involvement in the child care study made it a natural place to originate work on the project.

Before the end of the year, however, the project would take a new direction. In August 1986, James Richmond, formerly vice-president of the W. K. Kellogg Foundation in Battle Creek, Michigan, was named the new executive director of the Greenville foundation. Richmond had had experience in grantmaking and proposal preparation at the Kellogg Foundation, a foundation with assets of more than $2 billion.

At about the time Richmond arrived in town, Greenville's problems in the child care area merged with the community foundation's need for a very visible, documented issue to tackle to qualify for the Ford Leadership Grant. Richmond met with a group of community leaders, including some from the original task force on the child care problem. The Greenville foundation applied for the Ford grant on September 25, 1986, with the initiative, called Greenville's Child, as the centerpiece proposal.

Meanwhile, United Ministries had moved ahead with plans to address the issues raised in the child care study.

"We were the only agency willing to commit staff time to figure out what we could do about coordination," said the Rev. Elizabeth Templeton, Executive Director of United Ministries. "We started working on some aspects of the report and were beginning to look for money to try to get it up and off the ground."

A developmental board for Greenville's Child was appointed, and the fledgling program began with very limited funding under the United Ministries umbrella. United Ministries approached foundations and had plans to seek corporate funding for the project. The scenario changed, however, with the accelerating interest of the Greenville foundation and the possibility of obtaining the Ford Foundation grant.

Resolving Ownership Issues

The community foundation used the child care study and expanded its thrust, Richmond said. "We were fortunate to have the study and all the work that was put into it," he said. "We broadened the study into a community-wide framework that covered funding by the foundation, a separate board for Greenville's Child and a whole series of service-delivery relationships between Greenville's Child and local colleges and other service agencies."

The bridge carrying the project from its beginning at United Ministries to its place within the foundation framework was sometimes difficult to cross, say representatives from both groups. Numerous meetings were held between foundation and United Ministries officials to work out problems and disagreements over the scope and direction of the program, over exactly what Greenville's Child was, and who had responsibility for it.

"There were some early issues associated with the ownership of the name Greenville's Child and the ownership of the research study and who would implement the study findings and how they would be implemented," Richmond said. "United Ministries had one view and the foundation had another. There was some turf guarding, and there were some tense discussions. But over a period of time the two reached common ground, if not consensus, on how the project would move forward with Ford funding. I think it was all part of a natural, evolutionary kind of process."

In Templeton's view, confusion contributed substantially to the problems. "I'm not sure I'd call it turf problems as much as confusion," she said. "And part of that was because nobody new what Greenville's Child was. Was it the community foundation's grant request, or was it the entity we had been working with for a couple of years?

"There was some dissension, mainly about who had the right to speak for Greenville's Child and who had the right to set the direction. The community foundation's version of Greenville's Child wasn't always the same Greenville's Child that everybody had been working on. It was real frustrating, but there had to be a point where both sides had to recognize they needed the other. It happened because there were a lot of private conversations, one-on-one or three-on-one."

Templeton said United Ministries planned to continue the Greenville's Child program even if the Ford Foundation money had not appeared, although its visibility and impact would have been lessened because of limited funding.

Award of the Ford Foundation grant made the initiative move forward rapidly. Greenville's Child, Inc., officially began operation under its own banner on August 1, 1987. James became the executive director. The agency obtained office space on the fifth floor of Greenville General Hospital. It was an appropriate location: In previous years the area had served as the hospital's maternity ward, and the room that became James' office previously had been a pair of patient rooms where babies received their very first child care.

The Greenville plan called for a five-year program to improve child care availability and quality in the area. The major component of the initiative was the establishment of the Greenville's Child organization, with an initial grant of $43,000 of the Ford Foundation funds. While it sought I.R.S. clearance as a nonprofit agency, Greenville's Child was housed under the United Ministries umbrella. Duke Power Company, the area's dominant supplier of electrical power, the Greenville Junior League, and the United Way of Greenville also contributed funding in the agency's infancy. Project H.E.L.P. (Help Educate Little People), a United Ministries program that provided volunteer teachers, educational materials, technical assistance, and staff training to child care centers serving low-income families, became a part of Greenville's Child.

Funding for the abbreviated first year of the organization totaled $67,075, of which two-thirds came from the foundation. The foundation's contribution was $80,000 in 1988 and is budgeted at $90,000 in 1989, $70,000 in 1990, and $25,000 in 1991.

Greenville's Child approached the first program area—coordination of child care services and activities—with a goal of improving communication between agencies, providing parents with better information on child care providers, and boosting training opportunities for child care workers.

A computer service was established to provide quick answers for parents calling about information on available child care services.

"Often, our response to a parent calling about the available services is an educational process about the types of care that are available," James said. "They may not be aware of family-based child care or group child care homes. We talk to them about what they should look for when they go out to select good child care. It is not our prerogative to make the decision for the parent. They need to make that decision as parents. We provide a minimum of three names of licensed or registered providers for them to start with. And we follow up until they've found the child care they're looking for."

In the first ten months of 1988, the child care registry served 439 parents, and the agency recorded 11 new child care providers.

A Special Needs Child Care Registry provides a list of caregivers for sick children and for parents needing child care on weekends and evenings and during holiday periods.

Child care referrals and parent counseling have also been provided under contract to several businesses in the area. Workplace seminars on parenting issues are planned.

In carrying out its education component, the agency has attempted to improve training opportunities for child care workers and to spread the word about Greenville's Child and its mission to parents and the public at large.

Greenville's Child and Greenville Technical College developed two weekend training sessions for child care workers, and most of a $4,000 minigrant awarded to the college through the foundation was used to pay the workers a $50 stipend for attending the sessions. The workshops included sessions on discipline techniques, child growth and development, infant and toddler care, child abuse and neglect, and helping children though crisis situations such as divorce and separation.

The work of Greenville's Child benefited from the fact that Greenville Tech opened a new Child Development Center in September 1988 after three years of research and planning on needs in child development.

In its advocacy role, Greenville's Child seeks to mobilize community action on behalf of child care issues. Other organizations involved in child care have been identified and contacted, and work is going on in the area of studying legislation and policies for preschool programs, including licensing standards.

Corporate and Other Initiatives

Greenville's Child has performed child care research for clients such as IBM, Xerox, and Pitney Bowes. The agency's services to business and industry include assessing needs and recommending plans of businesses interested in pursuing corporate-sponsored child care. While fees for these are modest, they should provide a continuing financial base for the agency in future years.

As a result several corporations are taking tentative steps in the child care field."For example, some companies are looking at the possibility of having on-site child care facilities down the road, but they want to move slowly and to know what other viable alternatives they have now," James said.

The foundation's child care initiative went beyond the creation of the Greenville's Child agency. About $20,000 a year was reserved for minigrants to encourage local educational institutions and child care service providers to collaborate on improved child care. Eleven proposals were received by the foundation in the fall of 1987, and five grants totaling $21,350 were awarded in December.

For example, the foundation awarded $10,000 to the Greenville Young Women's Christian Association (YWCA) toward the cost of developing a child care center at the county's new governmental–social services complex located near downtown.

A $4,000 grant was awarded to Greenville Technical College for continuing education workshops and on-site training for employees of low-income child care centers.

A $4,800 grant was awarded to Family Service Greenville for a "morning care" service for non-toilet-trained children at the local Women In Crisis Shelter, which provides shelter, counseling, and other services for battered spouses and their children, and for pre-service training for child care students in collaboration with Greenville Technical College.

A fourth minigrant of $2,550 was awarded to the Greenville County Child Care Association, an organization of child care providers, for a one-day conference for area child care center workers, owners, staff, and teachers. Conference workshops included sessions on staff motivation, positive discipline techniques, liability insurance, and spending quality time with children. The association had been organized as part of the Greenville's Child initiative to serve as a focus for programs aimed at pre-service and in-service training of child care personnel, and for the encouragement of voluntary accreditation of child care centers.

The foundation also issued a $5,000 grant to the Community Planning Council to evaluate Greenville's Child during its first five years.

A pair of grants was approved for the 1989 calendar year. Greenville Technical College received $10,000 to assist ten Greenville child care workers in receiving their Child Development Associate credential, a mark of training and achievement approved by the National Association for the Education of Young Children. The grant was critically important, said college Child Development department head Linda Brees, because it helps child care workers who otherwise might not have been able to afford the process necessary to obtain the credential.

The second grant—$2,500—went to the Greenville YWCA to aid its Active Parenting program, which targets the problems faced by parents and child care workers in dealing with children of all ages.

The state government Interagency Committee for Early Childhood Development and Education chose Greenville's Child as a model program because it illustrated how a community could unite to attack a child-related issue.

"From the very beginning the foundation was concerned about insuring that there be measurable objectives in the program," Richmond says. "We encouraged and worked with the Greenville's Child staff and board to make sure as the project moves forward it will be able to identify such things as how many businesses have benefited in improved child care for their employees, how many parents have had access to the referral service, and what changes have been brought about in licensing and other standards."

Minor Shaw is president of the board of the foundation and a board member of Greenville's Child. A former president of the Greenville Junior League, she was very active in the planning process that preceded the development of Greenville's Child and the pursuit of the Ford Foundation grant. "I want to see Greenville's Child become more active in solving the problems of child care," she said. "If Greenville's Child were to document that we needed a low-income child care center in a certain area, then I'd like to see Greenville's Child pull together the people who could take care of that need, make the proposal and fund it.

"We also need to work on getting better known in the commu⸗ nity. It's not easy to gain the trust of all the child care providers. Some are nonprofit, some for-profit. You've got to try to get along with everybody."

Templeton, of the parent United Ministries agency, said Greenville's Child has "strengths and weaknesses. . . . It has taken a while to get a focus, and one of my frustrations is that I wish they could have gotten their focus a little earlier in the game. But it's a new baby, and it's going to take a while for it to figure out what it is to be a grown person."

Jack Cromartie, who succeeded Richmond as the Greenville foundation's executive director in October 1988, said the foundation has demonstrated its ability to unite disparate groups and agencies to ignite a major project. "We need more initiatives like Greenville's Child in the foundation field, and it's happening throughout the country—working with other foundations and corporations to bring about good things in the community. This gives this foundation a springboard to do other things here."

15

El Paso: The Expanding Philanthropic Pool

Bea Bragg

ASSET DEVELOPMENT THROUGH PERSONALIZED PHILANTHROPY

Attorney Richard Feuille is tall, slim and graying in a manner often described by ad merchants and novelists as "distinguished." He says a small prayer before every meeting, moving all his listeners, regardless of their religion or lack of it, to murmur a soft "amen" with his. Sincere, devoted to family and church, he regularly supports his alma mater and United Way, and has a family-named fund in the El Paso Community Foundation. But he is not without humor, as anyone can tell by watching his twinkling gray eyes—one of which droops slightly in a perpetual wink.

Feuille is one of the founders of the El Paso Community Foundation. A lifelong resident of El Paso, he equates the future well-being of his city with the future of the foundation and gives accordingly. He and his brothers and sisters have placed three separate family funds for general charitable purposes within the community foundation. He learned early how unrestricted giving could help meet the community's needs.

Darkly handsome Hector Holguin was also born and raised in El Paso, but his background is quite different from Feuille's. He became a top engineering student at the University of Texas at El Paso and highly proficient in the world

*of computers. Recently he sold one of his closely held local software companies
to a Fortune 500 international company, contributing a portion of the sale to
endow a large permanent family-named fund in the foundation. Holguin is
devoted to his family and his church, and contributes throughout the year not
only to his fund but over and above it to a variety of charities, all through
the foundation.*

As diverse as these two civic leaders are in their interests and
backgrounds, both heavily support the community foundation as their
personal philanthropy, regarding it as a legacy to their children and
to all the children of El Paso. Feuille, trustee and former president
of the board, feels he has a professional obligation as an estate and
tax lawyer to remind his clients of a moral obligation to leave something to the community. He jokes with his friends and associates that
there are no pockets in our shrouds.

Feuille practices what he preaches. In the midst of personal tragedy,
as in the recent death of his sister-in-law, he urges family members
to take time to name the El Paso Community Foundation in the obituary
to receive memorial contributions. In more tranquil times, he urges
his relatives, from in-laws to cousins, to match his year-end contributions.

In the beginning, Holguin weighed the advantages of forming a
private foundation over placing a family- and corporation-named fund
within the community foundation. As he saw the good the foundation could do, he placed a family-named fund for general charitable
purposes and one named for the Holguin Corporation within the foundation. Both funds are in excess of several hundred thousand dollars.

Janice Windle, executive director of the El Paso Community Foundation, believes that community foundations are particularly adaptable
to accommodating such diverse interests.

*Consuelo Fierro, a friend of the late Marie Brown, recalls the day in November
several years ago when the two of them received El Paso Community Foundation's Giving Catalog, a compilation of "wish lists" of nonprofit agencies published
annually. Wishes ranged from carpeting for the public library to medical supplies
for a maternity clinic to baseball bats for the Boys Club. The two friends examined
the catalog carefully and each made a decision on what she would contribute,
but Marie Brown made an additional decision. Profoundly touched by the catalog
and the opportunity for personal philanthropy that it represented, she willed
her entire estate to the foundation.*

Although this retired bookkeeper was attracted to the foundation
through the restricted form of giving the catalog represents, when

she died at 75, her modest estate of about $175,000, including her house, cash, and car, went to general charitable purposes.

The Giving Catalog exemplifies the overarching philosophy of personalized philanthropy that underscores every act, every project, of the El Paso Community Foundation. The catalog gives nonprofit agencies a chance to air their needs but, more important, it elevates the giving of the smallest of gifts by those of modest means to an act of pure philanthropy. And creating opportunities for everyone to become a philanthropist is the primary goal of board and staff.

"We have a mission to make philanthropy possible for everyone and to demonstrate the effectiveness of private sector giving in American society," Windle says. "Americans know the value of philanthropy, but do they know that they personally can be philanthropists?

"The very wealthy have their tax advisors to inform them, but it is up to community foundations to carry the message to those of more modest means."

In addition to its other uses, the Giving Catalog says to the public that the El Paso Community Foundation is an institution with a high profile as a generator and manager of endowment capital.

"Marketing" philanthropy includes, along with the catalog and other publications, the careful construction of the foundation's image as a responsible, but innovative, participatory and caring institution through the following:

1. Personal attention to donors' needs;
2. Emphasis on business and press relations;
3. Constant attention to community needs and demographics so as to determine the direction of projects and grants;
4. Special meetings, especially an annual meeting;
5. Encouraging responsible and creative leadership through board selection and training.

PERSONAL ATTENTION TO DONORS' NEEDS

John and Mary J. searched for a meaningful memorial for Mary's parents. They found it through El Paso Community Foundation's family-named funds program, with a beginning capital of $25,000. Later, they named another fund of $100,000 in memory of John's parents. Janice Windle carefully explained how they could create a charitable endowment fund bearing their family name and still have the income dedicated to general charitable purposes:

"I believe totally that donors should have the right, just as the donor of a private foundation has, to the personal satisfaction of giving back to their community," Windle says.

The success of this policy is indicated by the preponderance of family-named funds in the El Paso Community Foundation dedicated to general charitable purposes. What donors learn to appreciate most is that, by dedicating their gifts to general charitable purposes, their legacy will be shared throughout time no matter what changes occur in the community's charitable needs.

Mr. L. is a World War II refugee from Nazi Germany who came to this country absolutely penniless. Through hard work and the help of a social service agency that provided his basic needs until he could get a job, he gradually created opportunities for himself that led to personal wealth. He has found, through the foundation, the perfect answer to his desire to repay his adopted country. At first, he wanted to designate a specific number of agencies that he would name as beneficiaries in his will. The foundation staff arranged meetings with the directors of each. After about ten such meetings, he exclaimed, "Enough! I'm crazy about all of them. I need a general charitable purpose fund!"

"We find," Windle says, "that if a person is philanthropic generally, he or she is interested in all facets of community life, therefore a natural for a general charitable purpose fund."

While this sort of personalized philanthropy requires a lot of staff work and attention, it offers a large opportunity for asset growth. Other important rewards, Windle says, include the knowledge gained of population clusters. Two examples are prominent Hispanics and young professionals who lead a successful and financially comfortable life but who may not have the means to endow a private foundation.

Since the foundation was formed in 1977, its stake in the wider community of the two border cities, El Paso and Juarez, has been well understood. Affluent Hispanics on the U.S. side of the border have strong, sentimental, family ties to Juarez, and one of the first large-scale grants was awarded to Centros Maternos, a maternity clinic formed by volunteers in Juarez. Thus, they gained a favorable view of the community foundation and responded positively to board and staff efforts to interest them in American-style philanthropy. (The clinic has now been replicated throughout Mexico, thanks in part to the El Paso Community Foundation grants and guidance in seeking other grants from private and corporate foundations throughout the United States.)

Before she accepted a trusteeship on the foundation's board, Mary Carmen Saucedo was a member of the Federal Reserve Bank Board. She also had been a member of the foundation's Advisory Board of Trustees, an honorary group designed to enhance the credibility of the foundation, since her retirement as associate superintendent of El Paso Independent School District.

Because of her experience as an educator, the foundation called upon Saucedo to serve as an advisor to an environmental education project funded by the Ford Foundation, El Paso's Public Service Board, and Fred Hervey, a local philanthropist.

Hispanics now comprise well over two-thirds of El Paso's population. The figure is significant because it is estimated that 32 percent of all El Pasoans live under federal poverty guidelines. The poverty level for the Hispanics is far greater. While the city's planners cannot provide a precise figure, some have estimated as many as half.

When the foundation began its Hispanic family-named funds program in 1987, Saucedo could easily and confidently persuade other Hispanic families to join because she had satisfied herself that the foundation served Hispanics well.

"We are products of our parents who lived—and suffered—during the Mexican Revolution of 1917," she explains. "They lived from day to day because of the terrible uncertainties they endured. Planning for the future was a luxury they could not afford."

In the very first year, seven Hispanic family-named funds were established for general charitable purposes. Thirty-five more have been added. The foundation's goal is to have funds in the names of all the Hispanic civic leaders of El Paso.

One group, the Suntarians, is comprised of professional business people in the 28–45 age group. This association has been particularly aligned with the foundation in two projects related to downtown economic development. For example, Sunturians co-chaired with the foundation a successful fundraising drive to purchase the city's old Plaza Theater.

DISCOVERING COMMUNITY NEEDS

Marcia, 9, has a painful rash on her arms that worries her teacher. "I know her parents live in extreme poverty and speak very little English. They probably would not understand a note even if I sent it," she told the school health nurse.

Investigations by the City–County Department of Health revealed that Marcia and thousands like her live in Third World conditions on the edge of El Paso because they have no running water. In many cases, the water they haul to their homes is stored in barrels once containing carcinogenic chemicals, causing the rash. The situation was, in large part, brought on by land speculators who sold lots for homes—"the American dream," with the promise of "water soon"—to trusting refugees from crowded urban areas of both El Paso and Juarez.

El Paso is a sprawling, fast-growing city at least 250 miles from any city of its size. Its Hispanic character is spelled out by bilingual billboards before one reaches the city limits. It has other international characteristics. Neighboring Fort Bliss, with its huge air-defense school, brings in military students from all parts of the world. El Paso also attracts a growing population of retired people.

Across the Rio Grande in Mexico, Juarez is an international tourist attraction. About twice the size of El Paso, it is increasing its current population of 1 million at a dizzying pace.

A huge part of the Juarez population is plainly visible from the University of Texas at El Paso campus on the north side of the Rio Grande. There, Felipe Angeles, a Juarez *colonia* (suburban development) epitomizes Juarez' great problems—not enough water, not enough sewage facilities, not enough housing, not enough jobs. From the Mexican side of the border, life looks much better across the river in El Paso. Thus, illegal aliens cross the border into the city. They bring only the clothes they wear on their backs and calloused hands to work for the minimum wage or less so they can feed a hungry family. Others enter legally, eager for the American dream of economic success.

Growth has brought both violent changes and economic benefit. The biggest impetus to growth in Juarez, and to a large extent in El Paso, is the twin plant, *maquiladora*. Maquiladoras are known as twin plants because they typically include one or more plants in the United States to provide parts and a plant in Mexico that assembles them. Maquiladoras "are built in Mexico near the U.S. border, by multinational firms to take advantage of Mexico's cheap labor," according to the *El Paso Times*. Components (machinery parts), shipped mostly from the United States, are put together in the Mexican plant and returned. "Special tariff exemptions allow the manufacturer to pay duty only on the value added by the Mexican labor, not on the value of the components," the *Times* notes.

While some see only problems, others on both sides of the border see challenges. El Paso and Juarez have a long history of cooperation, exchange of culture, mutual assistance, and friendships, in addition to economic benefits.

The two cities have also shared revolutions, depressions, world wars, gold rushes, prostitution, and gunslingers. But that is all in the past. The primary challenge today is that the two cities share polluted air and a dwindling supply of water. *Colonias* springing up on all sides of Juarez are seriously contaminating what groundwater remains.

To actually obtain water and waste treatment plants for this vast area was clearly a task too great for a small community foundation with assets then (1986) of only $6.5 million. But when the Ford Foundation announced grants available to assist small community foundations, the challenge was irresistible.

Staff members quickly learned that the foundation could attack only one aspect of this mammoth environmental problem of contaminated water, polluted air, and in many areas, poor land use. Thus, their proposal to the Ford Foundation addressed the need for environmental education, with a strong element of individual responsibility for addressing the issues.

This project, "Living on the Desert: Conserving Our Natural Resources," was tailor-made for staff and board of the foundation. When the Ford Foundation awarded the grant, the mood in the community turned to optimism and provided a catalyst for dynamic changes. As a result, the El Paso Community Foundation was able to raise the required $1 million match in less than six months.

It was not raised by patiently waiting for a donor to make an offer. The first step was defining the project to one of El Paso's leading citizens, ex-mayor and wealthy developer of chain restaurants and convenience stores, Fred Hervey. Widely known as a citizen keenly interested in El Paso's water issues, he pledged $500,000 of the $1 million. The remaining half was raised by persuading new donors to establish general charitable purpose funds.

Research for the environmental education project meant enlarging the foundation's circle of relationships to embrace nearly all departments of local government and schools, including 12 West Texas school districts outside El Paso that spread over distances as great as 600 miles.

Steven E. Mayer, executive director of Rainbow Research, Inc., and evaluator of the project says, "This is a theme, more than an issue or a project. As a theme, it allows you to raise the consciousness of the community where they live, to teach them about 'place'—a subtext to 'community' that seldom gets explored. Every time you say 'Living on the Desert' to a roomful of El Pasoans, you add to their sense of interconnection. . . . "

The project is expected to rally all parts of El Paso, Fort Bliss, and Juarez into a cohesive whole that will support clean water and air for all, conserve the fragile desert, and protect El Paso's mountain wilderness that dips down into the very city limits.

Another large project the foundation accepted was the raising of funds to purchase a once splendid theater built in 1930 that was destined to make way for a parking lot. The planned demolition of the Plaza, with its twinkling stars, floating clouds, Spanish castles, fountains, and patios, made philanthropists of many El Pasoans. Elderly men and women on Social Security contributed $1 to $5; wealthy patrons of the arts, $50,0000 to $100,000. School children collected nickels and dimes. The required $1 million purchase price was raised in less than six weeks—this from the sixth poorest city of its size in the nation.

BUSINESS AND PRESS RELATIONS

This January morning, Barbara, 11, goes to school with a smile on her face and a tilt to her chin. During the Christmas holidays, El Paso Community Foundation made it possible for her to have a new dress, something she had never had before. It was a gift arranged through the foundation's Spirit of Giving program and carried out by the Melvin Simon shopping malls in El Paso.

Christmas trees decorating the malls had oversized, colorful tags in lieu of ornaments. On the backs of the tags were descriptions of individuals and their needs. For example, the tag for Barbara read: "Barbara, 11, has never had a new dress. Needs size 8, likes blue." The tag was coded to indicate the agency that had submitted the request to El Paso Community Foundation for Barbara. A shopper chose this tag, bought the dress, took it to a designated booth in the mall for wrapping and delivery to Barbara by the agency.

El Paso Community Foundation's relations with the shopping malls is based on the recognition that malls like nothing better than people flooding in. If a nonprofit group can persuade people to come to the malls and persuade them to buy things while they're there, then a good relationship is established.

Something resembling a cause-related marketing concept was designed by Muriel Hall, regional director of both Melvin Simon malls in El Paso, and foundation staff. Hall, an advisory trustee of the foundation, pointed out that between Thanksgiving and Christmas 800,000 to 1 million visits are made to each mall. Further, shopping malls throughout the year are social gathering places, especially for teenagers—the foundation's future philanthropists, as Windle sees it. Windle and Hall combined the agency's client needs and the malls' needs into the tag concept.

A similar close relationship exists with communications media. Charles Brumback, president of the Chicago *Tribune*, indicates in a report on media and philanthropy (June 2, 1987), that the press should establish as strong ties with nonprofits as it does with corporate America, inasmuch as this sector is responsible for 10 percent of all the jobs in the United States, owns 11 percent of all real estate, and spends $100 billion annually.

El Paso Community Foundation, for its part, took the initiative in creating strong ties with the media. Staff works hard to supply reliable information for reporters. The foundation's reputation for helpfulness has helped it gain many a story it might not have had otherwise.

A special opportunity for the media to understand what a community foundation is arose when the foundation assisted them in establishing a Press Club Fund devoted to raising money for journalism scholarships. Each year, their local Gridiron Show, spoofing the infrastructure of city and county government, brings in substantial new sums to their fund. After each show, El Paso Community Foundation invites the media to a party at which foundation trustees see a video of the spoof.

This cooperation between nonprofits and the media began many years ago when the Gannett Foundation, owner of the *El Paso Times*, gave one of its first grants to the El Paso Community Foundation. Other projects include broadcasts on KTSM-TV airing activities of agencies with funds in the foundation, and publication by the *El Paso Times* of the annual Giving Catalog.

MEETINGS TO MARKET: PERSONALIZED PHILANTHROPY

El Paso Community Foundation's highlight of the year is its annual luncheon meeting. It is a gala affair, personalized and dedicated to honoring its donors and to bringing them face to face with the agencies their funds support.

Never longer than an hour and a half and filled with dramatic vignettes of what donors have been able to do for recipients, the occasion attracts some 500 donors, grantees, and others interested in the foundation. The next day's papers have such front page headlines as "Foundation Gives Away $1 Million!" Major grants are often turned into feature stories for television and newspaper reports.

Small meetings are held year-round to carry out the philosophy of personalized philanthropy. After publication of the Giving Catalog each year, a donor reception is held in a private home. Donors include everyone from the reporters of KTSM-TV, who made a series of news features on foundation agencies, to people who contribute large sums.

Small conferences may be held for almost any purpose relating to foundation activities. Examples: an orientation session on how to use the special cards created for family fund donors, a conference for a group of accountants or stock brokers, a meeting of the advisory board of a supporting organization.

BOARD SELECTION

Cheryl McCown, who has served on nominating committees during her six-year term as trustee, says that trustees are selected to represent the wider community but that their commitment to philanthropy and to the foundation is even more important. The record of giving to the community foundation and attendance at foundation functions are also factored in by the nominating committee.

Since three-fourths of the 13 board members have their own family-named endowment funds in the foundation, this commitment is evident. The equally committed remainder contribute according to their incomes, from $25 a month to $1,000 a year. All recruit other donors, including the very first board members, all of whom are still active on the foundation's behalf. This may account for the unusually large percentage (about 98 percent) of living donors in this 12-year-old foundation as compared to older community foundations.

Dr. W. climbs into his station wagon hours before sunrise on this Wednesday morning. Today is just like last Wednesday was and like next Wednesday will be—his "day off." He is on his way to Dell City, an isolated desert village 120 miles east of El Paso. There he will tend to the medical needs of the elderly and the poor in a one-room clinic. Without El Paso Community Foundation, which responded to the clinic's urgent request for help to pay for utilities, rent, and medical supplies, his visits would not be possible.

"Although the medical clinic in a rural area is by no means a typical foundation grant recipient, the situation proved to us all that we could, if we tried, be creative about the intensely human and almost impossible problems that come to us," Windle says. "It also gave us a chance to become known in this vast West Texas area where, as our foundation grows, we may have an opportunity to relieve other aspects of rural poverty.

"If we don't grow into new programmatic and, yes, territorial areas, our philosophy of inclusiveness won't grow. I guess when we receive a contribution of *real* property, West Texas style, like a herd of longhorn cattle or an oil well, we will know we have succeeded."

16

Tacoma: Fundraising from Board Roots

Marion Woyvodich

Tacoma, the third-largest city in Washington State, has a population of 160,000. It is the hub of Pierce County, where over a half-million people reside in an area rich in nature's abundance. To the west is Puget Sound, whose deep natural waterways have long been a lure to the shipping industry and recently more of an attraction to traders from the Pacific Rim. To the east is 14,000-foot Mount Rainier, one of the nation's tallest peaks and a popular playground for hikers, climbers, skiers, campers, and other lovers of the outdoors.

Farmlands and pastoral settings still blanket much of the valley between the mountain and the sea, and lush green forests carpet much of the surrounding land, a credit to the century-old timber industry that is at the heart of the region's wealth.

Despite its natural blessings and recent efforts at revitalization, Tacoma is plagued by a poor public image. Popular Tacoma newspaper-columnist Denny MacGougan describes the city as "a little like a beautiful woman who is accident prone." Others are quick to add insults to her injuries. In a 1988 livability study conducted by a local university, residents described their city as "industrial and smelly," in large part because of the air pollution and industrial odors that permeate port/industrial properties in the heart of town.

In an assessment of community needs, United Way found that there are more street kids per capita in Tacoma than in Seattle, a city triple its size. Pierce County has 30 times more refugees, primarily of Asian descent, than neighboring King County, the home of Seattle. Nearly all efforts to administer services to Asians, Hispanics, and other minority groups are hampered by language barriers.

Like all populated areas, Pierce County has its hungry and homeless, its mentally ill, its street gangs and drug dealers, its prostitutes and pimps. It also has dwindling public funds and limited private resources to cope with the welfare challenges posed by such a complex mix.

Seeking to address some of these needs, a small group formed the Greater Tacoma Community Foundation in 1977 to serve all of Pierce County. The foundation took an uncommon route by building a $600,000 endowment to cover administration costs before building a grantmaking endowment. The administrative endowment yields enough to cover 40 percent of the foundation's annual operating expenses, ensuring a solid base from which it can carry out its work.

Today, the foundation is one of the fastest-growing community foundations in the country. It began full-time operation in 1981 with meager assets, and by the end of its eighth year had assets of over $7 million.

The work began in the fall of 1976, when three local citizens joined forces to create a community foundation to respond to the community's needs. They were Arleigh Jones, vice-president and trust officer for the Tacoma branch of Seattle First National Bank; Byron Johnson, a self-employed entrepreneur; and Lawrence Ross, an attorney. The three founders enlisted five other men and a woman to join them on the original board of trustees.

The trustees met infrequently during the next three years, "going in fits and starts," according to Ross. "We knew we had a good idea, but you have to appreciate that in reality, once we were founded, it took time to get people interested and to enlist community support."

Trustees also were taking their time to find just the right executive director. They wanted someone "mature and qualified, who was not looking to make a pile of money because we couldn't afford to pay much," Jones recalls.

Early in 1981, Jones met Paul Bender, a man he describes as "very caring, hard-working, and very dedicated to whatever he took on." Bender was a veteran of 24 years of military service and had retired from the Army nearly 20 years earlier. He had served in several executive and management positions in Washington, D.C., and in 1972 was appointed secretary of the Atomic Energy Commission. It was in that job Bender worked with Dixy Lee Ray, who headed the federal agency.

When Ray made a successful bid for governor of Washington State in 1976, she appointed Bender her chief of staff. Four years later, Governor Ray was upset by a Democratic challenger in the statewide primary election, and Bender, like many others, was out of a job.

Tacoma foundation trustees offered Bender the position of part-time executive director. "He had the right background, was well-known and qualified, had a good reputation and lots of goodwill," Jones recalls. When Bender took the job in June 1981, foundation assets totaled only $10,000. Soon thereafter, the Ben B. Cheney Foundation, a local private foundation, gave its commitment to provide first-year administrative funds of $36,000.

Bender and the foundation trustees quickly established their goals. They wanted to make sure the foundation was well received by other nonprofit groups and not seen as a competitor for the limited number of donor dollars. Their strategy was to have the foundation establish its role in the community by taking on significant projects that would cast it in a positive light.

The first opportunity to do so came in the recession of 1982, when the foundation helped to create an Emergency Food Network. Pierce County unemployment stood at 14 percent, and existing social welfare providers were having difficulty meeting the increased demand for food and services triggered by a weakening economy. The foundation convened those providers, representatives of the Rescue Mission, the Salvation Army, and FISH Food Banks, named after the Christian fish symbol. They gathered to devise a method for responding to what all parties felt would be a short-term crisis.

Since the foundation already was set up to collect donations and to administer programs, the parties decided it made good sense for it to serve as the focal point rather than create a whole new nonprofit organization devoted to feeding the hungry. Thus, under the auspices of the Emergency Food Network, the foundation solicited donations of food and accepted pass-through funds.

As the ranks of the hungry and homeless continued to grow, what all providers expected to be a short-term crisis turned out to be a long-term set of circumstances that the Emergency Food Network continued to meet. In 1988, more than $900,000 in cash, food, and in-kind donations were collected, enabling the network to distribute food for 3.5 million meals.

At about the same time the food network began, the foundation started using pass-through monies from anonymous donors to support the Dropout Education Project. Under the project a nontraditional school offered street kids remedial instruction and personal counseling so they could return to the public schools or compete more effectively for employment. The project operated through a state contract for three years.

In the meantime, the foundation's fundraising efforts were under way but yielding only meager response. By the end of its second fiscal year, in May 1983, assets totaled $171,700, and a year later reached $226,000. Permanent endowment assets held steady both years at $24,000.

Pending the development of its own funds to support a grant program, the foundation continued to use pass-through monies. It also decided to seek a grant from the Charles Stewart Mott Foundation under its Community Foundation Technical Assistance Program. The program was established to assist the development of new and emerging or revitalizing foundations.

After selecting Tacoma as a recipient for its help in 1983, the Mott Foundation sent consultant Eugene Struckhoff to advise on asset development.

Struckhoff met with the foundation's board of trustees to define challenges and identify opportunities for raising funds. Major goals were to bolster administrative and unrestricted endowments.

"We were all very much aware of the need to raise administrative funds," Bender recalls. "If we were forever saddled with raising money for administration, we would never have the base we needed to go out and solicit unrestricted funds. A continuing plea for administrative funds is just not a very good sales pitch for when you go back and ask for unrestricted endowments."

Struckhoff suggested that the foundation seek a challenge grant from another foundation, corporation, or individual to get a large-scale fundraising effort under way. Challenge grants usually were successful, he said, because they gave foundation board members courage and incentive to raise funds and donors an incentive to give because the challenge device stretches their dollars.

Finding a challenger was itself quite a challenge. Though there were pockets of individual wealth in Pierce County, the per capita income in the mid-1980s was less than $11,000. Of the 20 private foundations and trusts that served the county, only four made annual contributions of more than $500,000, and those grants were heavily counted on to meet an already demanding list of social needs.

While Struckhoff and foundation trustees explored their options, Frank Underwood, a private foundation consultant, approached them to discuss what the local donor community could do to help out. Underwood, who had just started Grantmaker Consultants and represented three private foundations, was aware of the fact that only a few grantmakers made substantial contributions to the community. He felt another strong player was needed "to add stability to the grantmaking pool and hold all of us more accountable for responsible grantmaking."

When Underwood learned that the board was examining the challenge grant concept, he discussed it with the board of trustees of the Forest Foundation, one of his clients, for whom he served as executive director.

C. D. Weyerhaeuser, an heir to the timber company's fortune, had formed the Forest Foundation in 1961, naming it in recognition of the source of the family's great wealth. Several Weyerhaeuser family members served on the Forest Foundation board of trustees. "They are not flamboyant people and don't need or seek recognition," Underwood says. "They prefer to do quiet philanthropy."

Underwood's suggestion that they issue a challenge grant to get the community foundation on its way was well received by the Forest Foundation trustees. "They understood the need," Underwood says. "They saw it as an all-or-nothing situation. They felt that the sum they would put up would be sufficient to move the community foundation forward or lead to the conclusion that the timing wasn't right for the community foundation to get off the ground."

Underwood returned to the Tacoma foundation board to issue a challenge on behalf of the Forest Foundation, which preferred to remain anonymous to all parties concerned.

"Up until then, I perceived the community foundation board was kind of sitting back and waiting for things to happen, instead of going after them," Underwood recalls. "It's as if they didn't know exactly where to begin. They didn't have a lot of passion. The challenge grant awakened that passion in them."

Linda BeMiller, currently program officer for Grantmaking Consultants, for nine months in 1983 had worked as director of development for the Greater Tacoma Community Foundation. Because she knew first-hand of the struggles the community foundation had faced in trying to raise administrative funds, Underwood turned to her to draw up conditions of the challenge grant.

Under those terms, the board was required first to raise money for its administrative endowment from among its own members. The Forest Foundation said it would match on a dollar-per-dollar basis what they raised up to $250,000. Monies raised beyond that point would be matched on a 25 percent basis up to a maximum gift of $290,000.

Before the grant would be paid, however, the board was required to raise funds from the community at large to establish an unrestricted endowment. Contributions from the community had to at least double the Forest Foundation's matching money. "The donor did not expect to support the foundation for all time but to make it possible for them to be in a rather healthy position on which to build," BeMiller said. "The donor felt that if the board itself could not get motivated through a challenge grant, how could we expect the community to get motivated to give?"

The challenge to make pledges was issued to Tacoma foundation board members on November 7, 1983. They had until December 31— seven short weeks—to make good on their intentions, though pledges could be paid off in annual increments over three years. Community fundraising for pledges for the unrestricted endowment had to be concluded by the end of 1984.

Tacoma's actions were unusual for two reasons, Struckhoff said. Few community foundations choose to ask living donors for monies to fund administrative endowments. Living donors typically prefer that their donations go directly to charitable causes. "To convince donors otherwise is truly a hard sell because few individuals are far-sighted enough to realize that a community foundation needs to be able to show it can exist in perpetuity in order to raise grantmaking endowments for the community's good," he says. It also was uncommon for a board to mount such a financially ambitious campaign, seeking between five- and seven-figure sums from a number of donors as opposed to soliciting a single benefactor or "angel," Struckhoff says.

"To start from scratch, without an angel, is very difficult. I don't know that it had ever been done before in a direct campaign."

George Davis, an architect, entrepreneur, and arts patron who chaired the board's fundraising efforts, said he took "a very autocratic" approach when the time came to solicit his peers.

He had known many of the members of the board, which by now had expanded to 12 men and three women, for years. He knew much about their livelihoods and financial positions. After considering each one, he wrote down a figure he felt each would be able to donate and put each person's figure in a sealed envelope. He then took the whole group out to lunch.

"I knew them all very well so I apologized for my method, but I felt it would work," Davis recall. "I handed each person their envelope and instructed them to open it. I felt that if everyone saw that everyone got an envelope and was being asked to donate, there would be an acknowledgment of our shared responsibilities and that all of us would be involved.

"I felt it would be good for me, as the chairman, to see that everyone got their envelope, opened it and read it. I also wanted to see the reactions on their faces when they did."

Davis's unorthodox style yielded substantial results. Three of the board members accounted for pledges of $225,000. With only one exception, each individual gave at least the amount Davis suggested in his or her personalized notes within the allotted time frame. Total pledges hit $330,000, qualifying the foundation for a matching grant of $270,000.

Before the Forest Foundation would match that sum, the board had to raise double the amount—or $540,000—from the community for the unrestricted endowment. The Forest Foundation gave the Tacoma foundation a $5,000 grant to hire a fundraising consultant to develop a campaign. They settled on a "select prospect" approach, choosing to solicit individuals capable of contributing $10,000 or more.

Bender recalls that the board was particularly well equipped to raise the additional $540,000 for the unrestricted endowment. "They were people of affluence who had the potential of giving large sums of money themselves and going out and finding others of affluence who could give large sums of money, too."

Among the board members was the head of the major local bank and individuals who had made millions in business, real estate, and other ventures. They represented old money in the form of timber interests, and new money in the form of an international pension investment company. Former Governor Dixy Lee Ray, a feisty and colorful politician, also served on the board. Though not as wealthy as other board members, she had been connected over the years to many individuals who were.

Board members approached their work "with wild anticipation, but also with some concern," Davis recalls.

"Fundraising in Tacoma has always been difficult because there are fewer dollars concentrated among fewer people than there are in bigger cities, so the same few people are always being asked to give. Also, the leadership has never been the same, and only a few leaders have the stature to persuade those of great wealth that it's their responsibility to give for the benefit of those who have not," Davis said.

At least two foundation representatives made each solicitation call. Usually it was one board member who was accompanied by Bender or Margy McGroarty, the foundation's associate director, who had joined the staff in September 1983. Along with a sales pitch, each prospect received a packet of information that explained the community foundation concept and urged donor involvement. Follow-up visits were made by board members, either in person or by phone because, "People give to people," McGroarty says.

Even so, just before the end-of-1984 deadline, fundraising was lagging and threatening to fall short.

"As salesmen, the board members were having a tough time closing," Bender recalls. "They sometimes were allowing themselves to be put off by potential donors."

A quick visit from Struckhoff turned things around. Bender says Struckhoff really "laid into" the board, but Struckhoff says he was only offering them some "strong words of encouragement" at the time. He recalls telling them: " You've got to get out there and do this. You have an excellent opportunity that you can't afford to lose."

Struckhoff's words apparently set up the big win. A total of $659,700 in community pledges for the unrestricted endowment was obtained by the end of 1984, exceeding the $540,000 requirement by nearly $120,000. Most of the 28 people who gave donated at the $5,000 level, for a combined sum of $354,800; eight corporations contributed a total of $81,000; nine foundations, including the community foundation of nearby Seattle, made gifts totaling $83,900; the Junior League of Tacoma donated $25,000 toward the effort; and ten banks contributed another $84,000.

By mid–1985, the assets of the Greater Tacoma Community Foundation had risen nearly six-fold in just one year, to a total of $1.4 million.

It appeared that Eugene Struckhoff's "take-off" strategy was indeed taking off. It continued to soar when Puget Sound National Bank in 1984 petitioned Pierce County Superior Court to appoint the foundation successor trustee to 11 charitable trusts totaling $1.2 million. The trusts were transferred to the foundation early in 1985.

John Cunningham, Puget Sound National Bank trust officer, says the action was a good thing for all concerned. "The bank was aware that the community foundation was trying to get off the ground, and we thought it was a good time to help them out. And it was a two-way street. Besides increasing the foundation's assets, the move reduced each trust's service fees and trimmed the number of tiny trusts the bank had to administer."

Moving into its fifth year in 1986, the foundation had an opportunity to increase its assets once again. The Northwest Area Foundation gave the foundation $25,000 and proposed to match dollar-for-dollar another $25,000 to establish an unrestricted revolving loan fund to meet the emergency needs of nonprofit organizations. The challenge was similar to one issued by the Northwest Area Foundation in several other communities. Under the terms of the challenge, the Tacoma foundation had one year to raise the funds; $25,000 was raised from 26 donors, and an emergency fund of $75,000 was established. "The appeal for emergency funds really struck a chord with a different set of donors," McGroarty recalled. "They were people who were able to give because the foundation wasn't asking for large amounts."

Nonetheless, Tacoma/Pierce County United Way donated $20,000 to the effort. In making the gift, United Way Board President David Scholes, said: "It represents an opportunity for United Way to form a unique partnership with the community foundation. The $75,000 will really help nonprofit organizations deal with emergencies."

Among the beneficiaries was the Hilltop Day Care Center, which received a $9,300 loan to cover employee payroll and payroll taxes for one year, and the Pierce County AIDS Foundation, which received $10,000 in seed money.

As the foundation's unrestricted endowment fund began to produce income, a grantmaking program was established. The foundation also decided to sponsor for three years an Excellence in Education Award program to honor Tacoma educators and schools for outstanding performance.

By mid–1986, assets had nearly doubled, to $2.7 million. The foundation then began to flex its programing muscles. It funded a study to determine how a revitalizing Tacoma/Pierce County could organize its resources to benefit from major trade shows, conventions, and concerts lured to town by the newly constructed 25,000-seat Tacoma Dome and Convention Center.

At the same time, the foundation purchased remainder interest in Lakewold, a ten-acre estate and gardens on beautiful Gravelly Lake, in order to preserve this private resource for public use. The Friends of Lakewold, a nonprofit corporation, was created as a supporting organization of the foundation to hold Lakewold's real property and manage the estate as a public garden. By mid–1988, the foundation had received over $1 million in cash and pledges in an endowment fund campaign for the Lakewold estate and gardens.

In 1987 the foundation received its largest single gift: $1.4 million, which established the Baker Family Fund, an unrestricted endowment. The Bakers, a longtime Tacoma family, had disposed of their newspaper and communications industry holdings in a sale rumored to be in excess of $200 million. Elbert Baker II, the *Tacoma News Tribune* publisher and one-time trustee of the Greater Tacoma Community Foundation, was 76 years old and the youngest of three heirs when the properties were sold. He joined with his two daughters in deciding to make the gift to the foundation.

"We were all very pleased with what the foundation was trying to do and felt it was the best place to put our charitable dollars," Baker said.

Struckhoff, the dean of advisors to community foundations nationally, said working with the Tacoma foundation taught him some new techniques that have proved useful in helping other foundations develop their assets in the years since.

"I learned it is possible to raise an operating endowment from the beginning," Struckhoff said. "Tacoma proved it. It's important to have such a model, and I've used it several times since with board members in other communities who believe strongly in their foundation and want to give it strong leadership. I believe we'll see this approach become more commonplace and be included as part of the fundraising strategy that future community foundations use."

17

Sonoma: Visibility Through Action

Wendy Ellyn

THE CHALLENGE

In March 1987 the fledgling Sonoma County Foundation had just $350,000 in assets, no grantmaking program, and zero visibility. Executive director Virginia Hubbell and a half-time secretary worked out of a donated office in downtown Santa Rosa, California. The foundation's goal was to build a $5-million endowment by 1992.

To establish the foundation's identity in the community and to build credibility among both grantseekers and prospective donors, Hubbell, who had been hired six months earlier, asked her board of trustees to sponsor and operate a project to address a key community need. Developing such a project, Hubbell told her board, would help to demonstrate the foundation's strengths as a catalyst for problem-solving and a convenor of community resources. That, in turn, would help it raise funds.

For the most part, the board was enthusiastic about the idea. However, some trustees feared that, by operating a project, the foundation would alienate local agencies. To avoid setting itself up as a competitor for precious community funds, the board decided that the foundation should tap new funding sources to initiate a project, and should involve existing community agencies in the project's ownership and long-term operation.

With these goals in mind, the board directed its needs committee to identify an appropriate project targeted at youth-related issues. Discussions with local educators and social service agency directors helped the committee determine that the most effective strategy in preventing a broad range of problems among young people in Sonoma County would be a project focused on family support and parent education.

By December 1988, a Parent Education Project had accomplished all of the foundation's goals and more. Sonoma County Foundation had increased its assets to $1.1 million, including nearly $210,000 in contributions to help fund the project. Publicity spawned by the project had catapulted the foundation into the public eye and generated cooperation and recognition from local businesses and social service agencies. The project had demonstrated that the foundation could produce tangible, positive results on a key community issue.

"We succeeded in identifying a real community need, bringing together a diverse group of organizations and community resources to help solve it, and pulling in new sources of funding from outside the county," Hubbell said. "Now we're working to spin the project off to the community. Through this project, we've given the community one concrete answer to the question, 'What *is* this thing called a community foundation?' "

THE PARENT EDUCATION PROJECT

Perhaps the most distinctive element of the project was that it gave businesses the opportunity to offer family education to their employees by bringing trained parent educators directly into the workplace. The parent educators presented one-hour classes for working parents during lunch or shift breaks, once a week for four to six weeks. Classes covered such topics as balancing work and family life, improving communication, building self-esteem for parents and children, instilling responsibility in children, and family problem-solving.

Both male and female employees from all levels attended: managers, engineers, clerical staff, production workers. Classes were offered free to employees, but at several sites parents were so appreciative that they contributed up to $25 each for the course. At some work sites, classes were held entirely on the employee's own time; at others, classes were split over paid and non-paid time. By the end of its pilot year, the Parent Education Project had served nearly 400 parents and provided about 1,000 additional employees with a list of nonprofit agencies that help families. Numerous community agencies and the Sonoma County Board of Education distributed copies of the list to interested parents and community leaders.

One mother said that the classes helped her to share child-rearing experiences and feel more solidarity with co-workers, while learning to communicate more effectively. Another said she learned "what our parents perhaps didn't realize—that self-esteem is the most important thing to teach our children."

The project also received high marks from employers:

"Family disorder is the number one problem that interferes with work," said Jeanne Ganas, vice-president of human resources at Sonoma County Medical Association, where most employees work as claims processors. "Projects like this help us chip away at long-standing turnover dilemma. The work climate improves when employees know management is not oblivious to their lives away from this place."

Seven mid-sized and large employers in the county's four largest communities participated during the project's first year. Pilot programs were held at Sonoma County Medical Association, Santa Rosa Memorial Hospital, and Hewlett-Packard, all in Santa Rosa; and at Sonoma Developmental Center, a state hospital in Sonoma. A second round of classes was given at the medical association and IMCO Realty Services in Santa Rosa, Sola Optical in Petaluma, and Hewlett-Packard in Rohnert Park.

The project's success encouraged the foundation to expand it to other locations. A $5,000 grant from Pacific Bell enabled the foundation to develop a pilot work-site program to reach monolingual Spanish-speaking parents, a growing part of Sonoma County's population. In addition, the foundation received a $180,000 grant from the James Irvine Foundation for expansion and for training staff of local agencies to teach parenting skills.

The project also became the springboard for the foundation's involvement in other efforts to promote the health of families. Public televison Channel 22 asked the foundation to convene a forum of business leaders to participate in a national teleconference on employers and child care; 11 major Sonoma County employers participated. Findings from this forum were presented by the foundation at a regional conference for child care providers at Sonoma State University. This group continued meeting to discuss child care issues, and along with the foundation, co-sponsored a day-long symposium on child care options that was attended by more than 100 local executives and human resource managers. It was the first such gathering of business leaders devoted to child care issues in the county.

WHY PARENT EDUCATION?

Parent education in Sonoma County has a long history. However, accessible, large-scale parent training in the workplace is new.

Since the mid-1970s, parenting classes and support groups in Sonoma County have been offered, primarily through three agencies. Together, they served about 3,000 families in 1988—3 percent of the nearly 100,000 families in the county.

These agencies have been the most successful providers of parent education. Other groups, including churches, nonprofits, and public agencies, offer education and support for families; however, their classes are often underfunded, access is often difficult for parents, and attendance fluctuates greatly.

In recent years, decreased government funds for health and human services, and rapid, heterogeneous population growth have swelled the need for additional efforts to help families in Sonoma County.

The county covers some 1,600 square miles; Santa Rosa, population 109,000, is its major city and its financial center. Since 1980, the county's population has grown by about 20 percent to nearly 350,000. Most growth has occurred in Santa Rosa, Petaluma, and Rohnert Park, which form a metropolitan corridor along Highway 101, the main route from San Francisco, 50 miles to the south.

Private sector employment has shifted dramatically in the last decade, from a predominantly agricultural economy to one dominated by service, retail, and manufacturing. Newcomers include workers relocating to take advantage of the area's boom in these industries, immigrants seeking seasonal agricultural work, and new families seeking alternatives to skyrocketing housing costs in the Bay Area counties of Marin, Alameda, and San Francisco. Often both parents work. Many commute to work from new bedroom communities that lack well-established neighborhoods, many are single parents, and many do not live near extended families.

Through the workplace-based program, Sonoma County Foundation was able to bring together the business and social service communities to provide a much-needed addition to existing family support services. By integrating the Parent Education Project into a variety of sizes and types of businesses, the foundation offered parent education to a cross section of the community not typically served by existing agencies. Because the classes were offered free and at times convenient for working parents, they attracted many parents who might not spend time or money to improve their parenting skills: parents in two-worker families, single parents, and low-income parents.

THE FOUNDATION'S ADVANTAGE

Previous attempts at workplace-based parent education had faltered for several reasons. Corporations were reluctant to endorse one parenting philosophy to employees above all others. In some cases, agencies failed to tailor programs to the company's circumstances. The Sonoma County Foundation project succeeded largely because of such advantages as the support and direct involvement of the foundation's board of directors, an executive director skilled at fundraising and project development, a project coordinator, and the foundation's standing as a neutral agency.

The foundation was launched in 1983 by community and business leaders who were concerned about the shortage of government funding for human services. By 1986, the trustees decided that the Sonoma County Foundation could become truly effective only under the guidance of a full-time executive director. After several unsuccessful attempts to secure grants, the trustees donated money to pay a director's salary for one year.

Today, the foundation has a 20-member board that includes prominent business owners and managers, bankers, educators, and attorneys. President of the board, Jean Forsyth Schulz, is a director of several local nonprofit organizations (see page 109); several trustees are leaders in local educational, volunteer, and political organizations. Executive director Hubbell is experienced in fundraising and nonprofit management, having worked for many years as a consultant to corporations, nonprofits, and foundations.

The board's support was critical in getting the Parent Education Project under way. Several board members worked to involve local businesses. Two board members donated a total of $15,000 for the project. These funds, plus $15,000 from McKesson, allowed the foundation to hire a part-time project coordinator, Janet Bankovich. A former program associate in urban affairs at the San Francisco Foundation, Bankovich worked as a liaison between social service leaders, the foundation, and business.

In addition, the foundation's position as a neutral agency helped it convene a diverse group of community leaders to design the project. The foundation invited several agency leaders to sit on a nine-member advisory board with foundation trustees and a representative of the business community. Several were from social service agencies that compete for funding.

"This group had the potential to be especially political and partisan," said Phyllis Kirk, an advisory board member and founder of a parent support group in Sonoma. "But Virginia and Janet prevented that by keeping us focused. They galvanized everyone around a common goal."

While the foundation's board members originally feared that taking an operating role would alienate the very agencies the foundation hoped to work with, the opposite proved true. The foundation received only one complaint challenging its operating role. As the project grew, agency leaders came to view the foundation as an effective, dedicated ally in the human service community.

Some leaders likely believed that their participation in the Parent Education Project would ensure favorable consideration should their agency ever apply for a foundation grant. But there was more at work here than self-interest. The foundation was in a position to pave the way for a new alliance between the business and social service communities, and many leaders recognized that.

"I appreciated that the foundation went after sanction and funding from the business community, which has not traditionally been a resource for supporting families," said Marjorie Helm, a member of the advisory board and division manager of youth services for Sonoma County Mental Health. Others understood that the foundation was able to do what a single agency could not: raise significant funds to support parent education, and secure grants from foundations that had never before funded in Sonoma County.

HOW THE PROJECT GREW

The advisory board reviewed a number of other parent education models from around the country, but ultimately designed a hybrid version that made use of qualified local parent educators and fit the needs of Sonoma County businesses.

Hubbell and Louise Levinger, a foundation trustee and advisory board member, invited a variety of businesses of different sizes, types, and locations to discuss the project. A handful said the project wouldn't work for them, either because of their shift schedules or because of small staff size. Several nonunionized companies also voiced concerns that the classes not become a forum for organizing. But a majority expressed interest. These meetings gave businesses a sense of involvement and responsibility for the project.

The business meetings led Bankovich to design a sheet of guidelines, advising managers to schedule the classes in the same room, on the same day of the week, and at the same time each day; to obtain approval from mid-level managers for each department; and to publicize the classes well in advance. She also created publicity materials and met with managers at their sites to discuss logistics.

"The foundation respected that we're running a business, and that our primary purpose is to make a profit," said Mike Ronstadt, manager of training and health services at Hewlett-Packard in Santa Rosa. "Janet made it very clear that the foundation was willing to work within our structure—to use our methods of publicizing events, and to make sure the classes fit in with our work schedules."

Through a bidding process, two Sonoma County parent educators were selected to conduct pilot programs over two months: Summerfield Counseling and Peter Krohn. Both work according to a similar model, which teaches parents to promote self-esteem and to encourage children's responsible behavior not through rewards and punishments, but through helping children to recognize the consequences of their actions. Summerfield's trainers featured more class involvement and role-playing; Krohn, more lecture and discussion.

The pilot sites included a variety of businesses. Hewlett-Packard, an electronics firm, had about 2,200 employees. Sonoma County Medical Association, a claims-processing business, had 200, mostly women in their 20s. Santa Rosa Memorial Hospital had 1,100; Sonoma Developmental Center, a state hospital for the developmentally disabled, 1,300, including many single parents of below-average income.

RESULTS

Pilot classes were well attended at Hewlett-Packard and the medical association. However, only two classes were held at Santa Rosa Memorial Hospital, largely because the hospital was in the midst of staff layoffs, and because it became difficult to find one room to use regularly for classes. At Sonoma Developmental Center, flyers and other publicity materials were not ready far enough in advance to reach a significant number of employees. For this reason, and because approvals were not secured from many mid-level managers, only about 15 employees attended each of four sessions.

Nevertheless, evaluations of the classes from those who did attend were very positive. Many parents reported immediate results at home, and said the techniques and insights they gained helped them arrive at work feeling less stressed. Parents were willing to offer constructive feedback as well. At one site, though, some parents found the wide-open nature of the discussion sessions intimidating, and suggested that class leaders ask for anonymous written suggestions of topics or problems for discussion. Others suggested that workshops feature longer classes or more class meetings as well as classes tailored to parents of specific age groups. Many parents requested ongoing support groups once the classes ended.

In January 1988, the foundation's board agreed to fund the project for an additional year, and directed Hubbell and Bankovich to begin searching for funding. Work began on a second round of classes at four firms.

MOVING BEYOND THE WORKPLACE

In addition to parent education classes in the workplace, the foundation also hoped to foster the emergence of parent leaders to link with other groups, empower parents to lead support groups, and spread parent education to other sites.

After working with leaders in the nonprofit community, including a committee of leaders of agencies that serve Hispanics, Hubbell and Bankovich wrote a comprehensive proposal for expanding the program. The foundation received a $180,000 grant from the James Irvine Foundation. Tom David, grant officer at the Irvine Foundation, said the foundation's proposal was funded because it "demonstrates a foundation's community collaboration, capacity building and convening functions, addresses children's issues, includes services for parents of color, and meets needs outside a major metropolitan area—all of which are high priorities of the Irvine Foundation."

The project will expand along "train the trainers" lines. Three groups in the parent training field will train staff from health and human service agencies to teach parent education classes and to lead parent support groups. To sensitize these parent educators to the special needs and styles of the populations being served, a parent or individual from each group will be paired with the parent educator.

The ambitious program will serve Hispanics, Southeast Asian refugees, Eritrean and Ethiopian refugees, Native Americans, and blacks; teachers and staff of public and nonprofit organizations that serve children, librarians who work with latch-key children; and such special groups as adoptive parents, homeless parents, parents who are prisoners or in half-way houses, parents involved in the Greater Avenues to Independence (GAIN) and Aid to Families with Dependent Children (AFDC) programs, abusive parents, parents who were abused as children, parents of dropouts, teen parents, and parents of teen parents.

In the meantime, the foundation is strengthening the workplace-based program. It hopes to create a marketing package to expand the number of employers reached, and to train parents who have participated to lead independent workplace-based parent support groups.

BUILDING A COALITION FOR THE FUTURE

Sonoma County Foundation would not operate the worksite project indefinitely, even if more funds and staff were available. The foundation's intent was to strengthen existing programs and agencies by initiating a project that these agencies felt was important, and in which they could participate jointly.

"Our board was naturally quite pleased that the foundation's role as advocate and umbrella was seen as the key to this project," says board president Jean Schulz. "But this project does not only belong to the foundation. From the beginning, we made it a priority to involve diverse agencies, and to make this a genuinely cooperative endeavor."

Thus, the foundation is in the process of handing the project over to an advisory board comprised of agency and community leaders who will direct it long after the foundation's initial financial commitment ends. Foundation trustees have not guaranteed full financial support or administrative assistance, but they may consider making limited grants to the project. Most future funding is expected to come from such sources as fees for services and grants from foundations, businesses, the county, and other agencies.

According to Hubbell and Bankovich, initial discussions indicate that creating this advisory board may be more diffiicult—and political—than the foundation envisioned. The foundation's success at gaining grants for the project has proved to be a double-edged sword: while it ensures funds for the project's expansion, it also attracts some agencies that may be less interested in promoting parent education than in associating with the foundation in the hope that some of its prestige—and funding—will rub off on them.

Whether agency leaders can work together effectively over the long run is another concern. Organizations in the social service community are fierce competitors for precarious public and private funding. While many agency leaders were able to put their differences aside to work on the Parent Education Project, cooperating on a long-term program without the foundation's neutralizing leadership may prove

more difficult. To overcome such obstacles the foundation is working to create a broader based advisory board and three subcommittees,
which will determine the fate of the Parent Education Project.

Whatever the project's future may be, it has had positive and
widespread results. Hundreds of parents have been helped to see
themselves and their children in a new, more positive light. To businesses and the county at large, the project publicized the need to
support parents in the task of raising the next generation. It helped
forge new alliances between businesses and social service agencies.
And, in a short time, it demonstrated the practical role a community foundation can play in tackling a critical community problem
and in attracting new and otherwise unavailable funds to the community.

In Hubbell's words, " Yes, this program was controversial, and yes,
it took a lot of daring and hard work. But it brought home an important
fact to a lot of people—that community foundations are different, and
can dream as big as they want to dream."

18

Atlanta: Teaching Someone How to Fish

Martin C. Lehfeldt

An oft-cited proverb notes that if people are hungry, you can help them in one of two ways: either you can feed them fish or you can teach them how to fish. The Metropolitan Atlanta Community Foundation, in keeping with its philanthropic mission, continues to give away "fish," but for the past several years, it has also been offering instruction and encouragement.

It all started in 1984, when a study by the Urban Institute identified 578 not-for-profit organizations in the 19-county metropolitan Atlanta area—and that figure excluded hospitals and institutions of higher education, of which there are many. The Atlanta foundation's own mailing list held about 900 names of nonprofits, including the branches and chapters of parent organizations. It all added up to a lot of people looking for private contributions and volunteer assistance.

Atlanta is not a poor town, and its citizens do give to a wide variety of institutions and causes. However, with the notable exception of personal generosity by Coca-Cola magnates Robert and George Woodruff, the giving of her citizens has never been characterized by nationally pacesetting contribution standards or multi-generation traditions of philanthropy.

How then, would the growing numbers of nonprofits in metropolitan Atlanta survive? By the mid-1980s, the situation was exacerbated by the shrinking amount of public dollars available for the arts, education, and social services. The Metropolitan Atlanta Community Foundation had perhaps the clearest sense of the problem. It often was, and remains, the first stop for newly formed nonprofits and those taking their first steps into the fundraising arena. However, although the foundation's total disbursements in 1983 totaled $4,950,499, only $274,537 came from unrestricted or field-of-interest funds (since many of its donors are living and prefer to advise the foundation about their giving preferences). The foundation began to ask itself—in light of limited funds, finite resources within the community, and a relatively young tradition of giving by the citizenry—how can we best help this growing collection of nonprofits to help themselves?

MANAGING FOR EXCELLENCE

The beginning of an answer to the questions came from the Support Center of America, itself a nonprofit, which has established 13 technical assistance offices around the country to help nonprofits. It had none in Atlanta, but it asked whether the Metropolitan Atlanta Community Foundation would co-sponsor and function as the local secretariat for a three-day series of seminars designed to offer nonprofits training in management and fundraising skills. One incentive was that the Support Center had received a commitment from The Equitable Life Assurance Society, which has a substantial financial investment and presence in the Atlanta area, to pick up the tab.

The foundation responded enthusiastically to the offer. Beginning in 1984 and annually since, some 200 staff and board members from metropolitan Atlanta nonprofit organizations gather in the fall for the Managing for Excellence Workshop Series—three days of three sessions each day. In 1988, the 252 women and men who attended the overflowing sessions represented 130 organizations.

The Equitable funded only the first round of the program, but continued support was no problem. So successful was the initial venture that the foundation has been able to find other corporate and foundation sponsors each year. C & S National Bank and the First National Bank of Atlanta have become annual donors, and their contributions have been supplemented by gifts from the Atlanta *Journal-Constitution,* Contel Corporation, Decatur Federal Savings & Loan, Eastern Airlines, Georgia Power Company, National Bank of Georgia, Rich's, and Trust Company Bank. The total cost for printing, mailings, and the seminar leaders supplied by the Support Center is about $15,000. The only expense for the participants is a daily lunch, and lodging if they choose to stay in downtown Atlanta overnight.

Workshop participants receive not just the experience of in-depth presentations and interaction with the leaders but also carry home voluminous amounts of supplementary printed materials.

Alicia Philipp, executive director of the foundation, especially likes the fact that attendance at the workshop series is not restricted to board and top staff members of the nonprofits. As she describes it, "It's one of the few courses of its kind that's also designed to meet the needs of secretarial and bookkeeping employees—the kind of people who usually aren't exposed to this sort of experience—and they *do* attend."

It is too early to measure quantitatively what impact these programs have had upon nonprofits in the Atlanta area. However, Valerie Montague, the foundation assistant director, who has the responsibility for supervision of the management workshops, sees that applications for regular foundation support seem to be displaying more sophistication than several years ago.

Philipp is quick to point out that the management workshop series is not designed to meet the needs of every person or organization. Nor does the foundation wish to compete with other training offerings that may be available to nonprofit personnel and trustees. However, as United Way in Atlanta has trimmed back its training offerings to focus upon its own staff and volunteers, the foundation's program has gained importance for the community of social service agencies.

The range of topics is comprehensive, covering such areas as bookkeeping and financial management, marketing, personnel management, fundraising, budgeting, board development, and strategic planning. Those who attend also have the opportunity to meet with representatives from the companies that sponsor the workshop and—for a change—to establish relationships that are not driven solely by a fundraising dynamic.

Another side benefit of the program is the chance it affords nonprofit board and staff members to meet their counterparts from other organizations and to exchange ideas. As a result of this informal exchange, several of them already are exploring cost-cutting ideas like joint purchasing programs. The foundation decided that this kind of brainstorming should be encouraged; in 1988, to promote the sharing process, it scheduled a reception as part of the three-day program.

The reception, sponsored by Digital Equipment Corporation, attracted about 100 participants, including many nonprofit board members.

OUTSTANDING NONPROFIT MANAGEMENT AWARDS

Virtue is said to be its own reward, and perhaps the same standard applies to good management. Nonetheless, the Metropolitan Atlanta Community Foundation has made the decision to go a step further in promoting administrative excellence. Each year it gives public recognition and cash awards to nonprofits that have improved their management practices or sustained good administration over time.

The idea originated in 1984 with Jane Hopson, a member of the foundation staff. (Ms. Hopson also had been the first community foundation intern in the country under a program of the Council on Foundations.) She learned of a similar program administered by a corporate foundation in the Midwest and thought it had merit for Atlanta. The local foundation's directors endorsed the concept enthusiastically and agreed to support it from unrestricted funds.

The Outstanding Nonprofit Management Awards had these initial goals:

- To call attention to well-managed nonprofit organizations.
- To offer other nonprofits a set of management standards to which they could aspire.
- To enhance the visibility of the foundation.

Behind these goals were some other particular hopes. One was that the identification and recognition of well-run programs, especially by organizations that were not household names, might help to validate them in the eyes of corporate and other donors and thereby enhance their fundraising capabilities. The foundation's board and staff also felt that this new program would be an excellent mechanism to broaden community involvement in foundation affairs. Accordingly, it used the opportunity to appoint nonfoundation board members (especially minority and younger leaders) from the business and nonprofit professional ranks to serve on the awards committee.

To ensure some rough parity in the competition for the awards, the foundation divides applicants into three broad categories: small (those with budgets of less than $250,000); medium ($250,000–$900,000); and large (budgets of more than $900,000). No other distinctions are made. As a result, social service agencies vie with arts organizations, and educational institutions compete with health services.

The application process is kept as simple as possible. Essentially it requires a two-page narrative that describes those management achievements the applicant wishes to be considered by the awards committee. This written synopsis, signed by the organization's chair and chief executive, is supplemented by appropriate financial documentation. The foundation staff pays site visits to those applicants they don't already know. Of particular interest to the reviewers are achievements in organizational structure, planning, fiscal management, facilities and equipment management, fundraising, and internal and external communications.

The applicants cite many changes in their operations, but several themes seem to dominate the narratives: strengthening of the board and recruitment of additional volunteers, from which have flowed longer range planning, more systematic fundraising, and tighter fiscal procedures.

Applications (usually between 60 and 90) are received in the late spring, and the foundation announces awards in the fall. Each of the three winners receives a $5,000 unrestricted grant, a commemorative plaque, and free admission to its representatives for one year to all foundation-sponsored seminars and workshops. The foundation also announces two Merit Award recipients in each of the three categories, each of which receives a plaque.

Within a year of beginning the program, the foundation determined that it needed to add yet another award category—for more established organizations that, as Philipp puts it, "were just plain good and staying good." Accordingly, it added the Sustained Good Management Award, for which agencies and institutions may compete on the basis of a three-year record of managerial accomplishment. The annual winner in this category also receives a $5,000 cash award.

A glance at the winners from the past three years shows that the awards program has captured the attention of a broad cross section of the metropolitan Atlanta area's nonprofit sector. It is also interesting that organizations that initially may have received only Merit Awards have reentered the competition in subsequent years and won Outstanding Nonprofit Management Awards:

1985 OUTSTANDING NONPROFIT MANAGEMENT AWARDS

Hub Counseling and Education Center; Georgia Council on Child Abuse; Visiting Nurse Association of Metropolitan Atlanta

MERIT AWARDS

The National Hemophilia Foundation, Georgia Chapter; Auditory Educational Clinic; Big Brothers/Big Sisters of Metropolitan Atlanta; Annandale at Suwanee, Inc.; Goodwill Industries of Atlanta

1986 OUTSTANDING NONPROFIT MANAGEMENT AWARDS

The National Hemophilia Foundation, Georgia Chapter; Big Brothers/ Big Sisters of Metropolitan Atlanta; Goodwill Industries of Atlanta; The Brandon Hall School

MERIT AWARDS

Crawford Center for Therapeutic Horsemanship; Wolfcreek Wilderness School; Atlanta Fulton County Zoo; Atlanta University; Morris Brown College; Ruth Mitchell Dance Company; Southeast Community Cultural Center—The Arts Exchange; Planned Parenthood of the Atlanta Area; The Sheltering Arms

1987 OUTSTANDING NONPROFIT MANAGEMENT AWARDS

Radio Free Georgia Broadcasting Foundation—WRFG; St. Jude's House; Atlanta Fulton County Zoo; Housing Authority of the City of Atlanta

MERIT AWARDS

Quinlan Art Center; St. Luke's Economic Development Corporation; Council on Battered Women; South Atlanta Land Trust; The Tommy Nobis Center; YMCA of Metropolitan Atlanta; Atlanta Jewish Federation; High Museum of Art

1988 OUTSTANDING NONPROFIT MANAGEMENT AWARDS

League of Women Voters of Atlanta/Fulton County; Christians Concerned About Hunger—SEEDS; Council on Battered Women; Georgia Tech Alumni Association

MERIT AWARDS

Community Design Center of Atlanta; Georgia Nurses Foundation; South Atlanta Land Trust; Nexus Contemporary Art Center; YMCA of Greater Atlanta; Atlanta Botanical Garden; The Junior League of Atlanta

What does it mean to win an award? There's no easy way to generalize, but responses from two of the winners are instructive.

WRFG-FM is a community radio station that provides a wide array of programing to audiences that include racial and ethnic minorities, bluegrass afficionados, jazz lovers, and the gay/lesbian community. It offers strong coverage of politically sensitive issues and events. Despite its management award, it constantly faces financial peril, yet the station's board resisted the temptation to plow its $5,000 grant from the foundation into the operating budget. Instead, it elected to use the funds to hire professional fundraising counsel for assistance with long-range planning and campaign organization. Now it is preparing to launch a $400,000 drive, toward which it has quietly raised the first $60,000 from board members and special grants over a six-month period while building a campaign organization.

Atlanta's zoo, a city-operated facility, had fallen onto such hard times in the early 1980s that its care of the animals became a nationally publicized disgrace. A recent retrospective newspaper article described it as "the worst zoological ghetto in the nation."

A fresh administration came on board in 1984, and, by the end of 1985, a new, nonprofit organization, Zoo Atlanta, was in place to begin a massive fundraising and restoration effort. With $16 million guaranteed by revenue bonds from the Atlanta Fulton County Recreation Authority and a $4-million campaign that eventually raised $7 million, the new zoo moved quickly from the status of municipal embarrassment to local treasure. The Friends of Zoo Atlanta, an outgrowth of the old Atlanta Zoological Society, now has more than 50,000 members, making it the third-largest support group of its kind in the United States. In 1986, its staff applied for an Outstanding Management Award but had to settle for a Merit Award. The following year it reapplied and won the top award for large organizations.

Obviously, notes Dr. Terry L. Maple, Director of Zoo Atlanta, the $5,000 award wasn't going to make or break the budget. But, he quickly adds, "The validation of our work and the credibility it gave us was essential, especially for our donors from both the public and private sectors." Maple's staff is, to say the least, proud of the award, and he remains a strong booster of the program. In 1989, he served on the application review committee.

FUTURE PROMOTION OF NONPROFIT EXCELLENCE

An even larger issue is involved: Is there a need in Atlanta for some kind of nonprofit resource center? Research Atlanta, a local nonprofit center that studies patterns and trends in the city's life, believes the need is very real. In its 1987 report, *Coporate and Foundation Philanthropy in Atlanta,* it notes that "half to three-fourths of both companies and foundations [that responded to a survey] also worry about nonprofits needlessly duplicating services, about the number and size of grant requests, and about the lack of information on nonprofit management and programming effectiveness. Over half the foundations are also concerned about the quality of grant applications."

The report goes on to say, "A non-profit resource center should be developed in Atlanta to provide workshops, management and diagnostic assistance, resource information, and clerical and technical support for area non-profits."

Whether such a center comes into being and whether it is housed at the Metropolitan Atlanta Community Foundation, the foundation's officers echo the need expressed in the Research Atlanta study. Alicia Philipp and her colleagues report that the phone calls pour in daily: "How do we obtain 501(c)(3) status? What does this letter I just got from the IRS mean? How should I go about firing somebody? What can I do with my board? How do I go about raising money?" They still take all of these calls—sometimes responding with direct advice; sometimes providing referrals to Volunteer Lawyers or Volunteer Accountants for the Arts; often giving directions to the Foundation Center's collections at the downtown public library.

It is encouraging, on the one hand, that the number of nonprofits in metropolitan Atlanta is expanding to provide essential services. On the other hand, though, there is not sufficient government funding to support them all, and private-source philanthropy still is not keeping pace with the need. Corporate giving in Atlanta has dropped, a pattern that has been accelerated by the number of business takeovers by absenteee national and international companies. Clearly, both the for-profit and not-for-profit segments of the private sector will need to find ways to meet the challenge.

In all likelihood, the Metropolitan Atlanta Community Foundation will give leadership both to the discussion about solutions and the solution itself. For the time being, from the relatively low cash outlay of $20,000 a year for the management cash awards and the time involved in raising another $15,000 to underwrite the management workshop, it is able both to provide technical assistance to nonprofit management and to provide tangible recognition for strong performance. By teaching and encouraging organizations how to fish, it is making a direct contribution to their long-term survival and thereby to the total well-being of the community.

19

Cleveland: Arts Renaissance

Bill Doll

One June morning in 1977, David Bamberger, a young college music professor foolhardy enough to have quit teaching for his dreams of building a professional opera company in Cleveland, found a letter in his mail inviting him to a meeting at the Cleveland Foundation.

Bamberger, along with the heads of a half-dozen other local arts organizations, was being invited to develop a five-year plan for his institution. Out of that meeting would evolve a series of events, quite unanticipated at the time, even by the foundation, that would transform the performing and visual arts landscape in Cleveland and northeast Ohio. It would expand the city's core cultural institutions, help define their character, launch a period of robust growth and, serendipitously, begin an era of unaccustomed cooperative enterprise among the arts.

The foundation's work with the arts would underscore that its role has as much to do with the nonmonetary resources it provides—the contacts, the consultants, and its staff's acute sensibility to what the city's corporate and philanthropic leaders would accept—as it does with the dollars it bestows.

THE FOUNDATION AND ITS CITY

The Cleveland Foundation is the country's oldest and second largest community foundation. In 1977, its commitment to the arts was only two years old; yet in taking on the arts as a program area, it was playing out the same pattern it had for over 60 years. Since its founding in 1914, the Cleveland Foundation's *modus operandi* has mirrored the nature of the community it was created to serve.

Cleveland works through communal action; the sense of pooling resources led to the community foundation concept itself. Cleveland was then a boom town, a Great Lakes dynamo bursting with energy and new fortunes in oil, steel, and manufacturing.

In its early years, the foundation surveyed local social conditions such as a study by Roscoe Pound and his young assistant Felix Frankfurter in 1923 of the city's criminal justice system.

Through most of the next four decades, the foundation's approach was reactive—funding requests that came to it and supporting social agencies and education—rather than taking the initiative in seeking out projects and engineering solutions, as it often does now.

Several forces converged to transform the foundation and its approach to its city. The city itself was declining. Like other Midwestern industrial centers, Cleveland was being pummeled by foreign manufacturing competition and inflation. Factories closed, bankruptcies mounted. Traveling the broad flat city, which fans out from Lake Erie's southern shore, was a despairing tour of hulking abandoned factories, windows broken, smokestacks crumbling, and plaintive "For Lease" signs ignored.

In 1970 the city had 750,000 people. Ten civic nightmare years later it was down to 575,000—a 24 percent decline—while the numbers living in poverty soared. Cleveland became a national joke: the crooked Cuyahoga River, which snakes through downtown, became so polluted it caught fire. The crowning disgrace came in 1979, when it became the first major city since the Great Depression to default on its loans.

The Cleveland Foundation began taking a more active role. In 1974, Homer Wadsworth arrived form Kansas City, after 25 years with private foundations, to become the executive director. Avuncular and folksy, his manner belied a man of tremendous drive and a canny patience in working the halls of power.

Wadsworth brought a vision of a community foundation tackling Herculean problems. "Homer is committed to big projects," one of his colleagues said. "He would always say, 'Think about where you would like to spend a million dollars.' "

THE FOUNDATION FINDS THE ARTS

"What I found when I came to Cleveland," Wadsworth said, "was a large, sophisticated town with a leadership group of refugees from New England—men and women with strong social concerns and a strong tradition of responsible community action."

The years of inflation in the early 1970s, as terrible as they were for the city and many of its citizens, had enlarged the foundation's assets. The Distribution Committee added cultural and civic affairs to its traditional concerns in health, education, and social services.

Wadsworth hired the first program officer in cultural affairs, Patricia Jansen Doyle. Pert, effusive, and impeccably stylish, Doyle is still the investigative reporter she was in Kansas City when Wadsworth met her. In her meetings with arts organizations, she is a woman with a firm agenda and the persistence of a polite diesel engine.

In this gritty industrial city struggling back from decay and obsolescence, the foundation's work in the arts has since been a cross between that of mother hen, midwife, and a polite but very sentimental college admissions office.

But this is not solely Wadsworth and Doyle's doing. They were the representatives of a Distribution Committee that itself was the representative of a score of institutions and interests, from corporations to city hall to the governor's office to newly wealthy Jewish entrepreneurs to black neighborhood groups. None of these alone, including the foundation, was sufficient to get the job done. But all were necessary.

The skill of the foundation has been its ability to guide the arts groups in certain directions while being acutely sensitive to the interests and sensibilities of the other critical players. Indeed, it is somewhat misleading to talk of the "Foundation" as if it were some Olympian force single-handedly rearranging the civic landscape. The foundation is more like a small-town country store where people come to get advice, give advice, and the storekeeper knows where they can find what they need to solve their problems. Of course, this country store now has the added advantage of having $27 million a year to hand out. That brings people seeking funds and gets the town's respectful attention; it doesn't solve the problems.

MAKING CHOICES, BUILDING BUSINESSES

The city's cultural pillars—the Museum, the Orchestra, the Play House, and Karamu, an interracial theater and community house— had all begun in those heady days between 1914 and 1918. No surviving professional companies had begun since. Furthermore, the boards of those venerable institutions were closed to newcomers. Yet, Doyle says, "a lot of new people with money and education, who cared about the community, wanted to create new institutions." Much of the support came from Jewish, Catholic, black, and other groups, eager to be involved but historically denied a place on many of the established boards. The new arts groups have served to open up the leadership ranks of the community.

As David Bamberger, the aspiring opera impresario, said, "When you have a new idea, you go to the foundation." The Cleveland Ballet was the first in what Doyle calls the "Second Great Wave" of cultural organizations. The ballet received $120,000 from the foundation in 1975, formed a company of 21 young dancers, and made its debut in the fall of 1976. Later, Bamberger's opera received $13,000, over a quarter of its first budget of $45,000.

Between 1974 and 1978, the foundation had authorized an average of over $825,000 in art grants each year, nearly tripling what it had given annually before then.

But it wasn't easy to do. The idea of expanding the arts palette in the city made some people uncomfortable. They argued that the economy wasn't strong enough or that new competing institutions would doom existing ventures. For example, the head of the foundation's distribution committee was also the head of the orchestra trustees. He feared that new groups would drain off potential support for the orchestra, which was facing a $1 million deficit.

In fact, several groups were planning to start opera and ballet companies. Instances where there are competing groups in a community not large enough to support more than one underlines the unavoidable, and at times resented, power of the Cleveland Foundation.

While the city has a number of other foundations and corporate resources, the Cleveland Foundation's funds and prestige loom so large that other sources of funds tend to take their lead from the foundation. To fail to get the imprimatur of the Cleveland Foundation is, therefore, to be effectively closed off from other sources of funding.

For example, two groups sought to start professional ballet troupes in the city. Doyle says that only the Cleveland Ballet seemed to have the managerial discipline and the committed board necessary to become a full-fledged professional troupe. The second group's effort never got off the ground.

THE ARTS ORGANIZATIONS

These opening forays weren't only with new organizations. Some established ones were either in trouble or were not what they should be. Karamu had seemingly endless turnovers in management, and its budget had shrunk by 30 percent in five years. The Play House, the nation's oldest resident theater company and once a required stop for Broadway producers traveling the Twentieth Century Limited between New York and Chicago, was a phlegmatic company with an aging audience.

On the city's west side, the Great Lakes Shakespeare Festival was a summer theater with professional potential but just making do in a high-school auditorium without full-time management.

And along Euclid Avenue, the city's main downtown boulevard, Playhouse Square stood forlornly, a single complex of four once breathtaking movie and vaudeville palaces, built in the Golden Age of vaudeville, with over 7,000 seats, now a nearly abandoned colossus.

Despite a devoted band who took the theater's restoration as a holy cause, the corporate community was reluctant to take on such an immense resuscitation. Said the head of the city's largest law firm, "There was a general and well-founded concern that we would be just pouring money down a hole."

In short, in adding cultural affairs to its civic mission, the foundation committed itself to challenges that would not be brief encounters. It had pledged itself to the long term, for these were expensive and perpetually fragile endeavors in the arts.

FROM SEED MONEY TO CHALLENGE GRANTS

In that first year, 1975, the foundation planted seeds and helped stabilize some of the older arts organizations. That effort also raised the delicate question of how a powerful local foundation helps the arts without its beneficiaries becoming either dependent on or subservient to their benefactor? "It was clear that they had to find other sources of support," Pat Doyle recalls. But how?

Long-range planning. That process would help the groups become more businesslike. That, in turn, would impress the corporate community, whose dollars and support were the ultimate object of the exercise.

If the approach sounds a bit condescending, it was not that the artistic heads of the organizations were head-in-the-clouds dreamers disdainful of sound business practices. They were simply not experienced in managing. Their expertise, understandably, was in the fine points of their art, not in planning, budgeting, and balance sheets.

Mary Bill, executive director of the Great Lakes Festival, who has been with the theater since the 1960s, remembers being "a babe in the woods in my mid-40s about arts administration in a theater where the trustees kept the books." Her naivete was not unusual.

Thus, over three or four months, whenever Pat Doyle saw anyone from these groups at meetings, intermissions, or cocktail parties, she would casually, but pointedly, proselytize the value of long-range planning.

The June meeting to which David Bamberger and his six counterparts were invited would be a watershed for most of them. A course of organizational self-analysis and metamorphosis would begin that, in less than ten years, would find the Ballet, Opera, and Great Lakes Festival with budgets double or triple what they were in 1977 and established arts institutions in three magnificent theaters in Playhouse Square.

FROM ARTISTS TO PLANNERS

The managers, artistic directors, and board presidents who gathered at that initial meeting were clearly "anxious," Doyle says. A request by a major funder for long-range planning raised a lot of unsettling questions. Was this planning process some kind of screening device? Was there the possibility here that their funding would be in jeopardy if they did not develop plans, or if the plans did not pass muster?

Bamberger says that, "To say the Foundation 'encouraged' us to do five-year plans is perhaps euphemistic." But, he emphasizes, Doyle and Wadsworth never told any of them what had to be in the plans or how to do it.

The foundation gave each group planning funds ($5,000 a year each for four years). It also commissioned its own studies of income patterns for each group, and of comparable organizations in other cities.

The issues varied from group to group. The ballet and the opera were new organizations—what did they want to be in five years? Whom did they want to be in league with? Did the ballet want to be seen as a classical troupe or (as they finally decided) one that was known for developing new works?

For others, the issues were more specific: should the Cleveland Play House leave its ancestral theater complex of 60 years and move downtown? (No, they built a new theater.) Should the Great Lakes

Shakespeare Festival build its own theater on the lakefront or move to Playhouse Square? (It moved.)

ENTER THE CORPORATIONS

In 1978, Wadsworth approached Allen Holmes, the head of the city's largest law firm, about organizing a corporate advisory committee to review the plans for the arts. "Wadsworth wanted us to evaluate what these organizations needed from a business perspective," Holmes recalls.

At a dozen 7:30 a.m. breakfast meetings at the patrician Union Club, the heads of each of the arts groups came before the chief executives of the city's most powerful corporations to present their plans for capital expansion. "We found gross shortcomings," Holmes says. "Failure to address the whole concept of budgeting was pretty universal."

These polite inquisitions across white linen quickly turned into remedial basic business tutorials conducted by the CEOs. "We brought home to them quite clearly what was expected of them if they were to run their fiscal and administrative affairs in a businesslike way and expect corporate support," Holmes recalls.

Wadsworth had an additional agenda. Except for the orchestra, corporate Cleveland had ignored the arts. Work on the advisory committee changed that. If the corporate community was not impressed with the business know-how of the arts leaders, they were impressed with what the groups were doing artistically and their importance to Cleveland. Moreover, they sensed the importance of the theater district's revival to downtown revitalization.

In less than three years, the foundation's influence had helped launch or strengthen these seven organizations. As important, it had helped its grantees weave themselves into the fabric of the business community, which would continue to be an important source of funds and of board members whose support would be an important credential in the eyes of other funding sources.

THE CHALLENGE GRANT

In the previous two years the National Endowment for the Arts had rejected challenge grant applications from several Cleveland institutions, but now it was encouraging a consortium request. By the happiest accident of seven groups working at the same time on five-year plans, an informal consortium had begun to jell.

This collegiality was not easily orchestrated. In fact, the most common memory most have about that first meeting was that people in the different arts groups didn't know each other. The foundation asked each group to determine its own challenge request. Each would need to match, three-to-one, whatever it might receive through the NEA.

Mary Bill of the Great Lakes Festival remembers that exercise as "very scary." Great Lakes needed a new theater and upgraded management. "Our contributions hadn't been much more than $178,000 in any year—and now we were asking for $400,000, including what we would have to match." Other requests ranged from Karamu's $100,000 to Playhouse Square's $750,000.

In December 1978, Doyle and Wadsworth, accompanied by Allen Holmes, hand-delivered the $2,148,000 challenge request to Livingston A. Biddle, Jr., the head of the NEA in Washington. Biddle was skeptical. Could down-on-its-luck Cleveland raise the nearly $7 million needed to match? "$7 million?," replied Allen Holmes. "That's nothing."

And indeed the city did. "The grant really energized everyone," Pat Doyle says. "It finally unlocked the big corporate dollars." To the actual grant of $1.75 million (the NEA's largest that year) the foundation tacked on $250,000, for an even $2 million challenge.

Cleveland raised $13 million over the three-year challenge period.

PLAYHOUSE SQUARE AND THE QUEST FOR A HOME

From the beginning, the groups shared a common problem: inadequate performance space. The Cleveland Opera and the Great Lakes Festival played in school auditoriums. The Cleveland Ballet performed in a rented theater. Eventually, Playhouse Square (now called the Playhouse Square Center) emerged as the obvious solution: three theaters of more than adequate size—the Ohio seated 1,000, and the Palace and State over 3,000 each.

But restoration would be a gargantuan $37 million task. The theaters were a physical mess. Seats had been ripped out. Plumbing had burst. Even in the two theaters that were still usable, the State and the Palace, delicately frescoed ceilings had been spray-painted red in their final, sad years as third-run movie houses.

Disagreements about what the theaters should be used for further obscured the center's possibilities. The group that had spearheaded the campaign to save the theaters was opposed to their becoming homes to fine arts institutions. They believed that only Las Vegas-style big name entertainers and Broadway musicals would draw the crowds necessary to pay the bills.

Finally, the corporate leadership, who would be asked to raise the money for the restoration, did not believe that the people who were running the Center could successfully operate such a large complex.

Pat Doyle thinks it was both the fact that these theaters were already built and might help revitalize the downtown core that convinced Holmes' Corporate Advisory Committee to change their minds about the odds for Playhouse Square's success. Eventually, two of the committee, the head of a major accounting firm and a major regional bank, joined the board of Playhouse Square, thus certifying its arrival in the arts establishment.

New management was brought into the center. By 1984, the opera and the ballet had taken up residence in the State Theater, the Great Lakes festival in the Ohio, and in 1988 the grandest of them all, the 3,200 seat Palace—an uninhibited tour of two millennia of Western architecture—was re-christened for commercial entertainment.

In 1980 the foundation made its largest grant ever from non-designated funds—$710,000—to Playhouse Square, and purchased an adjoining office building, which it considered critical to the district's economic development. The $3.8 million price was recouped when the foundation sold the complex in 1987 for over $6 million.

The center had become a community crusade. Fifty major businesses committed over $11 million, including such Fortune 100 companies as BP America, TRW, and the Eaton Corporation, along with 11 foundations and several hundred individuals. The federal government pledged $3.5 million, matched equally by the county. The State of Ohio added another $3.75 million.

By 1984, seven years after that fateful meeting, Cleveland's "Second Great Wave" now had homes.

FROM PARENT TO PARTNER

The foundation's relationship to its artistic charges had changed in many ways. Steven A. Minter, its new executive director, says, "We realized that we had some well-established arts groups now—how do we sustain and help them stretch?" The foundation now was less a quasi-parent and more a partner. The Ballet, the Opera, and the Great Lakes Festival have become multi-million-dollar operations. The ballet was touring nationally and the Great Lakes Festival was sending productions to Broadway.

The next major project, a regional marketing survey to assess the audience potential for other ventures, signaled a changing relationship.

Among the most intriguing findings, the more kinds of arts one attended (e.g., theater, ballet, and contemporary art), the more other arts one was likely to attend. Thus, the groups were wrong to fear that shared mailing lists led to purloined subscribers. Resistance to cooperation melted.

So in 1987, twenty-one local arts groups initiated, with foundation support, the Cleveland Arts Consortium and together applied for another NEA challenge grant specifically to foster cooperative audience-building activities.

That move led to a regional joint marketing campaign, called "Bravo! Cleveland." In 1988, when the Great Lakes Festival mounted an elaborate production of Spanish playwright Garcia Lorca's "Blood Wedding," 48 local arts groups joined in with 135 events, from a Picasso exhibit at the Art Museum to Spanish jazz on Cleveland's public radio station.

Of course, problems remain, not the least of which is fundraising. If the foundation is no longer midwife and mother hen, its position at the fulcrum of civic leadership requires it to persistently be talent scout and early warning system, as well as patron.

"The roles we play differed according to the circumstances," Minter says. "Convener, catalyst, sometimes educator, taking the philanthropic lead, and sometimes, as a last resort, managing the project itself."

THE PERPETUAL TIGHTROPE

The foundation's delicate use of its influence, Homer Wadsworth acknowledges, is played with caution. "Representing the Cleveland Foundation can be frightening," Doyle explains. This second largest community foundation serves a metropolitan area that is only twelfth largest in the country. As she points out, other comparably large community foundations—New York or San Francisco, for example—operate in much larger arenas peopled with so many more resources and countervailing forces.

The risks temper and shape the foundation's commitment. Still, in Cleveland, it has wrought a renaissance in the arts.

20

Bridgeport: Teenage Pregnancy

Steve Kezerian

Buried deep in a comprehensive report on ambulatory care by the Southwestern Connecticut Health Systems Agency in 1979 were some startling statistics on adolescent pregnancy in the city of Bridgeport. To the credit of the health officials and the local press, the report was given wide distribution and the statistics lifted out of the tables and publicized.

"City's Teenage Pregnancy Ratio Highest in the Nation; Family Planning, Medical Care Deficiencies Cited" was the four-column headline on the front page of the *Bridgeport Post* of Wednesday, July 18, 1979.

At a time when the ratio was declining in other urban areas in the country, Bridgeport's numbers had in six years jumped eight points: 82.5 out of every 1,000 females in the 15 to 19 age bracket were becoming pregnant. The ratio for the country as a whole was about 58/1,000.

The news article quoted Stephen Glover, an agency spokesman. The principal reason for the high rate, he said, was the lack of effective educational and medical programs in the inner city that would help prevent teenage pregnancy.

"While Bridgeport has a plethora of health care services, most are oriented to curative aspects of health care and to acute conditions. There is a great need for services directed to the preventive health

care," he said, and then warned, "Bridgeport has quite a bit to do
to get its rates down."

Community leaders were jolted by the report. They worried that
it would exacerbate racial and religious tensions already dividing the
city on the inflammatory issue of sex education. Catholics, along with
other conservative religious groups, had fought attempts by Planned
Parenthood to circulate pamphlets openly in the schools about birth
control and family planning. Proposed sex education courses for the
schools had been tabled by acrimonious debates. And raucous street
confrontations had occurred when Pro-Life advocates had picketed
the Summit Women's Center, which houses an abortion clinic. The
bleak intergroup situation in Bridgeport was a daunting challenge to
anyone trying to heed Glover's warning.

An old Yankee city of 142,000 people, Bridgeport is beset with the
heavy burdens faced by other industrial centers in the Northeast. Many
old smokestack factories are empty. Blocks of public housing built in
the post-World War II years are boarded up, their interiors gutted.
The city's black and Hispanic population, 40 percent of the total, makes
up 80 percent of the enrollment of the public schools, which have
a 37 percent dropout rate. And nearly 50 percent of the minority
students come from families that qualify for welfare aid.

Just 50 miles northeast of New York City, Bridgeport thrived as a
seaport and major manufacturing center in the first half of this century,
a mecca for the Italian, Irish, Polish, and other European immigrants
seeking work. In the past 25 years another set of immigrants have
poured into the city, the Puerto Ricans, seeking factory jobs even as
they were dwindling. Bridgeport also ranks in the top 25 cities with
the highest rate of families classified as poor.

But the picture was not all bleak. Bridgeport is at the eastern end
of Fairfield County, the most affluent county in the United States, in
the state with the highest per capital income. There is no lack of rich
resources in the county—funds, institutions, and trained professional
people.

THREE PROPOSALS

On the heels of the health survey report and the headlines of 1979,
three programs, each independent of the other, were proposed to com-
bat the escalating rate of adolescent pregnancy. One proposal had been
floated by the city's Health Department asking for funds to increase
its staff with professional people who would concentrate on promoting pregnancy prevention and helping teenagers who became preg-

nant. The second proposal originated with the Catholic Coalition on Problem Pregnancy (CCOPP). The Catholic Diocese, which is headquartered in Bridgeport (Catholics make up 45 percent of the city's population), had called for a stronger effort within its own ranks by organizing a coalition of some 20 Catholic offices and institutions— St. Vincent's Hospital, Natural Family Planning, Catholic Charities, and the parochial schools, among others—to deal with adolescent pregnancy.

Both proposals, from the city Health Department and from the Catholic Coalition, were submitted to the federal Office of Adolescent Pregnancy and Parenting programs in the spring of 1980. Neither proposal offered any new solutions, simply organizational expansion. Both were rejected.

The third proposal came from another direction. Colin Gunn, counsel for the Educational Foundation of America (EFA) and a resident of nearby Westport, offered his foundation's help.

EFA was founded in 1959 by the late Richard Prentice Ettinger, a New York publisher, to improve the quality of higher education and to assist deserving youth gain a college education. His interests and those of his charitable foundation subsequently extended into medical and social problems, with a special concern for population planning. EFA is directed by Ettinger family members whose own contributions have raised the foundation's assets above $80 million.

With the backing of EFA directors, Gunn contacted Edward E. Harrison, an old schoolmate and president of the Bridgeport Area Foundation (BAF). A prominent industrialist and civic leader, Harrison had founded the BAF in 1967 with relatively modest funding. He was enthusiastic about Gunn's idea and the prospect of a private foundation and a community foundation linked in a joint venture.

What kind of program would be appropriate? What services were needed? Who would be the participants? To observe an existing program said to be highly effective, Harrison and H. Parker Lansdale, executive director of the YMCA, visited Johns Hopkins University in Baltimore. Lansdale had served as community liaison for the BAF and United Way as well as chairman of the Ambulatory Care Task Force that had produced the 1979 report.

The Johns Hopkins University Adolescent Pregnancy program had been started with the assistance of EFA funds. It was an impressive operation, but it was not a suitable model for Bridgeport.

"We liked what we saw, but came home discouraged about replicating the program," Harrison recalls. Johns Hopkins University provides

Baltimore with the services of an influential, well-funded medical school and hospital, staffed by a broad range of experts who can organize and administer a special program on adolescent pregnancy. Bridgeport has no such institution. Three area general hospitals and the four colleges and universities (none of them with medical schools) lack the resources to attempt an endeavor similar to Baltimore's.

Officers of the two foundations, after lengthy deliberations, sought a new solution: if there was no single entity in Bridgeport strong enough to handle the broad responsibility of running a program on teenage pregnancy, then a new model had to be created using talents and services already in the community.

Over the next seven years, 1981–1988, EFA would make grants totaling $150,000 for such a project. The BAF, with a far smaller endowment ($6 million in 1981), had fortuitously received a special bequest in 1977, the Julia Palmer Fund, that could be used to help needy children. Income from this fund was allocated to the planning and administering of the adolescent pregnancy program. It amounted to $250,000 over the same seven-year period.

Both Harrison and Lansdale were longtime officers of United Way of Eastern Fairfield County (Bridgeport and its ring of five suburban towns). Both were certain that United Way would be the best conduit for funds to develop and oversee a new program. Richard O. Dietrich, executive director of United Way since 1973, had been a YMCA director in the midwest and in Bridgeport, and knew firsthand the distressing problems of young people in the inner city. Under his leadership, United Way had taken an increasingly active role by responding to the needs of the homeless and the elderly, and to the dangers of drug abuse. His belief is that "the character and scope of our social problems today require a new set of principles or rules in order to address issues. At the heart of these new rules or principles is the need for powerful collaborative intervention."

Edward C. Keane, professor of Psychology and Human Services at Housatonic Community College, had taken a two-year leave from his college to be Director of Planning and Research for United Way. One of his first assignments was a study of local resources for any comprehensive undertaking. Within the city and state health departments, the public and parochial schools, the sectarian and secular family service agencies, and the three hospitals were some 20 offices that listed adolescent pregnancy among their concerns. But these existing programs on the teenage issue were only a part (usually not a major part) of the broad health and welfare agenda of these offices.

The glaring weaknesses of a fragmented, attenuated approach to this critical community problem were revealed by the study. The existing programs were not adequate to handle the growing number of teenagers who needed help. There was no clearinghouse or central advocacy group for adolescent pregnancy in the city. Individual agencies were operating with little or no cooperation with each other. Probably the most disheartening aspect was that the agencies and institutions were in a sharp, almost self-defeating competition for funds.

There had to be a better way, based on cooperation among the different sectors. On the recommendation of Dietrich and Keane, the United Way board of directors approved the formation of an Adolescent Pregnancy Steering Committee of community leaders to develop a plan for uniting the many divergent organizations.

In the midst of this planning, another jarring headline broke in the press. The *Bridgeport Post* on Tuesday, February 3, 1981, ran a story across six columns reporting on the activities of the Summit Women's Center and its abortion clinic. More than 3,500 women had received abortions at the clinic in 1980. Thirty percent of them were under 19 years of age. About 10 percent of the teenagers were Hispanic or black. But it was the religious affiliation of the 3,500 women that made the headline: "51% of Center's Abortion Clients are Catholic."

The reaction of the Bishop of the Diocese of Bridgeport was swift and firm. "The attitude of the Catholic Church will not in any way be changed by any statistics," he declared in a follow-up news story. "The question of abortion is a moral problem transcending denominational lines. Catholics are reminded that regardless of public opinion, changing social attitudes and other social pressures, abortion is always morally wrong."

Prospects for a fully cooperative venture seemed dim. To rally the forces around a common goal, an ingenious conference was scheduled.

CONFERENCE STRATAGEM

With funding from the BAF and the EPA, the United Way sponsored a special conference on ways and means of solving the problems of adolescent pregnancy. The meeting was held at the Ryetown Hilton, 40 miles from Bridgeport and just across the state line in New York, on June 11, 1981. The meeting was being held on neutral ground isolated enough not to arouse local Bridgeport antagonisms. The 135 participants from Bridgeport had been invited not as official representatives of agencies, but as concerned civic leaders. Along with participants from Planned Parenthood and the Summit Women's Center were three Catholic officials: one from St. Vincent's Hospital, one from the parochial schools, and Sister Helen Clifford from the office of Catholic Family Services. She was to play a major role in later developments.

The problems and programs in other cities were presented by guest speakers. By placing the Bridgeport problems in national perspective, the conference aimed to raise the concerns of the delegates above their particular interests.

The task ahead for Dietrich and the Steering Committee was to design a format to get people to work together. Dietrich believed that such a format was possible by having separate "tracks" of operation under the umbrella of a benevolent and so-called neutral overseer. Each track would retain its independent functions without compromise of ideology, but at the same time cooperate in broad areas of agreement to reach out more effectively to teenagers and their families. The backing of the two foundations was critical. Both BAF and EFA had agreed that no new funds would be given without some evidence of collaboration. The commitment of the two foundations protected United Way from charges by its member agencies that monies that should be theirs were being diverted to the umbrella group.

One of the two tracks under Dietrich's format would be the Council on Adolescent Pregnancy (COAP), a combine of government, secular, Protestant, and Jewish departments and agencies. There was no difficulty in getting the council established, with Geraldine Johnson as chairman. Johnson had been Superintendent of Schools in Bridgeport from 1976 to 1981, the first black woman to head a public school system in a major Connecticut city. Adolescent pregnancies and resulting school dropouts had been one of her concerns as an educator, and she had been active in the early planning work of Keane's committee. The second track envisioned under Dietrich's format would be the Catholic coalition.

There was no precedent for such collaboration on community sex problems by the Catholic Church anywhere in the country. On being invited to a meeting to discuss the possibility of working together, the Bishop's office expressed skepticism, but agreed to talk.

Thus began in the summer of 1981 a series of intensive dialogues, which Dietrich came to regard as "friendly negotiations." Moral issues were involved and the Church stood by its principles. Who was to counsel the youngsters on premarital sex, birth control and contraceptives, and abortion, all sinful under Catholic doctrine? Nor would the Catholic Church let itself be placed in a position of direct cooperation with those who prescribed otherwise.

"Why don't you just give us the money and let us run our own program and let others do theirs?" was the appeal by the Bishop's office to Dietrich and Keane, the United Way negotiators. "There is no money unless there is collaboration," came the answer.

Dietrich was convinced that separate, non-collaborating programs would inevitably become competitors for funding and community support, and such competition would be destructive to United Way's mission of building better community cooperation. "Bridgeport, more than any other city I know, is fractionalized on racial and religious issues. The Catholic Church itself has had to deal with some bitter polarization among rival ethnic groups within the parishes," he said.

The United Way, according to Dietrich, could not support two opposing programs—the Catholic coalition and the council—that would add to the tensions that already divide the city. "The young people who need the help are caught in the middle of the battlefield," he said.

In what became the final session of negotiations, three cans of cola became pivotal. The soft drinks were on the table for refreshment, and Dietrich saw an opportunity to demonstrate the validity of the two-track format to Monsignor William A. Genuario, Vicar General of the diocese. "The first can is the Catholic coalition," Dietrich said. "The second can is the council, the other track." Placing the third can squarely between the two, he explained that "this can is the central agency that divides the two tracks. Each can does its own work. The middle can protects either of the other two from shooting off its track into the path of the other. At the same time, there are ties between the tracks for collaboration that each side wants."

Monsignor Genuario studied the three cans carefully, meditated a few moments, and said he would confer with the Bishop and report back the next day. Their answer was affirmative. A preliminary agreement, titled, somewhat starkly, the Principle of Remoteness, was drawn up, translating the metaphor of the three cola cans into a working policy statement. In effect, it defined and safeguarded the Catholic track in what was to be the Greater Bridgeport Adolescent Pregnancy Program. (GBAPP).

In a position paper that elaborated on the agreement, the Catholic coalition stated: "How could we, a Catholic pro-life agency, associate with agencies that have at the very least a pro-choice bent or 'abortion mentality'? Our answer has been that direct cooperation with what ultimately might occur is not possible because of the way the collaborative effort has been set up; i.e., there are built-in protections. In other words, even though someone may ultimately decide to get an abortion, we have tried our very best to counsel that person and get her to think twice about her action. . . .

"Catholic principles of moral theology teach us that we may never directly cooperate in another's sin. There are times, however, when for just reason, indirect cooperation with a person who may ultimately choose to sin (in our sense of evil action) is tolerated, especially when the cooperation itself is not evil and there is reasonable hope for the opposite to occur."

It would be another year after the Principle of Remoteness before the collaborative project would begin. In that transition period, Keane, Johnson, and Sister Helen Clifford were immersed in paperwork, drafting statements of agreement and tables of organization. They were working with 60 different offices—24 in the Catholic coalition and 36 in the Council—to fill the boards and committees. A careful system of checks and balances was built into the bylaws to prevent any encroachment on the integrity of either track. Even procedures for issuing news releases were spelled out in detail.

On March 12, 1983, Sister Helen, Johnson, and Keane went to the editors of the *Bridgeport Post* with a news release that had been scrupulously reviewed by committees of the two tracks. The editors had promised cooperation in publicizing the new project; nevertheless, the three remained in the newsroom into the evening hours until the story as rewritten by a reporter was punched into the printing computer. The next morning there was a five-column story, this time a headline with a positive note: "A New Network Blends Sectarian, Public Agencies In Efforts to Resolve Teen Pregnancy Problems." Illustrating the article was a cover of a GBAPP pamphlet bearing the names of the Catholic coalition and the council. In the center was the silhouette of a young woman in an obviously gravid condition.

It would require several more months of talking and planning before the coalition and the council would reach out collaboratively to help needy youngsters. But the heavy attention that had for three years been focused on adolescent pregnancy had prodded the two to revitalize their own lagging programs.

SEPARATE BUT COLLABORATIVE

On the Catholic side, Sister Helen had been instrumental in developing a family life curriculum for all 12 grades in the parochial schools. Catholic Family and Social Services founded a residential center for young pregnant girls. The coalition had started a fertility awareness class in the Catholic high school called Teen STAR (Sexuality Training in the Context of Adult Responsibility).

From the other track, the council, came a sex education curriculum for the public schools. After ten years of debate and waffling, the Board of Education voted for its adoption in 1983. The council sponsored workshops to train 30 teachers for the course and, with the help of BAF funds, helped develop course materials.

A second notable achievement was the establishment of Teen Health Centers in the three public high schools. These centers, staffed by a full-time social worker and a nurse practitioner, are adjacent to but separate from the regular school nurse. They deal with the whole range of a teenager's health—physical, psychological, and social. Drug abuse, sex-related ailments, and troubles in a student's home life head the list of problems. The centers do not dispense condoms or other contraceptives but have a direct line to other agencies and clinics where help is given quickly and confidentially. The two foundations, EFA and BAF, along with other agencies, provided the money to get the centers started. State and city funds now underwrite the costs.

A third program initiated by the council was the Adolescent Family Life Collaboration, serving teenage mothers with their babies in a family setting. A social worker makes regular visits to the young mother to help her with her new responsibilities, and brings in other agencies when support is needed. One of the objectives is to help the teenager remain in school; she can complete her high school education in special classes, with child care provided by the high school.

The first totally collaborative program under GBAPP came in the fall of 1983, the Teenage Fatherhood Project. It was a good choice for a kick-off, since the handling of young fathers engenders little or no controversy. Funded by the BAF and the Bank Street College, the project was assigned to the YMCA for management, and quickly gained national recognition because of the dedicated leadership of its director, Manuel Cardona. A social worker, he had come from Puerto Rico where he himself had been a father at age 17. He prefers working the streets and neighborhoods rather than from a desk to seek out the teenage fathers more likely to be found there than in school or on a job. In the course of a month, he works with 10 to 15 young men, persuading them to earn a high school diploma and helping them to get a job to support their family. The Ford Foundation has sponsored Cardona's program as one of eight national demonstration projects on teenage fathers.

In February 1985, the Greater Bridgeport Adolescent Pregnancy Program was formally incorporated as an independent nonprofit agency and certified as a member of United Way. Its gestation had stretched over four years from the time United Way had accepted the commission from BAF and EFA.

With the help, once again, of BAF and EFA, plans were drawn to open the Adolescent Resource Center as the official headquarters. There were still some prickly issues that tested the Principle of Remoteness. A directory listing all the programs and services for adolescent pregnancy had to be compiled. There were 44 in all, listed alphabetically starting with Birthright of Greater Bridgeport and ending with YWCA Rape Crisis Center. Planned Parenthood's listing would normally have fallen on a page facing St. Vincent's Hospital. The juxtaposition was unacceptable. (Planned Parenthood had not been on the original roll call of council members three years earlier because of Catholic opposition, "but as time went on we insisted on our right to have it included," Johnson said.) A minor crisis was averted by giving the agency its full regional title, "Greater Bridgeport Chapter Planned Parenthood," thereby placing it under "G" in the alphabetical listing and eight full pages away from St. Vincent's Hospital.

But there was no pussyfooting about speaking out to the public in clear, vivid language. Livelier nomenclature and publicity were used to get the message across. Adolescent Resource Center was too somber a title to attract the young, so the center was given a new working name, "Teen Place." On billboards, ad panels on buses, and on 25,000 wallet-sized plastic cards circulated to youths and families throughout the city was the legend: "Teen Place will answer your sex questions. Free and confidential."

Teen Place is in the middle of a block in downtown Bridgeport. Inside the first-floor facility are lounges for visitors and offices for the staff. To the rear is the desk of the social worker who handles the hotline for calls from teenagers (and others) asking for information and often for help about the myriad problems relating to sex, dating, pregnancy, the human body and its reproductive system. In addition to answering questions, the social worker has a number of services to offer—the secular and religious counseling agencies, free pregnancy testing, follow-up visits by social workers and health professionals. In its first 20 months, the hotline received 3,203 calls. Of these, 1,157 were from the usual cranks and disturbed persons who exploit hotlines. The other 2,046 were callers making an honest appeal for help and information.

The working relationship of the collaborative program is best symbolized by the two offices, side-by-side, of the codirectors: Johnson of the council and Sister Mary Bernard Wiecezak of the Catholic coalition, who succeeded Sister Helen Clifford. The two often assist on hotline calls and with drop-in teenagers, but are more concerned about going out into the city and delivering their message. GBAPP sponsors regular series of classes and lectures on human sexuality, one for teenagers, the other for parents and adults who are working with teenagers.

Has GBAPP made a difference? The most recent report on adolescent pregnancy in Bridgeport shows that the ratio has dropped only two points below the ratio of ten years ago. But the drop is encouraging to Keane. "The rate was predicted to increase. Any leveling off or decrease is a positive sign," he said.

The critical role of the community foundation and its private foundation partner is underscored by Dietrich, in words and in his own career. In January 1989, he moved over from United Way to become the first full-time president and chief executive officer of the Bridgeport Area Foundation. "The collaboration would never have taken place without the leadership and resources of the foundations," he said. "Only the foundations are willing to take risks in supporting important experimental programs. Our youth today are being torn apart by institutional protectionism and failure to find strong collaborative models that can address sexual matters, drug abuse, AIDS, broken families. Too many of our social service programs are using horse-and-buggy delivery systems to solve the problems. We need creative new ideas. The foundations must nurture these new ideas and use their money as leverage to put them into practice."

21

Arizona: At-Risk Children

Irene Rasmussen

Among the many roles community foundations play, rarely are they active participants and leaders in the state political process. But it did happen in the state of Arizona.

Arizona is a political maverick of sorts. For example, it is the only state without a formal Medicaid program; instead, the legislature has fashioned a unique indigent health care system that uses portions of Federal Medicaid monies with restrictions and qualifications painfully negotiated upon between Arizona legislators and federal officials.

The Arizona Community Foundation was organized in 1978 by community leaders. Three part-time executive directors served until 1983. In those early years the foundation gradually gained assets. It could not afford full-time regular staff; its slim operating expenses were paid by major banks, trust companies, and utilities. By 1983 assets had grown to only $2 million and the foundation was giving away less than $100,000 annually.

In 1983 the board hired the first full-time professional manager, Stephen D. Mittenthal, formerly with the Weyerhaeuser Company Foundation, and two years later undertook its first major capital campaign, for $5 million in permanent unrestricted endowment. Over the next two years the foundation continued a steady rate of growth as donors recognized how the 1986 tax reforms increased the advantages of giving to community foundations. By 1989 assets had climbed to $20 million.

Aiming at growth, the Arizona Community Foundation staff and board focused almost exclusively on the accumulation of capital and on traditional programming. A powerful incentive to shift focus came in 1986 with the Ford Foundation's competitive grant program to community foundations for significant attacks on priority community needs.

Since Arizona ranks right at the bottom of social service dollars expended in virtually every category, Mittenthal and his staff and board had a wide range of subjects from which to choose. Mittenthal solicited the advice and ideas of his board members, talked with community leaders in informal focus groups, and began to gather a consensus. Substance abuse, child abuse, and teen pregnancy were popular suggestions, but the topic mentioned most often was mental health in general and the mental health of children in particular. The area was, according to Mittenthal, "a virtual *tabula rasa.*" Practically no children's mental health funds were available, private or public; the programs were spotty and uncoordinated; and the impact was almost unmeasurable. It was an issue area with a pretty clear field; no one agency or entity dominated.

Armed with an informal consensus on a severe community problem, Mittenthal submitted a proposal to the Ford Foundation. The need was expressed in vivid data: "At least 125,000 children in Arizona ages 2–18 are 'at risk' of mental illness, by virtue either of genetic impairment, socio-economic status, family situation, chemical dependency, or exposure to other environmental stress factors. . . . Only 10 percent are currently receiving care. . . . Suicide is the second leading cause of death among 15- to 19-year-olds in Arizona, with a rate of 18.1 per 100,000 adolescents; Arizona's overall suicide rate is 40 percent higher than the national. . . . Arizona has one of the highest incidences of child abuse in the nation. . . . 9,000 women and children sought help at domestic violence shelters in 1984. . . . 500 children currently identified as seriously emotionally disturbed require placement in a psychiatric hospital or residential treatment center; state funding is available for only 30 not adjudicated dependent or delinquent." Finally, the most telling: *"Arizona ranks last in the nation in per capita funding for mental health services among the states."*

Mittenthal proposed that the Arizona Community Foundation deal with this problem through "a tripartite leadership development program: (1) grantmaking, (2) asset development, and (3) community education." He requested a $500,000 challenge grant that would create an Arizona Children's Trust Fund. The fund represented not only a rationale for the grant but also a true commitment by board and staff of the foundation to the issue of children's mental health. Specifically the board designated $320,000 from the community foundation's limited discretionary funds in order to give the Children's Trust Fund some economic momentum. The board and staff's willingness to put up other hard-earned monies would help ensure the success of the project.

While Mittenthal and the foundation began focusing on the issue of children's mental health, the mental health and political community had been busy, with little knowledge of what was happening within the Arizona Community Foundation. Both professional children's advocates and agency staff members and boards had introduced a series of legislative bills to improve funding for mentally ill children and their families over the preceding ten years, with little success.

At almost the same time Mittenthal was applying to the Ford Foundation for money to assist with children's mental health, Jesse McClure, Dean of the School of Social Work at Arizona State University, was appointed the Chairman of the Children's Mental Health Task Force by Governor Bruce Babbitt. To follow the work of this committee, one must recall the bizarre political events in Arizona at that time.

A POLITICAL MAELSTROM

Babbitt had been a great friend to children, working in behalf of children's legislation throughout his tenure, specifically in the areas of child abuse and foster care. In the spring of 1986 he informally leaked that he was going to run for President. Children's advocates urged him to appoint a committee that would be charged with studying the issue of children's mental health and producing a report before Babbitt left office in January 1987. The hope of the children's advocates was that the recommendations of this committee would set the children's mental health agenda for the next governor. Babbitt obliged by appointing McClure and the Children's Mental Health Task Force.

In the fall of 1986 a colorful campaign was held for governor, with the conventional wisdom saying that one of the Republican candidates, Burton Barr, would walk away with the big prize. Barr had been the majority leader of the Arizona House of Representatives for years and was one of the best-known and most powerful political figures in the state. His opponent in the Republican primary was Evan Mecham, an old-time conservative party worker who had run several times before but never won. Because of his extreme right-wing politics, his history of many losses and no wins, and several personal quirks, the press, the columnists, mental health advocates, and most other interest groups did not take him seriously.

However, the voters did, and he swept the Republican primary. The Democratic primary contest began with two candidates but one dropped out before the primary. Then, just before the general election, he re-entered the field as an Independent. This gave Arizonans three candidates on the General Election ballot—a situation they had never faced. After a campaign filled with charges of bigotry, racism, misuse of campaign funds, and daily mud-slinging and rebuttals from all three candidates, Evan Mecham won, with 42 percent of the popular vote.

Many of his campaign statements had been perceived as racist, sexist, and anti-Semitic by segments of the community. In his first speech after his election he promised that one of his first acts after being sworn in as governor would be to abolish the statewide holiday in honor of Dr. Martin Luther King, Jr. With a series of other statements including a statement on "our Christian nation," seen as anti-Semitic by the press, this led to a statewide recall movement to oust him from the governor's chair even before he had been sworn in.

Meanwhile the Children's Mental Health Task Force continued to meet, hear testimony, and gather information for recommendations but decided to defer delivery of a report. "We, along with everyone else in Arizona, were going to wait and see what was going to happen with the new governor," says McClure.

Around this time, in December, the Arizona Community Foundation received word that it had been awarded one of the coveted $500,000 leadership development challenge grants from the Ford Foundation. The *New York Times* picked up these grants as national news, the local papers reported the grants, and suddenly the Arizona Community Foundation was at the center of a swirling movement of community activists trying to change the children's mental health system in Arizona.

The professional mental health provider community in Arizona is a group of knowledgeable, experienced agency directors, board, and staff. Many of them were caught by surprise by the announcement of the grant and its size. Mittenthal fielded many phone calls. Some agency directors were suspicious, some were angered that they had not been consulted before such a large sum was requested for Arizona, and most were simply curious to find out who these new players were and whether the new money would be able to help in the long battle to upgrade the children's mental health system. Mittenthal talked at length with each one and eventually managed to win over all these potential opponents and put them squarely in his corner.

THE ARIZONA CHILDREN'S TRUST FUND

In organizing how work was to be done on children's mental health with the Ford Foundation grant monies, the community foundation created the Arizona Children's Trust Fund, a collection of permanent charitable endowment funds held within the Arizona Community Foundation and the Tucson Community Foundation. The trust fund was also to be the grantmaking arm of the Ford Foundation funds and would provide other grants to nonprofit, organizations that address "the social, health, educational, vocational, artistic, cultural, and other needs of children." The most significant aspect of the Children's Trust Fund is that the foundation chose to leverage the Ford funds with other Arizona Community Foundation monies ($320,000, as mentioned), thus creating a much larger aggregate fund.

During the spring of 1987 the political climate in Arizona was volatile. The recall movement against Mecham was in full swing, with constant press coverage of the new governor's activities, hostile and divided public opinion, and a growing unease in the State Legislature. Reports began to be leaked about possible improprieties in campaign funding and use of public monies for private purposes. Several charges were made that had criminal implications, and "indictment" began to be added to the already chaotic chorus for recall or impeachment.

In the meantime Mittenthal hired Gail Jacobs, an experienced child advocate and former employee of the Governor's Office for Children, as a full-time Development Coordinator for the Ford Foundation project. She was also to serve as liaison with a variety of private and government agencies, to staff an advisory committee for the Children's Trust Fund, and to coordinate the fund's grants and community education programs in children's mental health.

Jacobs's background in legislative and community relations work made her a natural information center for the children's mental health advocate community. Most of these people knew Jacobs, were aware of her new position, and began to call to see what role the foundation was contemplating in the coming legislative session. According to Jacobs, "During those intensely political spring months we laid low at the community foundation, steering clear of the Mecham mess at the Capitol, trying to get our own house in order first."

McClure continued to meet with his task force. "If we get this report done, we will need somebody to coordinate the activities that will make this a reality," he said. "The Arizona Council of Centers for Children and Adolescents should be that group. And let's get moving on legislation." Maria Hoffman, a long-time children's advocate and executive director of the council, was selected to be the main lobbyist for the issue with the legislature.

A BILL IS BORN

So a complicated and tedious process to create a bill began. It required finding sponsors and working with the legislature to sponsor an awesome request—a whole new coordinated and funded statewide mental health system for children.

At the same time the media began to cover the issue of children's mental health more intensely. Several horror stories were covered by both the papers and television—extreme cases of mentally ill children with poor family support and nowhere to get help within the fragmented children's mental health system. By the summer of 1987, children's mental health was the single hottest human service issue in Arizona.

The Arizona Community Foundation contracted with the Community Council, a United Way community planning and organizing agency, to run workshops around the state to gather advice and information as the foundation's board and staff planned and developed a grants strategy. There had been so little money in the past for children's mental health activities and such a great need that almost anything the foundation could do would be helpful. The difficulty was exactly where to start.

The foundation also contracted with Arizona Advocates for Children to organize community education and to link up with key mental health and children's groups throughout the state. So a second series of meetings sought to educate the diverse community of children's advocates on the status of the children's mental health system in Arizona.

These meetings firmly established the Arizona Community Foundation as a significant player in the field of children's mental health. The informal purpose of the meetings was to identify and solidify a constituency for positive action on children's mental health. Because Mittenthal had previously spent time with the leaders of these groups, his motives were not questioned. The group came away from these meetings as a strong, cohesive, and potentially powerful lobbying constituency for a coming legislative battle.

The Community Council consultant hired to facilitate the meetings, Steve Wise, summarized the professional community's reaction as follows:

- Some surprisingly strong support for spending money on efforts aimed at system change, coordination, information dissemination and advocacy.
- Support of the work being done by the Children's Mental Health Task Force, community education and prevention programs.
- Other public and private funds should be leveraged.

All of these forces began to converge in the hot Arizona summer of 1987. McClure's task force was about to issue a final report. The Arizona Legislature was in session, considering an impeachment of the governor, a process for which Arizona had no precedent. The media were caught up in the subject of children's mental health. The children's mental health provider community, reinforced by the community meetings sponsored by the Arizona Community Foundation, was becoming more vocal, organized, and active.

The Children's Mental Health Task Force, with its final report ready for presentation to governor Mecham, prepared a legislative plan. The strategy was to request a sympathetic legislator to add to any existing bill an amendment that would establish an informal interim committee on children's mental health. (In the Arizona legislature an interim committee is often used as a vehicle for getting public testimony and almost forcing the legislature to deal with an issue that is of great importance to certain segments of the public.)

But the legislative process was in almost total disarray, with the House of Representatives considering the possibility of sending Articles of Impeachment to the Senate for a trial. The normal process of legislation slowed down to a crawl. Hoffman, the lobbyist on the children's mental health issue, persuaded two legislators to go to the leadership and ask for an interim committee on mental health. The interim committee was created in August, and the issue of children's mental health was now officially on the legislative agenda.

A NEW PLAYER IN THE CORRIDORS

In the great confusion of possible impeachment, recall, and indictment, scheduled legislative committee meetings were abruptly cancelled, meetings were called with only the briefest notice, and legislators were in an extremely bad humor.

The lobbyists for children's issues, usually paid executive directors of agencies providing children's services, are well known to the legislators. At best they are seen as focused on single issues without a broad community-wide point of view. At worst they are seen as mendicants with their hands out for more money for their own agencies.

But this legislative session had a new player, the Arizona Community Foundation, which entered the fray with its own pot of money, the Ford Foundation grant, and its own independent set of issues. The legislature perceived greater depth than before. The Arizona legislators are used to being lobbied by human services advocates with little money, lightweight boards, bare-bones operating budgets, and almost no independent economic clout. The foundation was a different type of constituent. It had money, it had a significant board, and it had the promise of even more private sector money if the match money for the Ford Foundation grant was secured.

Mittenthal says of the Arizona Community Foundation's presence in the legislature's consciousness, "We stumbled on the scene and were in the right place at the right time. We were welcomed as a partner into an arena in which people had been struggling for years. The fact that we are an independent entity enhanced our credibility. Actually the resources we brought at that point were minimal in relation to the scale of the problem, but the advocates who had been working so hard to improve the situation for mentally ill children and their families were glad of any help that we could offer."

The interim legislative committee on children's mental health held a three-hour public hearing on November 23, 1987, and its recommendations and those of the Children's Mental Health Task Force were ready for Governor Mecham. Communication with the governor's office had been practically nonexistent during this time because it was almost in a state of siege; business like the Children's Mental Health Task Force was definitely on the back burner there.

The foundation had not formally testified to the interim committee, but its counsel was sought by Hoffman and the other active lobbyists, and its office was an informal center of the educational effort. Jacobs, with her broad connections in this community, served as an informal information point; she stopped rumors, passed information among the lobbyists, and assisted with her knowledge of the individual legislators and the legislative process.

Into this hectic, media-filled atmosphere of possible impeachment, recall and/or indictment, came the final report of the Children's Mental Health Task Force in December 1987. McClure and Hoffman took tall stacks of the final report to present to the governor and to the leadership of the legislature. As they approached the Capitol through the open governmental mall, they were mobbed by reporters who tore the reports out of their hands and began flipping through them. McClure and Hoffman were understandably confused; they knew the issue was important but they had no idea the media also gave it that much weight. But, surprise—the reporters mistook the task force report for a report to the legislature by a paid consultant that would define the potential Articles of Impeachment. In disgust, reporters threw down their copies and went back to waiting for something more exciting and newsworthy. McClure and Hoffman picked up the reports, went up to the governor's office, and presented them to his staff. To no one's surprise, the governor was not available to meet with them.

As the legislature opened in January 1988, the strategists for political action for children's mental health recommended that two bills be drafted and introduced, in spite of the chaos surrounding the governor:

House Bill 2335

- Creates a children's behavioral health council
- Mandates that a children's behavioral health council be appointed by the governor, President of the Senate, and Speaker of the House of Representatives

House Bill 2338

- Mandates that the Arizona Department of Health Services be responsible for delivering children's mental health services
- Allocates $5 million to begin services to children with mental health problems

These two bills waited as the long impeachment process unfolded. While the Senate conducted the impeachment trial, the House of Representatives went back to its regular workload. With almost no fanfare, no large public hearings, and minimal press coverage, these two bills passed the House and were sent to the Senate for discussion.

In March, Governor Mecham was convicted by the Senate, and Rose Mofford, Secretary of State, became governor by constitutional succession.

AMIDST RELIEF, A VICTORY FOR CHILDREN

The state began to mend. Perhaps as a part of a general feeling of relief, the Arizona State Senate passed the two children's mental health bills, creating the basis for forming a coordinated statewide, state-run children's mental health system, with initial funding of $5 million. It marks the beginning of a major change for the mentally ill children of Arizona and their families.

Several of the players credit the Arizona Community Foundation with being the catalyst that made it all happen. McClure says, "We had been working on this issue for years, but the foundation's entrance into the issue gave this thing some legitimacy and community support. They were doing the essential leadership work of educating the community. They used their funds to underwrite the development of community forums throughout the state. No one else could have done it."

During the campaign for the passage of the two bills, the varied constituency supporting changes in the children's mental health system solidified into a cohesive lobbying group. Simultaneously a group of child advocates based in the city of Prescott organized the first statewide children's mental health conference. In recognition of its contribution, the Arizona Community Foundation received the Advocate of the Year Award. This group of advocates for children recognized the worth of having a new player in the political mix and honored the foundation for its role in the political process.

In October 1988 most of the same advocates gathered at a foundation-sponsored conference in Casa Grande to examine the status of the children's mental health system and learn what the state's implementation strategies would be. During the long journey to passage of the legislation, the foundation concluded that there simply was not enough information available on the causes, possible prevention strategies, and treatments for children's mental illness. Therefore a study was commissioned from the Program for Prevention Research at Arizona State University. This study defines prevention, identifies risk factors, describes successful models, and proposes large-scale demonstration projects that include evaluation components. The grants strategy of the Arizona Children's Trust Fund is based on this study.

With this new solid basis of research and knowledge about what it will be funding, the trust fund issued a Request for Proposal (RFP) on December 15, 1988. It was the first time an Arizona grantmaker has publicly announced a substantial grants program in this area, and one with potential for coordinated funding with state and other private sources. Potential applicants were challenged with a detailed and rigorous set of guidelines that call for a more sophisticated level of response than is usual with grant applications. Thirty proposals requesting a total of $1.5 million were submitted from a wide range of applicants—mental health centers, hospitals, child care centers, school districts, and Indian tribes. The foundation is considering boosting its first-year allocation to over $150,000 to respond to these and other prevention projects.

Even before the RFP, the foundation had begun moving its funding toward children's mental health. In the grant distribution cycle that ended October 1, 1988, the foundation funded a variety of programs that all have elements of prevention aimed at improving life for Arizona's mentally ill children and their families.

During the long campaign for the creation of a new children's mental health system in Arizona, the foundation's board of directors and the Children's Trust Fund Advisory Committee were all kept informed, and many participated both in their roles as committee members and as interested citizens; in the background, the staff of the Arizona Community Foundation kept moving along—raising money to meet the challenge part of the Ford Foundation grant, raising money for their other essential projects, and projecting a professional, concerned image to the community.

Many times in the political process the image of what happens is more important than the reality; this time Arizona got both—the reality of a developing (though still seriously underfunded) children's mental health system and the perception that a new player in the political mix, the Arizona Community Foundation, was helping to create the new system.

Gaining the higher profile that participation in this legislative battle gave them has made changes in the foundation's viewpoint. "It became increasingly clear to us this year that the major audience for what needs to be done for most human service issues *is* the legislature," Mittenthal says. "We learned a lot and plan to continue to be involved. Informally there will continue to be contact with the legislature."

The community foundation is already deeply involved in defining ways to share information and insights with the legislature. "What can we undertake to help these 90 most essential people deal with priorities affecting the well-being of Arizona," he says. "The first thing we will do is ask *them!*" Thus he has begun meetings with individual legislators to ask them how the Arizona Community Foundation can best inform and help the legislators on issues on the foundation's agenda.

Mittenthal plays down the community foundation's leadership role in the children's mental health scenario. "It was more serendipitous than calculated," he says. However, the forces that came together to allow these significant bills to be passed were not accidental. The advocates needed the credibility of the Arizona Community Foundation, the foundation needed the public exposure that participating in this public issue would bring, and the legislators needed the evidence that the private sector was chipping in and not just asking for help.

The foundation may not have prowled the legislative cloakrooms promoting specific bills, but its credibility and stature were no less present through dollar support and moral encouragement of advocacy efforts, participation in the closing deliberations of the children's mental health task force, and association with several key legislators via the Children's Trust Fund. In a state like Arizona, private sector initiative is customarily valued. Knowing that a private grantmaker stands behind legislation and is prepared to use its own resources to help foster a public agenda lends cachet to the agenda and the foundation.

22

Boston: Poverty and Community Organizing

Michael Segal

In September 1984, the Sunday *New York Times Magazine* ran a controversial article headlined "Manchild in Harlem," written by Claude Brown, the noted black author and teacher. Brown, who 20 years earlier wrote the book *Manchild in the Promised Land,* an account of his Harlem youth, depicted life in New York City's black ghetto as being "persistently violent." The essay was labeled a fiction by some, prophetic by others.

One person who was deeply moved and troubled by the piece was Geno Ballotti, the director of the Boston Foundation. Since assuming the top position five years earlier, Ballotti had been nudging the foundation toward a focus on persistent poverty. Brown's tale of life on the mean streets of his native city suggested to Ballotti that perhaps a more aggressive approach to dealing with the problems confronted by the poor was necessary. He asked his staff to determine whether Brown's portrait of Harlem was at all reminiscent of life in Boston's black neighborhoods; if so, he wanted to know what the foundation and others could do about it.

A staff retreat in nearby New Hampshire was scheduled for the following month to discuss the problems of Boston's inner city, and to hear the reactions of youth service workers from the Roxbury section of the city, Boston's black ghetto.

While Boston was not viewed as being as dangerous as New York, what the staff learned was troubling enough: among Boston public school children, 38 percent came from families receiving AFDC welfare grants, and nearly 50 percent lived in public housing. A judge from the Roxbury District Court told the staff that the number of cases coming before him that were drug- and teen-pregnancy-related was rising dramatically. A pediatrician at Boston City Hospital reported increasing numbers of low-birth-weight children and poor pregnant women who receive inadequate or no prenatal care; and of significant growth failure in poor children under six years of age.

The staff retreat was postponed when, four days before the date, Geno Ballotti unexpectedly died. Named to succeed him was his deputy, Anna Faith Jones, who had served as a program officer at the foundation since 1974. Jones became the first black woman ever to head a major foundation in the United States.

Under the leadership of board chairman Dwight L. Allison, Jr., and Jones, the Boston Foundation, the fifth largest and one of the oldest community foundations in America, moved quickly early in 1985 to implement a new project, which became known as the Poverty Impact Program (PIP). It was both a tribute to Ballotti and a logical extension of the work that Jones and the staff of the foundation had been doing in the early 1980s.

In 1985, the foundation dispersed more than $8.8 million from assets of more than $135 million. By 1988, the numbers grew to $12 million in grants and more than $200 million in assets.

By 1988, the Boston Foundation was half-way into the ambitious, $10 million, five-year PIP program. Also that year, the foundation inaugurated a spin-off venture, the Community Organizing Initiative, which eventually became a separate, $1-million, five-year PIP program. The organizing initiative further refined, broadened, and strengthened the foundation's commitment to issues of poverty and race, and to developing new partnerships and leadership in the poor neighborhoods of Boston.

For the first time in the foundation's history, grants are being dispensed to enhance community organizing as a goal in itself. "Empowerment"—defined as skill-building, leadership development, and integrative educational opportunities—and "institutional change"—modification of actions or policies, and increased participation by the poor—are two criteria, among others, that the foundation has established for prospective grantees. In addition, the foundation has embarked on an ambitious drive to raise a $5-million endowment to make permanent the aims of the new organizing initiative.

The Boston Foundation is not the first to fund community organizing; a handful of other community foundations around the country, plus a few left-leaning private funding sources and religious foundations, support community organizing. What makes the work stand out is that a foundation of the Boston Foundation's age and size has targeted such projects as a major focus of its work.

"Rather than simply help improve a community health center, or rehabilitate some housing units, or modify some curriculum," said foundation program officer John Ramsey, "we decided to take a more frontal approach to poverty."

THE PULL OF TRADITION

From its inception in 1915, the Boston Foundation has grappled with ways to enrich the life of the people of Boston and its surrounding neighborhoods. But for much of its history, the foundation's contribution typically was in the realm of operating support to large, established health and social welfare institutions. Even when the city and the nation seemed to be imploding in the volatile 1960s, the response of the foundation was in keeping with the values and interests of its largely Brahmin donor base.

The speed with which the foundation moved in 1984 and 1985 undoubtedly would have surprised a previous generation of board members. In 1968, the Committee of the Permanent Charity Fund of Boston, as the Boston Foundation then was known, acknowledged the many crises of the year in the narrative portion of its Annual Report.

"It was a grim year," wrote the director, Wilbur J. Bender, in his opening to an unusually downbeat and introspective message to donors, grantees, and the general public. Bender went on to question the role of the community foundation. "Clearly it will share the widespread sense of urgency and will recognize the need for massive changes in the ways in which its community struggles with the monumental and unprecedented human and social problems which confront it. It will realize that it too must change."

Bender's sentiments were genuine, but they did not lead, that year or the next, or for many more, to a fundamental shift in priorities. Efforts to preserve historic buildings received a considerable amount of funding, as did suburban and waterfront open space projects. Support for the arts continued to increase, and one-third of all disposable income went to the capital needs of "significant Boston institutions"—teaching hospitals, museums, and the local public television station.

When change did come, it would take the foundation in directions never imagined. One decision made long ago gave the foundation the ability to respond to changing times and community needs: that is, its fiscal strategy was to amass the largest possible pool of unrestricted funds, as opposed to encouraging a large number of bequests, each with its own guidelines and constraints.

Thus, about 55 percent of the more than $12 million paid out in grants in 1988 came out of discretionary funds. The percentage of grant dollars generated from unrestricted funds by many other community foundations is about one-half that of Boston's.

In the early 1980s, the proliferation of local tax limitation laws in many parts of the country—including a rather draconian measure approved by Massachusetts voters that severely crimped the ability of local governments to raise property tax revenue—coupled with the federal government's policy of cutting taxes and social spending, aggravated the condition of the poor. The Boston Foundation's initial response included not only grants to groups waging a lonely and underfinanced local war against poverty—for example, the Poor People's United Fund and the Massachusetts Coalition for the Homeless—but also partnerships to address social issues. The partnerships formed included the Boston Compact, an effort that linked Boston public schools with the business community to improve the system; the Boston Housing Partnership, a plan to develop affordable rental housing that brought together large financial institutions, state and local governments, community development corporations, and others as packagers and managers of programs that salvaged buildings; and the Local Initiatives Support Corporation, a private, nonprofit enterprise that provides financial and technical assistance to housing projects sponsored by community development corporations.

With these commitments, the Boston Foundation, within a matter of just two years, became a major part of the social fabric of Boston. To Ballotti, Jones, others at the foundation, and in pockets of concern and activism throughout the city and state, poverty was viewed as a growing phenomenon that was being obscured by political optimism and a thriving local economy. Ugly and disturbing conditions were becoming evident to those who chose to look away from the impressive downtown skyline to the neighborhoods. Growing numbers of people, children especially, were being consigned to lives of poverty, illness, drug dependency, and even early death.

MAKING A DIFFERENCE

The Boston Foundation's new poverty project was introduced to the Greater Boston community through a public meeting and pamphlet called *Making a Difference.* Distributed in 1985 to roughly 3,500 community activists, issue advocates, and public opinion leaders, the 20-page booklet contained the foundation's rationale for committing $10 million over a five-year period.

"Poverty is a scourge that inflicts pain and despair upon whole communities," wrote the authors of *Making a Difference.* "It hurts people, particularly children, in devastating ways, while sapping the energy and confidence a people must have to build a hopeful future."

The long-term goal of the foundation was "to mobilize new resources, to build new alliances, and to spur new activity on behalf of the poor." To Anna Jones, this commitment was as important as the money. The foundation's message, she said, "was that democracy will fail if we allow the gap to widen between the haves and the have-nots."

The time frame was chosen because the staff and board gauged that five years was time enough to serve a significant number of people, and for people to learn something about themselves and of what works and what does not. Even if the programs that might be spawned in a resurgence of community activism with the help of the foundation were not to survive after five years, Jones suggested, "everybody benefits"—the effort would nonetheless be considered a success if a new generation of community leaders emerged.

Ten million dollars was designated for the program for two reasons: The amount would make a dramatic statement that the foundation was serious about its commitment to fighting poverty; and for internal purposes, it was decided that by spending down roughly one-third of the foundation's unrestricted funds, a significant amount would be left for other discretionary uses. Other, more traditional, grantmaking programs of the foundation were continued.

The foundation singled out four areas of activity for funding under the Poverty Impact Program—maternal and infant health care, teenage pregnancy, employment and training, and urban parks and public spaces.

These areas were selected after extensive discussions with community activists and academic experts, and a review of prior foundation grants. Early in the process it was decided that to avoid being accused of merely relabeling ongoing commitments, the foundation would not make grants in areas that had received significant funds in the past.

"The sleeper among the four was the open-spaces piece," says Jones. "I wanted to add a quality-of-life element because too often people tend to focus only on clothing, health, housing, and the like when they address the needs of the poor." It was important to Jones to include at least one item that dealt with the amenities of life in the city's poorest neighborhoods—"quiet and peaceful places."

The Boston Foundation sought through its new grant program not only to support new ideas and approaches to anti-poverty work but also to encourage more joint ventures of the type in which it had participated a few years earlier. With governments at all levels constrained by either deficits or the need to shift tax and spending burdens, calls for increased involvement by nontraditional players were widespread.

This pattern was not lost on the staff of the Boston Foundation or local community organizations. "People were beginning to come together after the federal government turned off the faucet," says Jones. "People who before had competed with one another for funds were now saying: We've got to work together; if our community is going to improve, we're going to have to do it ourselves."

POVERTY IMPACT PROGRAM GRANTS

By the end of 1988, the Boston Foundation had distributed about $5 million in the Poverty Impact Program: more than $1.25 million went out in 22 grants for health-care projects; almost $1.5 million went for 28 teen pregnancy efforts; nearly $1 million was allocated for job training purposes to 13 grantees; and 25 grants of almost $1.4 million were dispersed to preserve and protect urban parks and open spaces.

Typical of the maternal and infant health care dispersals were two grants made in 1987 and in 1988 to a group called "Networking for Life: Mattapan Infant Mortality Prevention." The Mattapan section of Boston has changed dramatically over the past two decades. Once a largely white, professional-class, suburban-like neighborhood bordering on the upper-middle-class town of Milton, Mattapan is now a poor community made up of African-American, Haitian, and West Indian peoples.

Networking for Life coordinates the activities of eight Mattapan agencies that provide a range of offerings, from general health care, mental health and housing, to day care and unemployment counseling. The staff identifies needs and capacities of participating agencies and provides a strategy for community outreach, volunteer mobilization, resource sharing, and staff training.

The Boston Foundation's most extensive commitment to combating teen pregnancy went to the Roxbury Comprehensive Community Health Center's Adolescent Life Options Center program. The project, a collaborative effort of the Health Center and the Planned Parenthood League of Massachusetts, seeks to prevent unintended pregnancy and to enable teens to make decisions that promote social and educational growth. Instruction in health care and sexuality has been provided to date to more than 1,000 teens. Career preparation, personal development counseling, and academic assistance eventually will be offered within a single freestanding facility that is being renovated. A planning grant of $75,000 was made in 1986, and a program grant of $75,000 in 1988.

In the area of employment and training, the foundation awarded $50,000 to the Boston Private Industry Council for the first phase of its "BostonWorks" program. The PIC, formed as part of the federal government's reorganization of job training initiatives in the early 1980s, seeks to expand educational and job opportunities for adults. Business firms played a major role in designing and implementing the program. With the Boston Foundation grant, over 1,200 adults benefited from their involvement in the more than 25 programs that constitute BostonWorks.

In the urban parks and public spaces funding category the foundation made a $125,000 grant to the Boston GreenSpace Alliance. The alliance, made up of 87 organizations concerned with outdoor recreational opportunities in the neighborhoods of Boston, coordinates activities in and promotes the use and maintenance of parks, urban gardens, and vacant lots for Boston residents of all ages. The grant was made to implement an "action agenda" that evolved from a seminar the foundation sponsored on the future of Boston's open spaces.

CATALYST FOR COMMUNITY ORGANIZING

The departure from 70 years of tradition marked by adoption of the Poverty Impact Program opened new possibilities not previously imaginable.

"What turned our heads around," says Jones of her board's willingness to spend less on direct services and more on antipoverty projects, "was the view that the programs are ends in themselves; they build skills and indigenous leadership." By funding these kinds of poverty programs, Jones adds, "you're building a capacity for the future," as opposed to funding the delivery of services, as needed as they may be.

Jones viewed the Poverty Impact Program only as a first step in using the resources, influence, and encouragement that an esteemed institution like the Boston Foundation can provide to develop leaders for the next wave of community-based self-help efforts.

When Jean Entine, a seasoned organizer from the Boston area, showed up looking for a job with the foundation, a concentration on community organizing had long been under discussion—"even before we gave out our first Poverty Impact grant," Jones recalls.

Among the arguments that Entine made to Jones to support her candidacy was that as a 70-year-old organization the foundation had earned a reputation as a safe and dependable entity for a certain segment of the donor community, but that others found the image a bit too stodgy for their tastes. Entine suggested that the foundation could not only make a decisive statement about its role in Boston by funding organizing, but that it could appeal to a new breed of younger donors—people influenced by the activism of the 1960s and beyond— who perceived the foundation as being too traditional to satisfy their philanthropic giving bent. In addition, Entine suggested, if a respected organization like the Boston Foundation funded organizing, other donor sources might begin to think of it as a fundable activity, as well.

THE ROLE OF THE FOUNDATION'S BOARD

The board of directors of the Boston Foundation was amenable to moving in new directions. Leadership was provided in the person of Dwight L. Allison, Jr., chief executive officer of the Boston Safe Deposit Company, the initial trustee of the foundation's funds. Allison brought energy and vision and a shared sense of values to the community activist-oriented staff.

During his first five years as chairman, from 1979 to 1984, Allison, working closely with Geno Ballotti, reorganized the foundation. Among other moves, he added four additional trustee banks. The capacity of the foundation to grow had been limited by its historic reliance on one bank; by adding others, Allison was able broaden the foundation's financial base. With Ballotti's death in 1984, and with the restructuring effort completed, the foundation began to focus more on programmatic activities.

For many organizations, when board members, let alone the chairman, start to ask questions about day-to-day operations, the inquiries are viewed by operational staff as being nothing short of intrusive. Not so at the Boston Foundation.

As Anna Jones is fond of saying, a gradual unfolding of a culture that included the staff and the board of the foundation enabled the programs of the late 1980s to emerge. Fundamental change had not come to the Boston Foundation as soon as Ballotti died. For years, he and Jones had spent considerable time working with the board, making certain that everyone was in agreement about where the organization was headed. The decisions to implement the Poverty Impact Program and, later, the community organizing initiative did not require a full-court lobbying effort by the staff.

Notwithstanding the board's willingness for the foundation to move in atypical if not radical directions, Jones approached the board before hiring Jean Entine to work on the community organizing plan. The hiring of operational staff normally does not require board approval, but since no commitment had been made to move into organizing, and since organizing was not a part of the Poverty Impact Program agenda, Jones wanted to proceed with full board awareness.

With the approval in hand to develop an organizing model and to hire Entine, Jones had her prepare a survey of the different kinds of community organizing that then were taking place in Boston. Entine spent six months in discussions with other funders, activists, and trainers, developing a proposed set of guidelines for a community organizing initiative. She reviewed more than 30 guidelines from other foundations that fund organizing initiatives, interviewed several dozen wealthy donors, met with about 15 individuals who provided training and technical assistance for organizers, and observed scores of organizing projects.

She also conducted an informal survey of local funding sources and determined that, for the most recent year for which information was available, five foundations in the Boston area made grants totaling $500,000 for organizing projects. In contrast, the 65 member foundations of the Associated Grantmakers of Massachusetts, a clearinghouse of local foundation activity, made social service grants totaling $59 million.

Entine, an organizer who had had difficulty finding money for her own projects not many years before, was hardly surprised by her findings. The vast difference in amounts of money being dispensed reflected the difference between "those who are interested in addressing systemic causes of poverty—the organizers—and those who are more focused on ameliorating the suffering—the service providers," she says. "Both are needed, but the imbalance is too great."

APPROVAL OF THE ORGANIZING INITIATIVE

In June of 1987, the board of the Boston Foundation approved the guidelines for the community organizing initiative that Entine and the operational staff had developed. Included among them were:

- Preference would be given to groups focusing on poor and low-income constituencies.
- At least 50 percent of those who plan, implement, make policy, and raise funds for the organization must be poor and low-income themselves.
- Projects should combine action and community education.
- Projects should be integrated in terms of race, class, and gender.

It was also decided that grants awarded under the organizing initiative would be made in amounts ranging from $5,000 to $25,000: The lower figure was picked to encourage fund applications from groups that traditionally do not approach large donors such as the Boston Foundation.

As always with a new and controversial initiative, a negative impact on a foundation's ability to attract donors is a possibility. While this potential was considered, Allison and the rest of the board were prepared to take the risk and live with the consequences of what they considered to be their morally correct choice.

"The special responsibility of the community foundation," Allison said when the new organizing program was announced, "is to seek out areas where change should be taking place and where there is no institution in the community that is both fostering that change and funding it."

As to the relationship between fundraising and controversial issues: "I think we ought not to put constraints upon ourselves because we think it may affect our ability to raise money," he said. "I don't think that if you do the noncontroversial thing you will raise money, and if you do the controversial thing you won't. You probably lose some donors no matter what you do.

"We really can't govern by trying to find the least controversial denominator. We have enough unrestricted money and good will and donors behind us that if we stand up and do what is right people will support us, even though they may not agree with every policy we have."

Through 1988, the Boston Foundation awarded 19 grants totaling $273,000 for organizing. The average grant size was about $14,400. They included $15,000 to the Commonwealth Tenants Organization to support a tenant organizer; a similar amount to the Chinese Progressive Association to further its work toward protecting the rights of laid-off Chinese garment workers in a section of Boston that is losing its manufacturing base and that is being encroached upon by the expansion needs of a nearby hospital; $19,000 to a group called IRATE, the Immigrant Rights Advocacy Training and Education project, to support the formation of an immigrant workers association; and $7,500 to the Massachusetts Association for Reform Now for its rape prevention program in the predominantly black Roxbury section.

ENDOWMENT

Inspired by each new step taken—from the homelessness initiatives of the early 1980s to the Poverty Impact Program of 1985, to the organizing initiative of 1988—the staff of the Boston Foundation decided late last year to institutionalize its most recent commitment. Upon the completion of a feasibility study by Entine and the foundation's donor relations specialist, Nancy England, the board approved a plan to establish a $5-million organizing endowment.

Surprisingly, Entine and England—the first fundraiser ever hired by the foundation—met little resistance when they proposed the special endowment to Jones and the board. "I don't think anyone thought it could be done," explained Entine of the ease of obtaining approval for this latest organizing proposal. "And I didn't know if it can be done, either."

Entine and England spent several months meeting with foundation consultants, bank trustees, community activists and large individual donors for their views and to gather the names of prospects for donations to the endowment. If the money is raised, the Boston Foundation would be the first community foundation to create a special fund to focus on full citizen participation and empowerment of low-income individuals and neighborhoods.

As yet unanswered is the question of how a community foundation convinces wealthy people who typically leave or donate money for arts and cultural projects to give for such a controversial program? The hope is that this field-of-interest fund will appeal to a sector of the donor community that otherwise might not give or leave money to a traditional foundation. Large and small donors are being approached to contribute to the fund, including individuals who are known to donate to similar projects out of personal or corporate-giving funds that they control. In addition, other foundations are being asked to make matching contributions.

England sees a slightly different way in which the foundation might benefit. "Some people do not like to give money that will be allocated at the discretion of a distribution committee," she says. She and Entine plan to market the new endowment fund to would-be donors as a somewhat restricted fund that can best meet the objectives of a small base of contributors. While the foundation has not abandoned its commitment to expanding its unrestricted fund, the organizing endowment represents a way to expand the donor pool.

Field-of-interest funds are not new to the Boston Foundation. If its experience with the Fund for the Homeless has predictive value, then the organizing endowment might in fact bring in the additional funds that are projected. When the foundation established the fund in 1983, no one knew for sure just how much would be raised. Within a few years, and with Kitty Dukakis, the governor's wife, serving as the fund's chairperson, more than $1 million was brought in from area corporations, civic groups, and individuals.

The community organizing endowment campaign is off to a good start with one anonymous gift of $250,000. The staff is determined to give this effort their best try. "We want to ensure that this commitment (to organizing) will endure beyond our lifetime here," says Jones. While the endowment is being raised over a five-year period, the foundation has agreed to allocate $200,000 for organizing in each of those years.

RESULTS

An outside evaluation firm, Educational Development Center, Inc. of Newton, Massachusetts, has begun to evaluate the Poverty Impact Program under a separate $100,000 grant from the Boston Foundation. The foundation was curious about the effectiveness of collaborative efforts and the assessments of grant recipients themselves of the role played by the foundation's staff. Questions that will be addressed are: Are the programs vital? Is the Poverty Impact Program important? Do the projects truly empower people? While their interim report is still months from being completed, some preliminary observations already have been discussed with foundation officials.

Many meetings with grant recipients, including scores of site visits, have revealed a concern with the multiplicity of poverty-related problems that their clients confront, and with the larger-than-anticipated number of clients that the grantees are seeing.

As for the separate community organizing grants, Jones estimates that it would take four to five more years to evaluate the skill-building and leadership-development goals of that program, which is still in its infancy.

While results of such studies will be informative, Jones believes that "sometimes we get too involved in looking at results." While it is nice to know if the prisoner is rehabilitated into a productive citizen, Jones suggests, there are other ways to gauge philanthropic programs. One "result" of the Poverty Impact Program, she says, is the creation of the organizing initiative. "We were trying to experiment with ways to use the money more effectively to promote systemic change."

Another measure is the relation of the poverty program to the foundation's ability to maintain growth of the fund. To date, the new programs have not adversely affected the level of contributions: In fiscal 1988, nearly $9 million was raised, compared to more than $11 million in 1987 and $6 million in 1986.

At another level, the foundation itself has become even more of a player in the public policy arenas of Boston's City Hall and the Massachusetts State House, a role that might not have been realized were it not for the focus on new programs. The staff is heavily involved with the Boston parks department in the effort to overhaul the city agency; through the Boston GreenSpace Alliance, the foundation plays an advocacy role at the city and state levels; the staff works with the city commissioner of health in developing maternal and infant health and child abuse and protection programs; and the foundation has provided the funds for a management reorganization of Boston City Hospital.

At the state level, the foundation is working with the state commissioner of public health to develop AIDS and infant mortality reduction campaigns; it has supported efforts that helped create legislation to assure prenatal care for poor women; and it was a principal backer of the consumer group that advocated successfully for passage of the nation's first cradle-to-grave compulsory and universal health insurance law in 1988. "These are things we would have been very reluctant to do a decade ago," according to program officer John Ramsey.

But perhaps of greatest significance, the Boston Foundation has established itself as a strong and committed partner in the effort to empower people from Boston's neglected neighborhoods. As Hubie Jones, dean of Boston University's School of Social Work and a leading human services and civil rights advocate, said in a recent Boston Foundation newsletter: " You're in the hope business. And it's important because you are the leadership foundation in Boston. The fact that you're standing up and saying that you're not going to solve this problem alone is crucial. You're trying to give sectors of the poor some hope that they are going to have access to some things they didn't have access to before."

23

Philadelphia: Grassroots Empowerment

Jennifer Leonard

"The Philly Foundation has been the one foundation that never abandoned our organization, even when we went through crisis," Johnny Irizarry reflects between bites of fried plantain.

Irizarry is executive director of Taller Puertorriqueño, a Latino gallery and arts workshop that weathered management turmoil in 1984 with Philadelphia Foundation assistance. "They knew us well enough to know that we'd come back: that the Puerto Rican community would not be without a cultural center," says Irizarry.

NEIGHBORHOOD DEVELOPMENT IN A CITY OF NEIGHBORHOODS

The City of Brotherly Love hosts the nation's third-largest Puerto Rican population, some 200,000 tomato and mushroom pickers, factory hands, students, and veterans clustered in eastern North Philadelphia. Philadelphia also boasts a community foundation some call "courageous" and others "anti-establishment," one that has set its sights foursquare behind the Johnny Irizarrys who seek to elevate and empower Philadelphia's growing numbers of poor, minority, and disadvantaged people.

In a city of 109 distinct neighborhoods, where people identify their heritage by street corners, the Philadelphia Foundation has fiercely aligned itself with grassroots community initiative. Its renewable general support grants offer start-up, sustenance, and sheer survival for small organizations serving blacks and Puerto Ricans, Asians, gays and lesbians, women, and welfare recipients.

Respected for its leadership in Philadelphia philanthropy, the community foundation's vision has been limited primarily by slow asset growth: 1988's $60 million endowment compares poorly with other mature community foundations serving populations much smaller than metro Philadelphia's 4 million. A stepped-up development effort, begun in 1987, will ultimately show whether the foundation's flaccid fundraising performance stems simply from its Quaker-like reluctance to solicit or from a rejection of its progressive policies by Philadelphia's elite.

EVOLUTION, NOT REVOLUTION

The Quakers who followed William Penn to the Delaware Valley three centuries ago came to do good and, the wags say, did well instead. With characteristic modesty, they quietly invested their wealth near home rather than market their city to the world. The result, says sociologist E. Digby Baltzell, was a city whose historical place became relegated to the eighteenth century as New York and Boston surpassed what had once been the Western Hemisphere's dominant urban center.

Conservatism runs deep in Philadelphia. Despite its reputation as the birthplace of the Declaration of Independence, Tories partied here till dawn with British officers while Washington's troops starved at Valley Forge. According to historian Dennis Clark, former director of the Samuel Fels Fund, Philadelphia's elite were "deeply suspicious of immigrants and ethnics and blacks and working class people" brought in to fuel the small factories of the city's diverse manufacturing economy in the 1800s and early 1900s.

The loss of 200,000 manufacturing jobs after World War II increased class and income disparities. By 1982, the average white Philadelphia homeowner earned 50 percent more than the comparable black homeowner, a disparity that census figures suggest has only grown worse. Although a growing service sector and new generation of non-native CEOs have shaken some dust off Philadelphia's economy, its poor remain little touched, their unemployment exacerbated by the residential stresses of gentrification and redevelopment.

In America's fifth-largest city, tradition still rules. The Philadelphia Foundation's commitment to the underclass represents its own kind of tradition, one distilled from progressive Quaker and Episcopal elements or what historian Clark calls "the good face of the power structure."

THE MODESTY OF FRIENDS

William P. Gest, president of Fidelity Trust & Safe Deposit Company (now The Fidelity Bank), sold the community foundation concept to his board of directors in 1918. In good Philadelphian style, Fidelity ran the trust quietly, efficiently, and with little risk, although board minutes do note a 1946 "experiment" to centralize services for the chronically ill. In 1958, the foundation expanded to a six-bank trust (now seven) and hired its first staff director, Richard K. Bennett. Thus began three decades of increased risk-taking and social experimentation spearheaded by Bennett and his successors, Sidney Repplier and John Ruthrauff.

Bennett staffed a powerful new Distribution Committee led by Graeme Lorimer, editor of the *Saturday Evening Post* and *Ladies Home Journal.* In a 1988 interview, Bennett recalled that the board's grantmaking agenda related to the "in-town establishment," and that its members "would have liked to keep money with the art museum and orchestra." But Bennett—a "convinced" (converted) Quaker and conscientious objector who served with the ambulance corps in World War II—instead set the tone for a community foundation that would heed the cries of the community's powerless.

Bennett recalls bringing the Distribution Committee a newspaper-article about nine people found dead of starvation on city streets. The board members showed little emotion around their drinks at the fashionable Rittenhouse Club. But later, every member discreetly telephoned Bennett to inquire how the foundation might help.

"The Quakers get along with and can maintain a dialogue with the most diverse elements in society," says historian Clark. "So the role of a man like Dick Bennett with the Philadelphia Foundation ... sort of represents philanthropy with a ... modest face: not the pushy, individualist philanthropy of the guys who name big buildings after themselves, but much more studied and low key. That suited Philadelphia."

In 1960 Bennett was selected to direct the much-enlarged Phoebe Waterman (now William Penn) Foundation. But before leaving the Philadelphia Foundation, Bennett ensured his legacy by recruiting as his successor a man he knew from their mutual work with the Indian Rights Association.

THE LIBERAL EPISCOPALIANS

Sidney N. Repplier, a newspaper and magazine writer, knew nothing of foundations but everything about need. A progressive Episcopalian, Repplier subscribed to democratic ideals of equity and harmony among races. During 22 years with the Philadelphia Foundation, Repplier realized what Bennett had begun: a series of risk-taking, compassionate investments in consumer, minority, welfare, and women's rights.

The foundation's patrician board gradually went along with his views of good grantmaking: cooling tempers raised by blockbusting, easing racial tensions in the schools, assisting The Moroccos street gang in publishing a teen newspaper, underwriting a feisty consumer activist named Max Weiner. Board minutes from the 1960s reflect expanding support for issues affecting the poor and minorities. A 1974 letter to the Filer Commission from Repplier's associate director, the Reverend Donald Gebert, stated that "almost every grant ... would fulfill your criteria as being for the powerless."

From the late 1960s, the foundation also took a firm stand for women's rights—and pro-choice on abortion, a plucky policy in a city by then full of second-generation Irish and Italian immigrants. Philadelphia's innovative federated women's funding group, Women's Way, accrued national renown some years ago when rebuffed for membership in the local United Way, which said it would not support programs that contravened "the teachings of the Catholic Church." The Philadelphia Foundation, in contrast, has opted to fearlessly support every single organization under the Women's Way umbrella, incuding those advocating that women have choice with respect to abortion, family planning, and divorce.

The Philadelphia Foundation was an early supporter of day care, of rape hotlines, of battered women's shelters. Jane O'Neill, who later became a donor, recalls that she first encountered the foundation in her role as president of Planned Parenthood in the mid-1960s: "There was a very hostile public out there. Nice people didn't talk about [birth control]. The Philadelphia Foundation had the courage to make the decision that population control was one of our most important issues."

A WILLING BOARD

Repplier credits his board members with having had the independence to take chances on groups that didn't come with a "social pedigree." He tells the story of board member Ernest Scott, a prominent local attorney who, in his capacity as chairman of the local United Way, was picketed one day in the late 1960s by an angry group of welfare recipients, protesting that United Way was doing too little for them.

Delayed by the protest, Scott arrived late for the foundation's semi-annual Distribution Committee meeting. When he asked how far the group had gotten on its agenda, Repplier replied, "We're considering a grant to the Philadelphia Welfare Rights Organization." Scott groaned. "If I had any sense, I would vote 'no.' But, doggone it, the people deserve a hearing," said Scott.

Repplier recalls that the board burst into applause before voting the grant. For two decades, until a recent $2,000 gift from the Pew Charitable Trusts, the Philadelphia Foundation remained the only foundation that supported this advocacy organization for poor people, although it operated with considerable support from the state.

Board members, who initially trusted Repplier as a fellow blueblood guided by religious motives, increasingly supported his programs as their ranks diversified in gender and race during the 1970s. The foundation asked the board's appointing authorities to select civic leaders with a demonstrated interest in low-income communities. By the early 1980s, what had begun as an all-white male board boasted two women and, for two years, a black majority, reflecting the city's 40 percent black population.

AN ANONYMOUS DONOR

Both Repplier and John Ruthrauff, who became director in 1982, attribute part of their success in expanding the board's grantmaking vision to a special woman who established the foundation's first donor-advised fund 20 years ago with two gifts totaling $2.7 million.

The Anonymous Donor—as she continues to be known, her identity preserved even from the Distribution Committee—recalls meeting fellow Episcopalian Sid Repplier at "something to do with welfare rights." In a telephone interview arranged to protect her anonymity, this self-described Main Line heiress said her interests in civil rights and in grassroots organizing fit well with the foundation's philosophies. Her willingness to listen to foundation suggestions provided staff with an alternative avenue for presenting controversial grants to the Distribution Committee.

The Anonymous Donor recalls that Sid Repplier "would present something [risky] to me, saying he didn't know if it would go through; but if it was coming from the Anonymous Donor, well, he said, 'We'll have more chance of it going through.' " Once approved by the board, which reviews all donor-advised grants, grantees could develop a track record and be presented again for funding, this time from discretionary monies.

"It gave us a tremendous amount of clout," recalls Repplier, "when you could say with complete truthfulness that we had discussed some of these projects and some were off the wall at the time but have turned out to be excellent social investments." Longtime foundation grantees first funded by the Anonymous Donor include the Women's Law Project; Women in Transition, a counseling program; and the Elizabeth Blackwell Health Center for Women.

With full-time staffing and multiple trustee banks, the foundation's assets grew from $5 to $43 million during Repplier's two-decade tenure. Most important for the foundation's community focus, the proportion of completely unrestricted funds rose from 3 percent to 18 percent.

The foundation's annual reports also promoted "preference" funds, in which donors name agencies to receive first consideration for grants but leave the Distribution Committee final say. Unlike designated agencies, which receive an automatic annual *pro rata* share of fund income, preference agencies must apply for grants, receive amounts similar to other applicants, and are urged to spend the money on the poor and disadvantaged. Unallocated income from preference funds is spent at board discretion, making them additionally attractive. By 1982, thirty-three percent of the foundation's grantmaking came from preference funds.

IMPLEMENTING EMPOWERMENT

Associate director John Ewing Ruthrauff became executive director after Sid Repplier retired in 1982. Much like Repplier, Ruthrauff was a well-bred activist for progressive causes. Before joining the foundation in 1975, Ruthrauff spent three years as a management consultant with Philadelphia's Health and Welfare Council, assisting nonprofit agencies and organizing welfare recipients. A member of the American Friends Service Committee's Latin American Panel since 1980, Ruthrauff has used his annual three-week leaves to lead six groups of funders and one Congressional delegation on tours of Central America.

While preserving the foundation's traditional focus on the poor, women, and minorities, Ruthrauff felt the foundation's giving could be better defined to emphasize projects that helped people help themselves. After six months of discussions led by new Distribution Committee chair David Brenner, who left shortly thereafter to serve as City Commerce Director, the board in June 1983 unanimously reaffirmed the foundation's support for the poor and disadvantaged. A new policy statement stressed the concept that has become central to the Philadelphia Foundation's discretionary grantmaking in the 1980s: "empowerment," which Ruthrauff defines as "learning by collective action and trying to address causes" of social problems.

Grant proposals must address a set of "empowerment criteria" to show that applicant organizations:

- primarily benefit low-income and/or minority communities.
- have an organizational structure that assures the active involvement of its constituents in defining the problems to be addressed, making policy, planning, and evaluating the program.
- address the causes of problems affecting the group.
- promote collective action and mutual support in solving economic and social problems.
- build leadership skills and improve an individual's ability to assert control over his/her life while also helping others.

The net effect of these policies has been that the foundation tends to emphasize advocacy over direct service; gives preference to small agencies; and requires meaningful participation by the poor or minority people who stand to benefit from the foundation's grants.

A VOICE FOR CONSTITUENTS

To demonstrate client involvement in planning, policy making and programs, applicants must submit a "constituency information sheet" listing racial, income, and gender breakdowns for staff, board, and beneficiaries. While many foundation grantees met the new guidelines, a few complained, including a cultural agency executive who claimed her theatrical presentations would suffer if she diverted attention to placing minorities on the board or to attracting them to her audiences.

In practice, the empowerment criteria have provided an incentive for grantees to become more representative: "By having this kind of a mission statement ... organizations that applied ... knew then that there should be a kind of special focus that they themselves had— and my belief is that organizations that want money will do anything to fit in," says Ione Vargus, former chair of the Board of Managers (the renamed Distribution Committee).

The foundation broadened its own "constituency" participation by adding grantee representatives to board and staff. With the help of an executive search service he also makes available to grantees,

Ruthrauff hired employees of community-based groups rather than staff of other foundations. Dr. Carmen Febo San Miguel, a physician who heads the board of longtime Philadelphia Foundation grantee Taller Puertorriqueño, became the foundation's first Hispanic board member in 1988. At her first board meeting, Dr. Febo illustrated the importance of diversity by questioning the small numbers of Hispanics served by Philadelphia Community Health Alternatives (PCHA), a principal local AIDS agency.

Staff pointed out that PCHA, originally founded by gay white men, had dramatically increased services to blacks after an earlier notice from the Philadelphia Foundation conditioned further grants on such an expansion. The board then reduced PCHA's multi-year request to a one-year grant and required that on reapplication the agency demonstrate increased services to Hispanics.

Discussions in that November 1988 board meeting made it clear that most board members understand and support the empowerment focus. Members expressed the usual concerns about applicant leadership changes, inadequate planning, and new organizations that duplicated existing services; but they also favored agency diversity, constituent policy participation, and advocacy activities that addressed causes rather than symptoms. The board denied funding to one longtime grantee, a homeless shelter, after staff pointed out that the agency's clients had virtually no say in the shelter's rules or operations. "The clients are more objects than subjects in the process," one staff member explained.

Yet overriding all of these factors was a dedication to the ultimate beneficiaries of the grants. Foundation staff had recommended against support for a new organization serving women ex-felons, pointing out that only one ex-felon served on the board and that it provided more service than advocacy. Foundation chairman Don Jose Stovall, a state welfare administrator, initiated a move to override the recommendation, and the board awarded $7,500 to the group from its $20,000-per-meeting discretionary pool. Noting that he recognized the agency's board wasn't up to the foundation's standards, Stovall said, "There needs to be a voice there for the female ex-offender," and asked for a report the next year on the organization's progress toward program and empowerment goals.

NURTURING SMALL AGENCIES

Since 1983, the foundation has provided discretionary grants primarily to organizations with annual operating budgets of less than $1 million.

Funding small agencies means more risk. The quality of Philadelphia Foundation staff investigations into management quality, program design, and community need is well regarded by local foundation colleagues, but staff say that in order to fund grantees that meet the requisite empowerment criteria and otherwise are the most qualified applicants, they sometimes have to settle for less than optimal fiscal stability.

The foundation contributes to the stability of the small agencies by providing executive search services when executive directors leave, by providing funds for staff and board training—largely in community organizing skills—and increasingly by providing fundraising information and referrals to technical assistance providers. In recognition that small agencies need flexible funds, particularly for the advocacy activities few other funders will touch, the foundation provides three-quarters of its grants in general support. "Why do I think the Philadelphia Foundation is so terrific?" asks Letty Thall, executive director of the Delaware Valley Child Care Council and a longtime grantee in various women's programs. "Number one, they will fund operating. They recognize that for $5,000, you shouldn't have to come up with a discrete project."

The Philadelphia Foundation's general support grants can last up to ten years, sometimes longer, before the agency is asked to wait two or three years before reapplying. Ruthrauff criticizes the widespread practice of making short-term seed grants, which he believes reflects "the need of foundation staff to find excitement, not a careful analysis of what's going to develop the best resources for providing for people." Consistent, long-term support is required to produce societal change, he says.

"We need more foundations that will take on our burdens like they have," says Joe Watts, founder and executive director of a low-income housing advocacy and development agency in suburban Bucks County. The foundation, which spends half a million dollars annually on housing and community development, has given Better Homes, Inc., $127,458 in general support grants since it became the agency's first private funder nine years ago. The organization has acquired and rehabilitated 55 homes for low-income families and successfully urged county construction of 132 subsidized townhouses. In 1987, it won a joint Philadelphia Foundation–Pew Charitable Trusts–ARCO Chemical Company award for excellence in community economic development.

"The Philadelphia Foundation was quite receptive to helping us help ourselves; they've taken a risk, and I think they've come out a winner," says Watts, who washed cars and ran errands for a car dealer before founding the organization, which had a 1988 budget of $158,000.

ORGANIZING AND ADVOCACY

About one in four Philadelphia Foundation grant dollars goes toward neighborhood-based empowerment programs. These grantees are encouraged to learn how to organize their constituents to become effective advocates for change. The foundation's staff also take training in community organizing through groups like the Midwest Academy and the Center for Third World Organizing, which Ruthrauff says prepares them to "look at a community in terms of which organizations and individuals have power to make changes."

Program officer Jaime Pullen uses questions like these to evaluate grantees' strategies in organizing: "Are there clear steps? Are you going after something you can win or are you just picketing a building? Is it a strategy that's been done over and over again? Is it going to lead to other things that you can win? Are you going to involve more people?"

One foundation-supported success in the advocacy arena has been the Eastern North Philadelphia Initiative Coalition, through which 37 community groups—half of them Philadelphia Foundation grantees—challenged the foundation's founding trustee, Fidelity Bank, for redlining. The coalition negotiated a $50-million reinvestment agreement in 1986. The foundation funded implementation of the plan, which finances nonprofit housing and economic development, home mortgages for low- and moderate-income families, small business loans, and bank affirmative action programs.

Critics question whether the foundation has ignored direct service in favor of advocacy. Under Ruthrauff, says Peter Solomon, a probation administrator and board member of several nonprofit agencies, "The foundation became more radical, more minority-oriented and more social change-oriented. A lot of more 'mainstream' stuff that is still important seemed to disappear. You can't ask people to get involved in movements for social change if they're hungry, ill-clothed or unhoused."

"We still fund a lot of direct service, but it can be empowering," counters Ruthrauff. "Poor people look around and see abandoned housing, drugs, kids on the streets; they set up housing, recreation, and anti-drug programs in response. When we look in minority communities for indigenous groups, these tend to be direct service. We haven't figured out how to get them to look more broadly, in an advocacy way."

Ruthrauff cites as an example the foundation's needs assessment in the Southeast Asian community several years ago, stimulated by a board member. The foundation acted on the study's recommendation to fund mutual assistance agencies led by the Hmong, Vietnamese, Cambodian, Laotian, and ethnic Chinese populations in Philadelphia, as well as their coordinating group, the Southeast Asian Mutual Assistance Associations Coalition. These organizations, Ruthrauff pointed out, began by offering English-language classes, a direct service chosen by the people destined to benefit from the grants. "The empowerment criterion comes out here fairly clearly—people in their community doing what they think is most important," says Ruthrauff.

As for funding mainstream agencies, says Ruthrauff, "I believe that innovation often comes from the fringes, not from the core. When rape became a big issue, it was not the universities or hospitals, but women's groups, that addressed it." He points out that the foundation still supports many traditional groups, including agencies named by donors as well as discretionary grantees, some 15 percent of which have budgets exceeding the $1 million guideline. He compares the empowerment focus to affirmative action:

"If you don't have a focus on something in the low-income community, you are going to end up making grants only to large traditional agencies. I think by having the focus we have, we certainly maintain a balance."

MODESTY IS NOT A MARKETING TOOL

One of the most serious questions facing the Philadelphia Foundation concerns fundraising. While the Philadelphia Foundation has met its public support test for new income every year, its asset-building has been noticeably lackluster, relying primarily on trusts generated in years past by its trustee banks. This has meant small grants (mostly in the $5,000 to $25,000 range) and, given the foundation's policy of multi-year support, few new grantees each year.

The slow growth in part reflects the foundation's preference for unrestricted funds: the board has some degree of discretion over a relatively high proportion (71 percent) of the foundation's funds. Another widely accepted reason for the slow growth has been that neither Repplier nor Ruthrauff liked to raise money.

The foundation, true to a Philadelphian style of modesty, never really tried to market itself to prospective donors until the mid-1980s, when some board members began to realize that their community foundation was lagging behind the growth rate in other cities. A first attempt to mount a development program failed six months after it was launched in 1985; a second development director, hired in 1987, has begun to produce the kinds of marketing materials and make the kinds of connections that eventually should produce results.

But will they? In a community where the tradition of the Philadelphia Foundation represents the most liberal face of the elite, a number of people worry that the foundation's progressive grants policy falls too far afield of the more conservative tastes of many donors. "I know a lot of people who definitely would not give anything to the foundation because it does things they disagree with," says one insider. "Radical" and "anti-establishment" are terms sometimes applied to its grantmaking. From welfare rights grants to the challenge of its first trustee bank, the foundation has supported groups that publicly challenge the status quo.

Although the foundation's current marketing effort is designed to reach a broad spectrum of donors, traditionally it has appealed to the already converted—people like the Anonymous Donor and Jane O'Neill, who share its progressive philosophy. "I know three people who I talked with have set up funds that will pay out [to the foundation] when they die," says Kathryn Smith Pyle, the foundation's former associate director. One, a lesbian woman, felt the Philadelphia Foundation had been open to proposals from lesbian and gay groups (two have been assisted). "Another was a woman from a social welfare background who felt that what we were doing with low-income and minority issues was more significant than any other way she could distribute her money," says Pyle.

Ruthrauff points out that community foundations in Hartford and Boston, which like Philadelphia provide substantial support for advocacy and community organizing, have each built assets exceeding $100 million. This supports the contention by Ruthrauff and some of his board members that inattention to fundraising rather than a progressive grantmaking focus has hindered the foundation's growth. "I can't say our policies affected development," says former chair Brenner. "Our fundraising was so poor through 1983.... We only got money because it showed up [from the trustee banks]."

EVIDENCE OF LEADERSHIP

Within the City of Brotherly Love, the Philadelphia Foundation has many admirers. "The Philadelphia Foundation has been working in the community in a grassroots way for so long that they are the door for many of the small organizations," says Fred H. "Bud" Billups, Jr., former executive director of the Pew Charitable Trusts, Philadelphia's largest foundation. "If it were just the William Penn Foundation and Pew, people would feel completely shut off from the sizeable foundation community and, frankly, most of the foundation community, because many of the organizations don't have the sophistication to know how to contact [family foundations]."

The Pew, William Penn, and Samuel Fels foundations have increased their support of grassroots efforts in recent years. Both supporters and critics suggest the Philadelphia Foundation influenced these changes. "It's almost as though there was this group of people who had a certain political philosophy, managed to install themselves in that foundation, and are slowly but surely changing the tenor of foundations in Philadelphia to a great extent," says Solomon, the probation administrator.

"I think the Philadelphia Foundation has played some role in prodding others into admirable behavior over time," says Professor Sandra Featherman of Temple University, board member of the Samuel Fels Fund and actively involved in both the foundation and nonprofit communities. "I wish all foundations had the kind of principled standards the Philadelphia Foundation exercises.... Some grantseekers occasionally criticize it [because it is] hard to get money for good things that are not innovative enough, but it's had very sensitive and caring and thoughtful leadership over a long period of time."

For 30 years, the Philadelphia Foundation has remained true to the needy of its city: despite the reigning forces of conservatism, the foundation and its people have vigorously pursued their own tradition of service. The next decade will prove whether the foundation can attract greater support from those with means in the city, in order that it may continue to advance the interests of less powerful citizens.

24

Charlotte: Discovering Poor Neighborhoods

Bea Quirk

The problems facing low-income neighborhoods—illiteracy, crime, drugs, teenage pregnancy—require massive efforts with large amounts of money and resources. Yet just as the mighty oak started out as a small acorn, poor people in Charlotte, North Carolina, are finding that one way to start attacking these issues is through small, locally led projects, ones that not only chip away at the problems but also teach neighborhood leaders practical skills and provide them with a sense of empowerment.

One route they have taken has been neighborhood beautification. Far from being a frill, beautification in these areas has gone far beyond new paint, flowers, and trash receptacles. For example, in the neighborhoods of Wilmore, Brookhill, and Southside, the effort led to successful lobbying for the creation of a neighborhood park. In Reid Park, beautification projects helped get teenagers together for leadership and educational seminars and led to the creation of an economic development council. And in Seversville, a clean-up project provided the impetus for several churches to join neighborhood leaders to take on further activities to improve the neighborhood.

These grassroots efforts are the result of an unusual collaboration between emerging neighborhood groups; the Foundation For The

Carolinas, a main-line establishment organization working directly with low-income neighborhoods for the first time; and the Urban Institute at the University of North Carolina at Charlotte (UNCC), the university's applied research and public service arm. They were brought together by the Charles Stewart Mott Foundation of Flint, Michigan, which included the Foundation For The Carolinas in its national small neighborhood grants program from 1984 to 1989.

"In the past, we had provided seed grants to well-organized groups that contacted us," says Carolinas Foundation vice-president Barbara T. Hautau. "But this program involved us in a new area (low-income neighborhoods) with a different approach. Instead of responding to requests for money, we took a proactive role and sought out budding neighborhood groups, most without formal nonprofit status, to fund."

These were big changes for the foundation, which started out as a vehicle to serve donors. Founded in 1958 with a $3,000 contribution from the United Way, the foundation was conceived by the United Way's Social Planning Council as a place where donors could set aside funds for future use when needed by the community. Until 1969, the foundation was almost completely donor-advised. In that year, foundation leaders slowed development efforts because changes in the tax laws made the status of contributions to community foundations unclear.

The regulations were clarified by 1974, giving community foundations a favorable status. Several board members, led by Edwin P. Latimer, retired chairman of American Credit Corp., revived and reactivated the foundation, and the United Way donated part-time staff. From 1974 to 1978, assets grew from $463,000 to more than $2 million. Staff grew to three full-time people.

With the revitalization came some change in direction. By 1988, fewer than half of its 450 funds were donor-advised, and 3 percent of the funds were discretionary. The staff numbered 11, assets were about $34 million, and annual distribution totaled about $5 million.

Through the years, discretionary funds have been used as seed grants for new organizations trying out new concepts. Among the groups the Foundation For The Carolinas has helped start are the Mecklenburg Council on Adolescent Pregnancy; the Metrolina Food Bank; Friendship Trays; Child Care Resources, a clearinghouse and advocacy group for child care; International House, a support organization for foreign nationals living in Charlotte; and Shepherd's Center, a senior center run by senior volunteers.

The foundation's board of directors has 40 members, including many of the "Who's Who" of Charlotte, such as bank presidents, CEOs of local companies, attorneys, and three former Charlotte mayors. There are four blacks and five women. About 100 volunteers serve on a dozen committees overseeing funds that require specialized knowledge, such as the Charlotte Housing Authority Scholarship Fund and the Children's Medical Fund.

NEGLECTED NEIGHBORHOODS

Charlotte, the county seat of Mecklenburg County, is located in the southwestern part of North Carolina. It serves as a regional hub for transportation, distribution, and financial services. The county's population is about 28 percent black.

In 1983, when the foundation applied for the Mott Foundation grant, Charlotte was experiencing a surge of economic growth and expansion that continues today. Most of the growth was occurring in the downtown business area and in the wealthy southeast side. Since then, growth has broadened into the northeast and southwest. But west and northwest residents—mostly black and many low-income, but also including white and middle-class neighborhoods of both races— did not feel they were sharing in the prosperity. Complaints centered on inadequate schools, improper zoning, the impact of a growing airport, poor maintenance of the area's major roads, and a lack of investment in the area by government and business.

These feelings have not changed dramatically, but citizens in the west and northwest now feel more a part of the system. They are appointed to boards and commissions, and district representation was introduced to the city council in 1977, a direct result of the neighborhood movement.

Charlotte has a history of being a commercial center (after all, it was founded in the mid-eighteenth century at the crossroads of two Indian trading paths), and business gets involved in many aspects of community life. The community's commitment to serving the needy is demonstrated by the fact that the local United Way has one of the best records in the country for consecutively meeting its annual fundraising goal on time.

But the progressive attitudes and good intentions of Charlotte's leadership have suffered from the same one-sidedness as the Foundation For The Carolinas: the problems they worked on were generally the ones seen by the city's white upper and middle classes. Their efforts have been effective in many ways, but hampered by the fact that their approaches and solutions have often not included blacks or the working class and poor of both races.

The Mott Foundation had two motivations in developing its neighborhoods small grant program. One was a commitment to low-income neighborhoods, and the other was a desire to be a catalyst for change within community foundations. Grants were awarded to seven other foundations: the Arizona Community Foundation, the Community Foundation of New Jersey, the Greater Worcester (Mass.) Community Foundation, the Dayton (Ohio) Foundation, the Greater Kansas City (Missouri) Foundation, the San Diego Community Foundation, and the Oregon Community Foundation. The grants were challenges, requiring each community foundation to match the funds.

From 1984 to 1989, the foundation in Charlotte received $175,000 for grants and technical assistance and $19,800 for administration. It also came up with a required $105,000 in matching monies, some of it raised from city and county governments, other local foundations, and corporations.

Although the Foundation For The Carolinas became the flagship of the Mott Foundation neighborhoods small grants program, it was not at first a match made in heaven. The community foundation's decision to apply involved much soul-searching and trepidation. This type of grantmaking approach was new to them; they had not before dealt directly with low-income neighborhood groups, and they were concerned about the foundation's ability to succeed.

"Gordon Berg (then the executive director) came back from the orientation session Mott had for prospective grant recipients very excited, and that excitement was shared by the Board," Hautau recalls. "No one else in Charlotte was doing it, but we had a lot to think about. Did we know enough about low-income neighborhoods? Did we have enough staff? We didn't want to start something and then drop it. We knew we were making a big commitment."

Philosophical issues were also involved. David Taylor, a retired Celanese executive and a former member of the community foundation's board of directors, felt strongly about its need to take a new direction.

"We approached the Mott program with obvious trepidation, but I believed we had to instill a sense of action, not reaction, in the foundation," Taylor says. "People came to us with money, but we hadn't struck out on our own or taken any initiatives. To me, we couldn't justify our existence if all we did was act as a conduit."

The foundation called in people with expertise in low-income neighborhoods and grassroots organization from the start. It met with representatives from the black community, the Charlotte Housing Authority, the United Way, and the university. The university's Urban Institute reported that there were some 200 low-income neighborhood groups in Charlotte alone.

The foundation asked businessman Sam Smith, a leader in one of Charlotte's first successful neighborhood groups, to organize a neighborhood grants committee to make recommendations on funding. As a member of United Way boards, chair of the Charlotte Housing Authority, and a member of the Planning Commission, Smith had credibility with several sectors, and it was felt that he could bridge both worlds.

To further ensure knowledgeable implementation of the program, the foundation turned to UNCC's Urban Institute, which helps carry out the university's strong commitment to public service. The institute had its own staff and had a reputation for its proactive stance, having administered and run Leadership Charlotte, a leadership development program, since 1979. The institute was also active in developing a 250-acre mixed-use development adjacent to the university campus that acted as a catalyst for redirected growth in the county. It had also done extensive research on Charlotte's neighborhoods.

COLLABORATION AND CREDIBILITY

Taylor, the only foundation director to serve on the Neighborhood Grants Committee, says, "I don't think we (the foundation) could have done it on our own," he said. "The cooperative effort of the foundation, the committee and the Urban Institute was a key."

Mott Foundation representatives didn't see it that way, however, and the university's involvement was one of their biggest qualms. "Because of past experiences, we were suspicious—academics often have no sense of what neighborhoods are all about," recalls Suzanne Feurt, program officer for the Mott Foundation. "So we looked at their technical assistance carefully in our annual evaluations, and to our surprise and pleasure, the arrangement worked out well. They truly developed a partnership."

Still, in the beginning, it was a leap of faith for many, including Smith. "Frankly, I had viewed the foundation as elitist," he notes. "This was the first time I saw them seeking involvement outside the close, affluent group who ran it."

"And with the Mott program, I saw an attractive way for neighborhoods to be involved in bettering themselves," Smith adds. "Their
ownership in the program appealed to me. So I wanted volunteers
on the Neighborhood Grants Committee who would be active and
who had differing perspectives."

That included 11 diverse members who knew the local political
process, who worked with neighborhood groups, who specialized in
low-income housing, who had a corporate background, or who had
experience being advocates for low-income groups.

The committee's first task was winning the trust of the poor neighborhood groups. It helped that its members were known to them,
but these groups had seen programs before, started by others with
the best of intentions, that failed to come through as promised. This
was cynicism born of experience.

The Bethlehem Center is a nonprofit community center that serves
as the focus and administrative agent for three neighborhood groups
that have applied jointly for grants from the foundation. Barbara
Dellinger, associate director of the center, says, "When I first read about
the program in the paper, I didn't think they'd really give direct grants
to low-income neighborhood groups. It was an innovative step, and
it paid off."

"I remember one of our first meetings with the neighborhood groups
when we told them about the program," the foundation's Taylor says. "It
was like a couple of fighters circling each other. Who was going to
do what? They wondered if we were for real, and if we were, how
it could benefit them. When they realized we were for real, confidence
and trust built up on both sides. They learned, and we learned."

It also took time to define and fine tune the application process.
First, the Neighborhood Grants Committee rejected the foundation's
usual grant proposal form as inappropriate for low-income neighborhood groups. So they simplified the process and developed their own
guidelines. In 1984, $50,000 in grants was awarded.

In those first years, the committee also realized that smaller grants
would be more effective. "Under the Mott guidelines, $7,500 was the
maximum grant we could give, and most of us felt there wasn't much
you could accomplish with that," says Dr. Bill McCoy, director of the
Urban Institute. " Yet that was more than many of the residents earned
in a year, and they didn't even know where to start in spending that
kind of money wisely. So we reduced the amount of the grants to
an average range of $1,500 to $3,000 and increased the number we
gave."

The lack of money management skills was indicative of another important need of the neighborhood groups: development of leadership skills. As a result, leadership training became a required part of the grants. The Urban Institute holds a series of workshops each year. In addition, an annual awards banquet is held, and once a year, all the groups receiving grants go on a retreat.

DEVELOPING YOUNG LEADERS

Another major concern of the neighborhood groups has been the need for younger leadership to take over when the current organizers step aside. So in 1988, the Urban Institute added leadership training for youngsters aged 12 to 16. The sessions range from challenge courses on beams and ropes to discussions of attitudes and values.

In 1988, $44,480 in grants was awarded to 14 neighborhood groups, eight of which have received grants every year of the program's five-year history.

Beautification projects, the most commonly funded in the neighborhood program, have had far-reaching effects each year. For example, one of the first grantees was a coalition of three groups representing the Brookhill, Southside, and Wilmore neighborhoods. The Bethlehem Center has acted as their fiduciary agent and handles administration. The first year, they began paying area teenagers minimum wage to clean up the neighborhoods. This, in turn, helped the groups develop better relations with city government agencies and with local businesses. However, it still took substantial lobbying of local officials and negotiating with the city's Parks and Recreation Department to get a commitment for a public park on a rundown vacant lot. The groups also got financial support from a local Rotary Club, and ground was broken for the park in 1988.

The Reid Park Association uses the clean-up days as a way of introducing teenagers to such programs as challenge courses, workshops, and career days. At first, organizers literally had to knock on doors to find participants; now they're forced to turn teenagers away.

"In a city that's beautiful (Charlotte is known for its trees and landscaped streets), if you don't live in a pretty area, it's a big deal when it becomes attractive. It says that you belong, and that's a place to start," McCoy says. "Plus it's doable, and you can immediately see the results. It also leads to more sophisticated projects.

"If one part of a neighborhood is cleaned up, the parts that aren't clean become more visible, and there's pressure on their owners to do something about it," Taylor says. "Goodness can spread as well as evil."

About half the neighborhood groups have developed crime watch groups. Another highly successful project has been the First Ward Full Court Press. It combines basketball competition with community service and education, in which teams win points not only by scoring baskets, but by participating in community service projects (such as distributing information on child abuse and crime prevention) and by learning about such issues as drug abuse and teenage pregnancy prevention.

The Crestdale Community Organization in Matthews (in southeast Mecklenburg County) has received grants since 1985 to leverage more money to renovate its community center, add equipment, and begin new programs. Pottstown (a neighborhood located in Huntersville, a small town north of Charlotte) received funding for a lawn-care service that developed into a small business for the community. Three participants then took the skills they learned to start their own lawn-care service. Local business development is one of the program's long-term goals.

In 1988, the association in Huntersville received funds from the foundation to implement a food-service program at its community center, which had received funds from the county's Community Development Program for a fully equipped commercial kitchen that no one knew how to use. Working with a local community college, the association used the funds to train residents to use the equipment and serve nutritious meals to large groups, thereby generating money for the community and preparing them for food-service jobs elsewhere.

In Reid Park, the project began by installing neighborhood markers at the entrance to the community. Now, in addition to youth clean-up and leadership training, the neighborhood group is starting a day-care center, exploring the possibility of forming an economic development council to encourage businesses to locate in the area, and finding ways to stimulate new housing.

DOING THEIR BEST ON THEIR OWN

"In many programs of the 1960s and 1970s, outsiders came in and told these groups what to do," McCoy says. "With this program, the neighborhoods decide what they want to do, and we let them do their best on their own. We help, but we don't do the work or the organizing. We encourage them to look to their own resources and to form linkages with other groups.

"It's up to the groups to succeed or fail on their own," McCoy continues. "And there have been a few failures, usually caused by a lack of group consensus, cooperation, or mission. We generally give groups two years to show some progress before funding is cut off."

Although all those involved in the neighborhoods program are proud of the success of specific projects, they share a larger satisfaction. "It goes far beyond a particular project," says Rickey Hall, a leader in the Reid Park Community Organization. "The program has given us credibility and visibility and validates us with the community as a whole. We've developed a network of people and groups to turn to.

"It's given us a focus and a vision and the ability to plan and come up with creative ways to approach the problems in our neighborhoods. Plus it's offered us opportunities for personal development, to learn leadership skills and refine our abilities."

Hall, who works in the county's elderly lunch program, is an example of what those opportunities can lead to. He grew up in Reid Park and had moved away, but became involved in revitalizing its community organization. In 1988, he was accepted into Leadership Charlotte and is now involved in a variety of community groups, including the Charlotte–Mecklenburg Citizens Forum. Now in his late 20s, Hall has become an up-and-coming leader in the city, one to watch in the future.

"The neighborhood leaders have always been the experts—they know their needs—but their talents and abilities have never been tapped," says the institute's Green. "The neighborhoods are becoming stronger, linkages are being created, contacts are increasing, and their base of support is growing."

Not only has the neighborhoods small grants program had a positive effect on these low-income neighborhoods, it has also changed the Foundation For The Carolinas.

Taylor says, "We've shifted from a reaction mind-set to one of taking initiatives. And now we need to get through to people to give discretionary, or undesignated, funds."

The Foundation has recognized the problems posed by restricted funds. "We don't do fundraising, but when approached by a donor, we rarely asked for discretionary funds. Now we'll be more expressive about the need for it," Hautau says. "The neighborhood grants program is a good example to show donors what can be done with money that's unrestricted. It has strengthened our hand in that area."

As a result, one anonymous donor who had a donor-advised fund, gave an additional $1 million in discretionary funds to the foundation's endowment.

The Mott Foundation's Feurt is impressed with the changes in the Charlotte Foundation. "They have a better knowledge of community-based issues, and they no longer see them mainly through the eyes of their board," she said. "They better understand the value of the minority perspective, and more democratic values have entered their structure. They're better stewards of the money they have and are responding better to community needs."

Others are beginning to recognize and take advantage of that capacity. Hautau reports that other foundations now turn to them, and that Charlotte city council members who represent low-income neighborhood groups work with the foundation.

The Mott Foundation ended its funding of its original neighborhoods small grants program with the 1988–1989 fiscal year. But its effects on the Foundation For The Carolinas will remain, as the local group continues to take the lead on more projects and raise more discretionary funds. It has also made a commitment to continue the neighborhood grants program without the Mott funds, a commitment that has not been shared by all of the other seven recipients of funds from the National Community Foundation Grant Competition.

These changes have won over many people who had their doubts about the foundation. Smith, the chair of the Neighborhood Grants Committee, now also serves on the foundation's Distribution Committee. "The foundation has become more sensitized to the needs of the community," he says. "That's one reason I have chosen to participate—to help make sure we keep making strides in that direction."

25

Kansas City: Black and Hispanic Funds

Kenneth LaFave

Greater Kansas City contains a sprawling metropolitan area of some 1.4 million people in seven counties of two states, Missouri and Kansas. Although downtown Kansas City, Missouri, is an urban hub of some vitality, the larger bistate environment is a Western-style complex of multiple downtowns, bedroom communities, and shopping malls, rimmed in all directions by farmland.

The Missouri side, established and urban, has a solid Democratic majority among the electorate. Kansas City, Missouri, in Jackson County, is the major seat of business and culture for both sides of the state line. The younger Kansas side is almost uniformly Republican and given to clusters of small towns, the oldest of which is the heavily ethnic Kansas City, Kansas, in Wyandotte County. Lately, neighboring Johnson County has experienced a boom in population (most of it white and professional) and has been cited by the Census Bureau as one of the fastest-growing counties in the nation.

Writing ten years ago in words that are apt today, British author Anthony Burgess called the Kansas City area "an elegant center of trade and culture with a great Jesuit college"—Rockhurst, where Burgess was a guest on the faculty—"and the best beefsteak in the world." Indeed, the cow and its commerce dominated Kansas City for over a century, as an illuminated plastic Hereford, designated a national monument by Kansas-raised President Dwight D. Eisenhower, attests. From its 100-foot-high pedestal in downtown Kansas City, Missouri, the Hereford overlooks the Bottoms, industrial land (now largely unused) abutting the Missouri River, that once was the domain of the notorious Mayor Tom Pendergast. During the Pendergast regime between World Wars I and II, a corrupt Kansas City flourished as the Western outpost of the Mob, and speakeasies lined its fabled 12th Street.

Kansas City since World War II has become a center of clean industry. Marion Laboratories, H & R Block, and Yellow Freight are major employers. The biggest single private employer of all is Hallmark Cards, Inc., the greeting card empire of the Hall family. Nearly 7,000 Kansas Citians write, illustrate, manufacture, or market Hallmark Cards. More than just an employer, Hallmark Cards is a symbol of the present Kansas City, with its comfortable middle-class homes and traditional values, an environment conducive to family life. The Hall Family Foundations, philanthropic wing of Hallmark Cards, is the best-endowed private charitable institution in the area, with assets of better than $200 million. Founded in 1943, it serves local interest only.

Well-mowed lawns and parks still frequented by the middle class are one legitimate image of Kansas City; but another is equally real. Kansas City was born in conflict and maintains severe minority divisions and tensions today. The area was a vortex of abolitionist and anti-abolitionist agitation before the Civil War and earned the label "Bloody Kansas." In the late nineteenth and early twentieth centuries, blacks settled largely in segregated areas of both Kansas Cities. This *de facto* segregation persists today for some 180,000 blacks who live in the area and is readily evident in Kansas City, Missouri, where Troost Avenue, cynically referred to by many as "the great divide," places black neighborhoods to the east, white neighborhoods to the west. Inevitable results followed in the strife-torn 1960s, when a half-dozen blacks lost their lives in rioting.

But neither violence nor racism stopped there. In 1979, Bernard Powell, a Kansas City civil rights leader who had marched with Martin Luther King and had been awarded the Jefferson Award for Public Service, was shot to death at a public gathering. In the February 1988 issue of *Harper's* magazine, an unflattering profile of Kansas City by the K.C.-born Pulitzer Prize-winning author Richard Rhodes cited an instance in which white private security guards ousted black youths from the prestigious shopping area known as the Plaza, apparently without legitimate provocation.

Hispanics constitute a second, smaller minority population that is no less segregated. Some 35,000 Hispanics live in the area, about 80 percent of them Mexican-Americans. The original Mexican-American population arrived as section hands on the railroads at the turn of the century. A Spanish-language newspaper was founded as early as 1914, and the Mexican-American population of the two Kansas Citys grew to 5,000 by 1930. Following some deportations of illegal residents during the Great Depression, the 1940s saw a new influx of Mexican-Americans, mostly braceros, or day-workers. Migrations of Puerto-Ricans, Cubans, and Central and South Americans came to the area after World War II. A part of Kansas City, Kansas, known as Argentine and a segregated section of Kansas City, Missouri, are home to a large number of Hispanics.

The divisions persistent among racial groups had their counterpart in a divided philanthropic community. By the early 1980s, black charitable institutions were well established and independent of the majority population institutions, while majority programs were frustrated in their attempts to reach blacks. An incident in February 1983 summed this up. A nonprofit organization called the Minority Development Corporation was founded with the stated intention of funneling profits from a downtown hotel project into minority-owned businesses. A group of civic leaders were invited to form the group's board, including black businessman Ollie Gates, founder of a highly successful chain of barbeque restaurants and a well-known source of charitable giving to black charities. Gates refused to join the board, and in well-publicized statements said he feared "the corporation could become a political tug of war." The corporation went forward without Gates, but he proved to be prescient. In 1987, a plan to bail out the troubled hotel project made chances of assistance to minority-owned businesses, in the words of a spokesman, "extremely remote."

Although neither the Gates incident specifically nor any notion of the entrenched segregation of the Kansas City communities generally has ever been mentioned as a reason, the Hall Family Foundations later that year faced head-on the fact of black and Hispanic separation from Kansas City's majority population.

"It was really very simple," recalls Bill Hall, president of the Hall Family Foundations. "We were having a discussion of our board one evening, expressing concern about not doing a good job reaching black and Hispanic organizations. We talked about various strategies, but it was unlikely that we could implement any strategy to reach those groups ourselves. We simply weren't in touch with the communities they served." Dr. Clark Wesco, chairman of Sterling Drug Co. and a Hall Family Foundations board member, suggested the establishment of separate funds for blacks and Hispanics, with boards composed of those minorities.

Thus were born the Black Community Fund and the Hispanic Development Fund. The initial plan called for $300,000 to be given to the Black Community Fund and $225,000 to the Hispanic Development Fund, stretched over three years. The sole responsibility of the boards of those funds would be making grants. All the other duties of a foundation board—investment decisions and legal, accounting, and other details—would be delegated to an organization already in existence and accustomed to that work. The choice of the Greater Kansas City Community Foundation, according to Hall, was an immediate and unanimous decision.

"The Greater Kansas City Community Foundation provided two big advantages," Hall said. "First of all there was a system of checks and balances. There is always a concern that charitable monies can become too political," and the Greater Kansas City Community Foundation would be a safeguard against that, Hall believed. "Then there was the matter of overhead, all the legal work, the filing, checking out an applicant's tax-exempt status. If the new funds had to be used for staff to handle all this, most of the money would be chewed up in administrative overhead at the expense of grants."

The funds became field-of-interest endeavors within the Greater Kansas City Community Foundation. Representatives of the respective minority populations set their own funding priorities. Chairmanship of the Hispanic Development Fund went to developer Tony Salazar, known for his championing of Hispanic causes as the "unofficial manager" of the city's West Side. William M. Washington, affirmative action officer for United Telecommunications, was named chairman of the black fund.

The Greater Kansas City Community Foundation had been established in 1978 by a group of civic leaders, among them Donald J. Hall, scion of the Hallmark dynasty. The idea had been discussed for months. Then, at a dinner of the Clearinghouse for Midcontinent Foundations, someone said, "Let's stop talking about it [the community foundation] and get started." A hat was passed and the foundation was initiated with $210. By 1983, the year the black and Hispanic funds were established, the community foundation had assets of just over $8 million. In January 1986 the Kansas City Association of Trusts merged with the Greater Kansas City Community Foundation. The former, with seven member trusts, had provided some $20 million in funding to Kansas City social, educational, arts, and health programs since 1949. The result of the merger was a leap in total assets to over $24 million, as well as a very large combined board. The official new name became the Greater Kansas City Community Foundation and Affiliated Trusts, although the old name is still used for brevity. The merged organization comprised more than 125 funds and seven trusts.

The pilot period for the two minority funds was 1983–1986. The Black Community Fund assisted such cultural and service organizations as the Black Adoption Program, Black Archives, the Kansas City Friends of Alvin Ailey, and the Kansas City Jazz Commission. The Hispanic Development Fund monies went to, among others, the Guadalupe Center, a 70-year-old service organization formerly headed by Salazar; the Westside Housing Organization; El Centro community center; and the U.S. Hispanic Chamber of Commerce. In 1986, after reviewing the work of the two funds, Hall Family Foundations proclaimed both successful and granted the black fund $1 million and the Hispanic fund $750,000 to permanently establish them and encourage them to build endowments. This still left open the possibility that the funds could receive money from other sources.

No controversy seems to have arisen at any time over the idea or implementation of separate funds for "separate" populations. Perhaps because the form and style of the program simply acknowledged the separations already in place in Kansas City, the success of the funds was greeted by hurrahs. A November 12, 1986, editorial in the *Kansas City Star* exulted, "A board that is familiar with the community which it serves may responsibly and discriminately address the grant requests made by minority organizations in the Kansas City area." The black community responded with equal enthusiasm. The Urban League presented the Hall Family Foundations its 1987 Equal Opportunity Award.

At Hall Family Foundations, Bill Hall had spied one possible negative result. "Our greatest concern early on," he said, "was that our foundation and others would mistakenly think that this took care of giving to the black and Hispanic communities. In fact, what has happened is that the two funds actually increased the amounts being given by other organizations." In a way, the small amounts (less than $80,000 given annually by each fund) encouraged the leveraging of other, larger sources, often including both Hall Family Foundations and the community foundation.

Over the five years since the funds were created, the Hispanic Development Fund has proved to be the more dynamic of the pair. It has researched and defined the needs of Kansas City Hispanics, providing valuable liaison among disparate Hispanic groups and indicating possible common directions. Salazar announced early to his board, "This fund makes us (Hispanics) players in the philanthropy game." Blacks had been players in that game for decades, even if they played mostly on their own because of Kansas City's racial divisions. Hispanics comprised a much smaller community which, spread over the sprawl of the Kansas City area, had lacked focus. Therefore, while the Hispanic Development Fund had leadership thrust upon it, the Black Community Fund entered an arena that had already produced local black leadership organizations such as the philanthropic arm of Alpha Kappa Alpha and the prominent charitable group known as The Gentlemen of Distinction.

Rather than lead in any traditional sense, the Black Community Fund has acted as a sort of safety net for applicants who might otherwise give up, intimidated by the bureaucracy of grantsmanship. Washington has found that one of the most valuable services he can offer is that of streamlining the grant process.

"This has worked to our advantage because members of the Black Community Fund are members of the black community," Washington says. "We're familiar with the wants and needs of the community and we're aware of what various organizations are doing to meet them. We do not necessarily have a lot of investigating to do of the agencies, or if we do, it's just a matter of a telephone call or dropping by to talk. We know all the directors of the organizations."

Urban planner Ken Bacchus, a noted leader among younger black businessmen in Kansas City, was for several years head of a black neighborhood improvement agency. He confirmed Washington's statement.

"If you go to one of the larger foundations, you may have to make your point in great detail," Bacchus says. " You may submit everything you thought was necessary and then have to submit more. You may be on the verge of receiving your grant when a site visit is decided on and the grant is put off a month. Bill Washington has kept the Black Community Fund a fund of relatively immediate access."

Yet Bacchus never once applied to the Black Community Fund while he headed a community organization. He didn't need to. Other philanthropic sources were open to him, sources with more capital at their disposal. He says he perceives the Black Community Fund as "more of a support group than a leadership organization," and believes it is an invaluable source for small, newer black nonprofits and for applicants who might be intimidated by larger, nonblack organizations.

Comfort is indeed an element working in the fund's favor. "We have people coming to us who would never approach a white-controlled foundation," Washington says. "We've funded a number of smaller organizations that were not affiliated with the United Way, that were not 501(c)(3) tax-exempt organizations. Black people coming to black people creates a sense of community ownership of the fund and makes applicants comfortable. If this fund had been set up another way, as part of a common pot, the money might still be there, but black people wouldn't have the access to it they have now." The Black Community Fund makes grants to some non-501(c)(3) organizations through other agencies while helping them apply for tax-exempt status.

Black Community Fund grants go mainly to social service agencies, small businesses, and cultural groups. The most visible minority cultural enterprise in the city is the Kansas City Friends of Alvin Ailey. In 1984, after a Kansas City appearance by Ailey's New York-based American Dance Theater, The Gentlemen of Distinction approached Ailey with the idea of a residency in Kansas City. Ailey's integrated modern dance troupe would do outreach programs in schools, prisons, and community centers, in addition to performing for the general public at Kansas City's Folly Theater. Ailey said yes, and a support group was founded, headed by prominent black businessman Allan S. Gray.

The highly successful first residency included the world premiere of an Ailey ballet about Charlie Parker, called "For Bird, With Love," and generated a great deal of press. Since then, the "Friends" has presented Ailey's main company every other year and his second company in odd-numbered years with at least as much success among white and black audiences.

"The Black Community Fund has buttressed the already existing philanthropic network," Gray points out. "We were one of the first organizations it assisted. It certainly helped us to leverage other money and attract new dollars in the black community. With the dollars limited, it's crucial that the Black Community Fund identify causes worthy of its dollars." The fund's identification of the "Friends" led to major funding directly from the Greater Kansas City Community Foundation.

But the situation in the Hispanic community was altogether different. It was smaller than the black community, at a further remove on account of language, and its population centers were more distant from the heart of Kansas City. There was another aspect of Hispanic experience that might be called "invisible minority status." Until 1960, the Federal Census did not officially differentiate Hispanic from "white."

"We have a problem in this city being identified as a minority," says Bernardo Ramirez, assistant director of the Guadalupe Center. "When minorities are talked about in Kansas City, it means talk about blacks. We've been lost in the shuffle, and we've needed something like the Hispanic Development Fund to help identify us."

El Centro community center is an archdiocesan program in Kansas City, Kansas, whose executive administrator Richard Ruiz put a spin on Ramirez's point. "We never got much help before the Hispanic Development Fund came into being. If the monies were there, why weren't we looked upon favorably? What has happened is that now the fund leverages for us; case in point, our capital fund drive. The Hispanic fund made a contribution of $27,000. We were then able to go to Hall Family Foundations and say, 'Can you put up $50,000?' When they did, we went to another foundation and said, 'Hey, Hallmark Cards is participating.'" They raised the remaining $32,000 they needed.

Bill Diaz, a program officer for the Ford Foundation, had a chance to look at the Hispanic Development Fund closely in 1985, when Hall approached him with the idea of establishing funds in other cities on the Kansas City model. Hallmark had just purchased Univision, a Spanish-language television network, and Hall's idea was the possible implementation of funds in larger cities serviced by Univision, such as New York and Los Angeles.

"We needed to involve the station managers, since we didn't want to do anything without their approval," Diaz remembered of the proposed plan. "We wanted to use the stations for fundraising purposes—telethons, for example. It didn't work for a range of reasons, but both Ford and Hallmark have talked about getting back together to reopen this."

Of the "range of reasons," the most crucial related to the size of the communities involved: "It worked well in Kansas City because it's a small Hispanic community there and more unified, mostly Mexican-American," Diaz says. "That way you could find a key leader like Tony Salazar who knew everybody. When you start looking at New York and Los Angeles—with vastly larger, less unified Hispanic communities—you have a lot of different leadership that won't necessarily rally round."

Yet Diaz believes the Kansas City model is still workable in other places, given more developmental work, and he echoes a familiar strain when he talks about the Hispanic Development Fund representing something new in local philanthropy for Hispanics.

"Ford has been funding Hispanic organizations at the national level for 20 years, yet at the local level funding has been virtually nil," Diaz observes. What hasn't been done by mainstream organizations in the past probably won't be done in the near future, Diaz believes, without the innovation of plugging directly into the Hispanic community.

"The notion of Hispanics making themselves philanthropists is the key to success," he says. "The greatest value of something like the Hispanic Development Fund is that it can network with other organizations on an equal footing, the same way I can call a colleague at another foundation."

Ruiz echoes Diaz on the significance of community ownership. "This is an endowment we can say is ours. Through it we control our own destiny; set our own priorities. We do what the community feels are the most important things," Ruiz says. It is especially helpful to El Centro, he adds, because El Centro's location in Kansas City, KS, is "not in Hallmark's backyard."

Attorney Ramon Murguia took over from Salazar in 1987 and, in conjunction with the community foundation, oversaw the research, writing, and publication of a massive, 500-page "Hispanic Needs Assessment" for the purpose of verifying that the fund's perception of priorities was "in sync" with the community's perception. Residents, agency representatives, and community leaders were surveyed. An extensive group of volunteers gleaned demographic information and inquired about opinions on everything from immigration laws to the probabilities for success of the various Hispanic subgroups.

The study was undertaken partially to confirm and elaborate a priority that was already in place: the Hispanic Development Fund's commitment to education.

A year after the Fund was formed, a pattern became apparent. Of all requests, monies for scholarships for Hispanics to go on to college were the most numerous. "We thought, 'wouldn't it be more efficient to present a united education front as an outgrowth of the Fund?' " said Murguia. So in 1985, a separate fund was established, the Hispanic Scholarship Fund. Its directors were identical with those of the Hispanic Development Fund, but fiscal resources were maintained separately, and it was also under the community foundation's umbrella.

In addition to providing overwhelming support for the priority of education, the study reached a number of other conclusions, including the following:

1. The Hispanic population in Greater Kansas City is apparently somewhat better off economically than Hispanics nationally, but less well off than the general Kansas City population.

2. Largely fluent in English, most Hispanics nonetheless continue to speak mostly Spanish at home.

3. Kansas City-area Hispanics cite low educational levels and high dropout rates as their most urgent problems, with high unemployment a related concern.

4. Teenage pregnancy and alcohol and drug abuse are seen as prime contributors to the high dropout rate; services addressing these problems are viewed as severely inadequate.

5. Hispanic civil rights and service organizations are viewed more positively by Hispanics than are most mainstream organizations, and the Hispanic press is viewed more positively than the mainstream press.

Point 5, taken with Washington's statement that "ownership" enhances the comfort level of applicants to the Black Community Fund, confirmed the validity of the Hall Family Foundations' intuition in establishing the funds.

Recommendations published in the assessment included the following:

1. Expansion of corporate giving and college participation in the Hispanic Scholarship Fund.

2. Provision of accurate demographic information on Hispanic children from the school boards.

3. Expansion of existing tutorial programs.

4. Expansion and strengthening of educational services for adult Hispanics, especially English as a Second Language and General Equivalency Diploma.

5. Publication of an information-and-referral guide to human services for Hispanics.

Since its publication in August 1988, the assessment has been widely distributed in the Hispanic and majority populations, and has attracted considerable press attention.

As with the Black Community Fund, two prime advantages of the Hispanic Development Fund's makeup are its knowledge of the community and the rapidity with which it can respond to a need. A particularly dramatic example concerns the new immigration law. The Hispanic population was aware well before the passage of the law that a change was imminent. Ruiz went to Salazar with the idea of hiring an attorney to follow the progress of the law as it took shape, and to advise the Hispanic community on its ramifications. The Hispanic Development Fund came up with $9,000 for the project, and the Hall Family Foundations added another $9,000.

Speed was the issue for Sacred Heart Day Care, Kansas City, Missouri, a nonprofit that lost its federal funding almost literally overnight. "It was the middle of the school year and they made a request to us for an emergency need," Murguia said. "Our advisory committee members met the next day and determined that the need was important. Within days they had the commitment; within a few weeks they had the money."

The two funds share a remaining barrier to full efficacy: the small amounts of the grants they make. For all the talk of "leveraging," and for all the difference the presence of even a small independent fund seems to make, it remains true that the $60,000 to $75,000 each fund realizes annually on its endowment is not enough for the job at hand. Both Washington and Murguia cite fundraising as a priority—but for the future, not the present. "The plan is to have a few years of successful grantmaking under our belts before raising more money," said Murguia. Neither Washington nor Murguia was specific about how future fundraising might proceed.

The relationship of the funds to the community foundation is strictly supportive, an observation shared by Murguia, Washington, and the foundation itself. The watchwords of community foundation president Janice C. Kreamer are "proactive" and "problem-solving," yet she stresses the foundation's hands-off attitude toward grant decisions by the community funds. "Our job is to provide the Black Community Fund and the Hispanic Development Fund cultural and financial liaison with mainstream funding organizations," Kreamer says. "We have the firm desire not to get in the way of their priorities."

As an example, Kreamer cites the publication of the Hispanic Needs Assessment. "We provided a neutral base for the publication and stood behind its findings," she said. The foundation convened meetings, participated on the advisory committee for the study, and assisted in the dissemination of the results. No one at the community foundation had a hand in designing the questions on the surveys or in assessing the results.

There is black representation on the community foundation board, but currently no Hispanics. It is a situation Kreamer says will be corrected as soon as a board position opens up. When the community foundation merged with the Kansas City Association of Trusts in 1986, it created, in addition to considerably more substantial assets, a very large board. There are no imminent openings, but Hall, as well as Kreamer, is committed to placing a Hispanic on the board. "We look for diversity at the foundation, and currently there is key minority representation on all disbursement committees. It's a matter of getting it on the agenda."

The attitude of the Hispanic community toward this seems to be sanguine but watchful. Murguia, for one, sees no reason to doubt that the next community foundation board membership will go to a Hispanic. "They've always lived up to their part of the bargain in the past," he said. "They know how important a Hispanic board member would be to the Hispanic community."

Ruiz also expressed trust in the community foundation's future board makeup, as well as in the security the foundation affords the Hispanic Development Fund. "It was the right thing to work this fund through the community foundation to be administered and monitored there," he says. "I sleep better knowing our money is safely invested. As for the lack of Hispanic representation on their board, I am confident that will change, and it won't be a battle. They recognize the need. Tony Salazar was right when he said this made us a player in the philanthropy game. "

26

Minneapolis: The Minnesota Women's Fund

Patricia Bill

- The young deaf girl in an isolated area of rural Minnesota assumed she would die before she grew up. She had never seen a deaf adult.

- A rural Minnesota woman drives a tractor, bales hay, feeds hogs, and balances the family's budget. But bank officers asked her to wait in the lobby while they negotiated a loan for the family farm with her husband.

- The 16-year-old Hmong woman is married with three children and a fourth on the way. When the baby is born, she will live with her in-laws, who want her to have as many children as possible to make their clan stronger. It is difficult to show them that more children mean deeper poverty.

Such situations are concerns of the Minnesota Women's Fund, both a grantmaker and an advocate.

Created in 1984 as a designated area fund of the Minneapolis Foundation (the donor specifies the area of charitable interest, and the community foundation selects grant recipients), it became a supporting organization of the community foundation in 1989. (A supporting organization is administered by the community foundation but has its own board of directors and makes its own grants compatible with the foundation's purposes.)

"The Minneapolis Foundation and the Minnesota Women's Fund are a natural fit," says Marion Etzwiler, president of the Minneapolis Foundation and an early leader of the Women's Fund.

Indeed, the foundation's mission statement comfortably includes the fund's aims:

> The mission of the Minneapolis Foundation is to attract and mobilize community and philanthropic assets to promote equal access to resources needed for every individual, family and community in Minnesota to reach full potential.

The foundation also offered the Women's Fund what any emerging organization, philanthropic or otherwise, seeks—stability and credibility, for Minneapolis's community foundation is one of the country's largest and oldest. For most of its 74-year history it served residents of the Minneapolis metropolitan area. In recent years, however, new programs such as the Women's Fund and others expanded its geographic interest to include Minnesotans statewide. It has combined assets of more than $110 million (1988), oversees six major grantmaking programs, and is a community catalyst, convening Twin Cities leaders to address issues.

The Minnesota Women's Fund was "a wonderful collaborative effort—something a community foundation can do," says Thomas Beech, executive vice-president of the Anne Burnett and Charles D. Tandy Foundation (Texas) and former executive director of the Minneapolis Foundation.

The affiliation is generally a happy story, but not without a few glitches.

Between 1983 and 1989, the Women's Fund went from an abstract idea to a recognized philanthropy. Starting with no financial base, its endowment reached $5.2 million in four years. Renewed fundraising efforts begun in late 1988 are expected to propel the endowment to its $10 million goal.

In its first three years of grantmaking, the fund awarded 86 grants totaling nearly $767,000 to Minnesota women's groups for (1) advocacy/public policy development, (2) education, (3) leadership/role modeling, and (4) support/empowerment.

One of the largest of 40 women's funds in the United States, it is one of the few that is statewide and endowed.

"The reason for its progress," says Ellen O'Neill, the fund's program officer, "is that the foundation board allowed the community to influence the shaping of the Women's Fund's program."

"I'm very proud of the grantmaking program," says Etzwiler. "I'm proud of the risk-taking we're doing. I'm proud the board of trustees of the Minneapolis Foundation has supported the recommendations of the advisory board of the Women' Fund, including some controversial ones."

A slightly different view comes from Lauren Weck, who has been involved with the fund from its beginning as chair of the task force that structured it: "Although I'm thrilled with the program, I'm disappointed the fundraising isn't where we thought it would be," she says. "I'm disappointed that some aspects of the fund were cumbersome.

"Is it worth it? Yes!"

SETTING UP THE FUND

The Minnesota Women's Fund is one of the best funded, best organized, and most businesslike, says Joanne Hayes, until recently president of Women and Foundations/Corporate Philanthropy (WAF/CP), a network of board members and staff of grantmaking organizations and fiscal agent for the National Network of Women's Funds.

Increasing funds for programs on behalf of women and girls is a goal of Minnesota's and the national WAF/CP. Many of the persons who started women's funds in various parts of the country are WAF/CP members.

From the time the Minnesota's WAF/CP network was formed in 1978, its members discussed the sparse funding for women. Data supported their contentions:

- Approximately 80 percent of the Minnesotans living in poverty were women and children.
- Minnesota women were earning 58.2 cents for every dollar earned by men.
- Half the women working full-time earned less than $12,500 a year.
- About one in five women over 65 years old was poor.
- Child care, affordable family health care, and reliable transportation were not accessible to many rural Minnesota women.

Despite discussion, it took several years for action. That came through a task force on a "Single Parent Self-Sufficiency Fund." The task force met several times to consider purpose, structure, and policy of such a fund. It recommended that the fund be housed at a community foundation.

"The discussion was very thoughtful," recalls Patricia Cummings, a member of WAF/CP and on staff at the Minneapolis Foundation. "It made sense for us (WAF/CP) to spearhead the fund. We saw members being involved in it, but not running it. We were not well enough organized to do that. We were—we are—a network. Nevertheless, we wanted to keep our oar in."

The WAF/CP task force, which had representatives of the Saint Paul and the Minneapolis community foundations, approached both foundations for advice on establishing such a fund. Then, in March 1983, feminist Gloria Steinem spoke in the Twin Cities. The Minneapolis Foundation head, Thomas Beech, was among those hearing her tell of the need for increased foundation and corporate support for women and girls.

The idea of a women's fund intrigued him, and Lauren Weck, a WAF/CP member who was seated next to him, reminded him of the task force's earlier meeting with the Minneapolis Foundation about such a fund.

"Right after that, Tom called a group together. Within two weeks, he sent a memo to the Minneapolis Foundation board about the possibility of creating a women's fund," Cummings says.

Beech invited seven women to a brainstorming session; it included Cummings, Weck, Nancy Latimer (who had worked with the Saint Paul Foundation's Community Sharing Fund), and Etzwiler, who then headed a nonprofit organization serving women.

"Tom was very careful to say he would only 'convene' the group," says Cummings. "He made it clear there were options on whether to affiliate with one of the community foundations or to become an independent foundation."

As discussions about starting a women's fund continued, the group, now numbering ten, leaned toward becoming part of the Minneapolis Foundation, but there were issues to be settled:

- Who would govern the fund? In 1983 the Minneapolis Foundation board was predominantly male, and members of WAF/CP wanted to be certain that the board would be sympathetic to women's and girls' problems.

- The fund was to be directed toward social change, and that meant tackling tough, and sometimes unpopular, issues. Would a community foundation staff and board be comfortable with controversy?

- Would the community foundation support the recommendations of an advisory committee of the fund?

ISSUES IN AFFILIATION

The women, now known as the Minnesota Women's Fund Task Force, met in late March with five trustees of the Minneapolis Foundation. Among the trustees was Mary Lee Dayton, who would become chair of the Minneapolis Foundation in 1987.

Several issues were considered at the meeting:

- How would money for the fund be raised?
- How would the fund be administered?
- What would be the impact on the foundation's distribution committee?
- What would be the purpose of the fund? To make grants? Generate information? Stimulate similar giving by others?

The task force then met five more times to draft statements of mission and focus. In the spring of 1983, as the task force was meeting, a separate and well-attended symposium on "Single Parents and Self-Sufficiency" was conducted in the Twin Cities. Issues raised at the symposium were incorporated into the mission and focus statements of the proposed fund.

In June, the Minnesota Women's Fund Task Force expanded to include women of various racial, economic, and educational backgrounds. Ronald McKinley, a staff member of the Minneapolis Foundation who was responsible for new program development, also joined the group.

Task force members sought advice from colleagues in other communities who had set up women's funds.

At a June 25, 1983 meeting, the Minnesota Women's Fund Task Force unanimously recommended that a proposal for affiliation with the Minneapolis Foundation be prepared and presented to the foundation's board of trustees. It included a list of operations issues, a fund-raising plan, and a mission statement. In addition, the foundation was urged to review its investment policy on social concerns.

The Minnesota Women's Fund became a designated-area fund of the Minneapolis Foundation on October 12, 1983, with a goal of raising $10 million.

FUNDRAISING

Then began what Weck calls "frenzied activity." Although the Minnesota Women's Fund now had the stature of being affiliated with the Minneapolis Foundation, it was a fund without funding, an organization that was not operational.

Two prongs, or parallel tracks, of the Minnesota Women's Fund emerged: fundraising and program. The fund's development office was set up in January 1984 in St. Paul—across the Twin Cities from the Minneapolis Foundation, where the fund's program office was set up a year later. The result was that the Women's Fund had two separate staffs—development and program—with offices about ten miles apart. The governing bodies were also separate: development reported to a fundraising committee, and program reported to the advisory committee.

The Minneapolis Foundation board decided not to do the fundraising for the Women's Fund because the foundation did not have the administrative capacity at that time to take on a $10-million campaign, says Cummings.

There is conjecture that there were additional reasons for separating fundraising from the foundation. Some say it was to allow the Women's Fund to establish an identity and visibility of its own, thus attracting funds specifically to its pot rather than to the community foundation as a whole. Others guess that some founders of the fund wanted to retain some control over it—or as Cummings had put it earlier, "to keep their oar in."

"The intent was, you raise the money, then the program will start," she says.

The task force did not see the double track as a big disadvantage, says Latimer. The fund received grants for its development efforts from the McKnight Foundation, Dayton Hudson, and General Mills.

"In the beginning it was fine," she says. "You have to remember, *all* the funds had to be raised. We had no track record."

"We wanted to raise the endowment and get out of the way for programming," Weck remembers. "In hindsight, we now know so much more."

"To show you how naive we were, we thought we could raise the money in a year," says Cummings.

The thinking was that a $10-million endowment would be raised in one year, invested, and development activities would end. Grants would be made from returns on endowment investment.

The endowment goal was not reached in a year, or—despite changes in development strategy and personnel—in four years. The fund's endowment, however, did reach $5.2 million by 1988.

Opinion differs on why the goal was not reached.

"One issue was what the endowment amount should be," recalls Cummings. Task force members talked about $5 to $6 million, then went to $10 million. "It wasn't carefully thought out."

Sandra Butler, board member of several private foundations and co-chair of the fundraising executive committee, says "The community was not ready for this kind of campaign. It was a departure from the way the local institutions usually did campaigns."

Traditionally, major campaigns were conducted by a known organization after months of board discussion and planning. By the time a campaign was ready to begin, it would be common knowledge in the community.

Butler said she and Dayton did not have experienced professional development consultants to do feasibility studies and coordinate the campaign.

"Everyone was kind of off on their own raising funds," she said. "The fund had no record—the mission was there, but not the agency or programs—and it would be supporting groups outside the mainstream."

In addition, she recalled, the campaign was a little different in that it was both a capital campaign for endowment and an annual drive to set up the fund and get it going.

Because the Minnesota Women's Fund was to benefit all the state's women and girls, its leaders hoped to create a sense of ownership by involving as many women as possible from throughout Minnesota in fundraising, as well as in setting the direction of the Women's Fund programs. In truth, says Butler, only a small group raised funds, and some sections of the community were missed.

Among the greatest assets to the fundraising effort were co-chairs Dayton and Butler, members of two of the Twin Cities' oldest and wealthiest families. Both were dedicated to the cause and to the Minnesota community.

"The whole feminist movement in its broadest sense, is the most exciting thing to happen," says Dayton, the mother of four daughters. "It is thrilling for women to have the opportunity to break out of the slot we've been placed in.

"I've been so fortunate as a woman—just plain lucky. It was instilled in me somewhere along the line to give something back."

She did. In addition to the time and expertise she volunteered to the Women's Fund, she and her husband donated $1 million to the endowment.

"The fact that the fund was a part of the Minneapolis Foundation made an enormous difference in our decision to make the gift. The credibility of the foundation, its expertise in the management of its endowment fund, and its excellent program staff gave us confidence that our gift would be wisely handled," Mrs. Dayton said.

As contributions began to come in, another problem arose. With gifts ranging from $1, $5, and $10 to $1 million, and coming from a wide range of sources, the Minneapolis Foundation's accounting system was burdened. But Etzwiler, who replaced Beech as the foundation's executive director in mid-1984 as the funding campaign officially got underway, found compensation.

Signing thank-you letters for contributions to the fund was often moving, she says: "The Women's Fund is important to *all* women, no matter what their walk in life. The $5 and $7 donations from economically depressed areas were almost sacrificial gifts. They really came from the heart. There were also the wonderful experiences when women of means would attend gatherings and tell why the Women's Fund is important to privileged women. They would speak of their daughters and granddaughters having an opportunity to live in a system where people are valued no matter what their gender. They were truly committed."

Several public fundraising events were conducted, and smaller gatherings took place in homes or private clubs.

"Among the returns were raising the level of awareness of women's issues, and a feeling of belonging," says Latimer.

Despite challenges, the Women's Fund has achieved what is considered one of the most important results of any funding campaign: providing enough money to establish the kinds of programs expected by donors.

"The people giving to us are pleased, I think," says Butler.

At least one fundraising decision is not argued: "It was brilliant of us to go for endowment rather than pass-through or annual fundraising," says Latimer.

Endowment gave the Women's Fund a stable financial base and an ongoing, identifiable amount of money that allows long-term planning, which was important to the systemic changes the Women's Fund seeks. Pass-through or annual fundraising would have meant continual fundraising and short-term programs.

PROGRAMS

From its birth, the Minnesota Women's Fund was to be more than a grantmaking organization.

"Our purpose is to work in partnership with women throughout the state to remove the barriers that keep us from participating fully in society," says Ellen O'Neill.

To do so, the founders believed they needed to tap the ideas of a broad spectrum of Minnesota women. The vehicle was the fund's advisory committee, which met for the fist time in March 1985. Six of the 15 members came from outside the Twin Cities area. The rules also called for six members from the Twin Cities metropolitan area, five women of color, five low-income women, and three members of the Minneapolis Foundation's distribution committee.

The advisory committee developed an outreach strategy and guidelines and funding priorities for grantmaking, subject to approval by the Minneapolis Foundation. It makes funding recommendations to the foundation's distribution committee and, with the foundation's investment committee and staff, keeps an eye on the fund's financial status.

To get the grantmaking up and running, O'Neill first studied the guidelines of other grantmakers. Fundamental questions were addressed: What does social change mean? What makes that happen? What is diversity in Minnesota?

Instrumental questions, too: How big will grants be? How many? "We didn't know because the fundraising determined that," explains McKinley, who represented the foundation in the early planning of the program.

The geographical logistics were also a challenge. Although it now has several statewide programs, the Minneapolis Foundation was then still a Twin Cities-area organization.

"We had to create a network around the state so we could reach out effectively," McKinley recalls.

Minnesota is a large state, and travel time and expenses for members of the advisory committee complicated the logistics of meeting and added to administrative costs.

In addition to fundraising and developing the fund's program, the Women's Fund conducted a needs assessment.

"I had an idea of barriers to women and girls in the metropolitan area, but not in Greater Minnesota," says O'Neill.

She found several factors unique to rural Minnesota:

- A lack of funding resources made it difficult to start and maintain nonprofit organizations.
- Because population is dispersed, it is difficult to deliver services and resources.
- There were few vehicles to inform rural Minnesota women about available services, opportunities, or resources.

To reach rural constituents, the fund divided the state into six regions previously defined by Minnesota's largest grantmaker, the McKnight Foundation. The fund also hired part-time staff who live outside the Twin Cities and understand the needs of women and girls within their areas. The fund also publishes a newsletter and conducts conferences in the various regions.

The fund created five program areas.

Information Gathering

The fund documents the needs of and barriers to Minnesota's women and girls and brings the data to the attention of the people who can change things—public policymakers, other funders, and community leaders.

Education

The fund works to educate other funders and the public about the status of Minnesota women and girls.

Technical Assistance

This includes holding grant application information sessions before each Women's Fund grant cycle to help women write proposals, leading general proposal writing workshops, and publishing a funding resource directory for Greater Minnesota programs.

Grantmaking

The fund's grants focus on matters such as child care, support to help low-income women move to self-sufficiency, enforcement of domestic assault laws, and information to women and girls on the need for an equal rights amendment to the U.S. Constitution.

Conferences

Seeking to break down their isolation and engage them in the process of change, the fund enables women to meet to share information, skills, resources, hopes, and dreams.

THE FUND'S CURRENT PROFILE

The Minnesota Women's Fund has chalked up an impressive record:

- It raised $5.8 million ($5.2 million of it for endowment) in five years, more than many community foundations themselves have accumulated over decades.
- $767,000 has been awarded in 86 grants.
- 29 percent of its grants serve all Minnesota women, and 42 percent serve only those outside the Twin Cities metropolitan area.
- 48 percent of the grants provided general operating funds, 10 percent start-up funds, and the remaining 42 percent went to special projects.

Women's Fund grants have gone to organizations serving a variety of women's and girls' needs. For example:

- The Women's Technical Support Project offers farm women management skills, emotional support, leadership, and encouragement, in addition to seminars explaining legal and financial transactions that affect their future in a rural crisis. In a culture where wives often share in chores but not in management decisions, the project promotes systemic change and gives practical information.
- Silk Wings, a group in Duluth, is setting up study/action groups in local churches to change the churches' response to discrimination and violence against women.
- Minnesota Child Support Coalition addresses problems of nonpayment and enforcement of child support.
- The Cass Lake–Bena School District's "New Horizons for Women" prevention project offers support groups, assertiveness training, and other methods to help young women, many of them Native Americans, break cycles of teenage pregnancy, truancy, and welfare.

A new phase of fundraising began in late 1988. The fund aims to raise an additional $4.8 million over five years to achieve a $10 million endowment by 1994.

Moreover, the fund's structure changed. Beginning in mid-1989, the fund is expected to become a supporting organization of the Minneapolis Foundation. The fund is incorporated as a nonprofit and will become a legal entity with its own board of directors—an autonomous organization approving its own grants. The Minneapolis Foundation will appoint 51 percent of the new board.

"This step frees resources for the Minneapolis Foundation and consolidates resources of the Minnesota Women's Fund," O'Neill explains.

The Minneapolis Foundation, which had absorbed the Women's Fund's administrative costs after the early grants ran out, spent about $68,000 to run the fund in 1988, O'Neill estimates.

The structural change brings the fund's fundraising and programming to the Minneapolis Foundation offices, with both reporting to the Women's Fund board. "It means the Minnesota Women's Fund has an even better opportunity to achieve our goals," says O'Neill.

INDEX

Interagency Committee for Early
Childhood Development and
Education, 211
Interchurch Council of Greater
Cleveland (Federated Churches
of Greater Cleveland), 26
IRATE (Immigrant Rights Advocacy
Training and Education pro-
ject), 295
IRCA (Immigration Reform and
Control Act) (1986) 170–72, 177
Irizarry, Johnny, 299
Issues, focusing attention on, 126

Jacobs, Gail, 277, 280
James, Jean, 202, 208–10
James Irvine Foundation, 174, 176,
235, 240
Jansson, Douglas, 7, 91–92
Jay, John, 2
Jewish Community Federation, 26,
102
Job training, 290, 291
Johns Hopkins University Adoles-
cent Pregnancy program, 263–
64
Johnson, Byron, 224
Johnson, Geraldine, 266, 268, 270
Joiner, Charlie, 186
Joint Center for Political Studies, 6
Jones, Anna Faith, 39, 286, 288–93,
295, 296
Jones, Arleigh, 224
Jones, Hubie, 298
Joseph, James A., 1, 9, 11–12, 124
Josephson, Michael, 124
Juarez, Mexico, 216, 218–20
Julia Palmer Fund, 264
Junior League of Tacoma, 230

Kalamazoo Foundation, 142
Kansas City, Missouri, black and
hispanic funds in, 323–34
Kansas City Association of Trusts
and Foundations, 37, 326–27,
334
Kansas City Community
Foundation, 37

Kansas City Star, 327
Kaplan, Mitchell, 198
Karamu, 253, 255
Kay, Gerri, 184, 187
Keane, Edward C., 264–68, 271
Kettering Foundation, 141
Kimball, Lindsay, 79
King, Martin Luther, Jr., 64, 276
Kingsley, Sherman C., 27–28
Kirk, Phyllis, 238
Kreamer, Janice C., 333–34
Krohn, Peter, 239

Lakewold, 231–32
Lansdale, H. Parker, 263, 264
Latimer, Edwin P., 314
Latimer, Nancy, 338, 342
Lawrence, Massachusetts,
community foundation in, 6–7
Lawrence University, 113
Leadership (leaders), 63–71. *See also*
Distribution committee
backgrounds and experiences of,
66–68
case studies of, 14–15, 169–346. *See
also specific cases*
aid to non-profit organizations,
16, 243–60
asset growth, 15–16, 213–42
catalytic leadership, 16–17,
261–84
community needs, 15, 169–212
neighborhood development,
17, 285–322
new philanthropists, 17–18,
323–46
collaboration and, 142–43
community, 98–99, 199
donor services and, 98–99
Foundation for the Carolinas,
319–20
grantmaking and, 98
Philadelphia Foundation, 310–11
postwar, 32–33
requirements of, 11, 64–65
sources of, 23–24
standards and, 24
types of 65–66